CONTEMPORARY BALKAN CINEMA

Traditions in World Cinema

www.edinburghuniversitypress.com/series/tiwc

CONTEMPORARY BALKAN CINEMA

Transnational Exchanges and Global Circuits

Edited by Lydia Papadimitriou
and Ana Grgić

EDINBURGH
University Press

Edinburgh University Press is one of the leading university presses in the UK. We publish academic books and journals in our selected subject areas across the humanities and social sciences, combining cutting-edge scholarship with high editorial and production values to produce academic works of lasting importance. For more information visit our website: edinburghuniversitypress.com

Edinburgh University Press Ltd
The Tun – Holyrood Road
12(2f) Jackson's Entry
Edinburgh EH8 8PJ

First published in hardback by Edinburgh University Press 2020

Typeset in 10/12.5 pt Sabon
by IDSUK (DataConnection) Ltd, and
printed and bound by CPI Group (UK) Ltd,
Croydon, CR0 4YY

A CIP record for this book is available from the British Library

ISBN 978 1 4744 5843 6 (hardback)
ISBN 978 1 4744 5844 3 (paperback)
ISBN 978 1 4744 5845 0 (webready PDF)
ISBN 978 1 4744 5846 7 (epub)

CONTENTS

FIGURES AND TABLES

Tables

ACKNOWLEDGEMENTS

Working on this book has been a truly collaborative enterprise and we would like to begin by thanking all the contributors of *Contemporary Balkan Cinema: Transnational Exchanges and Global Circuits* for their hard work and patience, and for sharing their knowledge and love of Balkan cinema. Without your invaluable input and critical insight, this edited collection would not have been possible.

The idea for this book was sown by the banks of the Danube during the Divan Film Festival in Cetate, Romania, where the two of us first met in 2013. Those long summer days and evenings, filled with Balkan films and endless discussions with filmmakers and scholars from across the region over delicious locally produced food and plentiful wine, made very clear to us how much in common Balkan neighbours have, and how far cinema can help communicate it across borders. We would therefore like to express our gratitude to Marian Ţuţui for inviting us to Divan, and for his inexhaustible energy and enthusiasm that made the festival and its annual symposium on Balkan cinema such memorable experiences. We would also like to thank Dina Iordanova not only for her seminal academic contributions to the study of Balkan cinema, but also for introducing us both to Marian and thus implicitly triggering the making of this book. Below are some of the filmmakers, scholars and friends that we had the opportunity to share fruitful exchanges with in Cetate, and who helped us expand our understanding of Balkan cinema: Martichka Bozhilova, Agron Domi, Dana Duma, Aleksandar Erdeljanović, Mihai Fulger, Magda Mihailescu, Eno Milkani, Petar Kardjilov,

Andreas Konstantinou, Constantin Parvulescu, Nikos Perakis, the late Lucian Pintillie, Slobodan Šijan, Electra Venaki, Vlatka Vorkapić, Aleksandar Zikov, the late Aleksandar Yanakiev, Wang Yao, as well as the contributors of this volume Nevena Daković, Gergana Doncheva and Aleksandra Milovanović. Yet it was a semi-casual conversation with the then Director of the Serbian Film Centre, Boban Jetvić, at the Thessaloniki International Film Festival in November 2017 that gave us the final impetus to turn the idea into reality and make this book happen. In perhaps a rather surprising way, we owe this book to him.

Gathering information about the different Balkan cinemas has not always been easy, and we would like to thank all the organisations and individuals who assisted us with sourcing data, especially for the compilation of the appendix tables. These include (but are not limited to) the Albanian National Center of Cinematography, Bulgarian National Film Center, Croatian Audiovisual Center, Film Center of Montenegro, North Macedonian Film Agency, Kosova Cinematography Center, Greek Film Center, Film Center Serbia and Slovenian Film Center.

Finally, we would like to express our gratitude to Gillian Lesley and Edinburgh University Press for giving us the opportunity to publish this book, as well as the editors of Traditions in World Cinemas, Linda Badley and R. Barton Palmer for considering it a valuable addition to the series. Last but not least, we would like to thank all our colleagues, friends and families who have supported us throughout our literal, metaphorical and editorial journeys across the Balkans that have led to the completion of this book. This project is the culmination of many years' engagement with Balkan cinema, and we hope that it will mark the dawn of a new era for its production, study and enjoyment!

CONTRIBUTORS

Melis Behlil is an Associate Professor of Cinema Studies and Chair of the Radio, Television and Cinema Department at Kadir Has University in Istanbul, Turkey. She was a visiting scholar at the Massachusetts Institute of Technology, a Research Associate at Stockholm University and a member of the Global Women's Cinema Network. Her book, *Hollywood Is Everywhere: Global Directors in the Blockbuster Era* was published with Amsterdam University Press in 2016. In addition to teaching and other academic duties, she writes film reviews for various publications, co-hosts a weekly radio show and is a member of the Turkish Film Critics Association.

Francesca Borrione completed her doctorate in Education and Humanities at the University of Perugia, Italy. She is currently pursuing her second PhD in English at the University of Rhode Island where she is researching Italo-American literature and cinema. She is the author of three monographs and three novels. Her essay, '*La Terrazza* on the Circeo: Ettore Scola, Pasolini, and the Critique of Roman Intelligentsia in Late 70s Italy' will be published in the volume *The Cinema of Ettore Scola* (Wayne University Press) in 2020.

Maria Chalkou holds a PhD in Film Theory and History (University of Glasgow), sponsored by the Greek State Scholarships Foundation (IKY) and an MA in Film and Art Theory (University of Kent). She is currently a post-doctoral researcher at Panteion University (CIVIL – Censorship in Visual Arts and Film, supported by ELIDEK) and teaches Film History, Film Theory and Documentary at the Department of Audio and Visual Arts at the Ionian University. She is the principal editor of *Filmicon: Journal of Greek Film Studies*. Her research interests focus on film cultures of the 1960s, Greek cinema, contemporary European cinema, film censorship, film criticism and cinematic representations of the past. She has also researched and co-directed the documentary *Oneira Mikrou Mikous (1960–1967)/Dreaming in 'Shorts' (1960–1967)* for the TV programme *Paraskinio* (2007).

Costas Constandinides is Assistant Professor of Screen Studies in the Department of Communications at the University of Nicosia. He is the author of *From Film Adaptation to Post-celluloid Adaptation* (Continuum, 2010; paperback by Bloomsbury) and co-editor of *Cypriot Cinemas: Memory, Conflict, and Identity in the Margins of Europe* (Bloomsbury, 2014). He is the Co-artistic Director of the Cyprus Film Days International Festival and a member of the European Film Academy.

Nevena Daković, PhD, is Professor of Film Theory/Film Studies (Department of Theory and History, FDA, University of Arts, Belgrade) and Chair of the Interdisciplinary PhD Art and Media Studies. She is author of *Film Studies: Essays in Film Texts of Memory* (2014) and *Balkan kao filmski žanr: slika, tekst, nacija* (2008), and editor of many books (*Film and /Screen/Media Studies: Serbia 3.0*, 2019; *Representation of the Holocaust in the Balkans in Arts and Media*, 2015). She publishes widely in the national and international framework (UK, Turkey, Slovakia, Italy, Austria, France, USA) and was a guest professor at European and American universities. She regularly participates at international conferences and is a committee member of international project groups (COST and TEMPUS projects). She is a member of *Academia Europaea*. Her main research themes are nation and representation, the Balkans, Shoah and cultural memory.

Gergana Doncheva, PhD, is an Assistant Professor at the Institute of Balkan Studies and Centre of Thracology at the Bulgarian Academy of Sciences. She graduated from Sofia University (Bulgaria) and holds MA degrees in Cultural Studies (2002) and Political Science (2003). In 2010, she obtained her PhD from the Institute of Balkan Studies, Bulgarian Academy of Sciences and a year later she published the monograph *The Image of the Balkans in Balkan and Western films: Strategies of Representation* (in Bulgarian) based on her doctoral thesis. This research was nominated by the Bulgarian Film Academy (2010) in the 'the best book' category. Her research interests focus on Balkan film and culture, memory of socialism constructed in movies, e/immigrations and identities in cinema.

Ana Grgić is a Lecturer in Film, Television and Screen Studies at Monash University Malaysia. She holds a PhD in Film Studies from the University of St Andrews, with a thesis on early cinema in the Balkans, archives and cultural memory (forthcoming monograph with Amsterdam University Press). Her work has been published in *The Film Festival Yearbook 5: Archival Film Festivals* (2013), *Frames Cinema Journal* (2013), *Divan Film Festival Symposium Papers* (2014, 2015), *Cinemas of Paris* (2015), *Studies in Eastern European Cinema* (2016), *Short Film Studies* (2017), *Film Quarterly* (2018) and *Images* (2018). She is co-editor of two special issues: on 'Albanian Cinema' for *KinoKultura* (2016) and on 'Women Editors in Central and Eastern Europe' for *Apparatus* (2018). She was also involved in the preservation of Balkan film heritage (*Archives in Motion* workshops), and a regional film literacy project funded by Creative Europe-MEDIA (*The 5C Project*).

Raluca Iacob is an independent researcher working as a film curator for the Astra Documentary Film Festival. She completed her PhD at the University of St Andrews with a thesis on post-communist Romanian cinema. She is currently developing her thesis into a monograph, as a comparative study of Romanian, Argentinean and Iranian cinemas. Her work has been published in the journals *Film Criticism* and *Apparatus* (2018), as well as the collective volumes *Actes du colloque international, La chanson dans les cinemas d'Europe et d'Amerique Latine (1960–2010)* (Peter Lang), *New Romanian Cinema* (Edinburgh University Press, 2019).

Dina Iordanova is a native of Bulgaria. She is Professor of Global Cinema and Creative Cultures at the University of St Andrews in Scotland. Her work is on the cinema of the Balkans in its transnational contextualisation; she is the author of *Cinema of Flames: Balkan Film, Culture and the Media* (2001) and *Emir Kusturica* (2002) and editor of the collection *Cinema of the Balkans* (2006). She has also published work on aspects of Bulgarian, Yugoslav and Romanian cinema. In the past decade, she has been engaged with jury service, has given masterclasses, and has moderated discussions at film festivals in Romania, Greece, Turkey, North Macedonia and Croatia.

Dijana Jelača is a faculty member in the Film Department at Brooklyn College. She is the author of *Dislocated Screen Memory: Narrating Trauma in Post-Yugoslav Cinema* (Palgrave, 2016) and co-author of *Film Feminisms: A Global Introduction* (Routledge, 2019). She co-edited several scholarly volumes, including *The Routledge Companion to Cinema and Gender* (Routledge, 2017) and *The Cultural Life of Capitalism in Yugoslavia* (Palgrave, 2017). Jelača's research interests include transnational feminist film studies, women's film history, South Slavic film cultures, and socialist women's cinema. Her essays have appeared in *Signs, Camera Obscura, Feminist Media Studies, Jump Cut* and elsewhere. She is a Programming Director of the Bosnian-Herzegovinian Film Festival in New York City.

Sanja Jovanović completed studies at the Faculty of Dramatic Arts (Cetinje, Montenegro) and obtained her master's degree at the University of Leicester (England) at the Department of Mass Communication. She was an associate professor in Audiovisual Production at the Faculty of Visual Arts, University of Mediterranean in Podgorica (2006–2018). She currently works as the Program Policy Manager at the Film Center of Montenegro and is responsible for film industry research: Gender Equality in Montenegrin Cinema; Viewing Habits among Children and Teenagers in Montenegro; and Cinema-Going Trends. She is a member of the Association of Film Producers and Directors of Montenegro. She is a national representative at the European Audiovisual Observatory, a member of EFARN, and a deputy representative at Eurimages. She is co-author of *Oreol i Omča Leni Rifenštal* (Admiral Books, Belgrade, 2014) and has published numerous articles in national and international journals.

Iva Leković graduated in Art History at the Faculty of Philosophy in Belgrade. She finished her MA studies at the UNESCO Chair for Cultural Policy and Management at the University of Arts in Belgrade with a master's thesis entitled *The Balkans – A Cinematic Self-reflection*. Her work experience includes curatorial practices, field production and event production at film festivals. She has published several catalogue texts, essays and research articles about contemporary art, photography and film. She also had experience as a filmmaker on short projects. She is a member of ULUPUDS's (Association of Fine Arts Applied Artists and Designers of Serbia) section of historians and theoreticians of visual arts, where she conducts exhibition projects. She is currently completing her PhD studies at the Faculty of Dramatic Arts. Her research interests include film theory and Balkan studies and her work uses an interdisciplinary approach.

Aleksandra Milovanović is an Associate Professor of Film Studies at the Faculty of Dramatic Arts, Department of Theory and History. She is the author of books *Towards the New Media: Transmedial Narratives Between Film and Television* (2019) and *Imaginary Field of Film Image, Cognition and Interpretation* (2011) (in Serbian). In addition to her academic interest in Yugoslav film history and knowledge of audio-visual archives, she has extensive experience editing high-profile documentary films, TV series and video installations: *Toward a Concrete Utopia: Architecture in Yugoslavia* (MoMa, New York, 2018–19); *The Other Side of Everything* (Mila Turajlić, 2017), *Cinema Komunisto* (Mila Turajlić, 2011), *Vukovar, Final Cut* (Janko Baljak, 2006), *Insider* (Brankica Stanković, 2008–14, 45 episodes). She is also a member of NECS and DokSerbia.

Albana Muco is currently a PhD student in Linguistic, Literary and Intercultural Studies in European and Extra-European Perspectives (German-Albanian Studies) at the University of Milan (Italy). She received her BA in Translation and Linguistic Mediation at the Scuola Superiore per Mediatori Linguistici di Perugia (Italy) and her MA in Translation at the University of Turin (Italy) with a thesis on 'German and Albanian as Pluricentric Languages' ('Albanian as a pluricentric language', Peter Lang, 2018). Her research focuses on sociolinguistics, colour studies, phraseology, contrastive linguistics and translation. She is also interested in (inter)cultural studies.

Kledian Myftari is a postgraduate student in International Security at Charles University in Prague. He originally studied Political Science at the University of Tirana and received a Certificate in European Studies and International Relations from the Université Saint-Louis – Bruxelles. Myftari regularly participates in conferences and internships internationally. His areas of interest include film as a vehicle for conflict resolution and the impact of media in the Middle East.

Yiannis Papadakis is a Professor of Social Anthropology at the Department of Social and Political Sciences, University of Cyprus. He is the author of *Echoes from the Dead Zone: Across the Cyprus Divide* (I. B. Tauris, 2005, also translated into Greek and Turkish), co-editor of *Cypriot Cinemas: Memory, Conflict and Identity in the Margins of Europe* (Bloomsbury, 2014) and editor of a 2006 special issue of *Postcolonial Studies* on Cyprus, among others. His published work on Cyprus has focused on ethnic conflict, borders, nationalism, memory, museums, historiography, history education and cinema. His recent work explores issues of migration and social democracy in Denmark.

Lydia Papadimitriou is Reader (Associate Professor) in Film Studies at Liverpool John Moores University. She has published extensively on different aspects of Greek cinema, including (digital) film distribution, co-productions, film festivals and documentary. She is the author of *The Greek Film Musical* (2006), co-editor (with Yannis Tzioumakis) of *Greek Cinema: Texts, Forms and Identities* (2011) and the Principal Editor of the *Journal of Greek Media and Culture*. She has co-edited special issues for *New Review of Film and Television Studies* ('Film Festivals: Origins and Trajectories') and the *JGMC* ('Contemporary Greek Film Cultures: Weird Wave and Beyond' and 'Greek Screen Industries'). Her publications have appeared in, among others, *Screen*, *Studies of European Cinema*, *International Journal of Media Management* and *New Review of Film and Television Studies*.

Jurica Pavičić is a film critic at the principal Croatian daily newspaper *Jutarnji list* from Zagreb. In addition to newspaper criticism, he teaches history of

Croatian and Yugoslav cinema at the University of Split. His volume *Post-Yugoslav Cinema: Style and Ideology* was published in 2012 and his collection of analytical essays *Classics of Croatian Cinema from the Yugoslav period* in 2016. His fields of interest include Yugoslav culture of the 1950s and cinema of the post-Yugoslav states. He is the author of seven novels, two collections of short stories and several books of essays. Based on his novel *Alabaster Sheep* (1997), Pavičić wrote the screenplay for Vinko Brešan's film *Witnesses*. The film won several prizes at the official competition Berlinale in 2004.

Polona Petek (PhD University of Melbourne, Australia) is an Assistant Professor at the Academy of Theatre, Radio, Film and Television (AGRFT), University of Ljubljana, Slovenia, and a Research Fellow at the Faculty of Arts at the same university. She is the author of *Echo and Narcissus: Echolocating the Spectator in the Age of Audience Research* (2008) and co-editor (with Nil Baskar) of *Phenomenology of Film: Traditions and New Approaches* (2014). Her recent research focuses on transculturation, cosmopolitanism and mobility in cinema, particularly on the intersections of these issues and gender in Slovenian and other European cinemas.

Aida Vidan holds a PhD in Slavic Languages and Literatures from Harvard University, and currently teaches in the Department of International Literary and Cultural Studies at Tufts University. Her areas of interest include East European film, ethnography and applied linguistics. She is the author of *Embroidered with Gold, Strung with Pearls: The Traditional Ballads of Bosnian Women* (2003), co-author of *Beginner's Croatian* (2009) and *Beginner's Serbian* (2009), and co-editor of *In Contrast: Croatian Film Today* (2012). Her articles have appeared in an array of European and American scholarly publications.

Vessela S. Warner, PhD, is an Associate Professor of theatre history and dramatic literature at the University of Alabama at Birmingham. Her research focuses on cultural representations in Bulgarian, Serbian and Macedonian post-communist theatre, film and performance. Her co-edited collection, *Staging Postcommunism: Alternative Theatre in Eastern and Central Europe after 1989* (2020) was published by the University of Iowa Press. Besides this international collection, Warner has contributed to *The Routledge Companion to Dramaturgy* (Routledge, 2015), *From Exsilium to Exile: Forced Migrations in Historical Perspective* (University of Gdansk Press, 2014), *International Women Stage Directors* (University of Illinois Press, 2013), *Performing Worlds into Being: Native American Women's Theatre* (Miami University Press, 2009) and *Theatre and Performance in Eastern Europe: The Changing Scene* (Scarecrow Press, 2008). Her articles have appeared in numerous academic journals.

Bruce Williams is Professor of Cultural Studies at William Paterson University. He has published extensively in film theory, cinema history, and language and cinema. His articles on Albanian cinema have appeared in such journals as *Framework* and *Studies in Eastern European Cinema,* as well as in numerous edited volumes. His work is mediated by diverse interpretative frames, among these Marxism, cultural cosmopolitanism, feminism and queer theory. He is co-author, with Keumsil Kim Yoon, of *Two Lenses on the Korean Ethos: Key Cultural Concepts and Their Appearance in Cinema.* Williams is currently completing a book-length manuscript on Albanian cinema.

TRADITIONS IN WORLD CINEMA

General editors: **Linda Badley and R. Barton Palmer**
Founding editor: **Steven Jay Schneider**

Traditions in World Cinema is a series of textbooks and monographs devoted to the analysis of currently popular and previously underexamined or undervalued film movements from around the globe. Also intended for general interest readers, the textbooks in this series offer undergraduate- and graduate-level film students accessible and comprehensive introductions to diverse traditions in world cinema. The monographs open up for advanced academic study more specialised groups of films, including those that require theoretically oriented approaches. Both textbooks and monographs provide thorough examinations of the industrial, cultural and socio-historical conditions of production and reception.

The flagship textbook for the series includes chapters by noted scholars on traditions of acknowledged importance (the French New Wave, German Expressionism), recent and emergent traditions (New Iranian, post-Cinema Novo), and those whose rightful claim to recognition has yet to be established (the Israeli persecution film, global found footage cinema). Other volumes concentrate on individual national, regional or global cinema traditions. As the introductory chapter to each volume makes clear, the films under discussion form a coherent group on the basis of substantive and relatively transparent, if not always obvious, commonalities. These commonalities may be formal, stylistic or thematic, and the groupings may, although they need not, be popularly identified as genres, cycles or movements (Japanese horror, Chinese martial arts cinema, Italian Neorealism). Indeed, in cases in which a group of films is not already commonly identified as a tradition, one purpose of the volume is to establish its claim to importance and make it visible (East Central European Magical Realist cinema, Palestinian cinema).

Textbooks and monographs include:

- an introduction that clarifies the rationale for the grouping of films under examination;
- a concise history of the regional, national or transnational cinema in question;
- a summary of previous published work on the tradition;
- contextual analysis of industrial, cultural and socio-historical conditions of production and reception;
- textual analysis of specific and notable films, with clear and judicious application of relevant film theoretical approaches;
- bibliograph(ies)/filmograph(ies).

Monographs may additionally include:

- discussion of the dynamics of cross-cultural exchange in light of current research and thinking about cultural imperialism and globalisation, as well as issues of regional/national cinema or political/aesthetic movements (such as new waves, postmodernism or identity politics);
- interview(s) with key filmmakers working within the tradition.

FOREWORD: CINEMA OF THE BALKANS – AN ENDLESS JOURNEY

Dina Iordanova

Theo Angelopoulos, the titan of Greek and Balkan cinema, died in 2012. He was hit by a motorbike while on the set of his last film, *The Other Sea*, and passed shortly thereafter in hospital. It was to be a film about crisis, anxiety and austerity, about migrations, misty border-crossings, about refugees and home longing: a film that would have continued Angelopoulos's eternal themes of exile and endless journeying. Many regarded the director's death as symbolic collateral damage of the Greek economic crisis itself.

In the years that followed, many of the other directors that had shaped cinema in the Balkan region also passed away – Bulgarian Rangel Vulchanov in 2013, Romanian Lucian Pintilie in 2018 and the great Yugoslav-Serbian Dušan Makavejev, in 2019. Even if revered, their last decade was often marked by experiences similar to Angelopoulos' meaningless death – they had difficulties financing projects, felt misunderstood and isolated. The unsettled atmosphere took over the better part of others, who had previously enjoyed the limelight – like Bosnian Emir Kusturica, who got involved in idiosyncratic angry politics and barricaded himself in the narrows of his Serbian mountain stronghold of Kustendorf, out of where he makes maverick theatrical pronouncements to the world.

However, new films were made. New filmmakers stepped in to fill the void that these cinematic titans left. There was a generational change, and here we have a book that takes the challenging but distinguished task to introducing the new developments and to telling the story further, as it continues evolving into the second century of Balkan cinema.

The chosen vantage point for the contributions in this collection is 2008, the year of the global economic crisis – as well as the year when the Greek economic crisis started to unravel. These events impacted the South East European region beyond Greece: and indeed, they did, even though many of the countries around the Balkans follow an economic logic of their own. The story in these parts is often marked by perennially underperforming economies or by crises that appear unrelated – like the one in Turkey in 2018, which was preceded by an unprecedented economic boom. In fact, many of these countries often display scarcity and continuous stagnation; people who live here struggle with the mundane logistics of survival – as reflected in the films of the Romanian new wave and beyond. In general, it is a region that is hard to pin down and poses a variety of narrative challenges.

Even if not uniformly, the Balkan countries are regarded as peripheral and insufficiently European; ascendance to the EU is neither smooth nor easy. In fact, from the thirteen countries covered in this book, only six are members of the European Union (Greece, Cyprus, Slovenia, Bulgaria, Romania and Croatia). The other seven countries are suspended in various stages of bureaucratic recognition by the EU, and it is difficult to predict how things would evolve (Turkey, Serbia, North Macedonia, Bosnia-Herzegovina, Albania, Kosovo, Montenegro). Countries themselves are quite different in territory and population size; there are linguistic and religious divides that often impede productive cultural dialogue. On zooming in, one can easily find simmering conflict in many corners. What in the 1990s used to be one country, Yugoslavia, emerged in the 2000s as a conglomerate of seven newly independent republics – and it is quite possible that some chapters in this collection may be the very first instance where the cinemas of new countries are written about in English as separate national entities. The choice of framework, then, circumvents the complicated and counter-productive question of how things moved during the preceding period of turbulence. By 2008, in spite of economic turmoil, the current national formations were more or less settled.

Likewise, in the context of European cinema the visibility of these cinematic traditions is not particularly high. Yet there are outstanding achievements that compensate on the international scene. In the 1990s, it was the films of Theo Angelopoulos (*Ulysses Gaze*, 1995) and Emir Kusturica (*Underground*, 1995) that helped Balkan cinema gain recognition and acclaim. In the new millennium, it is new waves in Romania and Greece, bold new female filmmakers and the likes of Cristian Mungiu (*4 Months, 3 Weeks and 2 Days*, 2007) and Nuri Bilge Ceylan (*Winter Sleep*, 2014) that keep cinema from South East Europe afloat. The story continues.

* * *

A balanced country-by-country survey must pay attention to as many phenomena that occur in the covered territory as possible. Many of the authors writing in this book observe that films that are most popular within a given country rarely sell well beyond its borders. What makes an impact in the annals of international cinema may not be as influential at home, so some of the trends that privilege the international playing field may remain overlooked. The dark minimalist realism of the Romanian New Wave, the emotional stupor found in the Greek 'Weird' Wave, the existential sensibilities of new Turkish cinema and the range of thought-provoking documentaries made across the region, need special singling out where the ambition is to foreground recent landmark achievements of Balkan cinema.

So even though it is the names of specific countries that associate with the waves of 'Greek' quirkiness or 'Romanian' philosophical bleakness, it is mainly specific feature films – as well as some remarkable documentaries – that make up for the most recognisable recent cinematic output from the Balkans. Some of the titles that are recognisable internationally include *Dogtooth* (2009), *The Lobster* (2015) and *The Favourite* (2018) by Yorgos Lanthimos, *Attenberg* (2010) by Athina Rachel Tsangari from Greece, as well as *The Death of Mr Lazarescu* (2005) and *Sieranevada* (2016) by Cristi Puiu, *4 Months, 3 Weeks, and 2 Days* (2007) and *Graduation* (2016) by Cristian Mungiu, or *12:08 East of Bucharest* (2006) by Corneliu Porumboiu from Romania. Then, there is the work of acclaimed Turkish auteurs which could be described as a 'contemplative' wave: it goes beyond Cannes-winning Nuri Bilge Ceylan to include directors of related existentialist sensibilities like Zeki Demirkubuz, Semih Kaplanoglu, Reha Erdem and Yesim Ustaoglu, as well as internationally acclaimed work by female filmmakers such as Bosnian Jasmila Žbanić (*Esma's Secret: Grbavica*, 2006), Romanian Adina Pintilie (*Touch Me Not*, 2018) and Macedonian Teona Strugar Mitevska (*God Exists, Her Name is Petrunija*, 2019).

And then, transnationally, there are discourse-defining films by documentarians like Adela Peeva (*Whose Is This Song?*, 2003), Želimir Žilnik (*The Old School of Capitalism*, 2009), Andrei Ujica (*The Autobiography of Nicolae Ceausescu*, 2010), Alexandru Solomon (*Kapitalism: Our Improved Formula*, 2010), Danis Tanović (*An Episode in the Life of an Iron Picker*, 2013), Žiga Virc's *Houston, We Have a Problem* (2016), and Mila Turajlić (*The Other Side of Everything*, 2017), which have gained world-wide recognition and acclaim.

* * *

Talking of identity and collective memory in the Balkans is always fraught with peril; each story can be told in different ways, so touching on sensitive subjects of sameness and otherness is generally avoided. Nonetheless, topics of identity and memory prevail and continue to occupy the minds of the region's cineastes. Films like the Serbian *The Tour* (Goran Marković, 2008) or the Croatian *Buick Riviera* (Goran Rusinović, 2008) but even Romanian *Niki and Flo* (Lucian Pintilie, 2003) and *Sieranevada* (Cristi Puiu, 2016) may seem full of incomprehensible petty bickering and are often declared by Western critics to display 'black humour' but they provide, in fact, a symbolic battleground where conflicting narratives on recent history clash and reconcile.

Each of the countries surveyed here has produced ambitious nationalist sagas that have been widely acclaimed and awarded in the respective domestic contexts. At the same time, daring directors have continued making films on 'undesirable' topics – as seen in films such as Reha Erdem's exploration of guerrilla war in *Jin* (2013) or Emin Alper's study of political violence in *Frenzy* (2015).

Then there are the films dealing with haunting topics that require truth and reconciliation approaches – like the war rapes that are continuously being revisited in films from Kosovo and Bosnia; Jasmila Žbanić's *For Those Who Can Tell No Tales* (2013) is one of the finest examples of these. Or films that revisit the traumas of war like *Ordinary People* (Vladimir Perisić, 2009), *The High Sun* (Dalibor Matanić, 2015), *Men Don't Cry* (Alen Drijević, 2017) and many others – but also those films exploring problematic and irredentist allegiances from the times of the Second World War or even earlier contexts – the First World War, the Balkan Wars and the Austro-Hungarian or Ottoman rule. While populist governments encourage the production of ornate nationalist sagas in many of the countries explored here, this is also the region that turns up the most consistently committed anti-nationalist films that expose profound moral deficiencies and segregation in areas like education (*Our School*, Mona Nicoara, 2009), the performing arts (*Srbenka*, Nebojša Slijepčević, 2018), at the workplace (*The Miner*, Hanna Slak, 2017), or in public administration and health (*Erased*, Miha Mazzini, 2018). In this line of work, recent films by Romanian Radu Jude's stand out – the features *Aferim* (2015), which exposed matters of Roma slavery in the region, and *I Do Not Care If We Go Down in History as Barbarians* (2018), which was a passionate call to contemporaries for facing historical responsibility, as well as the experimental documentary *Dead Nation* (2017), which brought Romania's suppressed Holocaust record back from oblivion.

The collection seeks to strike a fine balance in giving a true picture that brings together all kinds of cinematic narratives that circulate in the Balkans – glorifying historical sagas alongside films that reveal injustices of the communist period, as well as 'dissident' films that engage with the difficulties experienced by ethnic, linguistic or religious minorities. In that, it asks for reflection of the perennial duality of irredentist and populist tendencies on the one hand and cosmopolitan leftist leanings on the other. One of the authors makes an apt remark about the irony of a period which sees the production of massive new film histories in some of the smallest countries that struggle to keep film production going. There is recognition, however, that cinema is chronicling the experience of the nation. In that, the film archives based in the region remain important, even if sometimes impoverished, so the work of organisations such as the Albanian Cinema Project, the Nitrate Film Festival in Belgrade and the Istanbul Cinémathèque is recognised as a remarkable preservation effort.

As an extension of this preservation work, several important documentaries explore the specific fortunes of filmmaking in the region: Mila Turajlić's *Cinema Komunisto* (2010) chronicles the film industry of Tito's Yugoslavia, Cem Kaya's *Remix, Remake, Rip-Off: About Copy Culture and Turkish Pop Cinema* (2014) zooms in on Yeşilçam and questions the biased understanding of cross-cultural appropriation. And, Greek Nina Maria Paschalidou's perceptive investigation *Kismet: How Turkish Soap Operas Changed the World* (2014) delves into the wide international spread of female-authored Turkish soaps and the way in which they shape women's self-esteem across the Balkans and the Middle East.

*   *   *

This book recognises the importance of new policies, facilities and distribution channels; each and every chapter charts the specific industry landscape, an underlying factor for the evolution of a national film culture: film institutes, production companies, mainstream and arthouse cinemas, membership in international funding bodies and organisations like the European Film Academy. Whereas most of the countries in the region would comfortably fit in the 'small national cinemas' framework proposed by Mette Hjort and Duncan Petrie, there are also some 'micro' industries, like in the case of Montenegro or Cyprus, as well as some sizeable ones, like Turkey, which produces more than a hundred films annually. The smaller size necessitates pulling resources together and engaging in co-productions, and indeed these collaborations are charted across the board to reveal a thriving and convivial creative milieu – with a special attention to matters of majority and minority co-productions, as well as runaway business.

In the context of digital transition and profound changes in exhibition, television and new streaming platforms (some of them international, like HBO) have stepped in and play an important role as producers; they also provide opportunities for improved (and truly global) exposure – many Turkish films are available on Netflix, and so is the Croatian mini-series *The Paper* (Dalibor Matanić, 2016–) or Romanian film *Rocker* (Marian Crişan, 2012). Amazon Prime features the North Macedonian *Honeyland* (Tamara Kotevska and Ljubomir Stefanov, 2019) – a film which won at Sundance and gained two

Oscar nominations, as well as a package of Bulgarian AgitProp documentaries, including Andrey Paounov's *Georgi and the Butterflies* (2005).

But there is also awareness that transnational production contexts can occasionally backfire – as shown in Melis Behlil's interesting case study of *Mustang* (Deniz Gamze Ergüven, 2015), a Turkish-language French film set in Anatolia and purporting to represent specifically Balkan matters of gender. *Mustang* was acclaimed in the West, then entered into the Oscars by France and subsequently shortlisted for the best foreign language film award, yet in Turkey it was regarded as inauthentic and even ridiculed.

The Balkan film festivals are given true recognition. Not only does one learn of important events across the region – from the veteran festival of cinematography the Manaki Brothers in Bitola, North Macedonia, through to the dynamic new DokuFest in Prizren in Kosovo – but one receives a comprehensive overview of the festival scene. The largest such forums include the Thessaloniki Film Festival (a conglomerate of several events), as well as the festivals in Sarajevo and Istanbul, which play an important transnational role in showcasing the area's cinematic output. Thessaloniki's Balkan Survey, a comprehensive sidebar that also features retrospectives of specific directors, has been in existence for more than two decades. In the absence of strong regional distribution networks, the festivals, which also feature project markets, enable a variety of Balkan collaborations, often structured around linguistic trajectories. In that, they become an important transnational factor in the evolution of cinema.

The specifics of transnationalism here is assessed against categories suggested by Mette Hjort (2010), and the talk is mainly of a prevailing 'affinitive'/'milieu-building' stance that manifests in transnational collaborative choices and where the affinities once again evolve mainly along linguistic groups, even if one also comes across examples of occasional 'opportunistic', 'globalising' and 'epiphanic' transnationalisms that manifest in a wider European context where the 'Balkan' classification turns undesirable. The transnational approach permits authors to give attention to the respective national diasporas and the dynamics of in- and out-migration trends, as far as audiences and film personnel is concerned.

* * *

This collection is radically different from all previous books on Balkan cinema in that it departs from the traditional male-dominated historiography which tends to overlook the achievements of women and makes a decisive step toward properly recognising female-made films, both in the present and retrospectively. And this is not only about the women who won top awards and gained international visibility – Jasmila Žbanić, Adina Pintilie, Ralitsa Petrova or Mila Turajlić – but also many others, like Aida Begić, Sonja Prosenc, Pelin Esmer, Zornitsa Sophia, Marianna Economou, to name just a few, who enjoy a high international profile and festival accolades. It is a period of unprecedented push for women, and one that marks a radical departure from the time when only male directors would receive nominations or awards and when only male filmmakers would remain in film history. Finally, this collection signals an opportunity to start bringing out of obscurity the work of important female directors of earlier generations such as Bulgarian Binka Zhelyazkova (1923–2011) and Albanian Xhanfise Keko (1928–2007).

* * *

The screening of Greek documentary *Catastroika* (Aris Chatzistefanou and Katerina Kitidi, 2012) – a film analysing the complex causes and global beneficiaries of the Greek economic crisis – at the Subversive Film Festival in Zagreb presented an unforgettable experience. The auditorium was totally packed, with people overflowing from the balconies and reacting stormily. The Q&A with the filmmakers was heated and went on for a long time. The atmosphere of solidarity and sharing was intense. This is the way I have always imagined what May 1968 must have been, in Paris and at the interrupted Cannes film festival . . .

In the past decade, my travels have taken me to many diverse corners of the Balkans – be it for participation at film festivals in Turkey, Greece, Romania, Bulgaria, Croatia, Cyprus, North Macedonia and Serbia, or for visits with friends in cities like Skopje, Novi Sad, Heraklion or Izmir. I also enjoyed the inspiring beauty of these lands – on the marble pebble beaches below Pelion mountain in Greece, on the ferries that criss-cross Istanbul's waterways, on the boats that take off from Ohrid and float during spectacular sunsets over the lake. I walked cobblestoned streets in Piran in Slovenian Istria, strolled under the watchful rooftop 'eyes' of houses in old Sibiu in Transylvania and marvelled at the architectural genius of Mimar Sinan at Istanbul's Süleymaniye Mosque, majestic yet restrained. I had my share of exposure to the unsettled politics of the region – at the anarchist Exarchia in Athens, near the disputed Gezi Park in Istanbul and at downtown protests in my native Sofia. I sat in the shadow of the makeshift 'wall' that divides Nicosia and stood in front of Ceaușescu's mammoth People's Palace in Bucharest. Wherever I went, I encountered the same feeling of solidarity among ordinary people, accompanied by humble awareness of limited power and modest economic means yet showing integrity and willingness to support one another when it comes to difficult times. The Balkans may be confused and peripheral, but they are also full of dignity and tangible humanity: a site for endless journeys.

* * *

If I knew who I was, I would have stopped making movies. I make movies to know myself. And to know the world. And also to find a balance, to understand. And that keeps me standing; just having this curiosity and a desire to travel that never ends. A desire to know other places, other faces, other situations, and to always feel myself, on an endless journey.[1]
(Theo Angelopoulos, 2012)

---

[1] From the film *Letter to Theo* (Elodie Lelu, 2019).

INTRODUCTION

Lydia Papadimitriou and Ana Grgić

Twenty-five years ago, in 1995, as the war was still raging in the former Yugoslavia two films from the Balkans dominated the Cannes Film Festival, winning the Palme d'Or and the Jury Prize respectively: Emir Kusturica's *Podzemlje/ Underground* and Theo Angelopoulos's *To vlemma tou Odyssea/Ulysses' Gaze*. Throughout the 1990s and 2000s a number of films from the region won international acclaim: Milcho Manchevski's *Pred dozhdot/Before the Rain* received the Golden Lion at the Venice Film Festival in 1994, Danis Tanović's *Ničija zemlja/ No Man's Land* won the Oscar for Foreign Language Film in 2001 and, a few years later, in 2006, Jasmila Žbanić's *Grbavica/Esma's Secret: Grbavica* was awarded the Golden Bear in Berlin. Despite their stylistic variety, all these films dealt with ethnic conflict, violence, war and their repercussions. Balkan cinema, inevitably, became almost synonymous with such topics, reinforcing entrenched perceptions of the Balkans as a place of unruliness and symbolic darkness. As Maria Todorova ([1997] 2009) has shown, the Balkans have long been laden with such negative connotations, and the violent post-communist breakup of the former Yugoslavia helped them resurface again in media and political discourse. With peace returning to the Western Balkans, the global limelight on the region has gradually dimmed, and with it, considerations of Balkan cinema as a whole. Certain national film movements, such as the Greek and Romanian New Waves, and/or individual directors from the region, such as Nuri Bilge Ceylan or Ralitsa Petrova, have since gained the attention of critics, academics and film festivals, but Balkan cinema has gradually lost its currency.

This book counters this tendency. It argues that the notion of the Balkans remains a valid framework within which to examine cinemas from the region, but that Balkan cinema needs to be reconceptualised in order to take into account new geopolitical, institutional and technological circumstances. As such, this collection widens the geographic focus in order to provide an inclusive view of the region and disband narrow identifications of the Balkans with the former Yugoslavia. Concurrently, it brings the temporal focus to a recent historical period, taking as its starting point the 2008 global financial crisis rather than the collapse of communism in Europe which often initiates such accounts. In throwing the spotlight equally on all countries of the region, irrespectively of size, wealth or output, the book aims to redress the terms of engagement with these cinemas, inviting a fresh look at each country's cinematic activity while also placing emphasis on instances of collaboration and exchange within, across and beyond the region.

Some of the cinemas examined here are very little known outside their particular context, and this collection provides the first available critical and historical account in English. As such, the book serves a dual function as both a scholarly study and a reference text. It presents national profiles of the cinematic production and film industry in all thirteen countries of the Balkans, while placing emphasis on transnational links within and beyond them. The collection (re)positions Balkan cinema in the global cinematic map, not only by highlighting the various challenges cinemas in the region have faced (and in many cases still face), but also by underlining ways in which filmmakers and institutions have sought – and often succeeded – to overcome them by developing existing and forging new cultural, economic and political alliances.

The adoption of the collective term 'Balkan' to consider the films of the region, rather than the apparently more neutral and descriptive designation 'South-Eastern European cinema' serves a polemical purpose: to disperse some of the deeply rooted negative perceptions of the region, by throwing into light a number of ways in which post-2008 cinematic developments testify to a more positive, constructive and collaborative ethos. While financial, social and political difficulties persist in many Balkan contexts, the last decade or so is marked by the ever stronger realisation among filmmakers and cinema-supporting institutions that cross-border collaboration is crucial in enabling projects to materialise and reach audiences. Such an emphasis on transnational exchanges does not only support the argument for the meaningful existence of a Balkan cinema, but also undercuts the negative connotations of the term 'Balkan'.

The origins of the West's unfavourable perceptions of the region, emblematised in words such as 'balkanisation', lie in its history as part of the Ottoman Empire and its consequent breakup into a number of nation-states. As Maria Todorova explains, 'Balkan' is originally the Turkish for 'mountain' or 'stony place', which was gradually used to refer to the mountain range that crosses contemporary Bulgaria (Haemus, in ancient Greek), before giving its name to the whole peninsula in the nineteenth century (2009: 26–8). It was Western travellers during the eighteenth and nineteenth centuries that started spreading this word, which was at times accompanied by comments regarding the perceived decline or debasement of classical ideals under the Ottoman rule (22). The term's strong negative connotations, however, only emerged at the start of the twentieth century, around the time of the Balkan Wars and the First World War, when the term 'balkanisation' also started being used (32). Already from the 1930s there were attempts in the West to replace reference to the 'Balkans' with 'South Eastern Europe', but this term also became problematic as it was used by the Nazis (28). While the issue subsided in the communist era, the violent fragmentation of the former Yugoslavia brought back reinforced perceptions of 'balkanisation' and associations of the region with conflict, war and violence, as well as essentialist interpretations of the Balkans and its politics (Glenny 2012). In the West's perception of the Balkans, history became mixed with projected fears enhanced by myths surrounding the region (for example, Dracula), reproducing and reinforcing negative stereotypes concerning this 'other' Europe. As Larry Wolff (1994) has noted with reference to Eastern Europe more widely, the Balkans hold an ambivalent relation to Europe, being both inside and outside it. They are, in many ways, Europe's liminal zone.

By branding the cinema of the region as 'Balkan' the book takes its cue from existing scholarship in cultural, historical and film studies but goes beyond it by offering a fresh perspective on post-2008 cinematic activity in the light, especially (but not exclusively) of fruitful cross-border interactions. The work of Edward Said (1978) and Todorova has had a deep impact on critical approaches on the Balkans, with concepts such as 'nesting orientalisms' (Hayden and Bakić-Hayden 1992, 1995), 'self-exoticism' (Iordanova 2001) or 'self-balkanisation' (Longinović 2005) being developed to address issues around representation and identity in the region. More recently, Dušan Bjelić has combined postcolonial with psychoanalytical insights in his analysis of Balkan pathologies (2016), critiquing the role of Europe in adopting neo-liberal and neo-colonial strategies to perpetuate a social, political and symbolic subjugation of the Balkans (2019). Along similar conceptual lines, Kriss Ravetto-Biagioli (2017) has offered close readings of selected artworks from the Balkans as a means of unmasking the crisis of European identity. This book is less engaged with attempts to unravel the complex symbolic and political relationship between the Balkans and the West and more concerned with offering an empirically grounded account of the cinematic activity within and across the region.

In the realm of film studies, no existing study examines Balkan cinema within the same spatiotemporal and conceptual parameters, that is temporal proximity, geographical inclusivity and an emphasis on transnational exchange and global visibility. Anglophone literature has tended to either conflate the Balkans with the former Yugoslavia (Iordanova 2001; Levi 2007; Jelača 2016) or focus on national case studies (Suner 2010; Karalis 2012; Vidan and Crnković 2012; Nasta 2013). The same applies to publications in local languages (for example, Daković 2008; Pavičić 2011). The predominance of national cinemas is a result of many factors, including linguistic and political ones. The mutual incomprehensibility of many Balkan languages makes it difficult to delve into neighbouring cinemas, while the political situation of recently separated nations such as the case of former Yugoslavia reinforces the desire to create nationally distinct cinematic narratives. Most crucially, unlike the case of Nordic countries that have systematically developed transnational institutions to support their regional cinema (Nestingen and Elkington 2005), there is no equivalent institutional framework in the Balkans to reinforce cross-border accounts of Balkan cinema. As a result of the above, local film scholars tend to privilege national frameworks as opposed to comparative or regional studies. The only other book that has a similar geographic scope is Dina Iordanova's *The Cinema of the Balkans* (2006), which nonetheless consists of twenty-four analyses of individual cinematic masterpieces from the region rather than the more industrially and contextually informed approach offered here. This book extends and expands on Iordanova's premise, who noted the disregarded interactions between Balkan filmmakers during the Cold War and in the new millennium (2006: 10), by offering detailed and concrete accounts of the ways in which such transnational exchanges have been experienced from within each different Balkan country and in recent years. We are particularly grateful to the authors of individual chapters (most being based in the particular country under analysis), who have been able to provide invaluable insights and who were instrumental in helping us connect the dots to create a collective account of Balkan cinema. We would not have been able to do so alone precisely due to continuing difficulties of accessing cross-border information, linguistic differences and the fact that formal transnational links are in the process of development. To this end, we would like to stress how the fruitful results of this edited collection are truly a joint and collaborative effort between different Balkan cinema scholars.

Spatiotemporal delimitations of Contemporary Balkan Cinema

Our account of contemporary Balkan cinema starts with the 2008 financial crisis, which began in the United States and spread across the rich world, accelerating the eruption of the European debt crisis in the following year. Unlike more obvious demarcations or moments of rupture that have served as starting or ending points for scholarly examinations of local, national and regional cinemas, such as the Second World War, the communist period, the fall of the Berlin Wall or even the digital revolution, we have chosen to focus on the decade following the onset of the global financial crisis in order to investigate the newly witnessed synergies on the Balkan film scene. This is because we have observed that, for a variety of reasons, since 2008 the region has – and is still in the process of – experiencing dynamic and increasingly transnational move-ments in terms of cinema production, distribution and exhibition. This is partly the result of the so-called Europeanisation of the Balkans. We acknowledge that this process has functioned as a double-edged sword: on the one hand, it has resulted in collaborative, transnational projects on all levels of the social, political and cultural spheres – including a number of exciting and novel film-related initiatives such as those discussed in this book; at the same time, it has led to the realities of neoliberal market ideology, unemployment and emigra-tion, as well as, in some cases, the rise of nationalist, racist and right-wing ideologies – points of friction and concern that also manifest themselves through cinema, as is also evident in several chapters here. Indeed, recent schol-arship has critiqued this form of European neo-colonialism and the 'economic subjection' of the Balkans, which has reconfigured the economic, political and social landscape and resulted 'at once in global integration and local social dis-integration' (Bjelić 2018: 751–8).

While, broadly speaking, such changes have affected the whole region, it should also be noted that the impact of the financial crisis, specifically, has been experienced at different stages and with different degrees of intensity in vari-ous parts of the region, largely because of the different degrees of integration of the Balkan countries into the structures of global finance. The countries that were part of the Eurozone – Greece, Cyprus and Slovenia – were most directly and deeply affected by it, while for the majority of Balkan countries, with dif-ferent currencies and smaller economies, the crisis had little direct impact. Despite such differences, however, 2008 marks a shift towards an embrace of a more extrovert attitude in film production and distribution across the Balkans. Whether as a direct consequence of the crisis or more deep-seated reasons, the post-2008 period has been economically challenging, but cinematically reward-ing, for the Balkan region. For instance, a number of countries in the Balkans have established film centres or implemented important structural changes in cinema legislation and funding in the last decade. These include the Film Law and the founding of the Croatian Audiovisual Centre in 2007, the merging of Slovenian Film Fund and Slovenian Film Centre in 2011, the introduction of the new cashflow system for film productions in Serbia in 2014, the adoption of the international co-production funding scheme in Albania in 2015 and the founding of the Film Centre of Montenegro in 2017, among others. The book highlights the ways in which filmmakers fought for survival, the kinds of stories they told and the means by which both individuals and institutions responded to this changing landscape, by – among others – building on cross-border cin-ematic collaborations across and beyond the Balkans.

Returning to the question of 'what are the Balkans', we acknowledge that definitions of the geographical boundaries of the Balkans vary a lot. Narrow definitions tend to reinforce particular perspectives on the region and thus contain irreconcilable contradictions more easily. Often, as noted above, the term has been conflated with the countries of the former Yugoslavia, especially as it re-emerged in media and political discourse at the onset of the Yugoslav wars in the 1990s. At other times, the term is used to refer only to ex-communist countries, thus excluding Greece and Turkey. The relationship of some geographically liminal countries, such as Romania or Slovenia, is often particularly ambivalent towards the Balkans, and as a result these are often excluded from consideration. The variations are many.

This book opts for an inclusive interpretation based on shared geography, culture and history. Put simply, this consists of being in South Eastern Europe, feeling connected to both East and West, having historically belonged either to the Ottoman or the Austro-Hungarian Empires (or both), and sharing the cultural imprint left by diverse civilisations inhabiting the area. Based on the above criteria, and as the book is organised by country, the geographical boundaries of the region are defined for our purposes here by four limit points as follows. In the North is Romania – both an Ottoman protectorate and part of the Austro-Hungarian Empire before its national independence in the nineteenth century. In the North West is Slovenia – long under Austro-Hungarian rule, but also part of Yugoslavia which had a strong Balkan identity. In the South East is Cyprus – an island of the Eastern Mediterranean geographically far from the Balkan peninsula but culturally very close to two Balkan countries, Greece and Turkey. In the East is Turkey – by far the largest country in the region and geographically mostly outside Europe, but whose imperial past has left a deep imprint in the history and identity of the region. It should be noted, however, that beyond national boundaries, the liminal positioning of the region at the edges of East and West renders it into a fluid imaginary and geopolitical space with fuzzy contours that cannot be strictly defined. While the geographical space thus delimited consists of thirteen countries, all of which are individually examined in this book – Albania, Bosnia-Herzegovina, Bulgaria, Croatia, Cyprus, Greece, Kosovo, Montenegro, North Macedonia, Romania, Serbia, Slovenia and Turkey – this book does not restrict the cinema activities it examines within strict boundaries of identity, nationality or space.

The organisation of the book by national cinema, whereby each chapter focuses on one country, allows the individual authors to highlight transnational and global links starting from the specific, local and national, but does not stop them from reaching out beyond national confines when assessing cinema activities and movements of Balkan filmmakers. Such an organisation has a number of advantages, especially given the lack of existing publications in the English language on the cinemas of some of these countries (such as Montenegro, North Macedonia or Kosovo). It acknowledges the role of nation-states in supporting cinema through production subsidies and promotional activities (e.g. in international film festivals), while also providing autonomy and agency to each (transnationally framed) national cinema. Furthermore, the coexistence of nationally designated chapters alongside each other in the volume invites the reader to initiate their own comparisons, while the alphabetical organisation aims to challenge any pre-conceived hierarchies or conceptual priorities, and establish a level playing field for all the cinemas presented.

Let's explain further.

1. As there is no equivalent publication that provides fundamental information on the film-related activities and current state of the industry in all Balkan countries, and especially in the newest among them, a country-by-country organisation serves this initial reference function. However, the chapters are not just descriptive, but also critical, as the authors frame the account of each country's cinematic activity in the context of transnational collaborations while assessing, where possible, current and future global prospects. It is this combination of the informative and the critical that supports the book's dual function as both a scholarly and a reference work while offering the foundations for future research on Balkan cinema.

2. Both conceptually and in practice, the transnational depends on the national. While the global disregards national boundaries, the transnational involves interactions and collaborations across defined national entities. The collection positions Balkan cinema in relation to both concepts, with the emphasis placed on the transnational (i.e. mostly regional and European collaborations) as the global impact and circulation of cinematic activity from the region remains rather limited. One of the most significant transnational dimensions of such activity is co-productions. For so-called 'official co-productions' (Hammert-Jamart et al. 2018) national designations are essential as they determine the legal dimensions of the arrangements. It is therefore necessary to locate transnational collaborations in the context of different national policies, institutions and discourses.

3. A number of countries included in the book have only gained their national independence since the 1990s and are still in the process of nation-building. Cinema plays a major symbolic role in shaping their national image and identity, and to reinforce perceived and desired (European) values. This is expressed both with reference to the past (constructing a national film history), and the present/future (branding the country internationally through new films). To a certain extent similar concerns also affect more established film industries in the region. While the different countries' nation-building projects are not the book's main focus, they are, however, examined as part of the broader context of film production, and especially if they impact on film-related policies, practices and collaborations. The

book's implicit agenda is to suggest that creative, cultural and financial partnerships and exchanges (such as the SEE Cinema Network, the Balkan Documentary Centre, the Balkan Film Market and CineLink at the Sarajevo Film Festival) are the main ways forward for the survival of these otherwise fragmented and, in their majority, poor film industries. Cinema can and does function as a unifying force.

4. The chapters are organised alphabetically, which may seem conceptually random at first, but this organisation is in fact both meaningful and critical of pre-existing power structures and formations of national cinema historiographies. The aim is to encourage novel readings that enable the repositioning, revaluation and reassessment of the richness and diversity of Balkan cinemas in the global edifice. In a context so complex and sensitive as that of Balkan cinema, any alternative chapter organisation that would involve grouping them in subcategories would impose an interpretative structure that would prioritise particular criteria and foreground one specific approach and perspective. Possible groupings could be made on the basis of the countries' global cinematic presence to date (critically recognised 'waves' and/or film exports); by size (of their film industry and/or population); according to their pre-1989 political status; by EU membership; or by a combination of the above. However, any of these would interpretatively fix the relationship between different countries with each other and globally in a premature way, given the fluidity of the cinematic state of affairs in the Balkans and the ongoing movement of contemporary film productions.

The book starts from a position of respect for each country, presenting them equally alongside each other irrespective of size, wealth, longevity or the international acclaim of their cinema. Some of these countries are, or until recently have been, affected by political difficulties and impasse, often among neighbours. For example, a naming dispute between Greece and the (former Yugoslav) Republic of Macedonia was only resolved in June 2018 with the adoption of 'North Macedonia' for the latter, while Kosovo remains unrecognised by over half of the United Nations' states and, crucially, by some Balkan neighbours and EU countries. While acknowledging such points of tension, the book focuses mainly on the positive steps taken in many parts of the Balkans in order to find common ground through cinema – both in terms of production and representation.

TRANSNATIONAL BALKAN CINEMA POST-2008

Collaborations across different Balkan countries at the level of production are not always linked with explicitly Balkan topics and/or iconographies, but, as Iordanova argues, a comparative and cross-cultural perspective can reveal a number of thematic and stylistic affinities across Balkan cinemas. If, as she points out, constructing Balkan cinema as an object of study is a project of 'connecting a disconnected space' (2006: 3), by offering transnational profiles of all national cinemas of the region this book contributes to forging and strengthening such connecting links. It should be noted, however, that while collaborations and textual similarities are present across the cinemas of the region, Balkan cinema should not be conceptualised as a closed genre with fixed and repeating characteristics, but rather as an open and dynamic entity with both converging and diversifying themes and styles that express the fluidity and, in some cases, precariousness of these cinemas. Any attempt to adopt a more fixed definition of Balkan cinema leads to narrow and restrictive interpretations. For example, film scholars and critics have often identified the specific type of black humour and cynical world-view present in films by Emir Kusturica and Srđan Dragojević as quintessentially Balkan in a way that ultimately reproduces a stereotypical perception of the region.

Observing recent films from the Balkans explored in the chapters, it is clear that several themes recur across national boundaries. These include the exploration of the past (whether returning to national myths or questioning official historical narratives), war and its consequences, crime and corruption, the effects of a dysfunctional state, judicial and educational infrastructures on the individual and the family, poverty and migration. A recent Slovenian film discussed in the book as a successful example of a co-production, *Ivan* (Janez Burger, Slovenia/Croatia, 2017), focuses on a personal and social drama against the backdrop of societal corruption and demonstrates a distinct auteur style. Similarly, in the case of Bulgaria, Kristina Grozeva and Petar Valchanov's social drama *Urok/The Lesson* (2014), a coproduction between Bulgaria and Greece, is an outstanding social drama dealing with crime, which has garnered several international awards. The Serbian majority coproduction *Rekvijem za gospođu J. /Requiem for Mrs. J.* (Bojan Vuletić, Serbia/Bulgaria/North Macedonia/Russia/France/Germany, 2017), an intimate drama set against a decrepit and realistic urban setting, explores similar themes prevalent in post-communist cinemas. While different in style and approach, Mila Turajlić's documentary *Druga Strana Svega /The Other Side of Everything* (Serbia/France/Qatar/Germany/Hungary, 2017) which won the main award at IDFA, and Radu Jude's film *Îmi este indiferent dacă în istorie vom intra ca barbari/I Do Not Care If We Go Down in History as Barbarians* (Romania/Germany/Czech Republic/France/Bulgaria, 2018), which won the Crystal Globe award at Karlovy Vary International Film Festival, serve as effective and highly successful examples of very recent arthouse Balkan films that rely heavily on co-production models and have global outreach. Both films offer counter-narratives of national history and question historical memory, one from a personal family perspective and the other through that of an artist.

While a number of these films are made as co-productions, this is not always the case. It can certainly be argued, though, that transnational collaborations encourage themes that resonate across borders, and the fact that these have increased in recent years only serves to reinforce the transnational character of post-2008 Balkan cinema. It should be noted that the stories are not always explicitly transnational in the sense of taking place in different locations across national borders or involving characters of diverse ethnic and national backgrounds. However, the recurrence of common thematic patterns and cultural-historical references and, as will be shown below, certain stylistic trends, even if these are not explicitly promoted as Balkan, testifies to the increasingly transnational nature of contemporary Balkan cinema. A recent example of a film that reflects what can readily be identified as Balkan sensibility is the primarily Romanian/Bulgarian coproduction *Aferim!* (Radu Jude, Romania/Bulgaria/Czech Republic/France, 2015). A historical road movie set in nineteenth-century Wallachia, the film testifies to the multi-ethnic and multicultural status of the Balkans at the time, while also reviving a cinematic trope shared among many ex-communist Balkan countries, that of the Red Western. It also draws on the shared regional mythologies around the *haidouks* – peasant bandits and/or guerrilla fighters who troubled both Ottoman and Habsburg authorities and romantically represented the desire for freedom.

Shot in spectacular black and white cinemascope, and heavily dependent on dialogue that is based on nineteenth-century Romanian literary sources, the style of *Aferim!* is at once quite unique and quite typical of a certain naturalist urge that characterises a lot of contemporary cinema from the Balkans. While oversimplifications regarding a dominant Balkan cinema style should be avoided, we can certainly note the significant impact of the minimalist, neo-realist approach introduced by the Romanian New Wave across many recent art films in the Balkans. For example, non-mainstream Croatian films, as discussed in more detail in the relevant chapter, have adopted several stylistic (and thematic) tropes inspired by the Romanian New Wave, including the choice of everyday locations, the absence of non-diegetic music and the naturalistic use of dialogue. Another notable stylistic trend is the Greek Weird Wave, although its extreme stylisation and very distinctive aesthetic sensibility has proven less directly influential. Stylistic experimentation with a marked authorial stamp is evident in Balkan art cinema across borders, as evident in the work of Slovenian Sonja Prosenc (*Drevo/The Tree*, Slovenia, 2014), the Croatian Dalibor Matanić (*Zvizdan/The High Sun*, Croatia/Serbia/Slovenia, 2015), the Greek Yorgos Zois (*Interruption,* Greece/France/Croatia/Italy/Bosnia and Herzegovina, 2015) and the Romanian Adina Pintilie (*Nu mă atinge/ Touch Me Not*, Romania/Germany/Czech Republic/Bulgaria/France, 2018), among others. In popular cinema, the identification of a distinctive Balkan group style is harder to ascertain, as film style here tends to service genre and storytelling rather than mark itself through attempts at distinction.

In conceptualising the notion of Balkan cinema and the way in which cross-border fertilisation and exchange take place, it is important to take into account all levels of interaction, ranging from production to distribution and exhibition. While European co-productions have been formalised since 1989 with the founding of the Council of Europe's cultural support fund Eurimages, and then in 1992 with the European Convention for Cinematographic Co-production which regulates the legal framework for such cinematic collaborations, the last decade has seen an increase in the number of co-productions with partners from Balkan countries, as explored in the individual chapters and further evidenced in the Tables at the end of the book. With the exception of Kosovo, by 2019 all Balkan countries were members of Eurimages and signatories of the European Convention on Cinematographic Co-production. In 2018, a revision of the convention that lowered the minimum participation level for a co-producing partner to 5 per cent served to enable smaller territories to become co-producers on bigger projects from which they had been effectively excluded before, due to budgetary restrictions. The likely consequence of the revised convention will be an increase in European co-productions involving Balkan countries in the years to come. (As this book was going to print, the world was hit by the Coronavirus pandemic that caused serious disruption to the film industry globally. The extent to which the disruption will be long-lasting and affect co-production practices in the Balkans and beyond remains to be seen). While such 'official co-productions' (Hammett-Jamart et al. 2018; Papadimitriou 2018a, 2018b) often involve at least one large co-producing partner from Western Europe (usually France or Germany), as these provide not only significant amounts of funding but also increased access to distribution possibilities, there has also been an increase in co-productions across Balkan countries without Western European involvement. For comparative purposes and in order to observe the increase in the number of co-productions (majority and minority) since 2008, we provide reference tables for each country at the end of the book. These tables also include yearly data on the number of feature fiction and documentary films, animation and short films, as well as admissions and box office figures. All the above offer supplementary insights into the fluctuations of national film production, distribution and exhibition, and the economic situation of each film industry overall.

There is no doubt that the primary motivation for co-productions is financial – access to more production funds and markets. In an influential article that distinguishes between different types of collaboration, Mette Hjort (2010) characterises this kind of co-production 'opportunistic transnationalism', as it reflects the pursuit of financial opportunities rather than more organic needs emerging from a particular script or other cultural or artistic factors. However, even if their primary motivation is financial, the pursuit of such co-production opportunities often also reinforces pre-existing cultural links while also helping consolidate a stronger sense of regional identity, as evident in Hjort's categories of 'affinitive' and 'epiphanic transnationalism' respectively. While the former refers to collaborations among partners that share core cultural and often linguistic elements, the latter concerns the creation of deep transnational links at a regional level. The case of co-productions among countries of the former Yugoslavia offers good examples of both, as these are based on common cultural characteristics (including, in some cases, a common language) and pre-existing production, distribution and exhibition networks from Yugoslav times, while they also explore the desire to redefine commonalities on new ground. Titles of such co-produced films that explore themes related to memory and trauma from the Yugoslav wars include *Turneja/The Tour* (Goran Marković, Serbia/ Bosnia-Herzegovina/Croatia/Slovenia, 2008), *Krugovi/Circles* (Srdan Golubović, Serbia/Germany/France/Slovenia/Croatia, 2013), Matanić's *The High Sun, Teret/ The Load* (Ognjen Glavonić, Serbia/France/Croatia/Iran/Qatar, 2016) and *S one Strane/On the Other Side* (Zrinko Ogresta, Croatia/Serbia, 2016). Other examples of affinitive transnationalism include co-productions between (or including) Albanophone countries such as *Bota/World* (Iris Elezi and Thomas Logoreci, Albania/Italy/Kosovo, 2014) and *Martesa/The Marriage* (Blerta Zeqiri, Kosovo/ Albania, 2017); or between Greece and the Republic of Cuprus, such as *I istoria tis prasinis grammis/The Story of the Green Line* (Panicos Chrysanthou, Cyprus/ Greece, 2017), *Figadevondas ton Hendrix/Smuggling Hendrix* (Marios Piperides, Cyprus/Germany/Greece, 2018) and *Pafsi/Pause* (Tonia Mishiali, Cyprus/ Greece, 2018).

The increased embrace of co-production opportunities from Balkan countries is the result of increased extroversion facilitated by institutional changes within a number of national Film Centres, which designate the allocation of funds towards co-productions. This, in itself, is a result of both a wider overall desire for 'Europeanisation' among the vast majority of Balkan countries, but also the implicit recognition that increased global competition makes it ever more hard for cultural products from small countries to survive not only at the global, but also at the national and local levels. The advent of digital technologies and their impact not only on production but also on distribution is largely responsible for such intensified competition. Lower costs have led to the production of an unprecedented number of films, which in turn find it harder to reach audiences in this overcrowded global marketplace. While large global players, such as the Hollywood studios, continue to dominate by differentiating their products through expensive technological investments and innovations (for example, in special effects) and huge marketing costs for theatrical and online global distribution, films from small and low production-capacity countries, such as the majority of the Balkan countries (with the sole exception of Turkey which has a very large film and television industry), increasingly rely on film festivals to achieve visibility and reach audiences. A world premiere and, even better, an award at a major international film festival such as Cannes, Venice, Toronto, Berlin or Sundance guarantees that a film will be shown to many smaller festivals across the world, while also having the chance for mainstream theatrical distribution in different territories. Television, DVD and streaming rights will most likely also follow, at least for some territories, and the film will therefore succeed in reaching transnational and global audiences. Inevitably, films from Balkan countries that aspire to global visibility depend on film festivals, and increasingly, as already pointed out, national cinematic institutions offer support for festival exposure.

Aside from leading to an overall increase in the number of films produced globally, and to the proliferation of Internet-enabled forms of distribution through both global and nation/region-based VOD platforms, digital technologies also lie behind the exponential increase in film festivals globally. The simple fact that films do not have to be physically transported as prints in order to be shown at a film festival, in what was an expensive, slower and more difficult to coordinate system, has resulted in an increase of events that bring films to local and national audiences. This phenomenon is also evident in the Balkans and, as the individual contributions in this book show, it has had a significant effect in facilitating cross-fertilisation across Balkan cinemas and strengthening the bond between films and audiences. In fact, this book owes its existence to two such festivals (the Divan Film Festival in Romania and the Thessaloniki International Film Festival in Greece) where the editors initially met and, then, over repeated encounters, witnessed the increased dynamism of Balkan cinema, as well as the audiences' and filmmakers' desire to reach beyond national borders and explore commonalities in both heritage and prospects.

Apart from the proliferation of, often specialised, film festivals, which encourage cinephilia and expose audiences to arthouse and alternative films (an indicative example is Slovenia, a country of two million inhabitants that has twenty-nine active film festivals), the region's largest festivals serve as hubs for the promotion of Balkan films and the creation of further networking and development funding opportunities for filmmakers. Established in 1994, the Balkan Survey program at the Thessaloniki International Film Festival regularly screens a selection of the latest arthouse films from the region, and organises retrospectives of Balkan filmmakers (for example Romanian Cristian Mungiu in 2012, Serbian Želimir Žilnik in 2014, Romanian Mircea Daneliuc in 2015, Turkish Zeki Demirkubuz in 2016, Yugoslav Dušan Makavejev in 2019). Since 2005, Thessaloniki has provided networking opportunities for filmmakers from the region through the Crossroads Co-production Forum that is open to projects from Mediterranean and Balkan countries (Papadimitriou,

2016). A major player in terms of both promoting regional films in its competition programmes and supporting co-productions is the Sarajevo International Film Festival that was founded in 1995 during the siege of Sarajevo as a symbolic cultural counter-offensive to the atrocities of war. The festival has expanded to include professional activities, including the CineLink Industry Days (since 2003), a co-production market for regional feature projects in the development and financing stages, and Talents Sarajevo (since 2007, and in cooperation with the Berlin International Film Festival), which is an educational and creative platform for young professionals from the region. The Transylvania International Film Festival (est. 2002), one of the biggest film festivals in Romania, regularly features the Balkans in its country focus section: Bulgaria in 2018, Slovenia in 2017, Croatia in 2016 and Greece in 2013, while also having played an important role in promoting Romanian cinema within Romania. In Bulgaria, the Sofia International Film Festival, also established in 2002, is credited for the revival of the Bulgarian film industry and for the visibility of emerging Bulgarian filmmakers such Maya Vitkova (*Viktoria*, Bulgaria/Romania, 2014) and Ralitsa Petrova (*Bezbog/Godless*, Bulgaria/Denmark/France, 2016) within and beyond Bulgaria.

Film festivals function as alternative distribution networks for arthouse films, but they also serve as exhibition outlets, especially in the former communist countries where the dismantling of the vertical distribution system has left many areas, especially rural and suburban ones, without access to cinemas. A number of contributions (Bulgaria, Romania, Kosovo, Montenegro) point to the significant reduction in the number of cinema theatres in recent years, as well as to the fact the new multiplex cinemas that to a certain degree replaced capacity (and are usually located in shopping malls) exhibit mostly Hollywood fare and, occasionally, local popular genre films. European arthouse films are sometimes shown in a select few cinemas in city centres, while national arthouse films or – even worse – films from neighbouring countries (whether arthouse or popular) are usually unable to reach mainstream distribution.

Finally, we should point out the increasing economic but also upskilling significance of attracting major international film and television productions to shoot locally, especially for smaller countries. Several contributors have noted the increase in subsidies and incentives for foreign productions and the establishment of dedicated infrastructure (film commissions) to oversee this process. Notable examples of such productions which have also helped boost tourism, aside from providing work to local professionals, are the HBO TV series *Game of Thrones* (Season 2, 2012) in Croatia, action films such as the USA/UK co-production *November Man* (Roger Donaldson, 2014) starring Pierce Brosnan in Montenegro, or Luc Besson's *Anna* (France, 2019) in Serbia. The impact of the influx of foreign capital through foreign film productions is particularly visible in the small and newly independent (since 2006) country Montenegro, which has resulted in the creation of a large number of local film production companies (thirty-three in operation by 2018) and accelerated the overall professionalisation of the sector.

Balkans: The Future Is Cinema?

In lieu of a conclusion, given that we consider the transnational movements in post-2008 Balkan cinemas as an ongoing and open-ended process, we would like to draw attention to several positive developments that have occurred within the fabric of the cinematic landscape in the last decade: from institutional changes, to the digitalisation of film heritage, to the increased cross-border movement of filmmakers and the presence of arthouse films at international film festivals among others. The increasingly extrovert attitude of film centres, institutions and archives has led to charting new territories, evident, for example, in the more visible Balkan presence at the Berlin and Cannes film markets. It has also strengthened existing, and/or forged new, regional and international alliances, as indicated by the collaboration between the Tirana International Film Festival in Albania and the Apulia Film Commission in Italy, or the Bulgarian National Film Centre's financial participation in Serbian mainstream film productions. Most importantly, it has led to the emergence of a young generation of authors, such as Ivan Salatić from Montenegro, Sonja Prosenc from Slovenia, Tolga Karaçelik from Turkey, Ilian Metev from Bulgaria, or Hana Jušić from Croatia among many others, whose films received recognition at prestigious film festivals. The rise of women directors across the region is particularly encouraging (Bulgarian Maya Vitkova, Romanian Adina Pintilie, Slovenian Hanna Slak, Croatian Ivona Juka, Serbian Mila Turajlić, Cypriot Tonia Mishiali, among others) and the emergence of new stories and attitudes toward topics and themes that have traditionally been more difficult to broach, such as LGBTQ, women, refugee and minority issues (particularly in Greece, Kosovo, Slovenia, and Serbia).

Despite the growing tendencies of right-wing and nationalist conservative ideologies across Europe and the world, as mentioned earlier, the Balkans have recently witnessed positive changes on the socio-political front: the resolving of the name dispute between Greece and North Macedonia, the ongoing efforts towards reaching a mini-Schengen trade agreement between Serbia, North Macedonia and Albania, and the strong civic consciousness as evidenced from the wave of protests against corruption and crime, or those for education reforms and women's rights across the Balkans in 2019. Despite the economic difficulties, unresolved political issues and wavering unemployment levels evident across the region, we hope that this book will not only serve as acknowledgement and witness of the recent energy and movement in all areas of film production, distribution and exhibition in the Balkans, but also inspire a continuation of this positive and progressive ethos of collaboration and transnational exchange. Presenting itself as a broad historical account of the last decade that seeks to trace the relationships and synergies between the different countries and filmmakers in the region and beyond, the book establishes a unifying and complex picture of cinematic activities, by placing emphasis on the increasing fluidity, mobility and exchange of people and things. Ultimately, the book aims to attract more viewers for Balkan films, motivate future cinematic collaborations, and inspire further academic work. It does not consider Balkan cinema as a uniform and fixed entity, but as a dynamic and multifaceted one that deserves both the world's attention and a more positive (self-) image. Most importantly, it argues that Balkan cinema deserves to be known, understood, loved.

References

Bakić-Hayden, Milica (1995) 'Nesting Orientalisms: The Case of Former Yugoslavia', *Slavic Review*, 54 (4), pp. 917–31.

Bakić-Hayden, Milica and Hayden, Robert M. (1992) 'Orientalist Variations on the Theme Balkans: Symbolic Geography in Recent Yugoslav Cultural Politics', *Slavic Review*, 51 (1), pp. 1–15.

Bjelić, Dušan ([2011] 2016) *Normalising the Balkans: Geopolitics of Psychiatry and Psychoanalysis*. London: Routledge.

Bjelić, Dušan (2018) 'Introduction: Balkan Transnationalism at the Time of Neoliberal Catastrophe', *Interventions*, 20 (6), pp. 751–8.

Bjelić, Dušan (ed.) (2019) *Balkan Transnationalism at the Time of International Catastrophe*. London: Routledge.

Daković, Nevena (2008) *Balkan Kao (Filmski) Žanr: Slika, Tekst, Nacija*. Beograd: FDU.

Glenny, Misha (2012) *The Balkans 1804–2012: Nationalism, War and the Great Powers*, updated edn. London: Granta Books.

Hammett-Jamart, Julia, Mitric, Petar and Novrup Redvall, Eva (eds) (2018) *European Film and Television Co-production: Policy and Practice*. London: Palgrave.

Hjort, Mette (2010) 'On the Plurality of Cinematic Transnationalism', in Nataša Ďurovičová and Kathleen E. Newman (eds), *World Cinemas, Transnational Perspectives*. New York: Routledge, pp. 12–32.

Iordanova, Dina (2001) *Cinema of Flames: Balkan Film, Culture and the Media*. London: BFI Publishing.

Iordanova, Dina (ed.) (2006) *Cinema of the Balkans*. London: Wallflower Press.

Jelača, Dijana (2016) *Dislocated Screen Memory: Narrating Trauma in Post-Yugoslav Cinema*. New York: Palgrave Macmillan.

Karalis, Vrasidas (2012) *A History of Greek Cinema*. London: Continuum.

Levi, Pavle (2007) *Disintegration in Frames: Aesthetics and Ideology in the Yugoslav and Post-Yugoslav Cinema*. Stanford, CA: Stanford University Press.

Longinović, Tomislav (2005) 'Playing the Western Eye: Balkan Masculinity and Post-Yugoslav War Cinema', in Anikó Imre (ed.) *Eastern European Cinema*. New York: Routledge, pp. 35–47.

Nasta, Dominique (2013) *Contemporary Romanian Cinema: The History of an Unexpected Miracle*. London and New York: Wallflower Press.

Nestingen, Andrew and Elkington, Trevor G. (eds) (2005) *Transnational Cinema in a Global North: Nordic Cinema in Transition*. Detroit, MI: Wayne State University Press.

Papadimitriou, Lydia (2016) 'The Hindered Drive towards Internationalisation: Thessaloniki (International) Film Festival', *New Review of Film and Television Studies*, 14 (1), pp. 93–111.

Papadimitriou, Lydia (2018a) 'European Co-productions and Greek Cinema since the Crisis: "Extroversion" as Survival', in Julia Hammett-Jamart, Petar Mitric and Eva Novrup Redvall (eds), *European Film and Television Co-production: Policy and Practice*. London: Palgrave, pp. 207–22.

Papadimitriou, Lydia (2018b) 'Greek Cinema as European Cinema: Co-productions, Eurimages and the Europeanisation of Greek Cinema', *Studies in European Cinema* 15 (2–3), pp. 215–34.

Pavičić, Jurica (2011) *Postjugoslavenski film: Stil i ideologija*. Zagreb: Hrvatski Filmski Savez.

Ravetto-Biagioli, Kriss (2017) *Mythopoetic Cinema: On the Ruins of European Identity*. New York: Columbia University Press.

Stojanova, Christina (ed.) (2019) *The New Romanian Cinema*. Edinburgh: Edinburgh University Press.

Suner, Asuman (2010) *New Turkish Cinema: Belonging, Identity and Memory*. London: I. B. Tauris.

Todorova, Maria ([1997] 2009) *Imagining the Balkans*, updated edn. Oxford: Oxford University Press.

Vidan, Aida and Crnković, Gordana P. (eds) (2012) *In Contrast: Croatian Film Today*. New York: Berghahn Books.

Wolff, Larry (1994) *Inventing Eastern Europe: The Map of Civilization on the Mind of the Enlightenment*. Stanford, CA: Stanford University Press.

1. ALBANIA: CROSSING BORDERS WITH A NEW IMAGINARY

Bruce Williams and Kledian Myftari

Albanian cinema is undisputedly one of the least internationally known film cultures of Europe's former communist countries. This lack of global exposure is due to a number of factors, among which are Albania's extreme separatism under communism, its especially arduous path towards a market economy, and its relative size, both in territory and population. One can question whether the mere notion of Albanian cinema is a meaningful construct in an era of international co-production and globalisation, particularly given its meagre output and the small number of speakers of Albanian *vis-à-vis* other languages of Eastern Europe. However, the strong historical attention devoted to Albanian cinema within the confines of Albania, particularly under communism, coupled with more recent debates regarding the notion of transnational cinema indicate that a wider examination of Albanian cinema in Balkan, European and other broader contexts is long overdue. In 1952, when the communist government formally opened the state-run Kinostudio complex, directors and other film professionals were initially trained in other socialist countries. As Albania's isolation from the Soviet Union and the Warsaw pact increased, it began to educate its professionals at Kinostudio itself, and Albanian cinema became a truly national product, with very little influence from international cinema. Nonetheless, there has been considerable critical discourse in the last few years regarding Albanian cinema in the era of international co-production. Regarding the transnational phenomenon, which can be applied to Albanian film production of the better part of the past three decades, Elizabeth Ezra and Terry Rowden discuss the interface between the local and the global, arguing:

> As a marker of cosmopolitanism, the transnational at once transcends the national and presupposes it . . . From a transnational perspective, nationalism is . . . a canny dialogical partner whose voice often seems to be growing stronger at the very moment that its substance is fading away. (Ezra and Rowden 2006: 4)

More recently, Steven Rawle has framed the transnational in the context of the nationalist underpinnings of Brexit and Donald Trump's populist agenda. He asserted: 'At a time when borders have been more porous than ever, the intensified focus on nationalism restates the prominence of nation-states in popular consciousness' (Rawle 2018: xii). By extension, one can assume that Albania's emergence in the realm of transnational production and reception does not imply an effacing of the national.

Such national/international debates respond to the notion of cultural cosmopolitanism, which characterises the strong identification of people of a given culture with cultural or aesthetic products from outside of their local or national sphere. Cultural cosmopolitanism is related to both interconnectedness and the sharing of aesthetics, perceptions, forms of expression and cultural practices. This concept does not suggest the effacement of the local or the national, and when applied to the context of Albanian international co-productions of recent decades, it provides the driving force for our argument here.

This chapter will situate developments in Albanian cinema in the last decade in a historical context, briefly exploring the state of Albanian cinema under communism, the economic and political turmoil of Albania following the fall of the regime, and how this context affected film production. An examination of the impact of the global economic crisis of 2008 on the country and its cinema will lead readers to an analysis of Albania's present-day film context, which will bear upon production, exhibition and distribution, both at home and abroad.

From the Communist Era to the Financial Pyramid Scheme of 1997

The emergence of Albanian cinema as a subject of academic and critical examination is a recent phenomenon. During the communist period, Albanian films were only seen abroad in rare screenings by special interest groups[1] or on occasion at festivals such as the Giffoni Festival for children's films in Salerno, Italy.[2] Albania's Stalinist regime was far more interested in the role of film as a pedagogical tool in the construction of a new society than in spreading its cinema in international cultural circles.

Despite Albania's extreme isolationism following its breaches with the Soviet Union, the Warsaw Pact and ultimately with China, Enver Hoxha, who governed the country from 1946 until his death in 1985, was, to a certain extent, a man of the world. A product of francophone education and residence abroad, Hoxha's own background seems contrary to the isolation of his later regime. However, communist Albania was not always as isolated as it would later become. Especially during the 1950s, a number of key players of the communist Kinostudio enterprise were sent abroad for training in such countries as the Soviet Union, Hungary and Czechoslovakia. As the Hoxha regime grew more paranoid, fewer artists were granted this opportunity. This education abroad for the privileged few notwithstanding, foreign influences remained extremely limited during the Kinostudio period, and Albanian artists and audiences had minimal, if any, exposure to international cinema.

Following the fall of communism in 1991, Kinostudio was split into four sectors: Albafilm, Albafilm Distribution, Albafilm Animation and the Albanian Central State's Film Archive. With this change came a notable reduction in cinematographic output, due primarily to a dearth in funding. The few feature films made were still by and large national productions. However, during the mid-1990s, Albania made cautious steps into international co-production, and its films enjoyed accolades in prestigious film festivals abroad. A case in point is Kujtim Çashku's *Kolonel Bunker/Colonel Bunker* (1996), a co-production with France and Poland, which focused on the impact of the Hoxha era on the individual and the regime's paranoid campaign of bunkerization.[3] *Colonel Bunker* was selected as the Albanian entry to the Academy Awards.

A maverick in international co-production, Çashku is a perfect example of Albania's new brand of cultural cosmopolitans. Having studied in Romania at the height of the country's isolation in the mid-1970s, he received a Fulbright Grant to research human rights at Columbia University in 1993. Also in 1993, Çashku attended the *Rencontres Cinématographiques de Beaune*, where he met his co-producers. In many ways, Çashku, a veteran of the state-run Kinostudio, serves as a model for Albanian cinema of the 2000s. So much of Albania's film culture today depends upon like-minded cultural cosmopolitans who have lived abroad and studied the aesthetics of diverse film traditions. These individuals have encouraged Albanian cinema to transcend its once-closed borders, all the while reflecting the country's own social dynamics.

Unlike other post-communist nations, Albania was precipitated into economic turmoil and civil war in 1997 due to the collapse of multiple financial pyramids, Ponzi schemes, in which some two-thirds of the population invested. These pyramids had begun immediately following the fall of communism, and by 1997 some twenty-six of them had failed. Christopher Jarvis (2001) has articulated that these schemes were significant given that their scale in relation to the overall economy was 'unprecedented', and the political and social impacts of their collapse were tremendous. He attributes the popularity of the pyramids to a number of factors: the lack of familiarity among Albanians with financial markets; the deficiencies of the old financial system which allowed for the development of informal markets; and government failure (Jarvis 2001).

As catastrophic as the pyramid period was, Albania's involvement with international co-productions would soon be revitalised. In 2001, Gjergj Xhuvani made *Parrulat/Slogans* (France/Albania) which focused on a young schoolteacher in southern Albania at the height of the country's isolation, forced to lead pupils in constructing political slogans in stone on a mountainside. The film was arguably Albania's most complex co-production to date, having been financed by co-production agreements with multiple French partners.[4] It met with a limited degree of international theatrical exhibition, particularly in France. The following year, Fatmir Koçi directed *Tirana viti zero/Tirana Year Zero*, a comedy broaching a number of burning social issues, among these the impact of emigration on Albania. It was funded as a co-production among Albania, France and Poland. Again, its international exhibition was mostly in France. Both films have met with critical acclaim, at home and abroad, with *Tirana Year Zero* garnering first prize at the Thessaloniki International Film Festival in 2001.

Albania was one of the few European countries to display a positive GNP growth during the early phases of the 2007 financial crisis, only feeling a negative impact in late 2008. Ditmir Sufaj attributes this to the relative newness of the Albanian banking system, its eschewing of many advanced and sophisticated financial procedures, the country's lack of a stock exchange and the limited reliance of Albanian banks on external funding from the foreign market (2015:132). The return of one-sixth of the Albanians who had emigrated to Greece, a country particularly hard hit by the crisis, also contributed to Albania's initial economic growth during the period. These returnees reinvested their savings from abroad in Albanian banks. Such funds, however, eventually became depleted, and the impact of the crisis was finally felt in Albania (Sufaj 2015: 133). Sufaj further identifies the reduction of trade with countries that were deeply affected, such as Greece and Italy, as well as Albania's over-reliance on remittances from Albanians living abroad as factors ultimately leading Albania to be impacted by the global economic crisis (2015: 134).

Albania's initial resilience to the crisis can be evidenced by the six feature films it produced in 2009. These were obviously financed prior to or early on in the crisis. One of these films was exclusively Albanian, five were majority Albanian co-productions and one was a minority co-production. A significant film from 2008 is Piro and Eno Milkani's *Trishtimi i Zonjës Shnajder/The Sadness of Mrs. Schneider*, a co-production with the Czech Republic (Czech title: *Smutek pani Snajdrové*). The film follows a love affair between a married Czech woman and an Albanian film student at the prestigious FAMU of Prague in the early 1960s. It focuses on the human impact of the forced repatriation of Albanian students in the wake of worsening conditions between Albania and the Eastern bloc. *The Sadness of Mrs. Schneider* draws upon the education and international experience of Piro Milkani, a veteran Kinostudio director, known for such films as *Ngadhnjim mbi vdekjen/Triumph over Death* (Albania, 1967), and *Ballë për ballë/Face to Face* (Albania, 1979). Milkani would later serve as Albania's ambassador in Prague from 1992 to 1999. Spoken mainly in Czech, the film nonetheless contains extended sequences in Albanian. It was selected as Albania's entry to the Academy Awards.

A film made towards the end of the troubled economic period was Joni Shanaj's *Pharmakon* (2012), a production financed exclusively in Albania. Shanaj, a social anthropologist, draws heavily on his education in Sweden and his impressive knowledge of international cinema in the creation of a work that has garnered a high level of critical accolades. *Pharmakon* follows a young man's search for truth in the blighted social landscape of contemporary Albania. The film's dynamics recall Antonioni, and its static shots are akin to the early films of Chantal Akerman. It was Albania's selection for the Academy Awards, and was deemed a masterpiece in *Sight and Sound* by Mark Cousins (2013) (see Figure 1.1).

Figure 1.1   Klevis Bega and Niko Kanxheri in *Pharmakon* (Joni Shanaj, 2012). Courtesy of Joni Shanaj.

Recent Albanian Co-productions and the Present State of Albanian Cinema

In contrast to Shanaj's film, Iris Elezi and Thomas Logoreci's *Bota/World* (2014) was produced through a collaboration among partners from Albania, Italy and Kosovo. Like Shanaj, its filmmakers have highly international backgrounds. While Logoreci is an Albanian-American residing in Tirana, Elezi has a broad foundation in film theory and cinema studies from extended studies in the US. Since October 2017, Elezi serves as director of the Albanian Central State's Film Archive. *Bota* reflects the often-contradictory relationship contemporary Albanians have with the Hoxha dictatorship, and focuses on the impact of the discovery of a mass grave on the site of a former relocation camp from the perspective of a younger woman whose mother died in the atrocities. A work of cinematic poetry with haunting visual dynamics, *Bota* has been lauded at such festivals as Karlovy Vary, Reykjavik and San Francisco (see Figure 1.2).

Since 2015, the Qendra Kombëtare e Kinematografisë (QKK)/Albanian National Center of Cinematography has maintained in place a financial scheme for the funding of international co-productions in which the Albanian share of the production is in the minority. This special initiative considers projects from Albanophone authors in Kosovo, North Macedonia and Montenegro, as well as foreign projects which meet one of the following criteria: (1) an Albanian subject; (2) shooting, at least in part, in Albania; and (3) no less than 50 per cent Albanian dialogue. Support is also offered to projects 'of particular interest' – this is not clearly defined – which spend a 'considerable amount' of their budget in Albania, either for shooting or in other aspects of production. Certain conditions apply: the award is limited to a maximum of 6,000,000 Albanian lek

Figure 1.2   Flonja Kodeli in *Bota* (Iris Elezi and Thomas Logoreci, 2014). Courtesy of Iris Elezi.

(approximately 47,000 euros); at least 80 per cent of the funds must be spent inside of Albania; a minimum of 70 per cent of the total film budget must be in place prior to the application to the Albanian National Center of Cinematography; the production company must be a legal entity in the Republic of Albania and the project must have received financial support from public institutions in the co-production country (Qendra Komëtare e Kinematografisë 2017). The Center's website lists a total of six films funded by the scheme in 2015 and 2016, including one from North Macedonia, four from Kosovo and one from Italy. It further lists nine projects competing for funds in 2017, which originated in Kosovo, North Macedonia, Serbia and Greece (Qendra Kombëtare e Kinematografisë 2017). The Scheme underscores the 'Albanian-ness' of its productions. The elements of Albanian language, shooting in Albania or an Albanian subject are requirements which make, at least to the spectator, the films difficult to distinguish from majority or national productions. The requirements of the financing scheme render the distinction between majority and minority productions virtually indistinguishable.

Despite having been produced prior to the first year of the formal co-production scheme, two films directed by non-Albanians are of particular consequence. One is deemed by the Albanian National Center of Cinematography an Albanian majority production, while the other is not mentioned at all (Tafa 2018). Designated a majority co-production, Johannes Naber's *Der Albaner/Shqiptari/The Albanian* (Germany/Albania, 2010) is a collaboration among the European cultural channel ARTE, Neue Schönhauser Filmproduktion, and an Albanian partner OnFilm Productions. No statistics are available as to the percentage of Albanian funding; it is simply categorised as a majority co-production. Its German director notwithstanding, the film primarily makes use of Albanian actors, among these the young male star of *The Sadness of Mrs. Schneider* Nik Xhelilaj, and Kinostudio veteran Yllka Mujo. Naber's film is one of the first examples of a new phenomenon, that of foreign directors who opt not only to make films on Albanian turf but, moreover, as non-Albanian speakers, choose to direct films in Albanian. *Der Albaner* explores the plight of an illegal Albanian worker in contemporary Berlin. His experience in Germany runs the gamut from underemployment, to immigration scams, to corruption, and finally to murder. In this film, Naber opts for a high level of linguistic authenticity, filming the Albanian sequences not only in Albanian (a language of which he has minimal knowledge) but, moreover, in the specific language variety of the country's extreme north-east. In light of Naber's advocacy for social issues and his desire to integrate his film into the Albanian context, the film is a clear example of Mette Hjort's notion of 'affinitive transnationalism', given the 'shared commitments' and 'the discovery of features of other national contexts . . . relative to key problems experienced within a home context' (2009: 17).

In 2011, US director Joshua Marston made *The Forgiveness of Blood*, a feature foregrounding the persistence of Albania's ancient tradition of the blood feud in the country's Far North. Although *The Forgiveness of Blood* was primarily a US/UK co-production, it did make use of the Albanian partner, Lissus films, and hence might be deemed a minority Albanian production. The film's Albanian-ness is undisputed: its dialogue is exclusively in Albanian; it was filmed in Albania; the cast is entirely Albanian; and it made use of Albanian talent in a number of crew positions. Nonetheless, it does not appear on the list of the Albanian National Center of Cinematography, a fact most interesting in light of the controversy discussed below.

The Forgiveness of Blood was nominated by the Albanian National Center of Cinematography as Albania's official selection for the Academy Awards. This choice was protested by Bujar Alimani, director of *Amnistia/Amnesty* (Albania/Greece/France, 2011), who decried the heavy US hand in the production (Holdsworth 2011). Albanian artists and intellectuals spoke from both sides of the divide. Journalist Elsa Demo defended Alimani's position, arguing that Albanians feel that no truly Albanian product could stand a chance for the coveted Oscar (Holdsworth 2011). In contrast, Kujtim Çashku lauded Marston's transcendence of the exoticism of the blood feud and his focus instead on issues of love and human relations (Holdsworth 2011). In October 2011, the Academy of Motion Pictures disqualified *Forgiveness of Blood* as a foreign film, given that the Albanian creative presence was very limited.

Whether *Der Albaner* and *Forgiveness of Blood* are classified as majority or minority co-productions, or neither for that matter, they attest to the importance of language and culture in assigning a national designation to a film. Marston, though American, examined extensively an Albanian cultural phenomenon, and did so in a way that brought Albanian audiences to feel that it was, indeed, an Albanian film. In a slightly different manner, Naber spoke to burning social issues often ignored in Germany (we must note that the film's positive reception in Albania was not matched in Germany). In both instances, the directors made a strong case for the presence of Albanian language cinema even though they were not Albanophone themselves. After all, in today's transnational context, the distinction is blurred between Albanian directors using foreign funding to film in their own language, and foreigners like Naber and Marston, who, as non-Albanophones, opt as well to make films in Albanian.

Albanian cinema, albeit small, is very much alive today. The Albanian National Center for Cinematography lists the production in 2015 of five features, eight documentaries, four shorts and one animated film; in 2016, it catalogues three features, six documentaries, six shorts and two animated films; and in 2017, twelve features, two documentaries and four shorts were produced. These statistics refer exclusively to films supported by the Center and do not consider works that have been produced without official Albanian governmental subsidy.[5]

Together with feature film production, Albania releases a number of documentaries annually, as evidenced by the attached statistical chart. A number have been made by film students or by directors in the initial stage of their careers. Of particular consequence are Jurgen Agushi's *Gjyshja ime/My Grandmother* (Albania, 2014), a film focusing on an elderly Russian-born woman, who, following her marriage to an Albanian, spent her life in Albania, living through the Hoxha regime. The film was screened at DokuFest in Prizren, Kosovo, the Seanema Film Festival in Ulcinj, Montenegro, as well as at DocuTIFF (the documentary festival associated with TIFF) in Tirana, all in 2016 (see Figure 1.3). A recent work that is especially significant in its examination of Albanian cinema is Mevlan Shanaj's *Koha e pelikulës: Xhanfise Keko/Xhanfise Keko: A Woman Director in the Time of Celluloid* (Albania, 2017). This documentary, a portrait of the sole woman director of Kinostudio, was screened at New York's International Filmmaker Festival in 2018.

One characteristic of today's Albanian cinema is that it is decidedly an authorial cinema. By and large, works of popular cinema are not funded by the National Center for Cinematography. Eriona Vyshka, of the Albanian Central

Figure 1.3   Poster for *My Grandmother* (Jurgen Agushi, 2014). Courtesy of the Marubi Academy of Film and Multimedia.

State's Film Archive, argues that, although mainstream cinema production is very rare, the Centre did provide funding for two of the popular comedies of Erion Bubullima (Vyshka 2019). These films were *Sex, përrallë dhë celular/Sex, Storytelling and Cellular Phones* (Albania, 2015), which focuses on a writer of children's books who, when discovering that his wife is having an affair with a younger man, becomes an amnesiac, and *7 Ditë/7 Days* (Albania, 2016), which tells of a young lawyer who is abandoned by her fiancé seven days before the wedding. *7 Days* received funding from a pay-per-view channel, DigitAlb. Two recent comedies featuring comedian/singer Ermal Mamaqi have played to packed audiences in Tirana. Rudina Vojvoda's *Femrat – the movie/Women – The Movie* (2016) was co-produced by Roland Volaj in conjunction with New York-based Rucksack Productions. Turkish director Emir Khalilzadeeh's Albanian-language *Dy gisht mjaltë/Two Fingers of Honey* (2019), was produced by Mamaqi Productions in cooperation with Elvana Gjata, another pop singer. The box office success of these films is largely due to the popularity of Mamaqi and Gjata.

WATCHING ALBANIAN FILMS AND FILMS IN ALBANIA: FESTIVALS, CINEMAS AND TELEVISION

From 1976 to 2000, eleven editions of the state-controlled Festival of Albanian Films were held in Tirana. Natasha Lako has identified a specific theme prevalent in each edition of this festival; these range from happiness and accomplishments (1976) to social anxiety (1991) and euphoria (1995) (Lako 2004: 99–147). Today, the main festival in Albania is the Tirana International Film Festival (TIFF), which has taken place annually from 2003 to the present. TIFF not only provides an excellent vehicle for screening Albanian films but, moreover, has been highly instrumental in developing and strengthening co-production opportunities. The festival often invites foreign producers. Another festival of note includes the International Human Rights Film Festival Albania (IHRFFA), sponsored by the Marubi Academy of Film and Multimedia, which has been held annually since 2006 (see Figure 1.4). Other festivals include the A-Film Fest Rozafa, which foregrounds films for children and youth, and the Balkan Film and Food Festival, which celebrates Balkan culture in the lakeside town of Pogradec. Of special note is Giffoni, Albania, which was established in cooperation with Italy's Giffoni Festival. The festival, held in Tirana, Durrës and Shkodër, is intended to strengthen the relationship between Italy and Albania in the same way the original Giffoni had done for previous generations. The project's website states that some 9,000 children are involved in judging films from previous Giffoni competitions and engage in other activities that promote civilisation and democracy through the arts. The event also fosters cultural exchange and co-production opportunities with Italy (AnsaMed).

Figure 1.4   Poster for the thirteenth edition (2018) of the International Human Rights Festival Albania. Courtesy of the Marubi Academy of Film and Mutimedia.

Despite the emerging critical attention on Albanian cinema, the international commercial release of Albanian films is still in its early stages and most films remain limited to screenings in international festivals. In recent years, Albanian films have appeared at numerous festivals as widespread as Busan, São Paulo, Tallinn, Istanbul, Geneva, and Palm Springs. They have won major awards in Moscow, Prishtina and Karlovy Vary, to name but a few. Likewise, during the period 2015 to 2018, students of the Marubi Academy of Film and Multimedia have had some twenty films screened in Kosovo, Montenegro, Serbia, Croatia, Bulgaria, Greece, Italy, Hungary, the US and Colombia. Recent Albanian cinema, moreover, has been shown in free screenings held by universities and special-interest groups. In the US, Albanian films are viewed by the Academy of Motion Picture Arts and Sciences in consideration for the Best Foreign Film Oscar. To date, no Albanian film has made the final list of contenders. Nonetheless, viewings by members of the Academy indeed foster familiarity with Albanian cinema among the American film elite. The films that enjoy international release, however limited, are usually those where the majority of the production budget, or at least a significant part thereof, comes from foreign co-producers. Naber's *Der Albaner*, which won major festival awards in Moscow, Nuremburg and Saarbrücken, was released in the director's native

Germany. Marston's above-mentioned *The Forgiveness of Blood* also had a limited international release. Within Albania, however, it is difficult at best to determine national box office receipts.

According to the Albanian Law on Cinematography, the Albanian National Center for Cinematography has the obligation to keep box office statistics on national films. Nonetheless, no statistics appear to be publicly available. There are fifteen movie screens in Albania, yet, as Eriona Vyshka asserts, quality, authorial, Albanian films are far less successful than foreign films, or the few existing popular films, such as those of Bubullima and Mamaqi. Vyshka further explains that, following festival tours and their screenings in Albanian cinema, most Albanian films are shown on television, usually the public Radiotelevisone Shqiptar (RTSH). If RTSH sponsors a film, it is a contractual obligation that it be screened several times on television.

In Albania, there is considerable interest today in the works of Kinostudio, and despite current indictments of the tyranny of the communist era, these films are still very popular. Television is a major vehicle for the dissemination of Kinostudio work today. Radiotelevisione Shqiptar (RTSH) includes Kinostudio productions as part of their regular programming. Moreover, two private pay-per-view channels, Tring Shqip and DigitAlb, show films from the communist era as well as other Albanian-language programmes. Favourable public reception of Kinostudio productions has been confirmed by actress Elvira Diamanti, former director of the Albanian Central State's Film Archive, who stresses that the Albanian public prefers older cinematographic products, 'and still feels spiritually detached from brand new movies, shot only recently' (Diamanti 2010).

AFFINITIVE COSMOPOLITANISM AND INTERNATIONAL COLLABORATIONS

The Tirana International Film Festival has been instrumental in developing cooperation with the Apulia Film Commission in Bari, Italy, which has provided film funding for its neighbours, Albania and Montenegro. In the case of Albania, such ties are a type of affinity cosmopolitanism inasmuch as a number of Italy's southern province have been home to the Arbëreshë, Albanian-speaking communities, which fled to Italy in the late 1500s to escape the Ottoman occupation of their territory. In the early twentieth century, Italian was a language of prestige in Albania. Under communism, families in Shkodër concealed Italian-language materials intended to preserve the language from generation to generation.[6] Nonetheless, Albanians throughout the country clandestinely tuned into Italian radio and television broadcasts. Moreover, the fall of communism and the ensuing economic turmoil led to the growth of a present-day Albanian diaspora in Italy.

Another example of affinitive cosmopolitanism involves Albania's film ties with another of its neighbours, Kosovo. We must note that Prizren was the birthplace of the League of Prizren, one of the key entities fostering Albanian nationalism in the late 1800s. Today, Prizren is home to DokuFest, which enjoys a regular Albanian presence. Moreover, in 2018, the Albanian National Center for Cinematography provided funding for four films from Kosovo. Such projects suggest a context not unlike the nineteenth-century notion of 'Greater Albania', consisting of Albanophone territories presently located in Albania, Montenegro, Kosovo, Northern Macedonia and Greece. The undertaking is challenging, given a number of factors. Firstly, the standard language as spoken in Albania is derived primarily from the southern, or Tosk, variety of Albanian. The language as spoken in Kosovo adheres more closely to the Gheg or northern variety. Although Gheg speakers can easily understand standard Albanian, the reverse is not necessarily true. Secondly, despite their proximity, Albania had virtually no ties with Kosovo from 1948 until the fall of communism in 1991 as it was next to impossible to travel between Albania and Yugoslavia. Thus Albania remained as distant to its near neighbours as it did to the rest of the world. This would change dramatically following the fall of communism.

The second decade of the twenty-first century has witnessed an unprecedented international interest in Albanian cinema, both on a practical and on a critical level. One of the most noteworthy of these has been the Albanian Cinema Project (ACP), which functioned between 2012 and 2018 and was initially founded to assist the Albanian Central State's Film Archive in the preservation of the country's film heritage. Supported by the Albanian Ministry of Culture, the US Embassy in Tirana, the Association of Moving Image Archivists and other members of the international cinema and archive communities, ACP completed the restoration of Viktor Gjika's *Nëntori i dytë/The Second November* (Albania, 1982), which was screened domestically and internationally in 2012 to mark the one hundredth anniversary of Albanian statehood. Two years later, ACP restored Xhanfise Keko's *Tomka dhe shokët e tij/Tomka and His Friends* (Albania, 1977), and this restoration was screened in a number of venues in the United States and Europe, as well as in Albania. Nonetheless, it was instrumental in nurturing a broader appreciation for Albanian films that was already developing among academics and film critics. Mark Cousins, for instance, included a brief examination of the children's films of Xhanfise Keko in his documentary *A History of Childhood and Film* (2013), and this director has further met with academic recognition.[7] In 2016, a special edition of the peer-reviewed journal, *KinoKultura*, was dedicated to Albania, and its articles and reviews examine both Kinostudio productions and more recent independent films. The contributors to this special issue were scholars active in seven countries in Europe, the US and Canada.

A New Imaginary

Thus Albanian cinema has entered into a heretofore unfathomable two-way dialogue with the world beyond national borders. The life cycle of Albanian films today transcends the national through the context of international co-production and, albeit on a limited basis, international screenings. At the same time, this process *presupposes* the national, for it is the very 'Albanian-ness' of the products that renders them alluring for academic and critical circles. There is clearly a process of affinitive cosmopolitanism at play, through which the outside world shares commitments with the formerly isolated state (Hjort 2009:17). By virtue of this dynamic, the world is finally beginning to recognise Albania.

Dudley Andrew has eloquently argued, 'Borders are thresholds as much as walls' (2011: 1008). This affirmation can reframe our approach to Albania, in that a threshold implies free movement and, more often than not, in both directions. We must rethink Albania's frontiers and the country's exchanges not only with its immediate Balkan neighbours, but also with more far-flung places on the globe. Albania's borders, once sealed – albeit not as hermetically as traditionally thought – are now increasingly porous and cultural products flow readily to and from the small nation. Albanian films may well lack significant international distribution, despite the tributes they have earned on the festival circuit. Nonetheless, the very international co-production channels that assure their existence open new apertures between the local and the global. Albania has conceded to the need for international capital and transnational avenues of dissemination, yet it continues to tell its own stories and in its own language. Of equal or greater importance are those non-Albanian films that do the same. Albania is now on the radar of cultural cosmopolitans, be they in Europe, the US or Australia, who have found a new imaginary in the small Balkan nation, and celebrate its cultural traditions, social realities and language on the screen.

ACKNOWLEDGEMENTS

The authors gratefully acknowledge the assistance of the following individuals: Iris Elezi and Eriona Vyshka of the Albanian Central State's Film Archive; Majlinda Tafa and Kozeta Kullakshi of the Albanian National Film Centre; and Kujtim Çashku, Eol Çashku, and Magali Perrichet of the Marubi Academy for Film and Multimedia.

NOTES

1. Sergei Yutkevich's *Skanderbeg* (1953), a Soviet-Albanian co-production, was screened at a Franco-Albanian friendship organisation in Paris following its release. Two decades later, the Groupe de Travail sur le Cinéma Albanais of the Université de Paris VIII (Vincennes) during the mid-1970s, led by Marxist professor Gérard Girard, viewed Albanian films quite extensively and published in 1975 a short monograph focusing on their major themes. This work pre-dated a similar volume published by Kinostudio by two years. The two works constitute the first studies in languages other than Albanian on Albanian cinema.

2. Three of the films of Xhanfise Keko garnered awards at the Giffoni Festival in Italy: *Beni ecen vetë/Beni Walks on His Own* (Albania, 1975) received a special award in 1978; *Pas gjurmëve/On the Tracks* (Albania, 1978) was awarded a presidential medal in 1979 and *Kur po xhirohej një film/While Shooting a Film* (Albania, 1983) received a silver medal in 1983.

3. From 1967 to 1986 some 175,000 concrete bunkers were constructed throughout Albania due to Enver Hoxha's fear of foreign invasion.

4. For a discussion of the co-production of *Slogans* see Dina Iordanova's review of the film in *KinoKultura*.

5. Although pre-dating the period of the financial crisis, another example of the extensive use of the Albanian language by a foreign director is Angeliki Antoniou's *Eduart* (Greece/Germany/North Macedonia/Albania, 2006). The film details the return to Greece of a young gay hustler/murderer to atone for his crime.

6. For a discussion of the Italian language in Albania, see Bruce Williams, 'The Eagle Rocks'.

7. See Bruce Williams, 'Two Degrees of Separation'.

References

Albanian Nation Center of Cinematography (2018) *Film Production Guide 2015–2017.* Tirana: Albanian National Center for Cinematography.

Andrew, Dudley (2011) 'An Atlas of World Cinema', in Timothy Corrigan, Patricia White and Meta Mezai (eds), *Critical Visions in Film Theory: Classic and Contemporary Readings.* Boston and New York: Bedford/St. Martins, pp. 999–1018.

AnsaMed (2019) 'Thousands of Youth to Judge Films in Giffoni Albania', <http://www.ansamed.info/ansamed/en/news/sections/culture/2017/11/20/thousands-of-youths-to-judge-films-in-giffoni-albania_aff14f9e-79ce-4fd6-b2b5-fbe745f7b9e8.html> (last accessed 1 April 2019).

Cousins, Mark (2013) 'Terra Incognita', *Sight and Sound*, 23 (1), p. 14.

Diamanti, Elvira (2010), Personal contact, January 2010.

Ezra, Elizabeth and Rowden, Terry (2006) *Transnational Cinema: The Film Reader,* London and New York: Routledge.

Groupe de Travail sur le Cinéma Albanais (1975) *Le Cinéma albanais.* Paris: Université de Vincennes.

Hjort, Mette (2009) 'On the Plurality of Cinematic Transnationalism', in Nataša Ďurovičová and Kathleen E. Newman (eds), *World Cinemas, Transnational Perspectives.* New York: Routledge, pp. 12–33.

Holdsworth, Nick (2011) 'Albanian Oscar Choice Sparks "Blood" Feud: Helmer Bujar Alimani Makes Official Protest', *Variety*, 29 September <https://variety.com/2011/film/awards/albanian-oscar-choice-sparks-blood-feud-1118043617/> (last accessed 10 June 2019).

Iordanova, Dina (2016) 'Gjergj Xhuvani's *Slogans*', *KinoKultura: Special Issue 16 – Albanian Cinema* <http://www.kinokultura.com/specials/16/R_slogans.shtml>.

Jarvis, Christopher (2001) 'The Rise and Fall of Albania's Pyramid Schemes', *Finance and Development*, 37 (1) <https://www.imf.org/en/Publications/WP/Issues/2016/12/30/The-Rise-and-Fall-of-the-Pyramid-Schemes-in-Albania-3161> (last accessed 28 June 2018).

Kinostudio 'Shqipëria e Re' (1977) *The Albanian Film*. Tirana: 8 Nëntor.

Lako, Natasha (2004) *Energija filmika*. Tirana: Toena.

Qendra Kombëtare e Kinematografisë (2017) 'Bashkëprodhimet në minorancë'/'Albanian Minority Co-Productions' <https://nationalfilmcenter.wordpress.com/dbashkeprodhimet-ne-minorance-2/> (last accessed 27 July 2018).

Rawle, Steven (2018) *Transnational Cinema: An Introduction*. London: Palgrave.

Sufaj, Ditmir (2015) 'Global Financial Crisis of 2007: The Case of Albania', *Mediterranean Journal of Social Sciences*, 6 (1), pp. 130–7.

Tafa, Majlinda (2018) Personal communication, July 2018.

Vyshka, Eriona (2019) Personal communication, March 2019.

Williams, Bruce (2013) 'Two Degrees of Separation: Xhanfise Keko and the Albanian Children's Film', *Framework*, 54 (1), pp. 40–58.

Williams, Bruce (2016) 'The Eagle Rocks: Isolation and Cosmopolitanism in Albania's Pop-Rock Scene', in Ewa Mazierska (ed.), *Popular Music in Eastern Europe: Breaking the Cold War Paradigm*. London: Palgrave Macmillan, pp. 89–103.

2. BOSNIA-HERZEGOVINA: CHALLENGING PRECARITY, RETHINKING TRAUMA

Dijana Jelača

The cinema of Bosnia-Herzegovina (for brevity, hereafter referred to as Bosnia) has made a significant international and regional mark in the post-Yugoslav period, and continues to do so despite all the challenges the industry continues to face since the onset of the global economic crisis of 2008.[1] However, since Bosnia was already in a difficult social and economic position prior to 2008 – due to its ongoing struggles with the post-conflict and post-socialist transition to neoliberal capitalism – it could be argued that its economy was not affected as dramatically by the global crisis as the countries that were less peripheral to the global economic flows of capital. In the ensuing years, however, the Bosnian economy has continued to deteriorate which, unsurprisingly, has reflected unfavourably on the economic aspects of the country's film production as well. Due to the lack of any systematic material change for the better, the country and its citizens are perpetually stuck in the state of transition (*tranzicija*), but what the transition will lead to and when it will end, remains an open question. This is one of the reasons I refer to recent Bosnian, as well as regional post-Yugoslav cinema more broadly, as a cinema of transition (where transition becomes a permanent state), mapped along multiple intersecting meanings of the term: including cultural, political, economic, generational and historical (Jelača 2018). This chapter offers a broad contextualisation of the country's film industry and highlights the conditions for production, exhibition and film circulation in Bosnia in recent years. In the latter part of the chapter, I focus on some of the most prevalent themes and filmmaking practices, as well as prominent filmmakers who have left their mark on Bosnia's film industry and beyond with their feature narrative films in particular.

As an extremely small film industry that takes shape in a society still struggling with its recent history of violent conflict (the Bosnian war lasted from 1992 to 1995), the Bosnian cinematic output has nevertheless frequently garnered international attention and broader critical acclaim on an international scale. Jasmila Žbanić's feature debut *Grbavica/Esma's Secret: Grbavica* (Bosnia-Herzegovina/Croatia/Austria/Germany, 2006), for instance, won the Golden Bear at the Berlin Film Festival, while Aida Begić's debut *Snijeg/Snow* (Bosnia-Herzegovina/Germany/France/Iran, 2008) won the Grand Prix in the Semaine de la Critique programme of the Cannes Film Festival. Perhaps most memorably, Danis Tanović's *Ničija zemlja/No Man's Land* (France/Bosnia-Herzegovina/Italy/Belgium/UK/Slovenia, 2001) won what is generally considered one of the highest international recognitions for a non-English language film – an American Academy Award for Best Foreign Language Film – prompting the director to emotionally state upon accepting the award: 'This is for my country, for Bosnia' (2002). The country that Danis Tanović dedicated his Oscar to, however, remains ethnically and politically divided by the still dominant ethno-national guiding principles of its political elites. Officially, since the end of the war, the country is administratively divided into two separate entities: Bosniak Muslim-majority Federation of Bosnia and Herzegovina, and Bosnian Serb majority Republika Srpska. The vast majority of film production activity takes place in the Federation of Bosnia and Herzegovina, with the political establishment of Republika Srpska consistently making an overt effort to isolate its territory from any designation of 'Bosnian' (in line with their nationalist politics, Republika Srpska typically co-finances films with Serbia).[2] This calls into question the possibility of unifying Bosnian cinema under the umbrella of singular national cinema in the context where the political and cultural situation on the ground reveals a population represented by political elites more invested in furthering divisions along ethno-national lines than bettering the lives of their country's citizens, or supporting its cultural production outside of the incessant attention to ethno-nationalism.

This splintering is perhaps best illustrated on the example of one of the region's best known auteurs, Bosnian-born Emir Kusturica, the winner of two Palme d'Or awards in Cannes (for *Otac na službenom putu/When Father Was Away on Business* (Yugoslavia, 1985) and *Podzemlje /Underground* (Federal Republic of Yugoslavia/France/Germany/Bulgaria/Czech Republic/Hungary/UK/USA, 1995)), who left Sarajevo during the war and infamously sided with Serbian nationalism.[3] In recent years, Kusturica has received funding from the government of Republika Srpska to build 'Andrićgrad' in Višegrad – a city-within-a-city that purportedly honours the legacy of Bosnia's Nobel prize laureate, writer Ivo Andrić, but does so through a decidedly nationalist

Serbian lens, thereby completely ignoring the writer's own ideological dismissal of ethno-nationalism. The newly built 'town' has its own cinema and a film institute, although the institute's activities remain unclear. Moreover, Kusturica received funds from Republika Srpska to make *Na mliječnom putu/ On the Milky Road* (Serbia/UK/USA, 2016), a meandering revisionist meditation on war and on the misunderstood artistic soul of the main protagonist played by the director himself (his love interest is played by Monica Bellucci). 'Andrićgrad' becomes a particularly problematic revisionist project in light of the fact that the city that it is built in – Višegrad (an iconic place of Bosnian heritage from Ivo Andrić's best known novel, *Na Drini ćuprija /The Bridge on the Drina*) – was a site of horrific Serbian war crimes against non-Serb civilians during the Bosnian war (crimes that have since been systematically denied). As a poignant counterpoint to Kusturica's ongoing project of cultural and political denial, erasure and therefore continuation and justification of ethnic cleansing, Jasmila Žbanić's docudrama *Za one koji ne mogu da govore/For Those Who Can Tell No Tales* (Bosnia-Herzegovina/Qatar, 2013) restages the experience of Australian tourist Kym Vercoe (who plays herself in the film), who visited the region of Višegrad and gradually discovered the history of war crimes hidden behind the veneer of a bucolic town. As I have argued elsewhere (Jelača 2016), Žbanić's film poses as a powerful countermonument where official commemoration of the victims of such crimes is denied in physical landscape through the ongoing refusal of the Republika Srpska government to allow a memorial for the victims be put up in public space.[4]

The ongoing administrative and cultural splintering along ethno-national lines closely intersects with the fact that Bosnia occupies an unenviable status of one of the poorest countries in Europe, one whose economy, as noted earlier, appears stuck in the limbo of never-ending post-conflict and post-socialist transition to the global flows of neoliberal capitalism (moreover, as of this writing, Bosnia remains outside the borders of the EU). In this context, the country's film industry relies on extremely modest internal funds[5] and the number of films it puts out each year is small (typically one to three feature narrative films are finished in a single year). As a result of the economic dispossession and lack of state-funded financial support, most films are usually made through co-productions with other former Yugoslav republics, as well as with co-financing from Eurimages, a cultural support fund of the Council of Europe. One could argue that this is one of the factors – however unwitting – that makes Bosnian cinema inherently transnational, as both national borders and national identity appear unstable and unable to fully sustain the country's cinematic output. What is more, since regional film co-productions and industry cooperation have become a norm when it comes to the Yugoslav successor states, it could be observed that these film industries – which splintered into smaller national cinemas after the disintegration of Yugoslavia – often performatively re-enact the former Yugoslavia as a way to ensure the continued survival of the region's tradition of producing richly diverse cinema amid growing economic, infrastructural and political challenges. The importance of co-productions for the vitality of regional film industries was articulated by Amra Bakšić Čamo, one of the most important film producers in Bosnia. She emphasises the 'shared cultural space' that makes such co-productions organic, and argues that it is not the case of 'mere' Yugonostalgia, but rather an instance of 'practical thinking' and mutual support that guarantees the survival of all individual regional film industries (Vukobrat 2014) – a practice akin to what Mette Hjort has, in a different context, designated as 'affinitive transnationalism' (2010). While initially arising out of convenience, affinitive transnationalism can mark a political stance – implicit or explicit – of troubling the homogenising perceptions of national identity and national cinemas alike. In the section that follows, I discuss film festivals as one of the key frameworks through which Bosnian and regional cinema circulates and interacts with the globalising flows of world cinema more broadly.

Film Festivals as Transnational Circuits of Past, Present and Future

The international significance of Bosnia and Herzegovina on a global film map is further ensured by the Sarajevo International Film Festival (SFF), whose co-founder and director is Mirsad Purivatra. The festival was first organised by film workers and enthusiasts in wartime Sarajevo under siege (1995) and has since grown into one of the most recognisable film festivals in the world that screens some of the best contemporary work of world cinema and frequently attracts prominent film industry names from around the globe. In 2007, in close cooperation with the Berlin Film Festival, SFF created the Sarajevo Talent Campus (more recently renamed as Talents Sarajevo), a platform for training young and upcoming film workers from the region and beyond. Moreover, since 2003, SFF has featured a separate programme that showcases the latest achievements of Bosnian filmmakers under the name B&H National Film Festival. This programme is organised by the Association of Filmmakers in Bosnia and Herzegovina, an official body representing Bosnian film workers and making yearly selections for Bosnia's candidate for Foreign Language Academy Award (its current president, as of this writing, is director Ines Tanović). This association is a member of European Film Promotion, an organisation that promotes European cinema on a broader international scale, as well as Film New Europe, a networking platform for filmmakers from the region of Central and Southeast Europe, as well as the Baltic states.

Since 2016, Sarajevo Film Festival has featured a programming section titled 'Dealing with the Past', which features regional post-Yugoslav films that seek to actively redress the recent traumatic history in the region. This programme is trans-ethnic and transnational, created in collaboration with the relevant institutions from Bosnia, Croatia, Kosovo, Montenegro and Serbia.[6] With the inauguration of a designated section for films that provide an opportunity for working through collective and individual trauma, the festival acknowledges and actively supports the role of cinema and film festivals in the circuits through which to destabilise dominant (and simplistic) hegemonic narratives about war and ethno-national belonging on a transnational scale.

In the exilic and diasporic domain of the industry's transnational extensions, SFF and the Association of Filmmakers in Bosnia and Herzegovina closely cooperate with the annual Bosnian-Herzegovinian Film Festival (BHFF) held in New York City – a small but growing festival first started in the early 2000s that showcases the best of Bosnian cinema to both diasporic post-Yugoslav audiences living in the US and to the broader US-based public. This small festival has frequently been the first and often only place where Bosnian films are theatrically screened in North America.[7]

Throughout its duration, the Sarajevo Film Festival attracts many international guests but also domestic movie audiences in great numbers (according to some estimates, the festival annually attracts more than 10,000 tourists to Sarajevo, and is attended by more than 100,000 visitors overall), generating a lot of enthusiasm for the cinema-going experience (N1 Info 2015). However, that enthusiasm does not necessarily translate into domestic audiences seeing Bosnian movies on the big screen during the rest of the year. Globally, the numbers of movie-goers are diminishing in an era where the proliferation of digital screen technologies and alternative forms of access have replaced the primacy of movie theatres (as well as traditional television). And as elsewhere in the world, the kinds of movies that attract bigger audiences typically belong to the mainstream blockbuster Hollywood fare. Domestic films typically attract much lower numbers, as attested to by the representatives of functional movie theaters in several Bosnian-Herzegovinian cities. They note that audiences typically prefer lighter fare such as comedies, while domestic filmmakers frequently privilege drama and 'difficult' themes (Skenderagić 2018).

However, the lack of domestic movie-going audiences in Bosnia has infrastructural causes as well. While there are multiplexes in the biggest Bosnian–Herzegovinian cities such as Sarajevo, Banja Luka and Zenica, most smaller towns and municipalities do not have functional movie theatres. Rather, the inhabitants of smaller towns in Bosnia can typically attend film projections once or twice a month through companies that offer the so-called travelling cinema. These companies screen movies (they offer a mix of domestic films, commercial Hollywood fare and international art cinema) in old (socialist) buildings usually referred to as Cultural Centers (*domovi kulture*), which are temporarily, and often inadequately, refurbished into movie theatres monthly or bi-monthly.

Following the trend of travelling cinema in order to bring movies to the inhabitants of smaller towns in Bosnia, the Sarajevo Film Festival has partnered with Obala Art Center to organise 'Operation Cinema' ('Operacija kino'). In 2014, for instance, the months-long tour travelled 12,000 kilometres and visited thirty-two Bosnian cities, while in 2017 the number rose to thirty-six cities. According to their own estimates, in 2013 the travelling cinema was attended by 9,000 people around the country (Sarajevo Film Festival 2014). In their stated mission, the organisers of 'Operation Cinema' emphasise a special focus on 'promoting and understanding film', and note: 'With both local and cross-border cooperation, the project puts special emphasis on the importance of cinema for the education of young people; as a result, through our activities we aim to strengthen youth activism and their politics, with our end goal being the improvement of the position of young people in our society' (Operacija Kino).

Echoing a similar approach to travelling cinema but on the independent end of the spectrum, the Pravo Ljudski Film Festival is premised on 'the commitment to record, disclose, explain and question, but also to finally provoke thinking and inform through independent cinema and arts' (Pravo Ljudski Film Festival 2018). Since 2006, the 'anti-festival', as they dub themselves, has supported young filmmakers and under-represented themes. A pertinent example of their engaged work is an experimental short *Biti daleko/To Be Far* (Samira Kameli, Sajra Subašić, Bosnia-Herzegovina, 2017), which addresses the ongoing international refugee crisis through the lens of Kameli's own refugee status, as well as through the treatment of the refugees from the Middle East in Bosnia. While Bosnia's independent and/or experimental film scene generally arises out of individual amateur filmmakers creating and showcasing their work through accessible digital technologies and platforms, organisations such as Pravo Ljudski make a concerted effort to encourage young amateur filmmakers, bring them together and also showcase their work throughout Bosnia in the form of a travelling festival. In the following section, I offer a brief overview of Bosnia's experimental and documentary cinematic output. The final section of the chapter focuses on narrative cinema as the dominant and most visible form of filmmaking in the country, and one that has gained most attention both domestically and internationally.

ALTERNATIVE, EXPERIMENTAL AND DOCUMENTARY CINEMA

Alternative and experimental filmmaking within Bosnia's cinematic cultural production is difficult to fully account for because it garners less critical and public attention. A few notable exceptions include the works of multimedia artist Šejla Kamerić, Enes Zlatar, who is also a member of a Bosnian alt rock band Sikter, and Banja Luka-born Dane Komljen, whose experimental works of 'slow cinema' have screened at a number of international festivals, with his feature debut *Svi severni gradovi/All the Cities of the North* (Serbia/Bosnia-Herzegovina/Montenegro, 2016) receiving its world premiere at the Locarno Film Festival. What is more, a number of young Bosnian film students have tried their hand at experimental filmmaking under the guidance of famed director Béla Tarr, who started a doctoral-level programme of experimental workshops named Film Factory in Sarajevo in 2013, as part of the Sarajevo Film Academy (a branch of the Sarajevo School of Science and Technology). The programme attracted film students from all over the world, and Tarr acted as the chief mentor for four years.

Documentary film production has a long and famed history of socially engaged and innovative work dating back to the Yugoslav period – for instance, the famed Sarajevo Documentary School, roughly dating to the years between 1962 and 1978, provided a body of work that brought new cinematic realism to documentary filmmaking in the region (see Halligan 2010). While it continues to be fairly prolific for a small film industry such as Bosnia's (likely due to its lower budget costs), documentary film still rarely achieves the cultural prominence that narrative cinema does. For instance, documentary films, outside their festival life, usually do not receive regular theatrical distribution – rather, they are typically shown on television (or produced directly for television). On occasion, the documentary creative teams' own efforts bring theatrical projections of documentary films to broader audiences themselves – such is the case of Emir Kapetanović's *Djeca mira/Children of Peace* (Bosnia-Herzegovina, 2015) and Srđan Šarenac's *Dvije škole/Two Schools* (Bosnia-Herzegovina, 2017) (see Figure 2.1). The latter film depicts the life of students in an ethnically divided high school in the town of Travnik, and brings to the fore the necessity to reform an educational system that privileges ethnicity over quality of education. Regardless of its status as a strain of filmmaking with a lesser amount of cultural capital than narrative cinema, documentary film continues to be an important venue for addressing important political, cultural and social issues in Bosnia and the region, as exemplified in the documentary works of Srđan Šarenac, Ines Tanović, Samir Mehanović, Šemsudin Gegić, Sabrina Begović Ćorić, Nejra Latić Hulusić and Namik Kabil, or in autobiographical documentaries recounting personal traumas of the war in works such as *My Own Private War* (Lidija Zelović, 2016, Netherlands/Bosnia) and *U potrazi za porodicom/Finding Family* (Oggi Tomić and Chris Leslie, 2013, UK/Bosnia-Herzegovina).

And while documentary, experimental, amateur and independent film work in Bosnia, as elsewhere, continues to grow and expand due to the accessibility of film technology in the digital age, it remains largely overshadowed by more mainstream forms of narrative filmmaking, higher-budget productions and more prominent film names. The next section largely focuses on the latter group of films. Rather than offering a comprehensive overview of all narrative

Figure 2.1 *Two Schools* (Srđan Šarenac, 2017).

films made in Bosnia since 2008, the remainder of the chapter will identify dominant themes, film practices and filmmakers who have made their distinctive mark within the framework of recent Bosnian cinema and beyond.

Bosnian Film Post-2008: Transnational Flows of Memory, Affect and Precarity

Trauma remains one of the dominant themes in post-Yugoslav cinema more broadly, due to the region's recent history of violent conflict and, as I have argued elsewhere (Jelača 2016), due also to cinema's distinct position as a conduit of collective and individual memory of trauma. Since Bosnia was a site of the bloodiest conflict in the disintegration of Yugoslavia, it is no surprise that its small film industry is still frequently preoccupied with the themes of addressing and overcoming the traumas of the recent past – a past whose many wounds remain otherwise not meaningfully addressed by the society at large. It should be noted that most of these films actively work against an ethno-national codification or legitimation of traumatic affect (trends that are otherwise dominant in Bosnia's social and political discourse), namely the most illuminating treatment of war trauma and its aftermath in Bosnian film situates traumatic affect with respect to the ways in which a violent armed conflict *produces* ethno-national identity, as well as gender and sexuality, rather than merely reiterate them. To wit, Aida Begić's aforementioned *Snow* (see Figure 2.2), as well as her subsequent film *Djeca/ Children of Sarajevo* (Bosnia-Herzegovina/Germany/France/Turkey, 2012), meditate on the intersections of traumatic recall, the impossibility of closure around traumatic loss and women's lived experience of traumatic affect as a distinctly gendered domain. Next to Žbanić's *Esma's Secret: Grbavica, Snow* represents one of the defining cinematic treatments of women's (frequently unspoken) war trauma in regional cinema. *Snow* was co-written by Elma Tataragić (the head programmer of the Sarajevo Film Festival), who also co-wrote the screenplay for Teona Strugar Mitevska's *Koga denot nemase ime/When the Day Had No Name* (North Macedonia/Belgium, 2017) and directed her own trauma-themed experimental narrative short *Sjećam se/I Remember* (Elma Tataragić, Bosnia-Herzegovina, 2016). The trauma-themed films that focus on women overtly intervene in Bosnia's postwar reality where women's experiences are frequently considered secondary to those of men or subsumed under the (patriarchal) ethno-national framework of ideological interpellation in which women's trauma is a mere stand in for collective ethno-national trauma. This makes it even more poignant that, in Bosnia, women filmmakers continue to be prominent and often most innovative creative voices, whether through addressing collective and individual trauma – next to the works of Žbanić and Begić, we could highlight here Šejla Kamerić's experimental feature *1395 dana bez crvene/1395 Days Without Red* (Bosnia-Herzegovina/UK, 2011) and Una

Figure 2.2   *Snow* (Aida Begić, 2008).

Gunjak's narrative short *Kokoška/The Chicken* (Germany/Croatia, 2014) – or through addressing other forms of social precarity, as in the works of Ines Tanović and Aleksandra Odić, which I discuss in more detail below.

And while the focus on female trauma brought to the screen by these women filmmakers presented some of the most provocative and insightful critique of reducing collective traumatic experience to a reiteration of ethno-nationalist ideology, in recent years, masculinity and trauma became a prominent object of inquiry in Bosnian cinema through a similarly critical and unflinching lens. In 2017 alone, two feature films – Alen Drljević's *Muškarci ne plaču/Men Don't Cry* (Bosnia-Herzegovina/Slovenia/Germany/Croatia) and Elmir Jukić's *Žaba/The Frog* (Bosnia-Herzegovina/North Macedonia/Serbia/Croatia) – both addressed the ongoing struggles of war veterans to cope with their untreated PTSD. *Men Don't Cry*, the feature narrative debut of Alen Drljević (who is a protégé of Jasmila Žbanić), is based on a true story of war veterans from all ethnic sides coming together for a series of group therapies that included participatory re-enactments of each veteran's most traumatic war experience. This intense and unflinching drama assembles a diverse male cast from the post-Yugoslav region and offers illuminating insight into wounded masculinity and systemic social neglect of the postwar psychological well-being of the veterans, while it also addresses the ways in which the veterans cling to masculinity as a way to mask the deep wounds that hide beneath their performance of bravado. Here again, gender is produced through traumatic affect rather than being treated as an a priori given. In a similar vein, Jukić's *The Frog* – based on the eponymous and highly successful play by Dubravko Mihanović – focuses on Zeko (masterfully brought to life by one of Bosnia's most prolific and memorable actors, Emir Hadžihafizbegović), and his struggle to overcome unspeakable war trauma two decades after the war had ended. The film's claustrophobic *mise-en-scène* conveys a deep feeling of emotional and existential stuckness faced by Zeko on a daily level. Like many veterans of the Bosnian war, Zeko struggles to act as a meaningful social actor, isolates himself and frequently manifests violent outbursts that threaten to harm both him and those around him. What films like *Men Don't Cry* and *The Frog* effectively illuminate is a form of social death experienced by men who fought in the war and survived it physically, while affectively they appear anything but alive – they are numb, withdrawn and mostly invisible to the society at large.

Frequent focus on traumatic affect and memory is further reflected in a strain of Bosnian diasporic films made either by filmmakers originally from Bosnia and making films in their adoptive countries or by Bosnian-based filmmakers addressing the themes of diaspora, displacement and migration in their own right. These transnational films focus on identity itself as always being a form of transition, and therefore destabilise the notion of the purity of national identity. As such, they act as significant counterpoints and challenges to the dominant postwar regimes of truth regarding the unity of the national body. Examples of a growing body of such films include the Croatian-Bosnian co-production *Buick Riviera* (Goran Rusinović, 2008, Croatia/Germany/Bosnia-Herzegovina/USA/UK, based on the novel by Bosnian writer Miljenko Jergović who co-wrote the screenplay), *The Waiting Room* (Igor Drljača, 2015, Canada/Bosnia-Herzegovina/Croatia), *Min faster i Sarajevo/My Aunt in Sarajevo* (Goran Kapetanović, Sweden/Bosnia-Herzegovina, 2016) and *Ništa, samo vjetar/Nothing but the Wind* (Bosnia-Herzegovina, 2016), by the Bosnia-based Timur Makarević. All these films feature protagonists who struggle with their splintered, dual identity between 'here' and 'there', between one's place of origin and their adopted country. At the root of the protagonists' struggle is often unaddressed trauma, whose meaningful working through requires a return to its place of origin – namely Bosnia itself. These transnational films overtly demonstrate how (national) identity is both produced and reiterated through trauma as a defining experience.

In yet another register of transnationalism in world cinema more broadly, further transnational extensions of the Bosnian film industry can be traced in the examples of the country's prominent directors making films in other national contexts and about themes that do not directly relate to Bosnia itself – for instance, Danis Tanović's *Tigers* (India/France, 2016), based on a true story of a multinational company's widespread cover up of the harmful effects of their baby formula in Pakistan, or Aida Begić's *Bırakma beni/Never Leave Me* (Bosnia-Herzegovina/Turkey, 2017), which focuses on the precarity of Syrian refugee children based in Turkey. In her film, Begić worked with actual refugee children, all non-professional actors, and the film's narrative is informed by the children's own lived experience of loss, displacement, uncertainty and dispossession.

Many of the aforementioned films that focus on the lingering effects of unaddressed war trauma simultaneously address related forms of social precarity, particularly those rooted in economic stagnation and the ever-growing class-based distinctions. For instance, Aida Begić's *Children of Sarajevo* poignantly conveys the continued economic dispossession experienced by young Bosnians orphaned in the war, while Igor Drljača's *The Waiting Room* mixes fact and fiction to depict the story of Jasmin Geljo, an iconic Bosnian actor who plays a version of himself on the screen, and who immigrated to Canada and is now forced to work odd jobs to make ends meet. Social and economic precarity, as well as racial discrimination, is a prominent theme in Danis Tanović's documentary drama *Epizoda u životu berača željeza/An Episode in the Life of an Iron Picker* (Bosnia-Herzegovina/France/Slovenia/Italy, 2013), which focuses on the true story of a Roma family's struggle to get adequate healthcare and be recognised as social actors who are as entitled to equal rights as the non-Roma population. The film's innovative form – evocative of the unique film language of the iconic Yugoslav and Serbian filmmaker Želimir Žilnik – blurs documentary and fiction, as the family re-enacts the key events that transpired during the health crisis that threatened to destroy them. One of the most critically lauded and internationally recognised Bosnian films in recent years, *An Episode in the Life of an Iron Picker*, won the Grand Jury Award and the Silver Bear for Best Actor upon its world premiere at the Berlin Film Festival. Calling further attention to the deep roots of social and economic precarity faced by Bosnia's Roma population, the recipient of the Silver Bear for Best Actor, Nazif Mujić – who, in fact, plays himself in this docudrama – subsequently made headlines when he stated that the success of the film did not make any difference for the better in the precarious status of his family. Mujić died in extreme poverty at the age of forty-eight in 2018, leaving behind his wife and young children. Reportedly, before his death he sold the Silver Bear so his family could make ends meet (Radiosarajevo.ba 2018). This tragic real-life ending of a protagonist of one of the most successful Bosnian films in recent years speaks to the limitations of socially engaged cinema or of its international success. If anything, it highlights engaged cinema's inability to meaningfully change the lived struggles of its subjects if such struggle remains systematically ignored by the broader society beyond the film screen and film industry.

In a more standard film language, documentary and TV veteran Ines Tanović made her feature narrative debut with *Naša svakodnevna priča/Our Everyday Life* (Bosnia-Herzegovina/Slovenia/Croatia, 2015), which depicts the life of an ordinary Sarajevo family trying to make ends meet in contemporary Bosnia. The film addresses, among other things, the phenomenon of prolonged adolescence faced by many of Bosnia's citizens who are forced – due to economic dispossession and a staggeringly high rate of unemployment – to continue to live with their parents well beyond their actual adolescent years. A similar theme is depicted in Aleksandra Odić's narrative short *Kineski zid/Great Wall of China* (Germany, 2017), about a family in northern Bosnia whose daughter Ljilja secretly plans to depart for Germany in search of a better life – a story of economic migration intimately familiar to a growing number of Bosnian families post-2008 (see Figure 2.3).

In 2014, much of Bosnia's cultural production – including film – focused on the centennial of the assassination of Franz Ferdinand, the Archduke of Austria, by the hand of a Young Bosnia (*Mlada Bosna*) member Gavrilo Princip in Sarajevo on 28 June 1914. The assassination effectively triggered the start of the First World War, but the political motivations of Princip's act remain a matter of some disagreement and controversy in the region. For some, he was a pan-Yugoslav revolutionary and an anti-colonial freedom fighter, while for others he was a Serbian nationalist and a puppet of Serbia's political elites of the time. The centennial presented an opportunity for Bosnian cultural workers, including filmmakers, to reassess the country's and Sarajevo's historical legacy, as well as examine the continued role of the past in the present. The ongoing

Figure 2.3 *Great Wall of China* (Aleksandra Odić, 2017).

disagreements over Gavrilo Princip's status are echoed in Danis Tanović *Smrt u Sarajevu/Death in Sarajevo* (France/Bosnia-Herzegovina, 2016), based on Bernard-Henri Lévy's play *Hotel Europe*, a film which brings together an ensemble cast and balances many intertwined stories in a single hotel in Sarajevo, and was another Silver Bear winner for the director at the Berlin Film Festival. More experimentally, Jasmila Žbanić's documentary *Jedan dan u Sarajevu /One Day in Sarajevo* (Bosnia-Herzegovina, 2014) is a collage mix of footage shot in Sarajevo on the day of the centennial by Žbanić herself, her collaborators, random passers-by, as well as tourists. The crowdsourced documentary footage shows various parts of the city and different ceremonies marking the occasion and is further mixed in with clips from three narrative films that depict the assassination. The cinematic treatment of the centennial inadvertently reiterated the centralised nature of Bosnia's film industry: Sarajevo remains the location most frequently featured in Bosnian films, while smaller towns and rural environments – a few notable exceptions aside – continue to be heavily under-represented.

Speaking of exceptions, it should be noted that the Bosnian film industry's dominant tendency of producing dramas with heavy social themes is occasionally punctured by comedies which, in turn, enjoy higher commercial success with domestic audiences but are generally less favourably received by critics. *Hiljadarka/A Thousand* (Nenad Đurić, Bosnia-Herzegovina, 2015), for instance, is a fictional comedic account of the story of Atif Kurtović, a coal miner whose iconic status in Yugoslavia was sealed when he became the face on the bill for one thousand Yugoslav dinars. On a more provocative end of the comedic spectrum, Jasmila Žbanić's *Otok ljubavi/Love Island* (Croatia/Germany/Switzerland/Bosnia-Herzegovina, 2014), co-written with Aleksandar Hemon, assembles an international cast and focuses on a queer love triangle centred around sexual desire between two women. As LGBTQ themes are heavily under-represented in Bosnian narrative cinema (one other notable exception is Ahmed Imamović's *Go West* (Bosnia-Herzegovina, 2005)), *Love Island* was a welcome thematic shift that nevertheless, similarly to *Go West*, traded in stereotypes regarding both queer identity and Balkanist tropes about backward regional mentality (Dumančić 2013; Jelača 2016). However, such lighter fare remains necessary for maintaining the optimism of domestic audiences towards a movie-going experience that supports regional filmmaking and not just the latest that the world's most commercial cinema has to offer.

Perhaps paradoxically, the future of Bosnian cinema rests in the very thing that might also indicate its ongoing precarity, namely in the necessity and vitality of regional, transnational collaborations that both reflect and reaffirm the inability of maintaining a singular national space within contemporary regional and global flows of cultural production, politics, economy, labour and power. With the disconcerting global rise of populist movements that cling to nativist politics and conservative definitions of citizenship, challenging – as well as undoing – the notions of national purity through cultural production remains all the more pivotal and subversive.

NOTES

1. After the Dayton Peace Accords, signed in November of 1995, the war in Bosnia was effectively ended by the division of the country into two administrative entities whereby the postwar State of Bosnia and Herzegovina comprised of the Bosniak-majority Federation of Bosnia-Herzegovina and Serb-majority Republika Srpska. The two entities each have their own governments and presidencies, on top of which there is a shared Bosnian government and triple presidency of the entire state (comprising one representative from each constitutive ethnic group: Bosniak, Serb and Croatian). This administrative setup has shown itself to be highly inefficient and, in the two and a half decades that followed, has proved extremely susceptible to furthering ethno-nationalist politics and divisions.

2. Examples of such Republika Srpska/Serbia co-productions include *Turneja/The Tour* (Serbia/Bosnia-Herzegovina/Croatia/Slovenia, Goran Marković, 2008), *Sveti Georgije uviba aždahu/St. George Kills the Dragon* (Srđan Dragojević, Serbia/Bosnia-Herzegovina/Bulgaria, 2009), *Neprijatelj/The Enemy* (Dejan Zečević, Serbia/Bosnia-Herzegovina/Croatia/Hungary, 2011), and *Na mliječnom putu/On the Milky Road* (Emir Kusturica, Serbia/UK/USA, 2016). Note that in the countries listed on IMDb (and cited here) as co-producing partners, the involvement of the Republika Srpska is listed as Bosnia-Herzegovina (or not at all).

3. For more on the director's work prior to 2000, see Gocić (2001). For an insightful analysis of *When Father Was Away on Business*, see Jovanović (2012); for provocative analyses of *Underground*, see Keene (2001) and Galt (2006).

4. Jasmila Žbanić is, together with producer Damir Ibrahimović, a co-founder of Deblokada, an independent production house that has, since 1997, put out a number

of socially engaged narrative and documentary films. Next to Deblokada, another prolific independent production company in Bosnia is pro.ba (started in 1998), which produces and distributes documentary, narrative and experimental films, including collaborations with directors Aida Begić and Danis Tanović.

5. In 2018, the Foundation for Film Industry allocated film funds in the total amount of 1,232,000 Convertible Marks (approximately 630,000 euros) (source: <http://fondacijakinematografija.ba/index.php/konkursi-81>)

6. See the News Page on 'Dealing with the Past' project by Sarajevo Film Festival: <https://www.sff.ba/en/news/10377/dealing-with-the-past>

7. For the 2018 edition programme of the Bosnian-Herzegovinian Film Festival, refer to: <https://www.bhffnyc.org/2018program>

References

Bosnian-Herzegovinian Film Festival (2018) *2018 Program* <https://www.bhffnyc.org/2018program> (last accessed 13 August 2019).

Dumančić, Marko (2013) 'Hiding in Plain Sight? Making Homosexuality (In)Visible in Post-Yugoslav Film', in Narcisz Fejes and Andrea P. Balogh (eds), *Queer Visibility in Post-Socialist Cultures*. Bristol: Intellect, pp. 57–80.

Galt, Rosalind (2006) 'Yugoslavia's Impossible Spaces', in *The New European Cinema: Redrawing the Map*. New York: Columbia University Press, pp. 123–74.

Gocić, Goran (2001) *Notes from the Underground: The Cinema of Emir Kusturica*. London: Wallflower Press.

Halligan, Benjamin (2010) 'Idylls of Socialism: The Sarajevo Documentary School and the Problem of the Bosnian Sub-Proletariat', *Studies in Eastern European Cinema*, 1 (2), pp. 197–216.

Hjort, Mette (2010) 'On the Plurality of Cinematic Transnationalism', in Nataša Durovicová and Kathleen E. Newman (eds), *World Cinemas, Transnational Perspectives*. London: Routledge, pp. 12–32.

Jelača, Dijana (2016) *Dislocated Screen Memory: Narrating Trauma in Post-Yugoslav Cinema*. New York: Palgrave Macmillan.

Jelača, Dijana (2018) 'Sex and Uncivil Disobedience: Girlhood and Social Class in Transitional Post-Yugoslav Cinema', *Contemporary Southeastern Europe*, 4 (2), pp. 121–40.

Jovanović, Nebojša (2012) '*Futur Antérieur* of Yugoslav Cinema, or Why Emir Kusturica's Legacy Is Worth Fighting For', in Daniel Šuber, and Slobodan Karamanić (eds), *Retracing Images: Visual Culture after Yugoslavia*. Leiden: Brill, pp. 149–70.

Keene, Judith (2001) 'The Filmmaker as Historian, Above and Below Ground – Emir Kusturica and the Narratives of Yugoslav History', *Rethinking History*, 5 (2), pp. 233–53.

N1 Info (2015) 'Purivatra: Broj posjetitelja SFF-a porastao za 10 posto', *N1 Info*, 24 August <http://ba.n1info.com/Kultura/a57507/Porastao-broj-posjetitelja-SFF-a.html> (last accessed 13 August 2019).

Operacija Kino, 'Šta je Operacija kino?' <http://www.operacijakino.ba/sta-je-ok> (last accessed 13 August 2019).

Pravo Ljudski Film Festival (2018) *History* <https://pravoljudski.org/2018/home/about/history/> (last accessed 13 August 2019).

Radiosarajevo.ba (2018) 'Osvajač "medvjeda"/ Objavljeno u kakvim okolnostima je umro Nazif Mujić', 24 February <https://www.radiosarajevo.ba/metromahala/teme/objavljeno-u-kakvim-okolnostima-je-umro-nazif-mujic/292102> (last accessed 13 August 2019).

Sarajevo Film Festival (2014) 'Počinje velika proljetna turneja Operacije kino!' <https://www.sff.ba/novost/9790/pocinje-velika-proljetna-turneja-operacije-kino> (last accessed 13 August 2019).

Sarajevo Film Festival (2016) 'Dealing with the Past', <https://www.sff.ba/en/news/10377/dealing-with-the-past> (last accessed 13 August 2019).

Skenderagić, Mirza (2018) 'Kolika je gledanost domaćih filmskih ostvarenja u domaćim kinima', *Stav*, 31 May <http://stav.ba/kolika-je-gledanost-domacih-filmskih-ostvarenja-u-domacim-kinima/> (last accessed 13 August 2019).

Tanović, Danis (2002) ' "No Man's Land" Wins Foreign Language Film: 2002 Oscars', YouTube Video, Oscars, 16 July 2014 <https://www.youtube.com/watch?v=4LV1-DYGR5U&t=207s> (last accessed 13 August 2019).

Vukobrat, Budo (2014) 'Bakšić Čamo: Slobodni pad filmske industrije u BiH', *Radio Slobodna Evropa*, 7 February <https://www.slobodnaevropa.org/a/baksic-camo-slobodni-pad-filmske-industrije-u-bih/25254082.html> (last accessed 13 August 2019).

3. BULGARIA: REFRAMING CONTEMPORARY ARTHOUSE AND MAINSTREAM CINEMA

Gergana Doncheva

The years 2008–18 proved to be a dynamic and turbulent period for the development of contemporary Bulgarian cinema in terms of the international visibility of local film productions and the growing numbers in movie theatre attendance at home. This prompted Bulgarian scholars and journalists to start speaking enthusiastically of a fragile revival of the national film industry following the bleak years of the so-called transition period.[1] This auspicious development is not a happy accident; it is rather a consequence of a number of different factors.

The accession of Bulgaria to the European Union on 1 January 2007 deeply affected all facets of social and cultural life within the country, including cinema. The effects of the EU integration process can be examined from both a *discursive* and a *practical* perspective. The former refers to the redefinition and renegotiation of national identity in the context of European values, and the latter to the adaptation and compliance with processes of a supranational entity with stringent rules and a unique model of functioning. This move towards the European cultural space was a long-lasting process, which in terms of the film industry began in 1993, when Bulgaria joined Eurimages, the Council of Europe's European Cinema Support Fund, and was therefore able to formally collaborate in production and distribution with other European partners.

The adoption of new laws regarding film production and the gradual alignment with the European Union, entailed a different ideological perspective that included the transnational aspect, and legitimated film both as an art and as a commercial cultural product, resulting in a wider diversity of film productions. The policy of the Nacionalen Filmov Centar/Bulgarian National Film Center aims to keep a balance between the two by investing not only in arthouse cinema, but also in good-quality commercial film projects. The most successful examples of this relatively new type of institutional practice are films such as: *Misia London /Mission London* (Dimitar Mitovski, Bulgaria/UK/Hungary/North Macedonia/Sweden, 2010), *Love.net* (Iliyan Dzhevelekov, Bulgaria, 2011), *Voevoda* (Zornitsa Sophia, Bulgaria/Croatia, 2017), *Vezdesushtiyat/Omnipresent* (Ilian Djevelekov, Bulgaria, 2017), *Vazvishenie/Heights* (Viktor Bojinov, Bulgaria/North Macedonia, 2017), all of which were so successful in the Bulgarian box office to warrant the characterisation 'national blockbusters' (see Table 3.1). These films feature a diversity of cinematic styles and genres: *Mission London* is an absurd comedy, *Voevoda* and *Heights* are historical dramas set during the Ottoman occupation of Bulgaria, while *Love. net* and *Omnipresent* focus on the problems of prosperous urban individuals who are rarely represented on the screen.

The recent breakthrough of Bulgarian films reaching large domestic audiences is the result of many factors, including the diversification of the production models. These institutional changes and their positive effects are evidence

Figure 3.1   *Love.net* (Ilian Djevelekov, 2011). Courtesy of Ilian Djevelekov and Matei Konstantinov.

that the 'third identity crisis' of Bulgarian cinema, which had been the result of the expanding process of globalisation after 1990, is gradually overcome.[2] Bulgarian films of the 1990s were characterised by two distinct narrative paradigms: the awkward attempt to re-evaluate the communist past and the desire to define new visions for the present, referred to respectively as 'in search of lost identity' and 'in search of landmarks' by Bratoeva-Daraktchieva (2019). Most of the films produced in this period belonged to 'vulgar realism' – a local version of Russian *chernukha*, the 'black genre' that pessimistically depicted dark realities in the collapsing Soviet Union (Bratoeva-Daraktchieva, 2019: 7). For more than a decade, filmmakers focused their attention on the most marginalised strata of society – a tendency that still has disciples today, but as part of a broader and far more diversified generic and artistic regime. In fact, what separates the transition era (from 1990 to 2007) from the following period is a range of discursive, thematic, artistic and genre transformations that have led to the contemporary auspicious state of affairs.

This chapter argues that the rejuvenation of Bulgarian cinema experienced in the last decade or so has emerged from several necessary premises: Bulgaria's EU orientation and membership; the updated legislation concerning all aspects of the film industry; the emergence of a new generation of filmmakers who are ready to work in a transnational competitive environment; the gradual business-oriented professionalisation of producers who were forced to seek alternative funding due to the scarce state support; and last but not least the appearance of a heterogeneous cinephile audience.

BETWEEN ARTHOUSE AND COMMERCIAL CINEMA: NEW INSTITUTIONAL FRAMEWORKS AND FUNDING MODELS

The most internationally acclaimed Bulgarian film that acquired status of an emblem of high-quality arthouse cinema during the decade under examination is *Ága* (Milko Lazarov, Bulgaria/Germany/France, 2018).[3] Ironically, Milko Lazarov's second feature film was not connected to the reality in Bulgaria at all, but located in the severe winter landscape of a mythical North and shot in north-eastern Siberia. Visually and narratively referencing Robert Flaherty's *Nanook of the North* (USA/France, 1922) the plot tells a story with universal appeal – that of an isolated human family that appears to be the last on Earth, as epitomised by Nanook, Sedna and their daughter Ága. The impressive visual conception and cinematographic style, and the distinctive narrative model that combines the intimate with the epic, differentiate *Ága* from other award-winning Bulgarian productions, which fall under the dominant category of social realism – such as *Bezbog/Godless* (Ralitsa Petrova, Bulgaria/Denmark/France, 2016), *Hristo* (Grigor Lefterov and Todor Matsanov, Bulgaria/Italy, 2016) and others. The emergence and success of such an atypical Bulgarian

Figure 3.2 *Ága* (Milko Lazarov, 2018). Courtesy of Veselka Kiryakova and Milko Lazarov.

film can be explained with reference to a number of contextual factors. These include (1) the gradual increase in the number of films produced and their budgets compared to the transition period (see Table 3.1); (2) the diversification of financial sources comprising national and municipality funds, European programmes and private assets; and (3) the diversification of forms of filmmaking that range from experimental and arthouse to mainstream titles, and include curious hybrids that aspire to combine the communicative nature of popular cinema with art cinema conventions.

In this section, I focus on the institutional frameworks and funding models which led to the establishment and diversification of contemporary Bulgarian cinema. The gradual introduction of a new legislative framework not only ensured the institutional parameters for a sustainable development of the Bulgarian film industry, but also contributed to the redefinition of national cinema. For the first time, these new laws formalised co-productions, reconceptualising notions of national cinema by placing it within a European context and leading to radical changes. These laws had a dual effect: they privileged an ideological perspective which includes the transnational aspect as an important ingredient, and they also legitimated film both as an art and as a commercial cultural product. The latter turned out to be a necessary precondition for the emergence of diverse movies since the early 2000s and especially in the decade under examination. However, the new emphasis on the commercial appeal of state-funded films has intensified conflicts concerning the allocation of state subsidies between those who support the qualities of arthouse films and those who place more value on mainstream productions. This conflict has revealed a generational gap too, reflecting the contrasting ideas about cinema and its social and commercial dimensions that the older and the younger generation of filmmakers have. The crucial dividing line in this debate remains whether one conceptualises cinema as an art addressed to a small elitist audience or as a medium with the potential to reach a wider public. In order to illustrate the institutional and legal changes that enabled the recent growth of Bulgarian cinema, it is important to highlight the two key legislative frameworks that shape the organisation, management and financial mechanisms of national cinema. These emphasise the role of production in terms of cultural value, but also guarantee continuity and stability in film production funding.

The notion of 'producership in culture' was introduced for the first time in 1999 with the 'Law on Protection and Development of Culture', which allowed for the first time both public and private entities to gain equal access to state subsidies (Bulgarian Cinema 2017: 3). Four years later, in 2003, the 'Film Industry Act' was introduced. This is a special law that outlines the regulatory frameworks, models and specific practices for sustainable development of the Bulgarian film industry in accordance with European legislative norms. The Film Industry Act facilitates 'the overall process of making a film production, from the idea to the promotion and exhibition', ensuring financial stability through the annual state subsidy which guarantees no less than 'the total of the previous-year average budgets of 7 feature films, 14 feature-length documentaries and 160 minutes of animation respectively' (Bulgarian Cinema 2017: 3–4). In percentages, 'the state aid is divided as follows: no less than 80% for film production; no less than 10% for distribution and exhibition, up to 5% for support to Bulgarian films related to national events and celebrations of historical figures' (Bulgarian Cinema 2017: 3–4).

The institution responsible for implementing the Film Industry Act is the Bulgarian National Film Center, which is under the auspices of Ministry of Culture. The Bulgarian National Film Center was established on 6 June 1991 on the basis of the French model (CNC) and its main functions are connected to 'financial support, distribution, exhibition and promotion of Bulgarian cinema in the country and abroad', and 'the development of film culture' (Bulgarian Cinema 2017: 9).[4] The 2003 Film Industry Act changed the role of the Film Center into an Executive Agency with a MEDIA programme information office.

As mentioned earlier, the bone of contention in the Bulgarian film community is the annual funding allocations by the Bulgarian National Film Center. Three artistic commissions for feature, documentary and animation movies evaluate twice a year the submitted projects on a competitive basis applying a stringent set of selection criteria such as 'the artistic potential in the European context of cultural diversity, the commercial potential and prospects for international recognition, and the economic justification for the proposed budget', as well as the producer's strategic plan, and the professional experience and recognition of the key figures in the creative team (Bulgarian Cinema 2017: 6).

The most common accusation against the state system for allocating the financial recourses for film productions is the elusive process of lobbying and the presumable influence exerted on some committees' members that, in turn, arouses suspicion for lack of transparency in the decision-making procedures. Another reason for tension is the perceived privileging of arthouse films at the expense of mainstream ones which benefits directors who follow the traditions of auteur cinema and who mostly belong to the older or middle generation (although there are some exceptions, too). Their projects more frequently receive state funding in the 'high-budget' category – that is films with a budget exceeding 306,775 euros (600,000 levs).[5] The principal objection against investing public resources in arthouse films is their overall low popularity, reflected in poor box office figures and overall financial returns. Furthermore, these movies often fail to attract attention and acclaim at international festivals because their topics and narratives are too closely linked to the local context.

Unsurprisingly, in the last few years younger filmmakers and some producers have called for an amendment of the Film Industry Act asking for priority to be given to low budget films which would provide more opportunities for first and second films made by new directors, as these would otherwise *de facto* be excluded from the selection. The revised version of the Film Industry Act is still under consideration and is expected to be voted on by the national parliament in 2020.

The Effect of the New Generation on Bulgarian Cinema

To a great extent, the most recognisable characteristic of the period 2008–18 is the appearance of a new generation of filmmakers who contributed to the thematic and stylistic enrichment of Bulgarian cinematic traditions, while some even succeeded in attracting the heavily fragmented audiences. In this period there were fifty feature films by new directors – an unprecedented number of debuts which unambiguously testifies to a dynamic generational change in Bulgarian cinema.[6]

Yet to describe the typical profile of a first-time Bulgarian film director is a difficult task. During the immediate post-communist period, the average age of a debut director had been around forty years old or even older. This deplorable situation, determined by the chronic shortage of state financial resources, explains the existing tension between the representatives of the older and younger generations in the two decades following 1989. Therefore the emergence of a high number of films made by first-time, and mostly younger, directors in the last decade deserves special attention, especially as a considerable part of these films have proved to possess serious artistic merit and/or commercial potential.

A dominant characteristic that the current younger generation of Bulgarian filmmakers share is that most of them have graduated from Western European or North American universities and have also gained professional experience abroad. This specific circumstance places them in a completely new global context and exerts significant influence on their individual creative style. For example, acclaimed documentary filmmaker Tonislav Hristov admits that the Scandinavian documentary film had an enormous effect on him (Kanusheva 2019:115), while Yana Lekarska's short films have been strongly influenced by the Korean cinematic aesthetics (Mártonova 2019: 3). In other words, these young directors introduce and promote a diverse and different visual culture in the local context, which seems to crave for an original iconic repertoire, topics and imaginary. An additional dimension concerning debutants is the emergence of a great plenitude of female filmmakers, such as Svetla Tsotsorkova, Nadejda Koseva, Ralitsa Petrova, Kristina Grozeva, Maya Vitkova, Yana Titova, Mina Mileva, Vesela Kazakova, Slava Doycheva and Yana Lekarska, now known due to the international recognition and festival circulation of their films.

In broad terms, these first films could be divided into two categories: arthouse and mainstream. The former have garnered a breath-taking number of prestigious national and international awards, whereas the latter have managed to win the audiences' heart. Overall arthouse films receive much more media coverage due to their circulation within an international context, while the majority of these films represent a bleak reality of contemporary Bulgaria. For instance, *Godless* won a Golden Leopard at Locarno, while *Otchuzhdenie/Alienation* (Milko Lazarov, Bulgaria, 2013) received two prizes at the Venice Film Festival and the Best Film Award at the Warsaw Film Festival. Other films depicting complex and difficult family relations – *3/4* (Ilian Metev, Bulgaria, 2018) won a Golden Leopard of the Present at Locarno – while those reminiscing for the communist near past such as *Dzift/Zift* (Javor Gardev, Bulgaria, 2008) won the Silver St George for Best Director at the Moscow Film Festival, *Cvetat na hameleona/ The Colour of the Chameleon* (Emil Hristov, Bulgaria, 2012) was included in the 2013 EFA feature film selection and *Viktoria* (Maya Vitkova, Bulgaria/Romania, 2014) received a Special Jury Award at the Transilvania IFF.

Yet, these arthouse films lauded at international film festivals, form a negative perception in the minds of Bulgarian audiences. These films tend to be shown in local cinema theatres after a long festival circuit invested with the halo of international recognition, and while this stimulates interest and high expectations, Bulgarian spectators are often disappointed and cannot identify themselves with the unattractive characters depicted in most of these films. Some local scholars have remarked that the monotonous repetitiveness of themes and narratives revealing the post-socialist legacy – moral and spiritual degradation, poverty and state corruption – repels the audience, although this thematic preference seems to be a successful strategy for receiving national or European grants (Gotseva 2018b: 20). Maya Dimitrova has noted how for a director to be a film festival auteur it is a specific form of marginalisation, and questions whether the Bulgarian film community wants national cinema to be categorised under such a perspective (2018: 13).

In addition, nowadays, film development in Bulgaria depends on another crucial issue that both practitioners and theoreticians emphasise: a deficit of good scriptwriters and, consequently, the lack of quality scenarios – a prevailing problem since 1989, when many directors started writing their own scripts (Stoilova 2017:181; Gotseva 2018a:10; Mártonova 2020: 127). Naturally, this does not mean that all films made according to this model are necessarily bad, but it is also true that a number of successful arthouse films, such as *Zift, The Colour of the Chameleon, Ága, Snimka s Yuki/A Picture with Yuki* (Lachezar Avramov, Bulgaria, 2019), were made in close collaboration with talented scriptwriters. This practice of collaboration is also evident in mainstream cinema, while the most popular films are based on literary texts by prominent present-day writers, suggesting that prior familiarity of audiences with a story enhances a film's chances of success. The film adaptation of the cult novel *Summit* by Milen Ruskov (who was awarded with the European prize for literature in 2014) is an indicative example of this process. This bestseller is of cardinal significance in the Bulgarian cultural landscape because it is a glamorous example of a critical revision of the mythologised historical period defined as Revival – the period in which Bulgarians were emancipated from the Ottoman Empire. Ruskov's deconstruction of the most sacred tropes entrenched in the national imagination was sufficiently provocative in order to draw the attention of Viktor Bojinov to make a film version entitled *Heights*.[7] The film was produced by Ivan Doykov, an emblematic figure within the Bulgarian film landscape, who had contributed to the commercial success of *Mission London* seven years earlier.

It is worth noting that most directors whose films are popular with audiences (Viktor Bojinov, Zornitsa Sophia and Dimitar Mitovski) have a background in the television and advertising sector, and use their knowledge of audience viewing patterns when preparing their own film projects. The promotional strategy of mainstream productions is quite different to that of arthouse films. Usually, the creative team invest a lot of time and energy in media at an early stage, with the aim to create an atmosphere of eagerness and expectation, but they also host noisy and extravagant film premieres especially for the local audiences.

Despite its popularity, commercial cinema has traditionally received scarce attention within Bulgarian film scholarship because of the elitist tendency that privileges arthouse films at the expense of mainstream productions. In her study of Bulgarian cinema in a transnational context, Nedyalkova (2015) breaks this mould as she argues that directors' and audiences' exposure to American mainstream cinema has had a major impact on the development of recent Bulgarian cinema. Drawing on examples from films such as *Svetat e golyam i spasenie debne otvsyakade/The World Is Big and Salvation Lurks Around the Corner* (Stephan Komandarev, Bulgaria/Germany/Slovenia/Hungary/Serbia, 2008), *Mission London* and *Love.net*, Nedyalkova (2015) demonstrates how Bulgarian filmmakers have appropriated and adapted this prevailing model producing hybrid patterns which take audience preferences and expectations into consideration. She also illustrates that these movies are heavily affected by Hollywood's industry practices, especially in terms of the marketing and distribution strategies applied within a specific context (Nedyalkova 2015: 27–33).

Embracing the idea that the development of Bulgarian cinema today should be conceptualised within a wider transnational framework, I focus on those aspects in direct correlation with significant processes caused by globalisation. In contrast to arthouse films, the steady appearance of mainstream debuts proves the growing necessity of local popular cinema to meet the requirements of a broader audience. In the last decade genre film in all its variations has flourished in Bulgarian cinema:

1. comedy (*Mission London*, *Chuzhdenetsat/The Foreigner* (Niki Iliev, Bulgaria, 2012))
2. romance (*Love.net*)
3. action (*Pistolet, Kufar i tri smurdyashti varela/Pistol, Briefcase and Three Stinking Barrels* (Georgi Kostov, Bulgaria, 2012), *Korpus za burzo reagirane/Rapid Response Corps* (Stanislav Donchev, Bulgaria, 2012) and its sequel *Korpus za burzo reagirane 2: Yadrena zaplaha/Rapid Response Corps 2: Nuclear Threat* (Stanislav Donchev, Bulgaria, 2014), *Benzin/Broken Road* (Asen Blatechki Bulgaria, 2017))
4. thriller (*Vila Roza/Roseville* (Martin Makariev, Bulgaria, 2013))
5. teenage (*11⁻ᵗⁱ A/11ᵗʰ A* (Mihaela Komitova, Bulgaria, 2015))
6. gangster (*Tilt* (Viktor Chuchkov Jr, Bulgaria/Germany, 2010), *Otrova za mishki/Rat Poison* (Konstantin Burov, Bulgaria, 2014))
7. drama (*Omnipresent*)
8. historical drama (*Heights, Voevoda* (Zornitsa Sophia, Bulgaria/Croatia, 2017))

Beyond the examples analysed by Nedyalkova and discussed above, a wider examination of Bulgarian mainstream cinema from this period reveals an intensive process of appropriation and adaptation of Hollywood formulas and consequently the construction of new hybrid local forms. The storylines tend to follow classic genre conventions, with characters placed in an urban environment, conspicuously displaying the luxury and splendour connected to upper-middle-class lifestyles (*Love.net*, *Omnipresent*). Interestingly, this process of adaptation of Hollywood and Western European formulas is also present in arthouse films. For example, *Zift* is a spectacular parody of the film noir with a black-and-white cinematography characteristic of the genre.

In local mainstream films, this peculiar flirt with Hollywood and British popular cinema has different manifestations, for instance *Pistol, Briefcase and Three Stinking Barrels* is an overt reference to Guy Ritchie's comedy *Lock, Stock and Two Smoking Barrels* (1998). *Ombre* (Zahari Paunov, Bulgaria, 2014) uses the familiar narrative structures of the Western in order to construct a Balkan tragicomic Eastern. International celebrities also make an appearance in a number of films: for example, the actors Christopher Lambert and Michael Madsen perform in *The Foreigner* and in *Broken Road*, the lead vocalist of the legendary band *Uriah Heep*, John Lowton, stars in *Love.net*. Spectators also discover a playful resemblance between Filip Avramov's Dimitar Obshti from

Table 3.1   Top Bulgarian releases of local film by box office 2008–16.

Film	Admissions	Box office
Misia London/Mission London (2010)	376,809	2,626,156
Love.net (2011)	207,122	1,376397
Operatastia Shmenti kapeli/Operation Shmenti Capelli (2011)	181,461	1,208,704
Tilt (2010)	142,799	933,617
11⁻ᵗⁱ A/11 A	97,867	718,848
Voevoda (2017)	86,587	673,700
Zhivi legendi/Living Legends (2014)	91,447	661,702
Chuzhdenetsat/The Foreigner (2012)	56,651	384,421
Stupki v piasaka/Footsteps in the Sand (2010)	54,674	342,003
Pistolet, kufar i tri smurdyashti varela/Pistol, Briefcase and Three Stinking Barrels (2012)	45,898	326,954
Korpus za burzo reagirane/Rapid Reaction Corps (2012)	44,200	310,144
Dyakon Levski/Levski (2015)	39,783	296,340
Balgar: The Movie 3D (2014)	33,144	270,063
Ketsove/Sneakers (2011)	41,380	263,989
Dzift/Zift (2008)	35,166	255,896
Korpus za burzo reagirane 2/Rapid Reaction Corps 2 (2014)	32,915	234,845
Svetat e golyam i spasenie debne otvsyakade/The World Is Big and the Salvation Lurks Around (2008)	36,400	181,763

Heights and Johnny Depp's Jack Sparrow from the Hollywood blockbuster *The Pirates of the Caribbean*.

The appropriation of American and Western European models is not limited to the plot and style, but also to the overall attitude to film as a cultural commodity which has to be produced, distributed, promoted and exhibited. Indeed, the vast majority of local films made between 2008 and 2018 which enjoyed a Bulgarian release for the period 1998–2017 belong to the mainstream category with *Mission London* and *Love.net* leading the trend (see Table 3.1) (Bulgarian Cinema 2017: 35–6). The latest Bulgarian blockbusters were *Heights*, *Voevoda*, *Omnipresent* and *Duvka za baloncheta/Bubblegum* (Stanislav Todorov-Rogi, Bulgaria, 2017) which had great results during the first week following their official premieres. What is more, *Omnipresent*, the second feature film by the creative duo Ilian Djevelekov and Matei Konstantinov, received not only Box office success, but also recognition by film critics and the jury grand prize award of the Varna film festival in 2017 (Bulgarian Cinema 2017: 35–6).

In conclusion, both mainstream and arthouse Bulgarian cinema has successfully adopted and transformed Hollywood and Western European film styles and filmmaking practices, to ensure, on the one hand, the sustainability of the local film industry, and on the other hand, continuous support by local audiences.

Figure 3.3   *Omnipresent* (Ilian Djevelekov, 2017). Courtesy of Ilian Djevelekov and Matei Konstantinov.

THE MAJORITY/MINORITY CO-PRODUCTION DEBATES AND THE TRANSNATIONAL DIRECTION OF BULGARIAN CINEMA

The diversification of production models as a whole, and in particular the rapid adoption of co-production as an industrial practice in its two forms – majority and minority – is a characteristic trend of the last decade. While this model has existed since the 1990s, it was only when the Film Industry Act (FIA) was adopted in 2003 that the situation gradually moved in a more positive direction. Thanks to the majority co-production model, many directors such as Kamen Kalev (*Iztochni piesi/Eastern Plays*, Bulgaria/Sweden, 2009), Dimitar Mitovski (*Mission London*), Viktor Chuchkov Jr (*Tilt*), Kristina Grozeva and Petar Valchanov (*Urok/The Lesson*, Bulgaria/Greece, 2014), Maya Vitkova (*Viktoria*), Ralitsa Petrova (*Godless*), Antony Donchev (*Zhenata na moya zhivot/The Woman of My Life*, Bulgaria/North Macedonia/Iraq/Romania), Grigor Lefterov and Todor Matsanov (*Hristo*) and Viktor Bojinov (*Heights*) have been able to make their first films. Some directors were also able to ensure international distribution, for instance *Heights* was broadcast on TV channels HBO and HBO GO (Statulov 2018: 33). Alongside these promising debuts, there are also other remarkable examples of rewarding transnational cooperation: the great star of Japanese cinema Kiki Sugino participated as a co-producer and actress in the lead role in the film *A Picture with Yuki*.

Figure 3.4 *A Picture with Yuki* (Lachezar Avramov, 2019). Courtesy of Chouchkov Brothers.

Additionally, the minority co-production model has also evolved and proven to be very advantageous, especially within the regional, Balkan context as it has resulted in the production of a number of important films, some made by some distinguished directors, for example Srđan Dragojević's *Sveti Georgije ubiva azdahu/St George Slays the Dragon* (Serbia/Bosnia-Herzegovina/Bulgaria, 2009), Reha Erdem's *Kosmos/Cosmos* (Turkey/Bulgaria, 2009), Milcho Manchevski's *Majki/Mothers* (North Macedonia/France/Bulgaria, 2011), Radu Jude's *Aferim!* (Romania/Bulgaria/Czech Republic/France, 2015), Tudor Giurgiu's *De ce eu?/ Why Me?* (Romania/Bulgaria/Hungary, 2015) and Nae Caranfil's *6.9 pe scara Richter/6.9 on the Richter Scale* (Romania/Bulgaria/Hungary, 2016). Bulgarian professionals were also involved in Adina Pintilie's first feature film *Nu ma atinge-ma/Touch Me Not* (Romania/Germany/Czech Republic/Bulgaria/France, 2017) that won the Golden Bear at the Berlinale.

The advantages and disadvantages of co-productions form part of a wider debate on the concepts of national versus transnational cinema that dominated the Bulgarian film community in the period 2008–18. The producer and film critic Pavlina Zheleva, who has widely discussed the role of co-production in the development of Bulgarian cinema, maintains that co-productions are a viable industrial practice offering a favourable alternative for financial backing (2016: 2–9). Indeed, her professional career epitomises the figure of the new producer, one that has relevant business expertise and works within a transnational environment, willingly collaborating with international partners across the Balkans and Europe.

Founding the companies *Geopoly* in 1995 and *Geopoly Film* in 2014, Zheleva and her colleague Georgi Cholakov took an overt interest in participating in projects implemented at an international level. From the outset, they built a sustainable network with film professionals from the region and were involved in a few fairly successful enterprises, such as the film *Eskiya/ The Bandit/* (Yavuz Turgul, Turkey/France/Bulgaria,1996), listed among the twelve best Turkish movies of all time and with 2.5 million spectators. Their next significant production was *Homa kai nero/Earth and Water* (Panos Karkanevatos, Greece/Bulgaria/Luxembourg, 1999), selected for many prestigious film festivals in Tokyo, Rotterdam and Karlovy Vary. Furthermore, *Geopoly Film* broadened the scope of their activity in the Balkans with other ambitious projects such as *Rekvijem za gospodju J./Requiem for Mrs. J.* (Bojan Vuletić, Serbia/Bulgaria/North Macedonia/Russia/France/Germany, 2017) but also beyond, making beneficial contacts with foreign producers from Lithuania, Hungary, Great Britain and the Netherlands.

Through her engagement in debates with the film community and her production work, Zheleva calls for the need to overcome the entrenched negative attitude toward minority co-productions in comparison to majority co-productions. The apparent reasons behind this palpable resistance is that majority co-productions are considered better due to the perception of being closer to national cinema (usually the director and the leading members of his/her team are Bulgarian, the language is Bulgarian and in many cases the plot and issues considered are addressed to local audiences). On the other hand, minority co-productions tend to be seen as a menace in terms of national cinema, because of the conviction that they take advantage of limited state financial resources without contributing to local and national film culture. Furthermore, some perceive that Bulgarian film professionals are treated as inferior in minority co-productions, only hired for technical aspects in their capacity as well-trained experts but incomparably cheaper as a labour force. Zheleva, however, argues that, despite such problems, participation in co-productions of any kind offer a means for continuous professional improvement (2016: 3).

Recent Bulgarian films made as majority co-productions have received warm acceptance at international festivals, such as: *Godless, Slava/Glory* (Kristina Grozeva and Petar Valchanov, Bulgaria/Greece, 2016), *Prokurorat, zashtitnikat, bashtata i negovia sin/The Prosecutor, the Defender, the Father and His Son* (Iglika Trifonova, Bulgaria/Sweden/Netherlands, 2016) and *Hristo*. Zheleva maintains that some films made principally using state funds have also achieved success and visibility transcending the national borders, for example *Karatsi/Losers* (Ivaylo Hristov, Bulgaria, 2015), *Zhazhda/Thirst* (Svetla Tsotsorkova, Bulgaria, 2015) and *Potuvaneto na Sozopol/The Sinking of Sozopol* (Kostadin Bonev, Bulgaria, 2014) (Zheleva 2016: 7). Given that all the above fall within the 'art cinema' category, it appears that those filmmakers who receive less state financial support for their projects are compelled to look for alternative resources and tend to be highly motivated to reach a wider public.

For Zheleva (2016), film is a cultural product that should reach its maximum audience, therefore the involvement in a co-production seems to be the best mechanism for distribution and exhibition in two or more countries. Since the producer faces greater challenges in the process of a co-production than a national film (raising public funds from different institutions with various requirements, cultural policies and specific agendas) 'it means that the authors have succeeded to go beyond the domestic mindset and to offer a product with better possibilities for realization on the global market' (Zheleva 2016: 4). The best films made as co-productions are often authentically good auteur cinema and vice versa, films with predominantly national financial support in many cases remain local audiences' favourites (Zheleva 2016: 4). The younger generations have expressed a wish for the state financial resources to be invested in debuts, second films of directors and low-budget and short movies (Zheleva 2016: 9), which could be a viable means for Bulgarian cinema not just to survive in a strongly competitive environment but also develop its potential in tune with world tendencies in film and culture.

Finally, aside from the state-subsided national film and the two co-production models discussed above, there is a specific group of heterogeneous authors, incorporated under the category of independent cinema, who tend to work outside the official system and rely heavily on private assets. Among them there are known directors such as Nikolay Iliev, Maksim Genchev, Georgi Kostov and Val Todorov, but the most provocative and acclaimed filmmakers within this category are Vasil Goranov and Andrey Andonov. For his exceptionally original documentary debut – *Koraba slanchogled/Sunflower Spaceship* (Bulgaria/Italy/Netherlands, 2016) Vasil Goranov obtained the Golden Rose award at the Varna Film Festival in 2017, where he was formally recognised as a talented young artist by the Bulgarian film community. Similarly, Andrey Andonov drew the attention of the local public and critics with the movie *Nikoi/No One* (Bulgaria, 2017) which was later unexpectedly bought by the American TV giant HBO.

THE VISIBILITY OF NEW BULGARIAN CINEMA: FILM FESTIVALS AND EXHIBITION NETWORKS

When examining the changes in Bulgarian cinema since 2008, I wish to stress the role of the Sofia International Film Fest (SIFF) as an institution with enormous significance due to its contributions to the revitalisation of the Bulgarian film scene through: making local films internationally visible, promoting gifted and unknown filmmakers from the region, presenting the best of world cinema to local audiences, and slowly constructing a cinephile audience. The evolution of this festival is equally remarkable. It had a modest beginning in 1997 as a forum devoted to music films, but within two decades SIFF has transformed into a prestigious festival which *Variety* magazine put among the top 50 events in the global film industry in 2007.[8] SIFF is officially recognised by the International Federation of Film Critics (FIPRESCI) and in 2010 it was accredited by the International Federation of Film Producers Associations (FIAPF) acquiring, in this way, a unique status in comparison with the rest of the film festivals in Bulgaria.

Arguably, SIFF owes its rapid development to the ambition and endless energy of its long-standing director Stefan Kitanov and the members of his team, who have worked to build a multifaceted event of artistic, social and economic relevance. From the very outset, their aim was to attract different partners and sponsors – national and European, from both private and state sectors, local authorities and foreign cultural institutes – which would ensure sustainability and visibility of the forum. Further, Kitanov has invested tremendous efforts to establish close collaboration with the regional and European festivals and thus SIFF became a part of a viable transnational network.

The festival programme offers a plethora of art temptations (the international competition for first and second films and for documentary movies, the Balkan competition and the national competition for the Jameson Short Film

Award), presentations of Film Studies publications, cineliteracy formats (SFF for Students) and numerous press conferences. SIFF, however, also functions as an important platform for business contacts bringing together producers, distributors and exhibitors from the entire world, reportedly 'more than 150 industry executives from different parts of the world come in Sofia to discover new projects and films' (Sofia International Film Festival). Within the framework of fifteen editions, Sofia Meetings – the festival's official co-production market – succeeded in developing its potential and nowadays it is a vibrant commercial venue comparable with similar regional markets, such as Agora, at the Thessaloniki International Film Festival, and CineLink Industry Days at the Sarajevo Film Festival.

Sofia Meetings consists of 'Feature Film Pitching', in which applicants present projects for their first, second or third feature fiction film looking for financial support, and the 'Balkan Screenings/Works in Progress', where near-completed projects are presented in the search for completion funds and/or festival premieres. This initiative manifests the explicit policy for the support and promotion of local productions in a broader globalised context. The festival's public-facing screenings are organised according to different thematic rubrics (Balkan competition, retrospective tributes, country in focus), offering local audiences the golden opportunity to see films made by internationally acclaimed filmmakers such as Nuri Bilge Çeylan, Srđan Dragojević, Jasmila Žbanić, Milcho Manchevski, Cristi Puiu, Corneliu Porumboiu and Cristian Mungiu before they became festival celebrities, and in addition spectators can also enjoy the films of great Balkan auteurs such as Theo Angelopoulos, Emir Kusturica, Goran Paskaljević, Goran Marković and Nae Caranfil.

Perhaps most importantly, SIFF is a vital landmark on the professional path of many young Bulgarian filmmakers, who have achieved notable debuts with widespread resonance abroad: Javor Gardev (*Zift*), Kamen Kalev (*Eastern Plays*), Konstantin Bojanov (*Avé*, Bulgaria, 2011), Milko Lazarov (*Alienation*), Kristina Grozeva and Petar Valchanov (*The Lesson*), Maya Vitkova (*Viktoria*) and Ralitsa Petrova (*Godless*). What is more, Stefan Kitanov participates as producer in realising and promoting feature film projects such as *The World Is Big and Salvation Lurks Around the Corner* and *Irina* (Bulgaria, 2018) that established the names of their respective directors Stephan Komandarev and Nadejda Koseva beyond the frontiers of the country.

Furthermore, the festival has a special socio-cultural contribution beyond its duration through the initiative entitled 'Sofia Film Fest on the Road', which is aimed at the inhabitants of small towns and villages (similar to the project launched by the Bulgarian National Television – 'Travelling summer cinema under the stars'). Both endeavours try to bridge the gap between the spectators from the big cities and those from the province literally bringing the latest films to the most remote locations in the country. This is an important factor in increasing and maintaining film culture, due to the fact that, since 1989, the cinema theatre network in Bulgaria has collapsed and the vast majority of cinema theatres, which functioned during communism are now closed. The tangible inequality in terms of access to qualitative native and European movies for urban and rural audiences has generated two antagonistic types of cinema goers cultivated by different visual patterns: the first consists of proactive urban spectators educated enough to be open to different kinds of film, while the second includes audiences mostly exposed to Hollywood genre films and local versions of reality TV formats whose cinematic tastes are far more restricted. These travelling film festival initiatives also reflected the desire for an authentic communication exchange between Bulgarian filmmakers and the heterogeneous public(s) about the crucial topic that is the future of national film.

CONCLUSION

The recent trends in contemporary Bulgarian cinema, the diversification of production models and the gradual increase and participation in both majority and minority co-productions within the region and beyond, instil a moderate optimism. Recently, the Bulgarian National Film Center participated with 90,000 euro in a regional project with the Serbian production company Gargantua Films, the Croatian producer Maxima film, the Montenegrin production house Artikulacija, Sirena Film from the Czech Republic and the Bulgarian production company the Chouchkov Brothers, to make the Serbian majority co-production *Budi Bog s nama/Be God with Us* (FoNet 2019) directed by the veteran director Slobodan Šijan. This is a story of a Yugoslav film critic, Boško Tokin, who had worked in Zagreb and Belgrade, and examines the life of this intellectual during the transitional era from the Second World War to socialist Yugoslavia. Similar models of regional co-productions are likely to continue into the next decade, especially to support popular and authoritative directors such as Slobodan Šijan, known for his comedies in Bulgaria and across the region, but also genre films geared toward reaching the maximum audience.[9]

The steady increase of film productions over the last decade, both in arthouse and mainstream categories, is the result of the continuous effort of the Bulgarian National Film Center, the Bulgarian film community and the local film festivals in supporting and promoting contemporary Bulgarian cinema. The current state of Bulgarian cinema is closely related to the increasing volume of film productions based on the diversification of industrial practices, the appearance of a new generation of filmmakers and producers who are prepared to work within a transnational environment and are flexible enough to compete for spectators beyond the local cultural space. Furthermore, the emergence of new genres and the resurrection of older generic forms is another positive tendency, which indicates a continuous process of alteration and renovation in recent Bulgarian cinema.

NOTES

1. Bulgarian sociologists Andrey Raichev and Kancho Stoychev (2008) found that the transition in the country was completed in 2004. While this statement triggered a heated debate in Bulgaria, the question surrounding the final date of this endless transition remains open.

2. According to Bratoeva-Daraktchieva, the 'first identity crisis' was a direct consequence of the introduction and establishment of Socialist Realism in the 1950s as the dominant normative aesthetic system and the 'second identity crisis' was linked to the general crisis of all ideologies in the 1970s (2019: 7).

3. For his film *Ága*, Milko Lazarov received the Heart of Sarajevo prize at the festival in Sarajevo in 2018 and numerous awards from different festivals across the globe.

4. The Bulgarian National Film Center organises two important events: the Golden Rose Festival of Bulgarian Feature Films (in Varna) and the Golden Rhyton of Bulgarian Documentary and Animation Films (in Plovdiv), which have a vital presence in local film culture.

5. In a regulatory document (Zapoved No. 9/06.02.2018) concerning the work of artistic committees at the Bulgarian National Film Center, the difference between 'high-budget' and 'low-budget' films in the Bulgarian context is defined with precision: films with a budget exceeding 600,000 levs are classified in the category 'high budget' and, respectively, under 600,000 levs 'low budget' (Bulgarian National Film Center).

6. This information was collected from the annual catalogues published by the Bulgarian National Film Center in reference to the national festival Golden Rose.

7. In the Bulgarian language there is no difference between the name of the novel and the name of the movie (*Vazvishenie*), and the English translation does not entirely convey the metaphorical layer of the Bulgarian title (Gotseva 2018a: 6).

8. For more details, refer to the official website of the Sofia International Film Festival and Variety Staff (2007).

9. The Bulgarian National Film Center will also participate in another Serbian majority co-production with 112,437 euro (FoNet 2019), based on a popular novel, *Leto kad sam naučila da letim/How I Learned to Fly* (*Radivoje Raša Andrić*, Serbia/Croatia/Bulgaria, in production), belonging to the family/teenage genre. The film is set on the Croatian island of Hvar and tells the story of a teenage girl growing up in the post-Yugoslav transition phase. The production is supported by Eurimages, the Serbian Film Center and was developed through the Film TEEP co-production training programme in Romania, organised by ARTVIVA with the support of the Romanian Film Center.

REFERENCES

Bratoeva-Daraktchieva, Ingeborg (2019) 'Bulgarian Film 1988–2018: Crossing Borders, Conquering Territories', in Nadezhda Marinchevska (ed.), *Post-totalitarian Cinema in Eastern European Countries: Models and Identities*. Sofia: Institute of Art Studies Bulgarian Academy of Sciences, pp.7–16.

Bulgarian Cinema 2017: Facts, Figures, Trends (2017) Sofia: National Film Center.

Bulgarian National Film Center (2005–18) <https://www.nfc.bg/en/> (last accessed 9 September 2019).

Dimitrova, Maya (2018) 'Retsepti na Arta – Evropeiski Kontekst', *ARTizanin*, No. 15, December, pp. 11–14.

FoNet (2019) 'Filmski centar: Bugari finansiraju dva filma iz Srbije sa 200.000 evra', *Danas*, 26 June <https://www.danas.rs/kultura/filmski-centar-bugari-finansiraju-dva-filma-iz-srbije-sa-200-000-evra/> (last accessed 9 September 2019).

Gotseva, Elitsa (2018a) 'Ot Naroda – za Naroda ili za Ekranizatsiata v Nai-novoto Bulgarsko Kino', *ARTizanin*, No. 8, May, pp. 2–10.

Gotseva, Elitsa (2018b) 'Otvud Festivalnite Nagradi', *ARTizanin*, No. 15, December, pp. 19–21.

Kanusheva, Irina (2019) 'Toslav Hristov: Za Men Kinoto e Zversko Udovolstvie', *ARTizanin*, No. 20, May, pp. 114–20.

Mártonova, Andronika (2019) 'Vidimo i Nevidimo Otvud "Snimka s Yuki" razgovor s rezhisiora Lachezar Avramov I scenarista Dimitar Stoyanovich', *ARTizanin*, No. 18, March, pp. 120–7.

Mártonova, Andronika (2020) 'The World of Korea in the Bulgarian Films Directed by Yana Lekarska', *Orbis Linguarum*, Vol. 18, Issue 1, pp. 79–85.

Nedyalkova, Maya (2015) *Transnational Bulgarian Cinema – Pieces of the Past, Present and Future*. PhD dissertation, University of Southampton, Faculty of Humanities, School of Film.

Raichev, Andrey and Stoychev, Kancho (2008) *Kakvo se sluchi?: razkaz za prekhoda v Bulgariia 1989–2004*. Sofia: Public House Trud.

Sofia International Film Festival (2001–16) *siff.bg* <http://siff.bg/en/> (last accessed 9 September 2019).

Statulov, Deyan (2018) 'Modelat *Vazvishenie*', *ARTizanin*, No. 15, December, pp. 31–5.

Stoilova, Theodora (2017) 'Viktor Bozhinov: Opitvame se da ne Pravim Kompromisi s Duha na Knigata i s Duha na Vremeto', *ARTizanin*, No. 1, October, pp. 179–83.

Variety Staff (2007) '50 Unmissable Film Festivals. These Global Events Rank as Must-attends', *Variety*, 7 September <https://variety.com/2007/film/markets-festivals/50-unmissable-film-festivals-1117971644/> (last accessed 9 September 2019).

Zheleva, Pavlina (2016) 'Zashto sme Trugnali po Tozi Put', *Kino Magazine*, 5–6, pp. 2–9.

4. CROATIA: FILM UNDER IDEOLOGICAL PRESSURE – THE STATE, ITS CITIZEN AND THE FALTERING FUTURE

Jurica Pavičić and Aida Vidan

As every year, in July 2018 the coastal city of Pula was the site of Croatia's national film festival. The monumental arena built by the Roman emperor Vespasianus in the first century AD served as the venue for this event as it did for the Yugoslav national film festival since 1953 until the country's disintegration in 1991. The year 2018 marked not only its sixty-fifth anniversary, thereby making it one of the world's oldest national film festivals, but also celebrated a decade since the establishment of the Hrvatski audiovizualni centar (HAVC)/ Croatian Audiovisual Centre, the principal institution for financing, programming and promoting Croatian cinema.

Nearly seven thousand spectators who gathered in the Roman arena to watch the opening night cheered Hrvoje Hribar, the man who had served as the HAVC's Executive Director for six years. The long applause, however, expressed at the same time an ironic commentary on the political scandal which had been shaking the Croatian media and society for months (Gabrić 2017; Bobanović 2018). Approximately a year earlier, Hribar had had to resign from his position as the Centre's head owing to a scathing report by the State Audit Office. The auditors claimed that the HAVC's business reports were delinquent and negligent, and its director guilty of financial and professional misconduct. The main objection was the fact that the Centre financed films without prior written consent by the Minister of Culture, Nina Obuljen Koržinek. Despite the flimsy attempt to cloak the reasons for the audit in financial matters, it was discernible from the onset that the real motivation was political. The audit report came as the final chapter of a long-lasting campaign in which right-wing groups, nationalist politicians and war veterans accused the HAVC of corruption, conflicts of interest and, above all, unpatriotic programming. The focus of criticism was the HAVC's financing of films which, according to these allegations, cast a negative light on the Croatian war for independence in the 1990s, in particular the two minority co-productions: a Danish documentary entitled *Massakren i Dvor/15 minutes – The Dvor Massacre* (Denmark/Croatia, 2015) by Georg Larsen and Kasper Vedsmand, investigating an unsolved war crime from August 1995, and a Swiss animation documentary *Chris the Swiss* (Switzerland/Croatia/Finland/Germany, 2018) by Anja Kofmel. The latter, selected for the Cannes Critic's week programme and nominated for the European animation award, deals with the murder of a Swiss volunteer in the Croatian Army who appears to have been killed by the soldiers from his own unit.

The turmoil ensued after a lengthy ideological struggle starting in 2016 and carrying on throughout 2018 with numerous press conferences and protests against the HAVC headed by the former short-term Minister of Culture Zlatko Hasanbegović, a right-wing politician who insisted on the need to 'debunk the system' and dismantle the Centre (Vladić 2018). During the parliamentary hearing on the new Film Law, Hasanbegović, subsequently an MP, stated that 'the HAVC was supposed to be an instrument of the Croatian state cultural politics, which did not happen' (Šurina 2018). However, the directors' and producers' guilds stood firmly by Hribar and the Centre, emphasising that under his guidance the national cinema stabilised its finances and organisation, and gained international visibility for the first time since Croatian independence. After Hribar's resignation, numerous members of the European Film Agency Directors, themselves in charge of their respective national film agencies, voiced their support of Hribar, emphasising that his 'role has been paramount in making Croatian film a success story in Europe' (EFADs 2017). The arena in Pula welcomed him as such.

The consequences of political meddling in cultural affairs were multifold. In 2016 the government failed to provide budgetary funds for the rebate given to foreign productions filming in Croatia. This caused panic among investors resulting in a decreased export of production services from 166 to 50 million kunas (equivalent to 23 to 7 million euros) in just one year (Pavičić 2016: 44). Many interpreted this economically suicidal gesture as an attempt to crash the Centre's economic pillars. As of 2016, the right-wing protesters campaigned against particular films, including the two aforementioned titles as well as the moderately critical mainstream comedy *Ministarstvo ljubavi/Ministry of Love* (Pavo Marinković, Croatia/Czech Republic, 2016), which ridicules the system that allowed war widows to abuse veteran pensions. In January 2018 when the film was to be screened on the Croatian Public Television (HTV), a group of veterans organised a riot in front of the TV studios. It remains unclear whether it was an act of piracy or the producer's shrewd decision, but the film appeared promptly on YouTube where it became a huge hit. The comedy with a rather modest theatrical attendance was seen by more than 90,000 in only forty-eight hours, gaining visibility from its sudden political notoriety.

Despite these turmoils, the decade spanning 2008 and 2018 has been one of the most interesting periods for Croatian film culminating in a number of significant achievements, only to end with ideological perturbations which have endangered both the future growth and creativity. The goal of this article is to provide the socio-political framework for these developments and situate the most relevant films within this context while discussing trends in styles, genres and subject matter. In addition, it aims to investigate the institutional impact and influences of TV, factoring in the larger question of European film distribution. Towards this goal, the HAVC, as the principal facilitator of film production in Croatia, will remain the focal point for laying out both diachronic and synchronic perspectives.

Croatian Film and Shadows of the 1990s

It is not surprising that the Croatian professional film community reacted with rage to the proposal to diminish the autonomy of the HAVC. The Centre itself was founded in 2008 as a reaction of film professionals to the 1990s, a period customarily considered as the most shameful chapter in Croatian film history. During this time film production and financing were under the direct supervision of the Ministry of Culture which resulted in a cohort of superficial patriotic war titles that have been categorised as 'films of self-victimisation' (Pavičić 2011: 108–36). These projects, which depicted the nation as a collective hero, vilified the Other (the Serbs) and included pompous Christian iconography, were executed by a handful of mediocre directors without significant previous credits, who jumped at the opportunity to make films by offering the authorities the type of projects they desired. Equally loathed by critics, professionals and spectators, these films generated a counter-effect and alienated the local audience from the domestic production (Pavičić 2012: 51–2). With a change of political tide to the left in the early 2000s, films of self-victimisation gradually gave way to different projects and new directors. The overall quality improved which, in turn, brought Croatian films to festival programmes, mostly of Berlin and Karlovy Vary (*Maršal/Marshal Tito's Spirit* (Vinko Brešan, Croatia, 1999), *Svjedoci/Witnesses* (Vinko Brešan, Croatia, 2003), *Tu/Here* (Zrinko Ogresta, Croatia/Bosnia-Herzegovina, 2003), *Armin* (Ognjen Sviličić, Croatia/Bosnia-Herzegovina/Germany, 2007)). However, the industry was still dependent on the relatively poor administrative capacity of the Ministry of Culture. Keeping in mind the painful experiences of the 1990s, the Croatian film professionals led by the film scholars Hrvoje Turković, Ante Peterlić and Ivo Škrabalo for over a decade promoted the idea of a national film institute modelled on French and Scandinavian examples. Their efforts came to fruition during the subsequent right-centre government which passed the new Film Law in 2007. The person who drafted the bill, Albert Kapović, became the first Director of the newly formed film hub, the HAVC, established at the time when almost all European nations had similar institutions, some of them for decades. Still, this delay had some positive side effects, in particular a twofold financial structure consisting both of a direct state subsidy and obligatory contributions from cinema chains, TV subscriptions, commercial and cable television channels as well as cellular phone and Internet providers. Since the HAVC emerged at the moment when it was apparent that Internet providers were lining up as the most relevant players in the distribution market, their inclusion in the list of contributors was a forward-looking decision.

With the negative experiences of the 1990s still resonating, the creators of the Film Law made every attempt to distance executive politics from film programming as much as possible. The selection of projects became an autonomous task assigned to Artistic Councilors who were appointed for a two-year mandate, each overseeing a different type of film (feature, experimental, animation, documentary). Their decisions were confirmed by the Audiovizualno Vijeće/Audiovisual Council, the main professional body of the Centre. The government or the Ministry of Culture had no influence on the membership of the Audiovisual Council which consisted of appointed representatives from professional institutions (the Directors' Guild, the Producers' Guild, the Film Academy, the Film Archive, etc.). An interesting aspect of the HAVC's setup was that financial contributors (including telephone companies and commercial TV channels) had their representatives in the Audiovisual Council as well. This system was – possibly unconsciously – modelled on that of the *Samoupravna interesna zajednica* (SIZ, Self-managing Interest Unit), which was the basic organisational form in the final period of Yugoslav socialism, a concept rooted in the principle of *Udruženi Rad* (United Work) and invented by the Slovenian Marxist philosopher and Tito's informal ideologue Edvard Kardelj. Despite gaining a mocking attribute of 'the last living SIZ in the world' the Audiovisual Council functioned well in part because of its built-in safety mechanism which prevented ideological and political intrusion into programming. It was exactly this component that the right-wing politicians tried to undermine when in 2017 they called for a 'debunking of the system'. In the course of ten years, the HAVC changed the entire landscape of the country's audiovisual industry. When the film professionals in the early 2000s lobbied for a new organising body, they had hoped it would achieve a long list of goals, many of which (although not all) have been accomplished.

Between the Local Audience and
the International Scene

Dispersing the deep-seated skepticism that the local audience had for domestic film after the mediocre 1990s has been one of the greatest challenges for the Croatian film industry. While from 2008 to 2010 the market share for national films hovered between 1.6 and 0.8 per cent of the total box office, in the subsequent period Croatian films represented anywhere from nearly 2 per cent (2015) to 11 per cent (2013) (Hribar 2014: 3; European Audiovisual Observatory 2009–18). These broad oscillations point to a narrowness of the repertoire but also to the lack of digital theatres in the first years of the decade under scrutiny. This trend began to change between 2009 and 2016 with increased admissions for domestic, European (non-anglophone) and world film from 7.5 to 15 per cent. The figures overall also improved for domestic films, although not consistently: between 2011 and 2016 seven feature films sold over 40,000 tickets each while four had over 100,000 admissions (Croatian Audiovisual Centre 2017a: 24). After 2016 and the political turmoils in the HAVC, these numbers started declining again, in part owing to the smaller number of produced and distributed films. While in 2017 twelve Croatian feature films were distributed in cinemas, in 2018 only six reached theatrical screens and only one had a moderately solid attendance (*Osmi povjerenik/ The Eighth Commissioner* (Ivan Salaj, Croatia, 2018; 31,499 viewers)). The third on the list of best attended Croatian films was the thriller *F20* (Arsen A. Ostojić, Croatia, 2018), which had only 4,711 attendees.

However, to put things in perspective, one should consider the fact that arthouse film in general suffers from low market numbers in other national contexts as well. A prominent Croatian producer cites the much larger German production with an approximate output of some hundred and fifty fiction feature-length films from which only about twenty end up in wide theatrical distribution and two to three become hits (Tomljanović 2015: 46). Most films, in particular the arthouse (and the Berlin School has received its share of criticism on this account), end up with the viewership of several thousand sold box tickets. Still, a larger production output is more likely to yield a hit or two annually and would also have greater genre diversity. Despite these trends, a larger question affecting not only Croatian film but distribution of world film in general is the market share of Internet/VOD/cable/mobile providers which is on the rise in Croatia as in other countries (Croatian Audiovisual Centre, 2017a: 63–6). The Digital Agenda for Europe, an initiative of the European Commission, has observed the sevenfold growth of the digital economy and called for a new policy framework (including film distribution) needed to define these markets. Under these fluctuating circumstances Croatia is yet to position itself in relation to the unified European digital market.

As already stated, domestic films represent for the most part only a marginal percentage of national film admissions and major hits are infrequent. When they do happen, they almost exclusively belong to the genre of comedy. Examples of this line of production abound: *Što je muškarac bez brkova/What Is a Man Without a Moustache* (Hrvoje Hribar, Croatia, 2005), *Sonja i bik/ Sonja and the Bull* (Vlatka Vorkapić, Croatia, 2012), *Svećenikova djeca/The Priest's Children* (Vinko Brešan, Croatia/Serbia/Montenegro, 2013), *Narodni heroj Ljiljan Vidić/The People's Hero Ljiljan Vidić* (Ivan Goran Vitez, Croatia/ Serbia, 2015), *ZG 80* (Igor Šeregi, Croatia, 2016), *The Eighth Commissioner*, *Koja je ovo država!/What a Country!* (Vinko Brešan, Croatia/Serbia/Poland, 2018), *Posljednji Srbin u Hrvatskoj/The Last Serb in Croatia* (Predrag Ličina, Croatia, 2019). The latter is particularly interesting as a genre hybrid: a political zombie comedy about a dystopian future in Croatia where greedy corporations poison the only water source causing a zombie-epidemic to which only the Serbs are immune. Infusing his film with political irony, Ličina ridicules the 'blood' and 'genetics' foundations of Balkan nationalisms.

Popular Croatian comedies share many common elements: nearly all have a regional flavour, mainly using locations on the Adriatic Coast or Dalmatian hinterland and consequently relying heavily on dialects in dialogues (either regional speech or urban Zagreb slang). They invariably deal with cultural contrasts (the differences between urban and rural or young and old) and depict a clash of mentalities, often representing backwardness and irrationality as dominating forces in Croatian society. Many of these motifs are typical not only for popular cinema comedies, but pervade also TV sit-coms such as *Naši i vaši/Ours and Yours* (Vančo Kljaković, Croatia, 2000–2) or *Stipe u gostima/Stipe Visiting* (Ognjen Sviličić, Croatia, 2008–14). Croatian audiences are also occasionally attracted to children's films. For instance, in 2017 the three best-attended Croatian films included the crime adventure *Uzbuna na Zelenom Vrhu/The Mystery of Green Hill* (Čejen Černić, Croatia, 2017), the historic fantasy *Anka* (Dejan Aćimović, Croatia, 2017) and the animation feature in Czech-Slovakian-Croatian co-production *Neparožder/Lichozrouti/ Oddsockeaters* (Galina Miklinova, 2016). Still, the production of children's films is unsystematic and sporadic. Children-oriented projects do not have a separate fund or public tender but rather compete for the same funds as arthouse and mainstream projects.

In part owing to its limited output, Croatian production suffers from insufficient diversification of feature length films. It largely consists of middle-budget art dramas suitable for international festivals and the arthouse circuit, with moderate domestic admissions ranging between five and twenty thousand spectators. A customary budget for a Croatian film in relation to the targeted local market is for the most part insufficient to produce large historic epics typical of contemporary Polish or Russian cinema. The preponderance of art dramas nonetheless has had a stylistic side effect evident in the domination of a European, minimalist neo-realist approach. Many important successful Croatian films from this period – *Crnci/The Blacks* (Zvonimir Jurić and Goran Dević, Croatia, 2009), *Metastaze/Metastases* (Branko Schmidt, Croatia/Bosnia-Herzegovina/Serbia, 2009), *Ljudožder vegetarijanac/Vegetarian Cannibal* (Branko Schmidt, Croatia, 2012), *Takva su pravila/These Are the Rules* (Ognjen Sviličić, Croatia/France/Serbia/North Macedonia, 2014 (see Figure 4.1)), *Ne gledaj mi u pijat/Quit Staring at My Plate* (Hana Jušić, Croatia/Denmark, 2016), *S one strane/On the Other Side* (Zrinko Ogresta, Croatia/Serbia, 2016), *Sam samcat/All Alone* (Bobo Jelčić, Bosnia-Herzegovina/Croatia/Montenegro/Netherlands, 2018) – share the elements of this style, including a hand-held camera, frequent close-ups, realistic urban settings, minimal or no music, veristic dialogue, imperfect vision or framing and basic linear storytelling of intimate narratives.

Such domination of one stylistic model could be interpreted as a reaction to the global stylistic shift from the new Philippine film to the Berlin School or the Dardenne brothers, but also as an influence of the geographically, socially and culturally similar Romanian New Wave. There may be yet another explanation which considers the historical background: new Croatian film developed its attributes as a reaction to the stylistic excesses and ideological layers of the 1990s, in particular the 'Balkan cinema style' epitomised by the films of Emir Kusturica and Srđan Dragojević. During the 2000s their choices gained political

Figure 4.1 *These Are the Rules* (Ognjen Sviličić, 2014).

notoriety because of self-colonial, auto-exoticising and politically regressive implications (Jameson 2004; Pavičić 2011: 172–8). The Romanian New Wave thus came as a cleansing device that could purify Balkan cinema from the 'Balkan cinema style'. After ten years, the counter-model itself has become the norm which continues to dominate in Croatian feature production. It is debatable whether this stylistic tendency further alienates the local audience or vice versa – whether this particular stylistic choice reflects difficulties in finding one's own audience locally, prompting authors to aim for the international arthouse and festival circuit.

In terms of thematic range, in this period, the topic of the Croatian war for independence has come to the fore in several films as a personal ethical drama rather than an epic-scale narrative, but overall it has gradually been losing prominence in the national output. On the other hand, the subject of war has persisted in Croatian regional co-productions. The national thematic focus has increasingly shifted to the realities of the postwar period and its consequences. At the same time, a number of films deal with intergenerational clashes, often conveying a healthy dose of implied or overt criticism of patriarchy. The misery caused by dysfunctional public services, a conservative mindset and corruption is another recurrent subject matter. Gender and minority rights have also appeared as a thematic niche. Many Croatian films critique the dominant nationalist ideology and its fetishism of the nation/state, neglecting to scrutinise capitalism and its impact on transitional society. With the exception of titles such as Dalibor Matanić's *Blagajnica hoće ići na more/ Cashier Wants to Go to the Seaside* (Croatia, 2000) and *Majka asfalta/Mother of Asphalt* (Croatia, 2010), and Tomislav Radić's *Što je Iva snimila 21. listopada 2003/What Iva Recorded on October 21st, 2003* (Croatia, 2005), films addressing capitalist issues are surprisingly infrequent. Left-wing critic Boris Postnikov sums it up: 'For Croatian film, we live in the state where capitalism has not happened: no privatized banking sector, no telephone companies, no media hushed up by advertising money, no commercialization of education, concessions on public property . . . most of Croatian film production adheres to the notion that "true capitalism" still has not happened in Croatia' (2018). He attributes this to the domination of the generation of directors born in the 1960s who 'gained their formative experiences in the communist period, and at the beginning of the 1990s when the narrative on the clash between the individual and the state was subversive for the last time' (2018). This clash which dominates so many Croatian films possibly also reflects the reality in which the filmmaking community lives day by day, as illustrated by the previously discussed events.

Since 2012, the presence of women directors in the Croatian film industry has increased significantly and has brought about different types of projects which have resonated positively with the audiences. Despite the fact that equality of women was one of the declared (and, in many aspects, achieved) goals of socialism, Yugoslav cinema was notorious for being a patriarchal boys' club. During the forty-three years of socialist Yugoslav cinema, only two women directed features, neither of them in Croatia. The first Croatian female director was Snježana Tribuson who directed *Prepoznavanje/Recognition* (Croatia) as late as 1996. Between 1991 and 2007, women directed four out of 108 films, that is 4 per cent of the total production in Croatia. This gender landscape has significantly altered in the current decade. Between 2008 and 2017, women directed fourteen films out of seventy-eight, that is 18 per cent of all films (Croatian Audiovisual Centre, 2017b: 11). The democratisation in funding processes explained above gave a chance to many first-time directors, a number of which were women, allowing for an increased focus on female characters and new visual sensibilities (Vidan 2018). This generation of women directors prioritised themes dealing with everyday reality, interpersonal relationships and ordinary characters rather than grand political narratives and symbolisms. These include Vlatka Vorkapić (*Sonja and the Bull*), Irena Škorić (*7 SeX 7*, Croatia, 2012), Vanja Sviličić (*Zagreb Cappuccino*, Croatia, 2014), Ivona Juka (*Ti mene nosiš/You Carry Me*, Croatia/Slovenia/Serbia/Montenegro, 2015), Hana Jušić (*Quit Staring At My Plate* (see Figure 4.2)), Čejen Černić (*The Mystery of Green Hill*), Barbara Vekarić (*Aleksi*, Croatia/Serbia/Montenegro, 2018), Sara Hribar (*Lada Kamenski*, Croatia, 2018) and Marina Andree Škop (*Moj dida je pao s Marsa/My Grandpa Fell from Mars*, Croatia/Luxembourg/Norway/Czech Republic/Slovakia/Slovenia/Bosnia-Herzegovina, 2019, co-directed with Dražen Žarković). Several, including Sonja Tarokić, Dubravka Turić and

Figure 4.2   *Quit Staring At My Plate* (Hana Jušić, 2016).

Antoneta Alamat Kusijanović, presented their shorts in the programmes of prestigious festivals and are preparing their first features in 2019.

Similarly, feature documentary has seen increased viewership, in part owing to the internationally renowned ZagrebDox Film Festival (est. 2005). Like elsewhere, feature documentaries partly replace the role of mainstream media coverage which has lost its investigating capacity owing to its dependence on big business and advertisers. It is indicative that the number of feature social documentaries doubled and, in some years, even tripled (e.g. 2016) in relation to 2010 and earlier, and the same goes for the mid-length category. Several Croatian documentaries stirred society during this period: *Goli/Naked Island* (Croatia, 2014), Tiha Gudac's autobiographical account of her grandfather's internment in Tito's Goli Otok concentration camp for political prisoners; *Djeca tranzicije/Children of Transition* (Croatia, 2014), Matija Vukšić's documentary on Croatian teenagers searching for wealth and stardom, *Glasniji od oružja/Louder Then Guns* (Croatia, 2017), Miroslav Sikavica's film on patriotic wartime pop music from the 1990s, Goran Dević's *Na vodi/On the Water* (Croatia, 2018) portraying the past of a former industrial city through its river, and Nebojša Slijepčević's award-winning *Srbenka/Serbian Girl* (Croatia, 2018) which chronicles the staging of a controversial theatrical piece based on the murder of a Serbian family during the war in Croatia. Among the most interesting examples of this type of investigative documentarism is Dario Juričan's *Gazda/The Boss* (Croatia, 2016), which focuses on the rise and social status of Ivica Todorić, the wealthiest Croatian businessman who, at the time when the film was made, employed forty thousand people in four post-Yugoslav countries. The multiplex chains initially refused to include *The Boss* in their repertoires for fear of revenge by Todorić who was also their business partner and advertiser. The film was financed through the HAVC, screened in an independent theatre network and on the festival circuit, eventually hitting the bull's eye. The omnipotent, almost invisible 'boss' suddenly became the topic of the mainstream media that otherwise avoided reporting on his businesses. Six months later, Todorić's entire empire collapsed in a rollercoaster of debts and he escaped to London. At the time of writing he has been extradited to Croatia where he faces a series of charges which could also implicate numerous political figures. In this case, Juričan's film affected the economic and political circumstances in the country on the most profound level.

Before the HAVC appeared, a source of deep frustration for the Croatian media and film community had been the lack of international visibility of the country's cinema. Its films were rarely distributed abroad or played in the programmes of major festivals, which, in the contemporary art-cinema world, is a prerequisite for any distribution outcome. The only exception was the Berlin Film Festival, which frequently included films by Vinko Brešan and Ognjen

Sviličić (however, almost always in the less prestigious Forum programme), while the Venice Film Festival showed only one Croatian feature between 1990 and 2008. The last time Cannes Film Festival had shown a Croatian feature was as a part of Yugoslav production in 1981.

The past decade has seen a significant change in this respect. While Croatian films continue to be present in Berlin's sidebar programmes (*Obrana i zaštita/Stranger* (Bobo Jelčić, Croatia/Bosnia-Herzegovina, 2013); *On the Other Side*), after decades of absence a couple of features (*These Are the Rules, Quit Staring at My Plate*) won prizes in Venice. Additionally, Croatian features were included in the programme of the Toronto International Film Festival (*Kosac/Reaper*, Zvonimir Jurić, Croatia/Slovenia, 2014) and the International Film Festival in Rotterdam (*Kratki izlet/A Brief Excursion*, Igor Bezinović, Croatia, 2017) and won the main prize at Montreal World Film Festival (*Ustav Republike Hrvatske/The Constitution*, Rajko Grlić, Croatia/Czech Republic/Slovenia/North Macedonia, 2016) as well as official awards at festivals in Karlovy Vary (*Neka ostane među nama/Just Between Us*, Rajko Grlić, Croatia/Serbia/Slovenia/France, 2010) and Sarajevo (*Naked Island, Serbian Girl*). Croatian short films were presented or won awards in Berlin, Venice, Cannes and Sarajevo, with *Piknik/Picnic* (Jure Pavlović, Croatia, 2015) winning the European film award for best European short in 2015 and *Zvir/The Beast* (Miroslav Sikavica, Croatia, 2016), a special award in the Directors' Fortnight programme in Cannes. Finally, the longest and most bitter spell was broken in 2015, with Dalibor Matanić's *Zvizdan/The High Sun* Croatia/Serbia/Slovenia (see Figure 4.3) not only being selected for Cannes' Un Certain Regard programme, as the first Croatian feature in thirty-four years, but also winning one of the prizes. Croatian cinema, at least so it seemed for a while, was back on international track.

Figure 4.3 *The High Sun* (Dalibor Matanić, 2015).

Co-productions: From Han Solo to Regional Collaborations

One of the HAVC's first requirements was to implement a system of subsidies for foreign productions in Croatia. Although the Croatian rebate system (20 per cent initially; 25 per cent in 2018) has never been as generous as in some other European countries, a mix of rebates, skilled professionals, solid infrastructure and a spectacular variety of easily accessible locations immediately attracted big international productions. These range from the TV series *The Borgias* (USA/Hungary/Ireland/Canada, 2011–13), *Dig* (USA, 2015) and *The Terror* (USA, 2018) to blockbusters such as *Solo: A Star Wars Story* (Ron Howard, USA, 2018), *Mamma Mia! Here We Go Again* (Ol Parker, UK/USA/Japan, 2018) to *Robin Hood* (Otto Bathurst, USA, 2018). Among others, the list of foreign directors who filmed in Croatia includes Peter Greenaway (*Goltzius and the Pelican Company*, UK/Netherlands/France/Croatia/United Arab Emirates, 2012), Marion Hänsel (*En amont du fleuve/Upstream*, Belgium/Netherlands/Croatia, 2016) and Pawel Pawlikowski (*Zimna wojna/Cold War*, Poland/UK/France 2018). Of these productions, the vastly popular HBO TV series *Game of Thrones* has had the biggest social impact. Shot in various Dalmatian locations (mainly Dubrovnik, Trsteno, Klis and Split), the series has inspired a whole new branch of 'Game-of-Thrones' tourism with fans flocking to the historic city venues. In the centres of Dubrovnik and Split, specialised *Game of Thrones* fan-shops have opened, tourist agencies organise thematic tours based on the series and some of the guides are the former extras. *Game of Thrones* has attracted tourists to locations which were previously overlooked by tourist business such as the medieval fortress Klis near Split.

Between 2012 and 2018 more than forty foreign productions were filmed in Croatia, including projects from the USA, the UK, France, Belgium, Germany, Switzerland, the Netherlands, Finland, Denmark, Sweden and India. In addition, the HAVC developed a strong network of regional co-productions. From the 2000s on, it has become the norm that Slovenian, Serbian, Croatian and Bosnian-Herzegovinian films are produced in collaboration, but broader south-eastern film networks have emerged as well in recent years. As a minority partner, Croatia participated in a long list of successful films from South Eastern Europe, from *Krugovi/Circles* (Srdan Golubović, Serbia/Germany/France/Slovenia/Croatia, 2013), *Poslednata lineika na Sofia/Sofia's Last Ambulance* (Ilian Metev, Croatia/Bulgaria/Germany, 2013), *Ničije dete/No One's Child* (Vuk Ršumović, Serbia/Croatia, 2014), *Sieranevada* (Cristi Puiu, Romania/France/Bosnia-Herzegovina/Croatia/North Macedonia, 2016), *Muškarci ne plaču/Men Don't Cry* (Alen Drljević, Bosnia-Herzegovina/Slovenia/Germany/Croatia, 2017), *Teret/Cargo* (Ognjen Glavonić, Serbia/France/Croatia/Iran/Qatar, 2018), *Šavovi/Stitches* (Miroslav Terzić, Serbia/Slovenia/ Croatia/Bosnia-Herzegovina, 2019), *Gospod postoi, imeto i' e Petrunia/God Exists, and Her Name Is Petrunya* (Teona Strugar Mitevska, North Macedonia/Belgium/France/

Croatia/Slovenia, 2019). Many of these films were played in the programmes of Cannes, Berlin, Sundance or Venice, thus providing ample opportunity for greater visibility on the international scene, but also for creative exchanges.

Despite strong collaboration, the market share of regionally co-produced films did not increase in the period analysed. On the contrary, it appears to have diminished. Even in sensitive postwar years, some Serbian films were huge hits in Croatia (such as *Rane/Wounds*, Srđan Dragojević, Federal Republic of Yugoslavia/Germany, 1998), while Croatian films (such as *Karaula/Border Post*, Rajko Grlić, UK/Serbia/Croatia/Slovenia/North Macedonia/Bosnia-Herzegovina/Hungary/Austria, 2006) similarly had solid admissions in Serbia. The latter was directed by one of the most renowned Croatian directors and was the first co-production which included all of the former Yugoslav republics (at the time Montenegro was still not an independent state). It is surprising therefore that the interest for the neighbouring cinemas in Croatia has faded away climaxing in 2018 when only one Serbian feature film was distributed (*Južni vetar/Southern Wind*, Miloš Avramović, Serbia). The only opportunity where regional films can be seen in Croatia are thus numerous film festivals. This trend potentially has manifold explanations. Serbian films are no longer 'the forbidden fruit' as they were in the immediate postwar years. The generation raised in the ex-Yugoslav cultural space is getting older and visits movie theatres less frequently. Finally, the political climate has changed owing to the nationalist ideological throwback. Irrespective of the explanation, the fact remains that the increased local co-production has not boosted attendance of regional films in theatres.

POSITIVE AND NEGATIVE OUTCOMES

Contrary to the situation with regional co-productions, the visibility of Croatian TV productions has seen a marked increase. The HAVC has played a critical role in financing the development stage, and its funding programmes have helped revive TV series production in Croatia as they were open to all audiovisual formats. While previously Croatian television produced only sit-coms and soaps, the HAVC together with media pressure encouraged public television to change this policy, and to make possible the realisation of more ambitious TV products, such as *Patrola na cesti/Highway Patrol* (Zvonimir Jurić, Croatia, 2016) and *Čuvari dvorca/Guardian of the Castle* (Lukas Nola, Croatia, 2017). Two series garnered international success: the political thriller *Novine/The Paper* (Dalibor Matanić, Croatia, 2016–20), focusing on a local daily newspaper in the city of Rijeka, was acquired for distribution by Netflix thereby becoming the first Eastern European series in the Netflix catalogue. Similarly, *Počivali u miru/Rest in Peace* (Kristijan Milić and Goran Rukavina, Croatia, 2013–17), a spy thriller dealing with the intelligence underground of the former

Yugoslav security services, was purchased by the British distributor Global Series Network. While both had a respectable international distribution, on the local scene a major success was reaped by the TV series *Crno bijeli svijet/ Black and White World* (Goran Kulenović, Croatia, 2015–ongoing) which became popular in several post-Yugoslav countries. Taking place in the 1980s communist Yugoslavia, *Black and White World* exploited the ambience of New Wave music, youth subculture and youth journalism in Zagreb in the early 1980s. Even the name of the show (and a part of the opening title sequence) came from the title of a popular 1979 punk song by the band *Prljavo kazalište/ Dirty Theatre*. *Black and White World* appeared on Croatian public TV in the period when Croatian culture reinvestigated its socialist past through several museum exhibitions, documentary serials and artistic projects. The generation which matured in the 1980s had reached middle age and influential positions in many Croatian cultural, social and economic institutions and this TV show served as their collective generational statement.

Supporting distributors of independent and non-Hollywood films has been one of the HAVC's principal missions and towards this goal it initiated the digitisation of cinemas which resulted in an independent cinema network. Globally, the switch to digital theatres peaked in 2010 and Croatia was heading in this direction too (European Commission 2014). By 2011, ninety screens were digitally equipped. Most of these, however, were multiplexes, thus threatening the survival of small independent theatres. In response to the European initiative to preserve and highlight the local production suffering from competition with Hollywood blockbusters, the HAVC supported the digitisation of independent cinemas which, by 2016, had brought fifty-six screens and six film festivals up to new technological standards (Croatian Audiovisual Centre 2017a: 22). These cinemas were not only situated in big cities, but also in small towns such as Zabok (population 8,894), Vodice (population 8,875) or Imotski (population 4,757). This important step ensured diversity of programming and was a prerequisite for increased viewership of Croatian and world titles.

It is without question that during the HAVC's era there have been numerous palpable achievements; however, some important goals have not been achieved. Historically Croatian animation, functioning at the time within the Yugoslav context, was the most recognised part of its film industry in the 1950s and 1960s, triumphing with an Oscar in 1962 for Dušan Vukotić's *Surogat/Surrogate* (aka *Substitute*, Yugoslavia, 1961). Some Croatian animation films continue to be successful on the festival circuit such as those of the Split-based author Veljko Popović (*Ona koja mjeri/She Who Measures*, Croatia, 2008; *Dove sei, amor mio*, Croatia, 2011; *Biciklisti/Cyclists*, Croatia/France, 2018). Unfortunately, the Croatian animation industry has not found a sustainable model for the production of feature-length animation films, which has become a global production norm and an important part of theatre programmes in the twenty-first century. In part, this has been due to the HAVC's inability to come up with an adequate model for financing this (by far the most expensive) film genre.

Despite achieving the status of an important location for international productions from *Star Wars* to *James Bond*, the country still does not have a proper film studio. Although the HAVC's officials tried to find a way to build a new facility in the vicinity of Zagreb, these efforts were still in the early stages when the political turmoil of 2016 brought a slow death to this initiative. The old communist Croatian studio, Jadran Film, used to be the cornerstone of the local industry and an important partner of Hollywood productions in the 1970s and 1980s. In the course of the postwar transition in the 1990s, the studio was privatised in a questionable process with the new owner lacking any interest in new productions, a business model which has ultimately brought the company to the edge of bankruptcy. Jadran Film has virtually no role in today's Croatian production, on a technical basis or as a producer or co-producer. The most problematic aspect of this situation is the fact that Jadran Film still owns copyrights for nearly the entire Croatian national film heritage from the Yugoslav period. In practical terms, this means that the Croatian film community is unable to preserve, disseminate or promote these films which are gradually fading from the collective memory owing to their unavailability in physical or digital formats. The insurmountable legal obstacles pertaining to the rights for the older corpus of Croatian film are replicated in the administrative and technological sense in the Croatian Cinémathèque (Kinoteka) which is inadequately housed in the Croatian State Archive instead of being under the HAVC's purview.

As of 2017 out of the 300 titles stored there, only twenty-five have been digitally restored and from this group only twenty-three are available as DCP (Croatian Audiovisual Centre 2017a: 26). Similarly, abysmal statistics concern mid-length genres (only two films have been digitised), short narrative and short documentary films (seventy-six) and animated film (thirty-three). The original prints of some renowned films such as Nikola Tanhofer's *H8* (Yugoslavia, 1958) are deteriorating at a fast pace with no appropriate measures in place to solve the problem. The lack of a plan for the preservation of this part of the national heritage has been a source of deep concern for both the film and scholarly communities since it makes a direct impact on the education of both future film professionals and the general population, on domestic and international scholarship owing to availability, and ultimately on the local audiences' awareness of traditions, styles and craftmanship. Moreover, the ownership issues make the relevant EU resources for restoration and digitisation of audiovisual heritage unavailable. The legal knot that has compromised the level of knowledge about Croatian film from the socialist era is a regrettable circumstance which other East European countries have resolved in a far more expedient manner.

CROATIAN FILM IN THE ERA OF THE PENDING CONFLICT

At the point when the filmmaking community and the Croatian Audiovisual Centre became the target of ideological attacks in 2016, Croatia was already a member of the EU (since July 2013) and, as in many former communist countries, the entry to the EU eventually triggered a moment of ideological push-back. During the process of accession, Croatia had to negotiate in order meet the requirements, consequently consenting to a more moderate political trajectory. As was the case with Poland and Hungary, after its official acceptance into the EU, the country no longer had to 'behave properly'. Croatia had its own more moderate version of the Polish/Hungarian conservative revolution, and the flagship institutions leading that movement were the local Catholic church as well as numerous influential war-veteran organisations. In this climate, the HAVC was promptly singled out for its ideological disobedience. Perceived as an alienated self-regulated professional oligarchy supported by public funding, the Centre was characterised as a typical example of the liberal 'arm's length principle' loathed by the right-wingers who also criticised it for promoting a 'left' (i.e. liberal) position and adjusting its values to the international market, Eurimages and foreign tastes. The struggle between the film community and right-wing politics seems unresolved for now and the HAVC's image remains somewhat tarnished. After the State Audit Office report was issued, as previously mentioned, Hribar resigned, and the Ministry of Culture appointed Danijel Rafaelić, a film historian who resigned from the position of the Centre's Director half-way through his term. However, the Minister of Culture Obujen Koržinek in the end did not 'debunk the system': in the new Film Law from 2018 the architectonics of the Croatian Audiovisual Centre have been changed only in minor details. Still, the ideological attacks had their impact. Due to institutional instability, production in 2018 diminished significantly (only six features in theatres, compared to twelve in 2017). Hand in hand with lesser production came the loss of visibility too: in 2017 and 2018 not a single Croatian feature was screened in the programmes of the most important A-category festivals.

It is already evident that the political atmosphere has propelled the type of projects which previously did not command the same attention, such as the war epic *General* directed by Antun Vrdoljak (2019, Croatia/Bosnia and Herzegovina), the financing of which had already started in 2016. The eminent director known for his achievements particularly in the 1970s and 1980s was the former Croatian Vice President in the era of Franjo Tuđman and overviewed Croatian cinema in the late 1990s. *General* is a biographical film about the life of Ante Gotovina, a former member of the French Foreign Legion and the lieutenant general in the Croatian war for independence, apprehended for war crimes and eventually acquitted by the International Criminal Court in the Hague in 2012.

The budget for this politically motivated project is significantly larger than that of the average Croatian film and stands at 14 million kunas (2 million euros). From the late 1990s onward, the Croatian was first among the post-Yugoslav film industries to deal with the horrific aspects of war and postwar reality at an individual level, starting with the documentary output of Factum production house and moving on to a significant number of feature films such as *Witnesses*, *Živi i mrtvi/The Living and the Dead* (Kristijan Milić, Croatia/Bosnia-Herzegovina, 2007), *The Blacks* and *The High Sun*. Most recently, however, there are some indications that the prevailing atmosphere in society might be causing a self-censorship effect. After a period of socially charged cinema, in the last couple of years Croatian film has shifted towards intimist dramas and the private lives of (mainly young) characters prone to passivity and escape (*A Brief Excursion*, *Aleksi*, *Comic Sans* (Nevio Marasović, Croatia, 2018)). On the other hand, the tendency towards more personal everyday topics may be a natural generational shift coming from the younger directors, many of them women, who experienced the last conflict as children and are increasingly abandoning war themes for the issues they perceive as more pertinent.

Despite the turmoil that has shaken the Croatian film industry as of 2016, a whole new generation of filmmakers has appeared with fresh feature-length projects which are currently in production, bringing to the screen new sensibilities, styles and thematic choices. Many of them, such as Jure Pavlović, Antonija Alamat Kusijanović, Sonja Tarokić, Jure Lerotić, Tomislav Šoban, Marko Jukić, Josip Lukić and Jasna Nanut, already boast of important accomplishments and awards in the short film category. Many say that Croatia has never had such a gifted generation of mature young filmmakers at their professional entry point. The key question for the future of its film will be what this new generation might face down the road: a functional film industry or an ideologically ravaged wasteland.

REFERENCES

Bobanović, Paula (2018) 'DORH je stavio točku na prljavu, klevetničku priču', *Express*, 25 October <https://www.express.hr/top-news/hribar-dorh-je-stavio-tocku-na-prljavu-klevetnicku-pricu-18238> (last accessed 15 August 2019).

Croatian Audiovisual Centre (2017a) *Nacionalni program promicanja audiovizualnog stvaralaštva 2017–2021*, (eds) Hrvoje Hribar, Sanja Ravlić, Uroš Živanović, Daniel Rafaelić. Zagreb.

Croatian Audiovisual Centre (2017b) *Facts and Figures. Production and Exhibition Figures for 2016*. Zagreb.

EFADs (2017) 'The EFADs Praise Hrvoje Hribar Contribuition to Croatian and European film as Director of the Croatian Audiovisual Center', *EFADs*, 27 February 2017 <http://filmneweurope.com/press-releases/item/114091-the-efads-praise-hrvoje-hribar-s-contribution-to-croatian-and-european-film-as-director-of-the-croatian-audiovisual-centre> (last accessed 11 May 2020).

European Audiovisual Observatory (2009–18) *Focus. World Film Market Trends.*

European Commission, Directorate-General for Communication (2014) *Digital Agenda for Europe* <https://europa.eu/european-union/file/1497/download_en?token=KzfSz-CR> (last accessed 16 February 2019).

Gabrić, Toni (2017) 'Hribar je mrtav, živio HAVC', *H-Alter*, 10 February <http://www.h-alter.org/vijesti/hribar-je-mrtav-zivio-havc> (last accessed 11 January 2019).

Hribar, Hrvoje (2014) 'A Great Quest for the New Has Begun', *Croatian Cinema*, 1 (3).

Jameson, Fredric (2004) 'Thoughts on Balkan Cinema', in Atom Egoyan and Ian Balfour (eds), *Subtitles*. Boston: MIT Press, pp. 231–57.

Pavičić, Jurica (2011) *Postjugoslavenski film: Stil i ideologija.* Zagreb: Hrvatski filmski savez.

Pavičić, Jurica (2012) 'From a Cinema of Hatred to a Cinema of Consciousness: Croatian Film after Yugoslavia', in Aida Vidan and Gordana P. Crnković (eds), *In Contrast: Croatian Film Today*. Zagreb, Oxford, New York: Croatian Film Association & Berghahn Books, pp. 49–58.

Pavičić, Jurica (2016) 'Najuspješnije reforme u kulturi uvijek su dolazile "odozdo". Nadam se da će me pamtiti kao ministricu koja je znala slušati potrebe cijelog sektora', *Jutarnji list*, 30 October <https://www.jutarnji.hr/kultura/art/najuspjesnije-reforme-u-kulturi-uvijek-su-dolazile-odozdo.-nadam-se-da-ce-me-pamtiti-kao-ministricu-koja-je-znala-slusati-potrebe-cijelog-sektora/5196387/> (last accessed 15 August 2019).

Postnikov, Boris (2018) 'Hrvatska režijska laž', *Novosti*, 24 November <https://www.portalnovosti.com/neprijateljska-propaganda-hrvatska-rezijska-laz> (last accessed 16 February 2019).

Šurina, Maja (2018) 'Hasanbegović svim silama raspalio po HAVC-u i Hribaru', *Tportal*, 26 April, <https://www.tportal.hr/vijesti/clanak/hasanbegovic-prozvao-havc-i-hribara-stazic-ovo-je-fasisticki-govor-20180426> (last accessed 8 November 2018).

Tomljanović, Igor (2015) 'Ljestvica gledanosti visoko je podignuta. Možemo li je održati?', *Croatian Cinema*, 2, pp. 40–6.

Vidan, Aida (2018) 'Framing the Body, Vocalizing the Pain: Perspectives by the South Slavic Female Directors', *Studies in European Cinema: Recent Quality Film and the Future of the Republic of Europe*, 15 (2–3), pp. 125–45.

Vidan, Aida and Crnković, Gordana P. (eds) (2012) *In Contrast: Croatian Film Today*. Zagreb, Oxford, New York: Croatian Film Association & Berghahn Books.

Vladić, Aleksandra (2018) 'Žestoka rasprava o HAVC-u', *Jutarnji list*, 26 April <https://www.jutarnji.hr/vijesti/hrvatska/video-zestoka-rasprava-o-havc-u-hasanbegovicev-govor-izbacio-cijelu-oporbu-iz-takta-to-je-bilo-fasisticko-obracanje-on-je-sramota-za-sabor-i-hdz/7289680/> (last accessed 9 February 2019).

5. CYPRUS: TRANSNATIONAL CHALLENGES, OPPORTUNITIES AND COMPROMISES

Costas Constandinides and Yiannis Papadakis

'It is difficult to make predictions, especially about the future', the quote variously attributed to Nobel-winning physicist Niels Bohr cautions. In this chapter, we present the two major trends in the cinemas of Cyprus,[1] arguing for an emerging tendency towards a shift in thematic focus during the post-2008 period. This would be a shift from a sustained, obsessive even, yet also understandable, focus on the island's division known as 'the Cyprus Problem' that to a large extent dominated previous cinematic production towards a variety of new directions exploring other themes like gender, migration, domestic violence and alternative forms of artistic expression. This thematic shift, we suggest, has also led to a relative shift in the kinds of collaborations sought: from island-wide to transnational. Films focusing on the Cyprus Problem with a reconciliatory theme were often produced through seeking collaborations between Greek Cypriots and Turkish Cypriots across the island's divide. These we call 'island-wide' collaborations. A thematic shift away from the Cyprus Problem entailed fewer such collaborations, hence relatively more emphasis on collaborations with other states, i.e. transnational collaborations. Our analysis describes this shift while presenting the advantages, challenges and what, we consider as, the limitations of such collaborations.

Cypriot cinemas should be located within the category of the cinemas of 'small nations' (Hjort and Petrie 2007). Given an island-wide population of around 1.2 million (with 840,000 living on the Greek Cypriot side and 360,000 on the Turkish Cypriot side) neither side in Cyprus meets the 4–10 million population criterion for defining a small nation set by Hjort and Petrie, therefore they may be described as micro-states or extra-small states, a category introduced by the authors to discuss the example of Iceland (Hjort and Petrie 2007). The number of full-length fiction films made in the Greek Cypriot side since 2008 (to December 2018) is 30 out of a total of 264 films produced under all types of production (feature, documentary, short film and animation). Out of the 30 full length films, 26 were financially supported by the Ministry of Education and Culture (MoEC) through its film production support programmes with an annual budget currently at €1.25 million for the development and production of films. On the Turkish Cypriot side, to the best of our knowledge, no established channels for film support exist while three feature films were made since 2008. *Kod Adi: Venüs/Codename Venus* (UK/Turkey/Cyprus, 2012) and *Dr. Dilara* (Cyprus, 2016) were directed by Tamer Garip and co-produced with Near East University located in northern Cyprus. *Gölgeler ve suletrer/Shadows and Faces* (Turkey, 2010) was directed by Derviş Zaim and co-produced with the Turkish Radio and Television Corporation, the national public broadcaster of Turkey, with the Support of the Ministry of Culture and Tourism of the Republic of Turkey.

The issue of scale has consequences regarding the transnational dimensions of filmic production, the most obvious being the need for such collaborations for financial and practical reasons. These we discuss in light of Hjort's (2010) typology of cinematic transnationalisms (see also Constandinides 2015). In our chapter, we note the predominance of 'affinitive-type' links whether with Greece or Turkey, meaning links between states with a 'long history of close interaction' (Hjort 2010: 50), and/or with other European states. Yet, given that affinity is both a political and an affective notion, it so-to-speak lies at the heart of the beholder. Thus film producers and directors interested in reconciliation expressed affinity with those across Cyprus's division both in terms of their films' content and in terms of their production, through various kinds of collaborations across the island's divide. In this sense, both island-wide and transnational collaborations were predicated on affinitive links, yet of different kinds.

The Cinemas of the Cyprus Problem

Given the emphasis of Cyprus Problem-focused films on the recent tumultuous history of Cyprus, a short historical introduction is necessary in order to contextualise the ensuing discussion. After almost a century of British colonial rule, in 1960 Cyprus became an independent state, the Republic of Cyprus (RoC), with a population of 77 per cent Greek Cypriots (442,000) and 18 per cent Turkish Cypriots (104,000). During 1963, inter-ethnic fighting broke out in Cyprus with Turkish Cypriots bearing the heavier cost in terms of casualties and around a fifth of their population being displaced. In 1974, an ill-fated Greek junta-inspired coup launched with the help of extreme right-wing Greek Cypriots led to a military offensive by Turkey dividing the island, including the capital, Nicosia. This was followed by population displacements of most Greek Cypriots to the south and Turkish Cypriots to the north. July 1974 is the period cast in Greek Cypriot social memory as their most trau-matic in terms of people killed, missing and displaced. Subsequently, Turkish Cypriots declared their own state, the Turkish Republic of Northern Cyprus (TRNC), which, however, has not received international recognition, except by Turkey. Currently, the southern (Greek Cypriot) side is controlled by the RoC (which is why we use here Republic of Cyprus and Greek Cypriot side interchangeably) while the northern (Turkish Cypriot) side is controlled by the TRNC. After the 2004 entry of the RoC into the EU, the dividing line of Cyprus – a United Nations-supervised porous ceasefire line rather than a state border, yet one with a non-recognised state – became the EU's ambiguous border to the East. This violent divided past has given rise on both sides to filmic concerns with trauma, blame and reconciliation. We have explored elsewhere in more detail the thematic and formal similarities with Israeli cin-ema, while also suggesting similarities with other Balkan cinemas (Constan-dinides and Papadakis 2015b).

During the post-2008 period six feature films were produced which explicitly focused on the Cyprus Problem: *O teleftaios gyrismos/The Last Homecoming* (Korinna Avraamidou, Cyprus, 2008), *I istoria tis prasinis grammis/The Story of the Green Line* (Panicos Chrysanthou, Cyprus/Greece, 2017), *Clementine* (Longinos Panagi, Cyprus, 2018) and *Fygadevondas ton Hendrix/Smuggling Hendrix* (Marios Piperides, Cyprus/Germany/Greece, 2018) on the Greek Cypriot side with MoEC's financial support and involvement as co-producer; *Shadows and Faces* and *Codename Venus* on the Turkish Cypriot side. The fact that despite the devastation caused by the economic crisis which reached the Greek Cypriot side in 2013, a substantial number of films still focused on the past and the island's division is a good illustration of the obsessive focus on the Cyprus Problem. In this section, we focus on *Shadows and Faces* and *Smuggling Hendrix*.[2] *Shadows and Faces* by Turkish Cypriot director Derviş Zaim,[3] who has been mostly living and working in Turkey, explores the 1960s, the most traumatic period for Turkish Cypriots, focusing on life in a small mixed village. While it ostensibly tells the story of a girl who due to the inter-ethnic fighting is separated from her father, the real focus is on the efforts of the two major charac-ters, long-time friends and neighbours Anna (Greek Cypriot) and Veli (Turkish Cypriot), who try, and tragically fail, to keep the village peaceful in an atmo-sphere of rising paranoia, violence and fear. It has utilised actors and talent from both sides of Cyprus (for example the music was composed by Greek Cypriot Marios Takoushis) as well as Turkey, and was made with financial support from both the TRNC and Turkey and developed in cooperation with Crossroads Co-production Forum – Thessaloniki International Film Festival (2009), among other regional collaborations. It won the Turkish Film Critics Association Awards at the 2010 International Antalya Golden Orange Film Festival and the Best Film, Best Director and Special Jury Awards at the 2011 International Ankara Film Festival. Island-wide collaborations are exemplified in this case by the use of Greek Cypriot actors and music composer, which is not surprising given that Zaim had previously often collaborated with Greek Cypriots (Constandinides and Papadakis 2015b).

Smuggling Hendrix, a Greek Cypriot film co-produced and directed by Marios Piperides, received the 2018 Best International Narrative Feature Award at the Tribeca Film Festival 'for its unique, comedic exploration of a complicated, absurd political situation told in a clear, personal and compelling way' (Tribeca Film Festival 2018). This is the story of Yiannis, a Greek Cypriot man whose dog, Jimmy, runs away to the Turkish Cypriot side of divided Nicosia, leading to an unlikely cooperation between a Greek Cypriot, a Turkish Cypriot, a (Turkish) 'settler' and a Greek brought together, each for their own self-interested reasons, in order to help smuggle Jimmy back across (see Figure 5.1). In the process, each learns about, hence also humanises, the maligned 'other(s)'. This film squarely belongs to the Greek Cypriot 'reconciliation' cinematic tradition (Constandinides and Papadakis 2015b) while, politically speaking, it also breaks new ground for Greek Cypriots by casting a sympathetic gaze towards 'settlers' from Turkey. In terms of its transnational aspects, this film is typical of many Greek Cypriot films

Figure 5.1 *Smuggling Hendrix* (Marios Piperides, 2018): Greek Cypriot Yiannis (Adam Bousdoukos), second from left, forms an unlikely alliance with Greek ex-girlfriend (Vicky Papadopoulou), Turkish Cypriot Tuberk (Özgür Karadeniz), third from left, and 'Turkish settler' Hasan (Fatih Al) to smuggle Jimmy the dog. Courtesy of AMP Filmworks.

as a co-production with Greece and another European state (Germany) with state (e.g. Ministry of Education and Culture (MoEC) of the RoC and the Greek Film Center (GFC), regional (e.g. SEE Cinema Network) and supranational (e.g. Eurimages) support.[4]

The collaboration with Germany, however, necessitated a telling – for the purpose of our discussion – compromise. The choice of a Greek (German) protagonist (Adam Bousdoukos), who does not speak with the Greek Cypriot dialect yet is presented as a Greek Cypriot character, could alienate Greek Cypriot audiences; it definitely does not enhance identification with the protagonist. While this linguistic issue is not apparent to a foreign audience, it necessitated a complicated explanation that comes late in the film through the dialogue, pointing out that the protagonist was born in Cyprus, but due to the 1974 war his parents moved to Greece and then elsewhere. This choice of actor was in fact dictated by the German co-producer who wanted a well-known actor to play the protagonist in order to enhance the film's international appeal, irrespective of its local reception. As the director, Piperides, additionally pointed out, previous efforts to work with local actors for a Greek Cypriot audience were disappointing because the cinema-going public in the RoC is very limited, 'so we did something for a more international audience' (Kades 2018). This film then is a good illustration of cinematic production in the RoC characterised by limited financial resources and audience, and the growing need for collaborations which usually involve Greece and/or other European states in order to secure additional financial support from regional/supranational funds, as well as compromises entailed to increase the visibility/marketability of a production – which, as Piperides notes, begins its journey 'with a big disadvantage' being from a small film producing country (Economou 2018a).

New Directions: Post-crisis Cypriot Cinemas

The issue of limited financial resources was exacerbated by the economic crisis which led to shifts in cinematic focus, while it raised new challenges. It was in fact during 2013 that the Republic of Cyprus was severely affected by the economic crisis leading to harsh economic measures, unemployment, and welfare and budgetary cuts, yet no significant public protests or the kind of political polarisation seen elsewhere. In her *IndieWire* article titled 'What It's Like to be a Woman Director in a Country with a Tiny Film Industry', the South African Greek Cypriot producer/filmmaker Stelana Kliris wrote that the 2013 banking crisis in Cyprus forced filmmakers to seek other directions, and that her first feature film *Committed* (Cyprus, 2014) was created in an 'inhospitable environment' (2014). The web portal, recently developed by the Cultural Services of the Ministry of Education and Culture exclusively dedicated to film production in the Republic of Cyprus, categorically yet discreetly informs its visitors that for the period 2013–14 no state funding was granted due to the financial crisis (Filming in Cyprus 2013–14). Kliris notes that the lack of state support gave her no option but to work with a micro-budget and a central crew of twelve members (2014). With producer Marios Piperides of AMP Filmworks, they could finance the film through crowdfunding and a private investor. *Committed* is an English language romantic road movie with a twist about a young man, reluctant to commit to a long-lasting relationship with his girlfriend, meets a runaway bride while driving in the countryside.[5] Kliris describes her film as the 'first post-crisis independent film to be produced in Cyprus' (2014) and adds that her response to the crisis may have inspired other filmmakers to take creative risks (i.e. explore ways to practise their art effectively with a lower or no budget).

Indeed, in 2015 the (Greek Cypriot) Cyprus Film Days International Festival (CFD), introduced for the first time a Cypriot films competition section comprised of four Cypriot films, a record number of full-length Cypriot films completed in the same year.[6] Three out of the four films (*Melos oikogeneias/ Family Member* by Marinos Kartikkis, *Ta magika fasolia/Magic Beans* by Theo Panayides and *Conveyor Belt* by Alexia Roider) were independent Greek Cypriot productions completed with Greek Cypriot funds and supported by the Independent Film Productions Funding programme of the MoEC (Republic of Cyprus Ministry of Education and Culture 2018). The fourth film, Kyros Papavassiliou's debut feature *Oi endyposeis enos pnigmenou/Impressions of a Drowned Man*, which also participated in the International Competition Section 'Glocal Images' of Cyprus Film Days (CFD), is a RoC, Greece and Slovenia co-production with financial support by the MoEC and the South Eastern Europe (SEE) Cinema Network. *Impressions of a Drowned Man* is the first post-crisis Cypriot film that secured a world premiere at a renowned international film festival, namely the Rotterdam International Film Festival. *Impressions of a Drowned Man* is a fictionalised account of the last day of the Greek poet Kostas Karyotakis, who committed suicide in 1928. The title is borrowed from Karyotakis's suicide note; however, the film is not a period piece and the main character (portrayed by Greek actor Thodoris Pentidis) returns in what seems to be the present day to relive the last day of his life knowing that he will eventually commit suicide. *Impressions of a Drowned Man* is another example of Hjort's definition of the affinitive transnationalism paradigm (2010) which informs most Cypriot films (discussed extensively in Constandinides 2015a). The affinitive transnationalism apparent in the context of Greek Cypriot cinema with Greece describes the following arrangement: Greek Cypriot production and Greek participation as a co-production or financial support by Greek state funds with the participation of talent (e.g. the main actor in *Impressions of a Drowned Man*) and experienced crew members from Greece or based in Greece.

The domestic commercial release of *Committed* in 2014 and of the Cypriot films made in 2015, namely *Family Member* and *Magic Beans*, was not well attended, especially when compared to the record-breaking 60,386 tickets sold for the Cypriot comedy *To pouli tis Kyprou/The Bird of Cyprus* (Nicolas Koumides), a privately funded commercial film released in 2014 in Cyprus, starring popular Cypriot and Greek TV actors. This illustrates Piperides's as well as Kliris's (2014) observations about the difficulty in finding local audiences due to the smallness of the population and the lack of funds, which hinders the possibility of developing films in Cyprus as a commercial enterprise. Cypriot cinema is essentially sustained by the limited government funds, therefore locally made films hope to reach audiences through their festival journeys. For example, *Committed* sold 405 tickets at the domestic box office but was distributed on DVD and VOD by Tiberius Film in Germany and was well attended at Greek-themed festival screenings in the US and Australia. The film is currently available via Amazon Prime video.

A common characteristic of the films that participated in the first CFD Cypriot Films competition section in 2015 is that they do not revisit the dominant theme of the Cyprus Problem but explore instead existential issues or the generic tropes of family drama (e.g. Kartikkis's *Family Member*). Family drama with a touch of (psychological) thriller describes three recent Cypriot films, *To agori sti gefyra/Boy on the Bridge* (Petros Charalambous, Cyprus, 2016), *Rosemarie* (Adonis Florides, Cyprus, 2017) and *Pafsi/Pause* (Tonia Mishiali, Cyprus/Greece, 2018). The films move the action away from visible and verbal references to divided Cyprus to bring to the fore what Kamenou (2015) described as 'exclusions' produced by the predominance of the Cyprus Problem – issues, in other words, un(der)represented previously in Cypriot films. Unlike the cinemas of the Cyprus Problem, the characters' motivations, family obligations or betrayals and the abuse of women in *Boy on the Bridge*, *Rosemarie* and *Pause* do not stand for nationalist aspirations or collective suffering. These films focus on domestic abuse as an attempt to comment on the violence of patriarchal structures.

Boy on the Bridge is a coming of age whodunit film set in 1980s rural Cyprus, loosely based on a book by English Cypriot Eve Makis titled the *Land of the Golden Apples* (2008). Makis co-wrote the script with Stavros Pamballis, a rare event, if not the first case in the history of Cypriot cinemas, where the director of the film was not involved in the scriptwriting process and the film is an adaptation. Charalambous's debut feature premiered as part of Rome Film Festival's autonomous section Alice in the City in 2016, which is dedicated to children and youth. The film tells the story of an adventurous boy, Socrates, who in his attempt to avenge his uncle for mistreating his aunt and cousin, unearths secrets that upset the idyllic setting of village life.

The leading character of Florides's *Rosemarie*, Costas, a TV soap opera scriptwriter, suffers from writer's block. The character has a brother in a vegetative state cared for by their older sister; Costas's brother fell into a water tank when they were small children, and Costas is convinced that he is the one responsible for this, even though he cannot remember what happened as he was only a little older than his brother. Costas begins to draw inspiration from the dysfunctional family that lives in the apartment next to his and begins to follow the daughter of the family, who secretly visits a baby; he eventually discovers the evil nature of the father of the next-door family, who surprisingly holds the answer to the question that haunts Costas (see Figure 5.2). The film premiered at CFD and became the first Cypriot film completed only with Cypriot funds and that won the Glocal Images Best Film Award of CFD's international competition section. *Rosemarie* also won the Best Film Award from the Greek Film Critics Association at the 58th Thessaloniki International Film Festival 2017 for a film in the Greek Films section, another illustration of affinitive transnationalism based on presumed shared ethnicity since *Rosemarie* is a Greek Cypriot film with no financial support from Greece.

Pause had its world premiere at the 2018 FIAPF (International Federation of Film Producers Associations) accredited Karlovy Vary International Film Festival in the East of West competition section. The film focuses on Elpida, who is going through menopause and imagines herself reacting to her husband's alpha male habits as one of the symptoms she experiences. Elpida's desire to free herself from a relationship where her happiness is secondary to her husband's basic needs grows, and the imaginary outbursts of anger or sexual urge begin to influence her actions in reality (see Figure 5.3). *Pause* is a Greek

Figure 5.2 Costas (Yiannis Kokkinos) haunted by his past struggles to cope with his work and social life in *Rosemarie* (Adonis Florides, 2017). Courtesy of AMP Filmworks.

Figure 5.3 Elpida (Stela Fyrogeni) enjoys one of her rare moments of freedom at a karaoke bar in *Pause* (Tonia Mishiali, 2018). Courtesy of A. B. Seahorse Film Productions.

Cypriot and Greek co-production with the support of the MoEC and SEE Cinema Network. The film credits Stelana Kliris as one of the producers of the film, who has previously collaborated with Mishiali (who acted as the producer) for the making of the former's short film *To the Moon and Back* (Cyprus) completed in 2018.[7] Both female filmmakers have been active in recent years and have created opportunities for the local film community by becoming involved in unpaid or symbolically compensated tasks outside the production of films. For example, Mishiali and Kliris acted as members of the CFD three-member artistic committee in 2015. Mishiali continues to be a member of the CFD artistic committee and also served as vice president of the Directors Guild of Cyprus board. Kliris (2014) notes that 'being a woman hasn't affected my working process [. . .] Cyprus may be a traditionally patriarchal country, but our film community is made up mostly of young, progressive people and we have a decent balance of male and female directors.' Female filmmakers are currently leaders in the areas of documentary and short film production. Greek-Cypriot Danae Stylianou has directed three documentary features (*To nisi pou moirazomaste/ Sharing an Island*, Cyprus, 2011; *A Haircut Story*, Cyprus, 2014 and *Birth Days*, Cyprus, 2018). Greek Cypriot Myrsini Aristidou's latest short *Aria* (Cyprus/France/Greece) premiered at the 2017 edition of Venice International Festival and competed at the Sundance Film Festival's short film competition the same year. The Australian-born Turkish Cypriot Yeliz Shukri directed two documentary features (*Murid*, Cyrpus, 2010 and *Missing Fetine*, Cyprus, 2017) in collaboration with Greek Cypriot producer Stavros Papageorgiou, another example of an island-wide collaboration. Aristidou's short *Aria* participated together with eighteen other Cypriot films (out of which thirteen are directed or co-directed by female filmmakers) under the Cypriot films competition section of the 2018 International Short Film Festival of Cyprus (ISFFC), winning first prize for best Cypriot short film. The ISFFC is the second major state-funded competitive festival, running since 2011.

Elena Christodoulidou, MoEC's senior cultural officer and head of the Cyprus Cinema Advisory Committee, in an interview she gave to Vassilis Economou of *Cineuropa*, notes that despite financial limitations, 'we have seen some great success stories recently' (2018b). Mishiali and Kliris along with Marios Piperides (*Smuggling Hendrix*) can, arguably, be regarded as promising examples of artistic initiative and leadership. It is important to note that these filmmakers (who have already had a successful journey as short film directors or producers of feature films[8]) managed to succeed within and not by 'exiting' (Hjort 2011) their small-state cinema context, unlike other Cyprus-born filmmakers who were forced due to pragmatic considerations to seek opportunities and inspiration elsewhere (e.g. the Greek Cypriot director Yiannis Economides who is based in Greece).

CONCLUSION

'News of my death have been greatly exaggerated', famously quipped Oscar Wilde. We are not suggesting here the end of the cinemas of the Cyprus Problem; rather, we posit a – welcome in our view – relative shift towards the exploration of other themes and other politics previously marginalised. This, shift, however, also has further political consequences given the diminishing needs for, and practices of, collaborations across the island's divide. We have discussed elsewhere how cinematic cooperation between Greek Cypriots and Turkish Cypriots has led to films that have managed to convey the recent violent history of Cyprus in the most balanced and multi-perspectival way, while the very act of collaborating carried its own political symbolism (Constandinides and Papadakis 2015b). This is not to say that all films dealing with the Cyprus Problem entailed island-wide collaborations (for example see *Smuggling Hendrix*), nor that island-wide collaborations were mobilised only for films dealing with the Cyprus Problem (for example see *Missing Fetine*). Yet, it is to be expected that if there is less emphasis on Cyprus Problem-focused and especially reconciliation films, there will be less of an ideological impetus for collaborations across the Cyprus divide, hence also less island-wide practices and consequently relatively more emphasis on transnational ones. We have also noted the compromise that the director of a politically orientated Cyprus Problem-focused film (*Smuggling Hendrix*) had to make, whereby international success through transnational collaborations could entail less of a political impact within Cyprus.

When it comes to transnational collaborations, it should be noted that even though various manifestations of the affinitive transnationalism model described above may have given birth to sustained and not one-off collaborations, this cannot be described as a model designed to build capacity. Greek

Cypriot filmmakers rely heavily on the arrangements we described because of underfunding (which also means not being able to travel extensively to participate in co-production forums) and their government's failure to recognise film as an industry; therefore, given the geographic proximity and linguistic identity it is much cheaper and easier to collaborate with Greece. Only recently, in September 2017, the (Greek Cypriot) Council of Ministers approved an incentives programme, supervised by the Cyprus Investment Promotion Agency (CIPA), to boost the audio-visual industry in Cyprus, which aims to attract international productions to Cyprus and includes incentives such as cash rebates, tax credits, VAT refunds and tax deductions on investments in infrastructure and equipment. CIPA, the Cyprus Tourism Organisation (CTO) and the Press and Information Office (PIO) of the Republic of Cyprus organised the Cyprus Film Summit 2018[9] to officially announce the Cyprus Film Scheme to international audiovisual professionals, hoping to introduce the RoC as a business partner to those interested in filming in Cyprus. The organisers dubbed this new government-oriented enterprise 'Olivewood' in their attempt to promote Cyprus as a natural film studio. In addition, the MoEC introduced a minority participation of a Cypriot co-producer programme in its 2017 regulation for the support of cinematographic works.

Economically speaking, but also creatively, there is no doubt that the Greek Cypriots have profited enormously from links with Greece and other European states, which have their own rich cinematic traditions. By contrast, Turkish Cypriots, not being recognised as a state and not being part of the EU, have had little choice than turn towards Turkey when it came to financial support and, rarely, to the MoEC of the RoC and EU funds through collaborations with Greek Cypriot producers (for example, the post-2008 collaborations between Greek Cypriot producer Stavros Papageorgiou and Australian-born Turkish Cypriot director Yeliz Shukri). Entry into the EU and its filmic structures, while undoubtedly beneficial for Greek Cypriots, has further distanced them from other possible collaborations with Africa and the Middle East. It should be noted, however, that while it is far from certain that such collaborations would have been financially advantageous for producers from Cyprus, there is also no sustainable policy to further them. The only hopeful exception in this regard is the current effort to enter into an agreement with Israel in the area of cinema – a first sign for creating sustainable transnational cinematic links beyond Europe.

NOTES

1. On the definition of 'cinemas of Cyprus' or 'Cypriot cinemas' which we use interchangeably see Constandinides and Papadakis (2015a) and especially Constandinides (2015a).
2. For a detailed discussion of the films by Avraamidou, Zaim and Garip, see Constandinides and Papadakis (2015b).

3. For Zaim's life, politics and influences see Raw (2017), while for a broader discussion of this film see Raw (2015) and Constandinides and Papadakis (2015b: 139–42).
4. *Smuggling Hendrix* was made with the support of the MoEC, the MDM Regional Fund in Germany, the Greek Film Center, ZDF/Arte, ERT (Hellenic Broadcasting Corporation), Media Desk – Creative Europe, SEE Cinema Network and Eurimages. The film was made with a budget of €1.3m, making it the most expensive Cypriot film made in post-crisis Cyprus, and secured a world sales agent, namely Match Factory, and distribution in Germany and Greece before its completion. The film continued to earn noteworthy accolades after its world premiere at Tribeca, including Best Screenplay at the 2019 Hellenic Film Academy awards and Best Cypriot Film at the 2019 Cyprus Film Days International Festival.
5. Kliris explains that 'while the official languages of Cyprus are Greek and Turkish, I was raised in South Africa with English as my first language and I have only experienced Cyprus as an expat, so I chose to make my characters from the large community of expatriates in Cyprus' (2014).
6. The Festival is organised by the Cultural Services of the Ministry of Education and Culture of the Republic of Cyprus and Rialto Theatre and is held annually in the two major cities of Cyprus: the coastal city of Limassol, which also serves as the festival's guest office/centre, and Nicosia, the capital city of Cyprus, where most of the industry-related activities take place. In 2011, CFD organisers introduced the first international competition section of the festival titled 'Glocal Images'. CFD (formerly known as the Cinema Horizons Cyprus Festival) has been running since 2001 and is dedicated to the showcasing of festival-oriented full-length fiction films from across the globe with a special interest in films originating from the three continents surrounding the island.
7. It is also worth noting that the director of photography of all three films is George Rahmatoulin, a Cyprus-born director of photography based in Greece.
8. Marios Piperides also produced *Rosemarie* and *Boy on the Bridge* among other key Cypriot films and his company AMP Filmworks is currently one of the most successful film production companies in Cyprus, predominantly focusing on the production of films in recent years.
9. See the Cyprus Film Summit website for further information: https://www.cyprusfilmsummit.com/

References

Constandinides, Costas (2015a) 'Postscript: Borders of Categories and Categories of Borders in Cypriot Cinemas', in Costas Constandinides and Yiannis Papadakis (eds), *Cypriot Cinemas: Memory, Conflict and Identity in the Margins of Europe*. London: Bloomsbury, pp. 207–36.
Constandinides, Costas (2015b) 'Transnational Views from the Margins of Europe: Globalisation, Migration and Post-1974 Cypriot Cinemas', in Costas Constandinides and Yiannis Papadakis (eds), *Cypriot Cinemas: Memory, Conflict and Identity in the Margins of Europe*. London: Bloomsbury, pp. 151–79.
Constandinides, Costas and Papadakis, Yiannis (eds) (2015a) *Cypriot Cinemas: Memory, Conflict and Identity in the Margins of Europe*. London: Bloomsbury.

Constandinides, Costas and Papadakis, Yiannis (2015b) 'Tormenting History: The Cinemas of the Cyprus Problem', in Costas Constandinides and Yiannis Papadakis (eds.), *Cypriot Cinemas: Memory, Conflict and Identity in the Margins of Europe*. London: Bloomsbury, pp. 117–50.

Cyprus Film Summit (2018) *cyprusfilmsummit.com* <https://www.cyprusfilmsummit.com/> (last accessed 22 August 2018).

Economou, Vassilis (2018a) 'Interview: Marios Piperides – Director', *Cineuropa*, 24 April <http://www.cineuropa.org/en/interview/352733/> (last accessed 22 June 2018).

Economou, Vassilis (2018b) 'Interview: Elena Christodoulidou – Senior Cultural Officer, Ministry of Education and Culture of Cyprus', *Cineuropa*, 3 May <http://www .cineuropa.org/en/interview/353414/> (last accessed 22 June 2018).

Filming in Cyprus (2013–14), *filmingincyrpus.gov.cy* <http://filmingincyprus.gov .cy/2013-2014/?lang=en> (last accessed 22 June 2018).

Hjort, Mette (2010) 'Affinitive and Milieu-building Transnationalism: The Advance Party Initiative', in Dina Iordanova, David Martin-Jones and Belén Vidal (eds), *Cinema at the Periphery*. Detroit, MI: Wayne State University Press, pp. 46–66.

Hjort, Mette (2011) 'Small Cinemas: How they Thrive and Why they Matter', *Mediascape: UCLA's Journal of Cinema and Media Studies* <http://www.tft.ucla.edu/ mediascape/Winter2011_SmallCinemas.html> (last accessed 22 June 2018).

Hjort, Mette and Petrie, Duncan (2007) 'Introduction', in Mette Hjort and Duncan Petrie (eds), *The Cinema of Small Nations*. Edinburgh: Edinburgh University Press, pp. 1–22.

Kades, Andrea (2018) 'Smuggling Hendrix: The Cyprob Via a Dog', *Cyprus Mail*, 13 May <https://cyprus-mail.com/2018/05/13/smuggling-hendrix-the-cyprob-via-a-dog/> (last accessed 22 June 2018).

Kamenou, Nayia (2015) 'Women and Gender in Cypriot Films: (Re)-claiming Agency amidst the Discourses of Its Negation', in Costas Constandinides and Yiannis Papadakis (eds), *Cypriot Cinemas: Memory, Conflict and Identity in the Margins of Europe*. London: Bloomsbury, pp. 181–205.

Kliris, Stelana (2014) 'What It's Like to Be a Woman Director in a Country with a Tiny Film Industry', *IndieWire*, 3 January <http://www.indiewire.com/2014/01/what-its-like-to-be-a-woman-director-in-a-country-with-a-tiny-film-industry-207581/> (last accessed 22 June 2018).

Raw, Laurence (2015) 'Cyprus Past, Present and Future: The Derviş Zaim Trilogy', in Costas Constandinides and Yiannis Papadakis (eds), *Cypriot Cinemas: Memory, Conflict and Identity in the Margins of Europe*. London: Bloomsbury, pp. 91–116.

Raw, Laurence (2017) *Six Turkish Filmmakers*. Madison, WI: University of Wisconsin Press.

Republic of Cyprus Ministry of Education and Culture (2018) 'Programme to Fund Independent Productions of Fictional Feature Films, Short Films, Documentaries', *filmingincyprus.gov.cy* <http://filmingincyprus.gov.cy/wp-content/uploads/2018/02/ Indipendant-Productions-Regulation-EN-BOOKLET.pdf> (last accessed 22 August 2019).

Tribeca Film Festival (2018) '17th Annual Tribeca Film Festival Announces Juried Awards', *Tribecafilm.com*, 26 April <https://www.tribecafilm.com/press-center/festival/press-releases/17th-annual-tribeca-film-festival-announces-juried-awards> (last accessed 22 August 2019).

6. GREECE: TRANSNATIONAL DYNAMICS IN GREEK CINEMA SINCE THE CRISIS

Maria Chalkou

The idea of an authentic Greek national cinema and the notion of Greekness have been passionately and recurrently debated by filmmakers, critics and scholars alike, while inspiring the creation of important films. However, despite being local and national in various ways, Greek cinema did not grow in isolation but has always been in dialogue with international developments. This chapter illustrates how a new and distinctive emphasis on the European, the transnational and the cosmopolitan has gradually become an overarching and, in my view, the most representative characteristic of Greek film culture of the past ten years. It focuses on how different levels of transnationalism (political, cultural, industrial, textual) helped redefine Greek cinema and reintroduce it in the domestic and international markets. It thus provides a contextualising overview of the flourishing post-2008 Greek film culture aiming to briefly explore its major trends and patterns. By doing so, the discussion points to how these trends Europeanise and transnationalise the Greek experience, secure international funding and address non-national audiences, while simultaneously renegotiating national identity. In the process, issues regarding (co-) production, circulation and consumption practices, as well as critical and audience reception, are also considered.

It is worth noting that this marked transnational turn in Greek cinema intensified at a time when the financial crisis, which hit the country particularly hard, reinforced nationalism and destabilised the Greeks' sense of belonging to the European community. Greek cinema developed as a counter-balancing cultural tendency that embraced the European and the global, while for the first time in its history it was acknowledged internationally as a dynamic force in European cinema.

THE WEIRD, THE POPULAR, THE NOSTALGIC AND THE REAL

When mapping out post-2008 Greek cinema four major tendencies in film production stand out: a surprisingly innovative arthouse trend, mainstream films of various genres, the in-between category of heritage films that attempt to combine art and commerce and an abundance of documentaries. Of those, by far the most celebrated development in this period has been the emergence of a vibrant arthouse strand, commonly termed as Greek Weird Wave or Greek New Wave, whose discovery, naming and consolidation originated outside Greece in the transnational environment of film festivals and Anglophone film criticism (Elsaesser 2018). The debt crisis played a pivotal role in the constitution of the Weird Wave as it abruptly turned Greece into a 'political hotspot' (Elsaesser 2018: 27), increasing the curiosity of international festival and arthouse audiences. A number of Greek films, however, received international recognition before the manifestation of the crisis in the country: *Strella* (Panos H. Koutras, Greece, 2009), *Kynodontas/Dogtooth* (Yorgos Lanthimos, Greece, 2009) and *Akadimia Platonos/Plato's Academy* (Filippos Tsitos, Greece/Germany, 2009), among others, won critical acclaim and major awards at international festivals – such as *Dogtooth*'s Un Certain Regard prize at Cannes – as early as 2009, when the economic downturn was global news, but not as yet a distinctly Greek problem. Yet, it was only after the crisis hit Greece that these and more films were recognised as part of a national cinematic wave.

The term 'Weird Wave of Greek cinema' was coined in 2011 by *The Guardian* critic Steve Rose who not only identified 'strangeness' as a shared quality in the new films coming from Greece, but importantly linked it to the country's socio-economic decline. 'Weirdness', hereafter, has been understood as 'a sign of the crisis' (Basea 2016: 64), as a response to, and reflection of, the national turmoil. Stylistic and thematic 'weirdness' linked to a nation in crisis produced specific expectations from Greek films in relation to their form and content, imposing a highly restrictive national and political frame for their reception and interpretation. This, not only encouraged reflective readings of the films, but also fostered the recycling of crisis-related subject matter and of particular stylistic, narrative and thematic norms.[1] Although filmmakers were initially resistant to being grouped as members of a crisis-triggered wave, and a 'weird' one at that, the usefulness of such a scheme in the promotion and visibility of Greek films abroad was soon recognised and practically embraced.

The Greek New/Weird Wave represents an enduring – already for over ten years – Greek national wave of universal appeal as an unprecedented number of films of various themes and styles are now shown in festivals and gain the-atrical and/or digital distribution beyond Greece, while continuing to attract critical attention and prestigious awards. Nevertheless, while such an ongoing encounter of arthouse Greek cinema with European and global audiences is unique in Greek cinematic history, the New/Weird Wave is notoriously unpop-ular at the domestic box office. Furthermore, the critical and scholarly privi-leging on the trend has produced a reductive image of Greek cinema as it has disregarded a much wider national film production that does not fall under the label. It obscures the variety of films produced in terms of genre, content, aesthetics and political discourse, ignores previous generations of filmmakers who are still active, and overlooks the commercial sector, which is popular in the national market and has given remarkable works.

After decades of alienation from the general public, Greek commercial cinema revived throughout the 2000s, when a notable number of comedies and nostalgic films set in the past achieved phenomenal box office success. At that point, new invigorating synergies between cinema and private televi-sion channels were introduced: TV channels became actively involved in film production while films employed TV writers, directors and stars to capitalise on previous successes and attract large TV audiences (Chalkou 2012: 246–7). Although during the crisis (i.e. in the early 2010s) domestic TV channels expe-rienced an unprecedented deterioration in terms of both quantity and quality of output, leading to a notable drop in the number of TV-funded films, popu-lar fiction films relying on the wider television culture exhibited remarkable resilience. Their generic range extended beyond comedy, including romantic and dramatic contemporary stories, adventures, thrillers and neo-noirs shifting from predominantly feel-good films towards darker contemporary narratives. Particularly successful in their commercial appeal, but also in terms of renew-ing the content and style of Greek popular film, was the debut and sophomore features of popular TV writer/actor/director Christopher Papakaliatis, *An . . ./ What If . . .* (Greece, 2012) and *Enas allos kosmos/Worlds Apart* (Greece, 2015), that feature painful romantic stories set in a nostalgic or crisis-ridden Athenian backdrop. Both films revitalised the struggling domestic film mar-ket and had international impact: *What If . . .* was remade as a Turkish film (*Bir Ask Iki Hayat/One Love, Two Lives*, Ali Bilgin, Turkey, 2019), while *Worlds Apart* participated at international festivals and was commercially released in a significant number of countries including the USA.

If contemporaneity in post-2008 Greek fiction film has been addressed mainly by the New/Weird Wave and the above discussed popular genres, past and history have been explored by the so called heritage film (period and cos-tume dramas, literary adaptations and biopics), the other major invigorat-ing strategic gesture of domestic industry to secure commercial viability and exportability. Balancing between commercialism and cultural credibility, high production value heritage films formed a dynamic trend throughout the 2000s further restoring the popularity and respectability of Greek cinema in the local market (Chalkou 2017). The trend can be seen as a response to the European heritage film which represents one of the highest-grossing genres, and alongside auteur cinema the most exportable type of contemporary European film (Vidal 2012: 4). During the crisis the heritage trend proved particularly persistent producing ambitious and bestselling works, such as Yannis Smaragdis's biopics *O Theos agapaei to haviari/God Loves Caviar* (Greece/Russia, 2012) and *Kazantzakis* (Greece, 2017), and Pantelis Voulgaris's female-oriented melodrama *Mikra Anglia/Little England* (Greece, 2013). By employing subjective memory, emotive narratives, nostalgia and colourful spectacle as the key ways of readdressing the national past, Greek heritage films of the time managed to reach large national audiences while receiving some recognition at international festivals. It is notable that since the beginning of the crisis a number of heritage narratives have manifested a return of the political,[2] and expressed a claustrophobic, bleak and painful, rather than bitter-sweet and nostalgic, prevailing mood. Indicatively, veteran filmmaker Pantelis Voulgaris's *To teleftaio simeioma/The Last Note* (Greece, 2017) takes place at a concentration camp during the Occupation and presents the distressing story of the execution of 200 imprisoned communists by the Nazis.

Such coexistence of continuity and rupture between the pre- and post-crisis years can be also found in documentaries, which from 2000 onwards have developed into a recognisable and prolific cinematic entity of considerable popularity. After Athens's street riots in 2008, caused by the assassination of a fifteen-year old boy by a policeman in the centre of the city, and the implementation of the austerity policies in 2010 due to the first bailout package, documentary became increasingly politicised and more influential on public opinion. Since 2008 three important documentary trends can be identified. First, documentary film has taken a strong radical turn often 'at the intersection of journalism and activism' (Lekakis 2017: 29) aiming to challenge official narratives on the economic crisis by exploring its multifaceted transformative impact on society and its international dimensions. Independent documentaries, such as the hugely popular crowdfunded and online-distributed *Debtocracy* (Greece, 2011) and *Catastroika* (Greece, 2012) by journalists Aris Chatzistefanou and Katerina Kitidi, emerged as part of the anti-austerity movement in Greece and against mainstream media journalism, shaping alternative public perceptions of the Greek debt crisis both for local and global audiences (Papadimitriou 2016a; Lekakis 2017). Second, the near-obsessive concern with history and unexplored traumas of the past that has been evident in multiple print publications, TV programmes and fiction films is also reflected in documentary. Such films privilege both oral history and archival research and occasionally polyphonic narratives, often focusing on Second World War-related issues such as the Occupation, the Holocaust and the Resistance that revive memories of national struggles, suffering and solidarity (*Kalavryta: Anthropoi kai skies/Kalavryta: People and Shadows*, Elias Giannakakis, Greece, 2014; *Oi partisanoi ton Athinon/The Partisans of Athens*, Xenofon Vardaros and Giannis Xydas, Greece, 1918). This trend seems to have been partly encouraged by the strained relations between Greece and Germany, as the harsh austerity imposed under memorandum obligations led to the widespread feeling among Greeks that they had been colonised. Third, there is an increasing interest in difference and marginality, in producing representations of Greek society's alien Others, from immigrants and refugees to community outsiders and invisible outcasts, such as Roma, imprisoned, elderly, LGBTQ+ or disabled people (*Proti yli/Raw Material*, Christos Karakepelis, Greece, 2011; *Roughcut*, Eliana Abravanel, Greece, 2013).

All major strands of post-2008 Greek cinema – the New/Weird Wave, popular genres, the distinctive category of heritage films and documentary – have arisen from legislative, production and funding structures that became increasingly transnationalised in the crisis years, during which, an entirely new landscape for filmmaking and film consumption for Greek films at home and abroad emerged.

Industrial and Institutional Strategies: Transcending Limitations, Expanding Horizons

During the crisis, domestic funding opportunities, both public and private, were substantially reduced and the ability of the country's film institutional system to support creativity was decisively undermined. The Greek Film Center (GFC) – the major source of public funding for Greek films – almost suspended subsidies that were only partly recovered after 2014. At the same time, the sizable drop in box office receipts (about 40–45 per cent) and the decline in the advertising market brought about structural transformations in the distribution/ exhibition sector and the collapse of the private TV channels whose income relied on commercials. Moreover, during the years 2016–18 a major shift took place in the operation of the privately-owned television channels, where key older players disappeared and newcomers emerged due to the introduction of a new law demanding provisional broadcasting licences to be replaced by permanent ones. As a result distribution/exhibition/advertising-led and private TV investment in film, which previously played a crucial role in both popular and arthouse film production, was dramatically decreased. The abrupt closure of the public service broadcaster (ERT) in 2013, which had been a prime funding body for Greek cinema, further deprived filmmakers of vital resources and threatened the completion of films, especially those that required these funds as part of international co-production agreements. The situation worsened in 2015 due to the new memorandum agreement that involved the suspension of the tax on box office revenues that was used to finance films.[3] Although

ERT reopened in 2015 and public money gradually returned, the Greek Film Center's structural weaknesses, internal tensions and frequent director/board changes brought about institutional stagnation and long delays.

Nevertheless the exposure of Greek films at international festivals and their rise in the global scene boosted the Greek film community's self-confidence and opened up new networking, funding and market possibilities. Under growing financial and institutional pressure at home, producers and filmmakers took advantage of international festivals and European film institutions to fully explore alternative resources and attract foreign money. In this respect they were systematically involved in international workshops and talent labs, project-development forums and pitching events, works-in-progress and co-production markets, securing international co-production deals and distribution agreements (Papadimitriou 2017b: 171).

As a result, in the last decade, a notable and growing number of Greek art-house, commercial and documentary films were co-produced with the participation of a major or minor international partner, including, apart from Eurimages and MEDIA support, a wide range of European and regional national agencies, private companies and television channels. Recently, there has been also a considerable diversification in the national origin of Greek cinemas' co-financing partners including a range of European, Mediterranean, Balkan and other former socialist countries (Papadimitriou 2017b: 170–1). Although during the years 2007–16 Greek majority co-productions represented a small share of the total number of national productions – about 15 per cent (European Audiovisual Observatory 2018: 12), in the crisis era co-productions have greatly contributed towards the financial viability and artistic sustainability of Greek cinema, and become a key tool for arthouse films to reach global audiences, especially given the low box office potential of the local market.[4] Co-productions have not only enabled filmmakers to continue making films and become more visible, but also to increase their productivity and work on significantly higher budgets.[5] These brought about a remarkable shift in the visual texture and the creative choices of many New/Weird Wave films and documentaries, expanding their representational strategies and raising the level of ambition.

Having started before, but culminating during the crisis years, the Greek official cultural policy encouraged transnational opportunities and the promotion of Greek cinema abroad. The two major state-sponsored film institutions, GFC and the Thessaloniki International Film Festival (TIFF), have been actively engaged in initiatives that aim to enhance cross-national collaboration for over a decade. The appointment in 2016 as TIFF's director-general of Elise Jalladeau, the French former director of Festival du film francophone de Grèce, is a recent testament to such transnational orientation. TIFF has been instrumental in advancing a sustainable international networking and co-production culture in Greece and the wider geographical territory, as in 2005 it initiated the industry section Agora and the Crossroads Co-production Forum.[6] Both TIFF and the GFC have encouraged collaboration between countries from the Balkans and the broader south Mediterranean and Eastern European region with initiatives such as the Balkan Fund (TIFF, 2003–10), dedicated to script development, and the South Eastern Europe (SEE) Cinema Network (est. 2000), a GFC-initiated cross-border regional fund that supports projects in development among the Network members. Similarly TIFF's special section Balkan Survey (est. 1994) that showcases highlights from the annual production in the region has helped put Balkan cinema on the international film festival map, while creating a site for inter-Balkan communication and exchange (Kerkinos 2013). Initiatives supporting transnational collaboration led by the GFC include the introduction of a funding programme for Greek minority international co-productions (2010), the bilateral French-Greek co-production treaty (2014), the mutual distribution deal between Serbia and Greece (2017) and the alliance with the Torino Film Lab (2018). The script development workshop led by the Mediterranean Film Institute (MFI) (est. 1998), supported by MEDIA, GFC and ERT, has provided valuable networking opportunities for over two decades, strengthening regional and European collaborations. In the context of a wider plan to promote Greek films abroad, in the past ten years the GFC has also supported a number of Greek festivals around the world (such as in London, New York, Los Angeles and Montreal).

The rise of a young generation of Greek filmmakers and the transnationalisation of Greek cinema has been also marked by the emergence of a new generation of (executive) producers whose international orientation and professional training abroad helped build transnational collaborations and a co-production culture. Exceptional among them is cinephile entrepreneur Christos V. Konstantakopoulos, who in 2008 established Faliro House Productions, 'a frontrunner in the re-emergence of Greek cinema' (Faliro House 2019), as the company's website claims. Konstantakopoulos has been the producer and direct (co-) financier of many of the most distinguished New/Weird Wave feature and documentary films, while by adopting an outward-looking approach to filmmaking has become a respected international player. He has established international co-production and distribution alliances (such as with US-based FilmNation supporting independent filmmaking) and, since 2017, he has initiated (with Athina Rachel Tsangari) annual Faliro House/Sundance Institute Mediterranean Screenwriters Workshops in Greece and been involved in the co-production of internationally acclaimed features such as *Only Lovers Left Alive* (Jim Jarmusch, UK/Germany/Greece/France, 2013) and *Before Midnight* (Richard Linklater, USA/Greece, 2013).[7]

In terms of opening up opportunities and promoting Greek films internationally, special mention is due to Dimitris Eipides, former curator of TIFF's New Horizons section (1992–2003), festival director of TIFF (2010–15) and founder of the Thessaloniki Documentary Festival (1999). Apart from cultivating a high-quality cinephilia and familiarising younger filmmakers and cinephiles with new and aesthetically challenging feature films and documentaries from around the world, as regular Toronto IFF programmer and director of the Reykjavik IFF (2004–10), he offered festival screening slots to young Greek filmmakers in their early steps. Lanthimos's *Kinetta* (2005), for example, that premiered in Toronto was a discovery of Eipides.

Overcoming geographical restrictions, reaching global audiences and liberating the funding, circulation and content of the films were developments facilitated by technological innovation and the new digital landscape, including the Web. Since the early 2010s, a notable number of filmmakers have explored new forms of film financing offered by social media, Internet networking and online platforms. Crowdfunding[8] and the possibilities of free content dissemination through the Internet gave impetus to low-budget independent filmmaking, and in particular to cross-media and web documentaries (*The Prism GR: Krisis,* Nikos Katsaounis and Nina Maria Paschalidou, Greece, 2011) marked by collective and participatory work, direct engagement with the surrounding Greek reality – as the films responded to the crisis with a sense of urgency and immediacy – and the articulation of alternative political discourses.[9]

Finally, in 2017 a new incentive scheme was introduced and two parallel official initiatives have been taken to encourage international filmmaking and co-production activity in Greece. The GFC formed the Hellenic Film Commission, a member of the European Film Commissions Network (EUFCN), while the Ministry of Digital Policy, Telecommunications and Media established the National Centre of Audiovisual Media and Communication (EKOME), including a network of regional film offices that aim to facilitate local and international producers to film on location in Greece. In particular EKOME seeks to attract large-scale foreign investment in cross-national co-productions by providing a 35 per cent cash rebate and offering additional tax incentives of 25 per cent.

Transnational Mobility and Creative Talent

In the new landscape examined above for film activity in Greece, the mobility of Greek filmmakers and other creative talent across the borders is a remarkable phenomenon that lies 'beyond the narrow political categories of emigration and exile' (Elsaesser 2018: 26). Film professionals travel abroad to raise funds, showcase their films, serve as jury members and work in non-Greek projects as celebrated professionals. The most distinguished example is BAFTA-awarded and Oscar-nominated Yorgos Lanthimos, who quickly established an auteur status that enabled him to enter the international film industry. Today he is UK-based, pursuing an international career that already includes three prestigious and much acclaimed English-language films. Although some of his key collaborators have regularly been Greeks (screenwriter Efthymis Filippou, cinematographer Thimios

Bakatakis, editor Yorgos Mavropsaridis, Faliro House Productions and Greek actors), Lanthimos's recent films do not invest in the national. Without compromising his identity as an idiosyncratic filmmaker, an identity that was fundamental in labelling the Greek Weird Wave as such, Lanthimos's works are now detached from a Greek socio-political and cultural context, moving smoothly through different nations, budgets, genres and topics.

Aside from Lanthimos, a notable number of other filmmakers, film practitioners and actors share their time between Greece and other countries, embracing opportunities to work abroad: Filippos Tsitos has built a career as film and television director in Germany, Athina Rachel Tsangari has a contract to direct the BBC TV series *Trigonometry* and Alexandros Avranas made *Dark Crimes* (UK/Poland/USA, 2016), while editor Yorgos Lamprinos's work for *Jusqu'à la garde/Custody* (Xavier Legrand, France, 2017) won him the French César Best Editing Award (2019). It should be noted that many of the filmmakers of the younger generation have a strong cosmopolitan background as they were trained in film schools and lived, worked and developed international networks abroad before the rise of the New/Weird Wave. Indicatively, both Tsitos's and Tsangaris's debut features, *My Sweet Home* (Germany/Greece, 2001) and *The Slow Business of Going* (USA/Greece, 2001) respectively, were shot outside Greece – it is worth noting that *My Sweet Home* competed at the Berlinale as a German entry – featuring foreign languages and addressing the very issue of socio-spatial and cultural mobility under conditions of globalisation. This long-running and ongoing exposure of younger generations of Greek filmmakers to cosmopolitan experiences and the educational, cultural, professional, communication and networking opportunities offered by an increasingly globalised world could be understood as another important parameter that has given rise to New/Weird Wave and to the 'transnationalisation' of Greek cinema as experienced today.

Outward and inward mobility of creative talent takes several forms in Greek cinema, complicating issues of representation and cultural ownership. Greek filmmakers move to other countries making films that feature the realities they find there, such as Thanos Anastopoulos and Davide Del Degan's documentary *L'ultima spiaggia/The Last Resort* (Italy/Greece/France, 2016) about a beach in Trieste. Others return to capture Greece's experiences under conditions of crisis, such as US-based documentarists Nikos Katsaounis and Nina Maria Paschalidou or London-based editor/director Yannis Sakaridis (*Plateia Amerikis/Amerika Square*, Greece/UK/Germany, 2016). Producers and directors from the Greek diaspora make both fiction and documentary films either focusing on Greece-related themes (*Mana* (Greece, 2015) by Valerie Kontakos; *The Waiter* (Greece, 2018) by Steve Krikris) or reflecting upon distant societies such as Greek-South African Etienne Kallos's *Die Stropers/The Harvesters* (South Africa/France/Greece/Poland, 2018), while also financing and directing ambitious heritage projects such as *Echoes of the Past* (Nicholas Dimitropoulos, Greece, 2019) that deals with the Nazi massacre of Kalavryta and Second World War reparation claims. Greek cinema has also indigenised a number of Greek-Cypriot filmmakers, such as Yannis Economides, whose work has become highly influential, or Elias Demetriou. A number of filmmakers also have chosen to be known with foreign-like names (Nikos Labôt, Manuel de Coco) suggesting either a cosmopolitan background or a deliberate distance from the national.

Over the last thirty years the demography of Greece has changed dramatically since, from the early 1990s onwards, the country has experienced varied and massive migration flows, either from the former socialist countries after the collapse of communism or from Asian and African countries in the ongoing refugee crisis. It has also witnessed regular inter-European mobility. Greece's rapid transformation into a multi-ethnic and multicultural community is reflected in its cultural life, including its film industry. German cinematographer/director Jan Vogel, French-born actor Ariane Labed and documentarist Marco Gastine, professionally nurtured in Greece Albanian director Bujar Alimani, Greece-born Albanian short filmmaker Neritan Zinxhiria and Iranian-Greek actor Vassilis Koukalani are a few representative examples that confirm the transformation of Greek cinema's creative talent into a colourful transnational body. However, apart from a few exceptions, such as the Eurimages and SEE Cinema Network-supported co-production *Agon* (2012) by Albanian director Robert Budina that deals with the experiences of Albanian youth in Greece, migrant and diasporic voices are still marginal. The prospective emergence of images of self-representation by immigrant/diasporic filmmakers through the eventual rise of immigrant/diasporic cinemas *within* Greece as well as the formation of an increasingly diversified, in terms of ethnicity and culture, domestic audience can be seen as major opportunities for Greek cinema in the near future.

Transnational Texts: Shared Histories, Inclusive Narratives, Hybrid and Abstract Forms

Aside from industrial, working and consumption practices, transnationalism is a textual approach (Shaw 2013: 51) evident in a wide range of Greek arthouse, popular and documentary films. Textual transnationalism can be read either as the inevitable result of the systematic exposure of Greek films to European fundraising and co-production practices, or as a conscious strategy of domestically funded films to fulfil the expectations of international markets and appeal to international audiences. Simultaneously, however, it can be understood as a genuine reflection of/upon the rich transnational experiences of the Greeks, the increasingly multicultural character of contemporary Greek society and the destabilisation of the concept of national/cultural identity in the contemporary globalised world.

In terms of content, there has been a strong thematic tendency in both fiction (*Hora proelefsis/Homeland*, Syllas Tzoumerkas, Greece, 2010; *Tungsten*, Giorgos Georgopoulos, Greece, 2011; *Wasted Youth*, Argyris Papadimitropoulos, Jan Vogel, Greece, 2011) and documentary film (*Oi katharistes/The Cleaners*, Konstantinos Georgousis, Greece/UK, 2012) to explicitly address socio-political realities in Greece. However, austerity, financial precariousness, political instability, the rise of far-right extremism and huge flows of refugees are not only endemic to Greece but urgent issues of broader European and global concern. Paying particular attention to these links, Rosalind Galt argues that the very rise of the New/Weird Wave can be understood as a desire to discover a cinematic form that could respond to the political questions of contemporary Europe at the intersection with globalisation and neoliberal politics (Galt 2017: 11). *Debtocracy*, a documentary which received international media coverage and global visibility, is most conscious of those interrelations and, by deliberately building on interviews with internationally recognised experts, such as philosopher Alain Badiou, it communicates the Greek crisis as a structural problem of the global economy (see Figure 6.1).[10] Notably also the topics of economic repression, xenophobia and Neo-Nazi violence were major vehicles for the nationally funded mainstream *Worlds Apart* to overcome the usual distribution barriers and circulate in more than ten countries and a number of festivals.

A dominant trend in both feature and documentary films consists of engaging with themes that are by definition transnational, such as multiculturalism

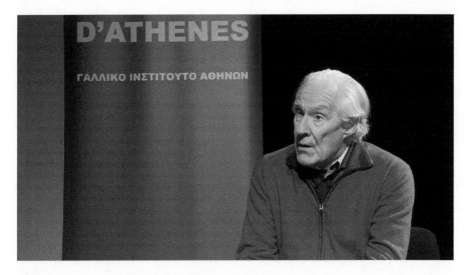

Figure 6.1   By featuring internationally recognised experts such as philosopher Alain Badiou, *Debtocracy* (Aris Chatzistefanou and Katerina Kitidi, 2011) articulates the Greek crisis as a problem of the global economy.

and border-crossing, while often situating them in a crisis-related context (*Tetarti 04:45/Wednesday 04:45*, Alexis Alexiou, Greece/Germany/Israel, 2015). These films place an emphasis on Greece as a site of intense multi-ethnic and multicultural encounters, on Greeks as diasporic and cosmopolitan subjects, and on various forms of dislocation and cross-border mobility such as migration, travelling and tourism, which include the depiction of foreign lands. In this respect, fiction films have opened up a new and diversified space to explore images of Otherness while addressing issues of identity and self-hood. They focus on the struggles of immigrants, especially from the former socialist countries, to integrate into Greek society (*Sto spiti/At Home*, Athanasios Karanikolas, Germany/Greece, 2014) or of refugees to cross the borders and flee to Europe (*Amerika Square*). They privilege 'Othered' subjectivities, with the narratives often being told from the perspective of immigrant characters not only to articulate stories of marginalisation and victimisation, of xenophobia and racism, but also to destabilise the very notions of identity and of national-historical-cultural belonging. Occasionally narratives blend national-identity boundaries, either by fusing Greek ethnicity with the national Other, as in the case of the young Greek-Albanian brothers in *Xenia* (Panos H. Koutras, Greece/France/Belgium, 2014), or by questioning the Greekness of their subjects as the narratives ambivalently or explicitly turn Greek characters into Albanians (*Plato's Academy*) or half-Turks (*Roza of Smyrna*, Kordellas George, Greece/Turkey, 2016) when their secret real national self is suddenly revealed. Moreover, cross-national love (*Worlds Apart*; *Roza of Smyrna*; *Polyxeni*, Dora Masklavanou, Greece, 2017) often within vacation settings such as exotic Greek islands (*Suntan*, Argyris Papadimitropoulos, Greece/Germany, 2016), journeying and expatriation (*Forget Me Not*, Yannis Fagras, Greece/USA, 2014; *Still River*, Angelos Frantzis, Greece/France/Latvia, 2018) or return stories of diasporic Greeks (*To dentro kai i kounia/A Place Called Home*, Maria Douza, Greece/Serbia, 2014) are common narrative motifs that explore complex identity issues and old traumas, foregrounding multicultural and multi-ethnic human, spatial and aesthetic territories that potential international audiences can identify with.

Another dominant way of articulating the transnational is to draw on shared past histories and cultures. Following the European model, most Greek heritage films, for instance, address both local and foreign audiences by employing a common European or transnational past (Vidal 2012), such as the German Occupation (*The Last Note*; *Echoes of the Past*) and the Holocaust (*Ouzeri Tsitsanis/Cloudy Sunday*, Manousos Manousakis, Greece, 2015), while also capitalising on national specificity. Just as in films set in the present, in heritage films too, Greeks are often depicted as part of a broader multicultural and multi-ethnic landscape. In *Little England*, for example, the island of Andros, alluding to the British naval empire, stands as a culturally hybrid microcosm where domesticated upper- and middle-class women consume foreign cultures (languages, music and fashion) while local men as sailors travel across the world mediating cosmopolitanism (see Figure 6.2). Issues of geographical mobility and border-crossing are pivotal to Greek heritage films with narratives often transcending the Greek borders to situate the action in lost motherlands, such as Asia Minor and Istanbul (*Roza of Smyrna*; *Polyxeni*), travelling destinations or host countries.

The evocation of a common European and/or transnational heritage is a key way of framing contemporary stories as well. Such stories often construct aesthetic and narrative spaces of competing or interlaced cultural and historical memories referencing shared historical legacies and political traumas, such as European dictatorships and totalitarian regimes (*Norvigia/Norway*, Yannis Veslemes, Greece, 2014) or the political legacy of May 1968 (*Silent*, Yorgos Gkikapeppas, Greece, 2015). Often the film narratives make creative uses of intertextuality and subtle allusions to a varied spectrum of shared intellectual and popular materials that range from literary to pop culture and film history: Bram Stoker in *Norway*; Knut Hamsun's *Hunger* in *To agori troei to fagito tou pouliou/Boy Eating the Bird's Food* (Ektoras Lygizos, Greece, 2012); Sir David Attenborough and Monty Python in *Attenberg*; *Rocky* (John G. Avildsen, USA, 1976), *Flashdance* (Adrian Lyne, USA, 1983), *Jaws* (Steven Spielberg, USA, 1975) and Frank Sinatra in *Dogtooth*; 1960s Italian singer Patty Pravo and an adaptation of the river scene of *Night of the Hunter* (Charles Laughton, USA, 1955) in *Xenia*; *Sliding Doors* (Peter Howitt, UK/USA, 1998) as an underlying narrative fabric in *What If . . .* and so on. Elina Psykou's *O gios tis Sofías/Son of Sofia* (2017), a painful coming-of-age drama that attempts to address the historical, political and cultural heritage of Eastern Europe, is

Figure 6.2   In *Little England* (Pantelis Voulgaris, 2013) the island of Andros stands as a culturally hybrid microcosm where women consume foreign cultures.

highly allusive and intertextual. While the narrative focuses on a Russian boy's painful adaptation to life in Greece, the *mise-en-scène* is populated by cultural and political references originating in former communist countries, but also familiar in Western Europe. This includes, among others, Misha, the mascot of the 1980 Moscow Olympic games (see Figure 6.3), Cheburashka, the famous Soviet animation character, musical scores such as the Russian song *Dorogoi dlinnoyu* ('By the long road' or, as it is commonly known, 'Those were the days') as well as the historical trauma of the failure of Communism. The film relates all these with fragments of Greece's cultural and political memories in order to contemplate on a disintegrating European vision.

Inevitably, the depiction of all the above interrelations involves multiple locations in different countries, extensive use of a variety of foreign languages (English, Turkish, Russian, Spanish, French, Arabic, Albanian, Italian, German and so on) and international casts. The European and often global star appeal of a number of actors, such as Catherine Deneuve (*God Loves Caviar*), François Cluzet (*Eteros ego/The Other Me*, Sotiris Tsafoulias, 2016), Max von Sydow and Richard Chamberlain (*Echoes of the Past*) or academy award winner J. K. Simmons (*Worlds Apart*) are evidence to their filmmakers' desire to increase international marketability and exportability.

As far as non-fiction is concerned, similarly to fiction films, documentary has largely embraced marginality, difference and divergence – often in relation to human mobility and border-crossing. Featuring Greece and dealing with

Figure 6.3 The *mise-en-scène of Son of Sofia* (Elina Psykou, 2017) is populated by cultural references originating in former communist countries, such as Misha, the mascot of the 1980 Moscow Olympic games.

multiple types of migratory, marginal or overlapping identities, there are films that focus on specific ethnic groups, such as docu-drama *Attractive Illusion* (Petros Sevastikoglou, Greece, 2012) on the experiences of illegal Nigerian immigrants in Greece, on underground multi-ethnic communities such as scrap metal collectors in Athens (*Raw Material*), or on expat communities such as a Russian group of Chernobyl-survivor scientists living on the island of Gavdos (*Oi athanatoi sto notiotero akro tis Evropis/The Immortals at the Southern Point of Europe*, Yiorgos Moustakis and Nikos Labôt, Norway/UK/Greece, 2013). Portraits of displaced characters struggling to set a new life in Greece such as a transgender Filipino hairdresser (*Roughcut*), a German activist and artist (*Xypnise o Sultan Ahmed/Sultan Ahmed Has Awoken*, Nikos Ligouris, Germany/Greece, 2012) or a Japanese woman married in Crete (*Sayome*, Nikos Dayandas, Greece, 2012) foreground multiculturalism and hybrid identities.

Moreover, cross-national dialogues and cultural hybridisation, and more precisely the interaction of Greek culture – language, music, theatre, orthodox Christianity – with other national traditions are celebrated both within and outside the Greek boundaries. In particular, issues of the historically troubled relation of Greece with neighbouring Turkey and Greece's Ottoman past – a topic that is often encountered in fiction films as well (*Roza of Smyrna, Polyxeni*) – recurrently surface either to throw light on painful historical issues (*Smyrni: I katastrofi mias kosmopolitikis polis 1900–1922/Smyrna: The Destruction of a Cosmopolitan City 1900–1922*, Maria Iliou, Greece, 2012) or to put emphasis on shared cultural experiences and cross-cultural exchanges. Nina Maria Pashalidou's *Kismet* (Greece/Qatar/France/Croatia/Bulgaria/Sweden/United Arab Emirates/Serbia/Canada/Finland/Singapore/Cyprus/Hungary, 2014) on Turkish TV soap operas, which were extremely popular in Greece during the early years of the crisis and in other territories across the Balkans and the Middle East, Marianna Economou's *Koudounia, klostes kai thavmata/Bells, Threads & Miracles* (Greece/Turkey, 2009) where Muslims enact religious rituals in a Greek monastery in Turkey, and *Kanarini mou glyko/My Sweet Canary* (Roy Sher, 2011), a Greek-French-German-Israeli co-production that follows the journey of three musicians from Israel, Turkey and Greece across the three countries and Britain tracing the music and life of Jewish-Greek rebetiko singer Roza Eskenazi, are representative of the complex cultural convergences and interactions in the broader region that documentaries bring to the fore. Furthermore, there are documentaries that move beyond Eastern, Balkan and Mediterranean identities to trace the tensions and intersections of the Greek with the Northern European and to meditate on the notion of European identity per se (*O dialogos tou Verolinou/Dialogue of Berlin*, Nicos Ligouris, Greece, 2017).

Pursuing their mobile characters and distant topics, documentaries travel, often to remote lands, either tracing reverse journeys from Greece to the character's birthplaces (*Sayome, Qadir – Enas Afganos Odysseas/Qadir – An Afghan*

Ulysses, Anneta Papathanasiou, Greece, 2008) or following the expeditions and wanderings of their Greek subjects. *Exotica, Erotica, Etc.* (France/Greece, 2015) by Greek-born and France-based visual artist Evangelia Kranioti, for example, traces the long journeys of Greek and other Mediterranean trade sailors across the world, and their romantic encounters with prostitutes at ports, to discuss issues of rootlessness, loneliness and erotic desire. Often loosely related or completely detached from the Greek context, documentaries travel to deal with hot political, environmental and human-rights topics of global concern, such as women's rights and Taliban violence in Pakistan (*Oi nymfes tou Hindu Kush/The Nymphs of Hindu Kush*, Anneta Papathanasiou, Greece, 2011), queer cultures in Rio de Janeiro carnival (*Obscuro Barroco*, Evangelia Kranioti, France/Greece, 2018) or the friendship between two ex-lovers and HIV-positive men in New Orleans (*Lamboun sto skotadi/They Glow in the Dark,* Panayotis Evangelidis, Greece, 2013).

Greece's own migratory, diasporic and cosmopolitan histories have also become important. There is a focus on portraits either of everyday characters, such as an elderly woman of Greek origin working as a maid in Cairo (*Katinoula*, Myrna Tsapa, Greece, 2012), or of distinguished Greek-diasporic individuals such as *Etel Adnan – Exoristes lexeis/Etel Adnan: Words in Exile* (Vouvoula Skoura, Greece, 2008) on the life and multicultural memories of the eponymous Lebanese-American-Greek-Syrian poet and artist. Particular emphasis is placed on diasporic and cross-national political subjects, a trend encouraged perhaps by the socio-political crisis in Greece and the rise of the Left. Forgotten pages of Greek-American labour history, for example, have been recurrently revisited (*Palikari: O Luis Tikas kai i sfagi tou Ludlow/Palikari: Louis Tikas and the Ludlow Massacre*, Nikos Ventouras, Greece, 2014), while the personalities of Greek-American cinephile intellectual and leftist activist Dan Georgakas (*Dan Georgakas – Epanastatis tis diasporas/Dan Georgakas – A Diaspora Rebel*, Costas Vakkas, Greece, 2015) and of a Greek communist fighter who fought for the Independence of Vietnam (*Viet Kostas – Ypikootis: Akathoristos/Viet Costas – Citizenship: Undefined*, Yannis Tritsibidas, 2012) are celebrated.[11] Likewise in the essay film *Imerologia amnisias/Amnesia Diaries* (Stella Theodorakis, Greece, 2012) the filmmaker's exploration of the collective crisis-ridden national present is mediated by her personal past and her subjective travel and cosmopolitan memories.

The transnational textuality and the international scope of post-2008 Greek cinema are apparent also in the titles of the films. On the one hand, there is a notable number of foreign-language original titles (*Tungsten, Wasted Youth, Forget Me Not, Silent*) addressing not only international markets but also a domestic, primarily young audience that has been persistently exposed to globalisation. On the other hand, many titles have international points of reference (*To thavma tis thalassas ton Sargasson/The Miracle of the Sargasso Sea*, Syllas Tzoumerkas, Greece/Germany/Netherlands/Sweden, 2019), allude to shared cultures (the short highly acclaimed *Ektoras Malo: I teleftea mera tis Hronias/Hector Malot: The Last Day of the Year*, Jacqueline Lentzou, Greece, 2018) or put emphasis on Othered, estranged and precarious identities and on the notion of not belonging (*Xenia*, *Polyxeni* – a female name which also means 'a stranger in many ways'). Some titles merge the national with the ethnic Other and the international using intertextuality: *Qadir – An Afghan Ulysses*, *When Tomatoes Met Wagner* (Marianna Economou, Greece, 2019) or *Little England*, the latter emphasising a peripheral status and simultaneously a strong identity as a European colonial centre. Particularly performative of an ambiguous, hybrid and transnational identity is the playful name *Attenberg*. It merges the city of Athens with the popular British documentarist Sir David Attenborough (Walldén 2017: 92) adding the Scandinavian and German ending '-berg' (implying also iceberg) to create a new autonomous and inseparable entity. The title and the content of *Ti nyhta pou o Fernando Pessoa synandise ton Konstandino Kavafi/The Night Fernando Pessoa Met Constantine Cavafy* (Stelios Charalampopoulos, 2008) are perhaps the most illustrative examples of identity hybridisation and of an articulation of the national through the transnational and the European. It is a hybrid film between fiction and documentary that delves into history, past cultures and actual archives, to narrate a fictional encounter of two major poets of the early twentieth century, the Greek Cavafy and the Portuguese Pessoa, who are now seen as parts of a common cultural European heritage. The two men meet the day of the 1929 stock market crash, on a transatlantic ocean liner carrying immigrants to the USA, among them a Greek, who interacts with and connects the two poets (see Figure 6.4). The narrative constantly mirrors the ports of Alexandria and Lisboa, as well as the poetry and the lives of the two men, to argue on precarious, mobile, fluid, multiple, overlapping and shared identities, and to contemplate the idea of Europe.

Textual transnationalism is also discernible in the formal traits of the films, especially as far as New/Weird Wave is concerned. As Walldén has put it, New/Weird Wave has reintroduced into Greek cinema an 'intense awareness of form' (2017: 80) and it is precisely this quality that was noticed by international festivals. In the short period before the crisis complicated their reception, Greek films attracted critical attention at festivals due their striking visual styles and inventive narratives – a set of internationally appreciated aesthetics that made them valuable 'festival films'. Notably non-Greek critics perceived and analysed them in relation to European cinematic trends, such as Dogme 95, and European auteurs such as Haneke, Lars Von Trier, Antonioni and Godard. Additionally, a considerable number of these films have exhibited a hybrid and aesthetically playful engagement with genre (vampire film, musical, melodrama, neo-noir) (Nikolaidou and Poupou 2017: 99) as a transnational vehicle of form and narrative.

The employment of recurrent thematic and iconographic patterns that function as abstract and empty schemes, marked by a deliberate sense of a-temporaneity,

Figure 6.4 *The Night Fernando Pessoa Met Constantine Cavafy* (Stelios Charalampopoulos, 2008) narrates a fictional encounter of two major European poets of the early twentieth century, the Greek Cavafy and the Portuguese Pessoa.

a-topicality and dystopicality, open to multiple and allegorical interpretations, is another key way of the New/Weird Wave to transnationalise film narratives. The emphasis, for example, on oppressive and abusing patriarchal families that has been identified as a major thematic preoccupation of New/Weird Wave films relates to global concerns rather than to strictly national iconographies (Aleksić 2016: 156). Likewise, the aesthetics of the space and of the chosen locations tend to work as symbolic forms and as universal *topoi* deprived of national references. Confined and claustrophobic spaces such as isolated houses and islands, tourist relics, ruined hotels, neglected villages, decadent buildings, the usual settings of New/Weird Wave films, function as wastelands and sites of dystopia (Poupou 2018). Even desirable tourist destinations such as a Greek island in *Suntan* – usual scenery to 'perform the national' (Elsaesser 2018: 30) – emerge not as an exotic and picturesque place but as a desolate dystopia. Likewise the wounded by the crisis and social violence cityscape of Athens, as part of the iconography of the Greek crisis, functions as an abstract metaphor of the capitalist world and as a neo-liberal urban dystopia. Commenting on the location choice of *Park* (2016), her film that is set in the deserted Athens Olympic Village inhabited by young people of various ethnic backgrounds, Sofia Exarchou emphasises the intentional a-temporaneity and a-topicality in the choice of the setting, pointing out that viewers can relate to it as a timeless 'no-man's land' ('Interview with the Director of *Park*', 2017). Despite emerging from Greek experiences, the recurrent motifs of the New/Weird Wave films on the wasteland and the repressive family, foreground a symbolic and universal texture, a shared experience of dystopia, that transcends Greece.

Conclusion

Regardless of the financial collapse and political instability of the post-2008 era, Greek cinema not only managed to survive but also to improve its cultural and political standing, strengthen its international position and overall rejuvenate and creatively restructure itself. This is the first period in the history of Greek cinema, when filmmaking and the film market were understood by professionals, institutions and government policies as primarily transnational and global terrains. From their inception, many Greek films of all types (arthouse, mainstream, heritage and documentary) are now consciously made to address international funding bodies, festivals and audiences taking the risk, according to some scholarly criticism,[12] of compromising their identity by internalising the expectations of international markets and funding schemes.

As has been demonstrated, all types of Greek film construct a variety of fluid, complex and hybrid identities which appear not only as representations of the contemporary experience but also as being embedded in the films' own cultural self. The national is constantly questioned and examined not simply through, in relation to or in interaction with the international but also as having itself multiple transnational dimensions. Although dismissive views on other nations and cultures are traceable, for example in comedies made for domestic consumption and even in some heritage films (*God Loves Caviar, Kazantzakis*), this is rather an abnormality. Contemporary Greek cinema as a whole, and at all possible levels (creative talent, production, content, form, modes of address, distribution and consumption) challenges the national. It integrates Greeks into European or global communities and Greek culture into the European/global heritage. At the same time it perceives Greece as a globalised community and constructs European and global cultures as part of the Greek heritage. This renegotiation and redefinition of the national through the transnational and the European is perhaps the most distinguished characteristic of Greek cinema today.

Notes

1. On the link of the New/Weird Wave with the Greek crisis, see Kourelou et al. (2014), Basea (2016) and Galt (2017).
2. On the return of the political in Greek films set in the past, see Kornetis (2014).
3. For a detailed discussion of the financial state of Greek cinema and of issues of production, distribution and exhibition in the crisis years, see Papadimitriou (2017a).
4. According to European Audiovisual Observatory (2018: 24), in 2015 co-productions represented 85 per cent of Greece's film exports.
5. For detailed studies on European co-production and Greek cinema since the crisis, see Papadimitriou (2018a, 2018b).
6. On the internationalisation of TIFF, see Papadimitriou (2016b).

7. On 'extrovert' producers and Konstantakopoulos, see also Papadimitriou (2017b: 171).
8. On crowdfunding as a practice of financing Greek films during the crisis, see Papadimitriou (2017b).
9. See Papadimitriou (2016a) and Lekakis (2017).
10. On *Debtocracy*, see Papadimitriou (2016a, 2017b).
11. See also *Kapetan Kemal, o syntrofos/Captain Kemal, A Comrade* (Fotos Lamprinos, Greece, 2008), the portrait of a Turk communist fighter who joined the guerrillas in the Greek Civil War.
12. On issues of orientalisation, self-exoticisation, uniformity and lack of self-determination in relation to New/Weird Wave, see Kourelou et al. (2014), Nikolaidou and Poupou (2017) and Elsaesser (2018).

REFERENCES

Aleksić, Tatjana (2016) 'Sex, Violence, Dogs and the Impossibility of Escape: Why Contemporary Greek Film is so focused on family', *Journal of Greek Media and Culture*, 2 (2), pp. 155–71.

Basea, Erato (2016) 'The "Greek Crisis" through the Cinematic and Photographic Lens: From "Weirdness" and Decay to Social Protest and Civic Responsibility', *Visual Anthropology Review*, 32 (1), pp. 61–72.

Chalkou, Maria (2012) 'A New Cinema of "Emancipation": Tendencies of Independence in Greek Cinema of the 2000s', *Interactions: Studies in Communication and Culture*, 3 (2), pp. 243–61.

Chalkou, Maria (2017) 'Memory, Nostalgia and Cosmopolitanism: The Greek Heritage Film', in Maria Paradeisi and Afroditi Nikolaidou (eds), *From Early to Contemporary Greek Cinema: Methodology, Theory, History*. Athens: Gutenberg, pp. 261–81 (in Greek).

Elsaesser, Thomas (2018) 'National, Transnational, and Intermedial Perspectives in Post-2008 European Cinema', in Betty Kaklamanidou and Ana M. Corbalán (eds), *Contemporary European Cinema: Crisis Narratives and Narratives in Crisis*. London: Routledge, pp. 20–36.

European Audiovisual Observatory (2018) *International film co-production in Europe*, <https://rm.coe.int/brochure-cannes-2018/16808ae9fa> (last accessed 10 July 2019).

Faliro House (2019) *falirohouse.com* <http://www.falirohouse.com/aboutUs/> (last accessed 20 July 2019).

Galt, Rosalind (2017) 'The Animal Logic of Contemporary Greek Cinema', *Framework: Journal of Cinema and Media*, 58 (1–2), pp. 7–29.

'Interview with the Director of *Park*, Sofia Exarchou' (2017) *YouTube*, SaFtAs GrEeK tEam Nea Peramos Senior High School, published on 13 February 2017 <https://www.youtube.com/watch?v=A_7RmPxtpII> (last accessed 20 July 2019).

Kerkinos, Dimitris (2013) '20 Years "Balkan Survey": The Establishment of a Formerly Unknown Cinema', *Filmicon: Journal of Greek Film Studies*, Blog, 2 November <http://filmiconjournal.com/blog/post/2/20_years_balkan_survey_the_establishment_of_a_formerly_unknown_cinema> (last accessed 10 July 2019).

Kornetis, Kostis (2014) 'From Politics to Nostalgia – and Back to Politics: Tracing the Shifts in the Filmic Depiction of the Greek "Long 1960s" Over Time', *Historein*, 2 (14), pp. 89–102.

Kourelou, Olga, Mariana, Liz and Vidal, Belén (2014) 'Crisis and Creativity: The New Cinemas of Portugal, Greece and Spain', *New Cinemas: Journal of Contemporary Film*, 12 (1–2), pp. 133–51.

Lekakis, Eleftheria (2017) 'Documentary, Media Activism and Anti-austerity in Greece: The #greekdocs Archive', *Journal of Alternative and Community Media*, 2, pp. 28–44.

Nikolaidou, Afroditi and Poupou, Anna (2017) 'Post-weird Notes on the New Wave of Greek Cinema', *Non Catalog*. Thessaloniki: 58 TIFF, pp. 88–105.

Papadimitriou, Lydia (2016a) 'Politics and Independence: Documentary in Greece during the Crisis', in Yiannis Tzioumakis and Claire Molloy (eds), *The Routledge Companion to Cinema and Politics*. London: Routledge, pp. 469–80.

Papadimitriou, Lydia (2016b) 'The Hindered Drive toward Internationalization: Thessaloniki (International) Film Festival', *New Review of Film and Television Studies*, 14 (1), pp. 93–111.

Papadimitriou, Lydia (2017a) 'The Economy and Ecology of Greek Cinema since the Crisis: Production, Circulation, Reception', in Dimitris Tziovas (ed.), *Greece in Crisis: The Cultural Politics of Austerity*. London: I. B. Tauris, pp. 135–57.

Papadimitriou, Lydia (2017b) 'Transitions in the Periphery: Funding Film Production in Greece since the Financial Crisis', *International Journal on Media Management*, 19 (2), pp. 164–81.

Papadimitriou, Lydia (2018a) 'European Co-productions and Greek Cinema since the Crisis: "Extroversion" as Survival', in Julia Hammett-Jamart, Petar Mitric and Eva Novrup Redvall (eds), *European Film and Television Co-production: Policy and Practice*. Palgrave Macmillan, pp. 207–22.

Papadimitriou, Lydia (2018b) 'Greek Cinema as European Cinema: Co-productions, Eurimages and the Europeanisation of Greek cinema', *Studies in European Cinema*.

Poupou, Anna (2018) 'The Poetics of Space in the New Wave of Contemporary Greek Cinema', *Parabasis*, 16 (1), pp. 295–313.

Rose, Steve (2011) 'Attenberg, Dogtooth and the Weird Wave of Greek Cinema', *The Guardian*, 27 August <www.theguardian.com/film/2011/aug/27/attenberg-dogtooth-greece-cinema> (last accessed 10 July 2019).

Shaw, Deborah (2013) 'Deconstructing and Reconstructing "Transnational Cinema"', in Stephanie Dennison (ed.), *Contemporary Hispanic Cinema: Interrogating Transnationalism in Spanish and Latin American Film*. Woodbridge: Tamesis, pp. 47–65.

Vidal, Belén (2012) *Heritage Film: Nation, Genre and Representation*. London & New York: Columbia University Press.

Walldén, Rea (2017) 'The Spatio-Temporality of the Avant-Gardes: Feminist Avant-Garde U-Topoi in Greek Cinema from Transition to Crisis', in Tonia Kazakopoulou and Mikela Fotiou (eds), *Contemporary Greek Film Cultures from 1990 to the Present*. Oxford: Peter Lang, pp. 71–100.

7. KOSOVO: CINEMATIC DEVELOPMENTS BETWEEN CONFLICTS AND SOCIAL TRANSFORMATION

Francesca Borrione and Albana Muco

Kosovar cinema is relatively young and only recently recognised as a distinctive entity, so the literature on the subject is minimal and limited to a few pages in Robert Elsie's *Historical Dictionary of Kosovo* (2011) or in popular travel guides. When looking at the history and evolution of Kosovar cinema in the last decade, it becomes clear that the themes of ethnic conflict and specifically the 1998 war have dominated genres and narratives.[1] Kosovar cinema is a cinema of war, trauma, catharsis and resilience; it mirrors the population's need to deal with the past and the desire to move on. Kosovar cinema is bound to the country's political and cultural history and reflects the challenges in shaping a new Kosovar identity while overcoming ethnic, religious and linguistic differences.[2]

Kosovo unilaterally declared independence from Serbia on 17 February 2008. Ten years later, the country is still in the process of defining its own identity within a climate of social and cultural problems while struggling to be recognised as an independent state.[3] In these post-independence ten years, Kosovo has made significant progress in democratic consolidation, improving public financial management (USAID Final Report 2017) and establishing international collaboration agreements. However, it also faces many internal challenges: lack of economic development, corruption and abuse of power, discrimination against the LGBTQ community and under-resourced educational system, as well as persisting ethnic divisions and hostilities (USAID Final Report 2017; European Commission Kosovo 2018 Report).

Historically, Kosovar identity has been 'determined by the relations between nationalities inside Kosovo (Albanians, Serbs) and by the relations between these single nationalities and other nation-states and symbols outside Kosovo (Albania, Serbia and so on)' (Albertini 2012: 10). For this reason, Kosovo has been a territory marked by binary oppositions (Serbians versus Albanian Kosovars, offensive versus defensive nationalism, unification versus separation, dominant versus subordinated part), while its new official status since its independence in 2008, is that of a multilingual, multicultural, and multi-religious country in Europe.[4] Given that 'post-national citizenship implies fluid and multiple identities that transcend binary oppositions' (Ivic 2016: 101), Kosovo can be understood as a 'post-national state' (Muco 2018: 177), that is as a heterogeneous and pluralist society that is trying to overcome ethnic divisions focusing on intercultural dialogue, rights and social issues. Committed to sensitising the public to ethnic, gender and political issues, cinema and film-related institutions are playing a key role in this process.

This chapter provides insights into the Kosovar film industry since the 2008 declaration of independence. It explores the films made, the funding institutions and production contexts that enabled them to be made, and the ways they are distributed and seen by audiences. The chapter relies predominantly on primary research, that is materials provided by the Qendra Kinematografike e Kosovës/ Kosovo Cinematography Center (KCC), by the staff of film festivals running in Kosovo and by film producers and filmmakers, as well as institutional reports and articles published in newspapers and online film magazines.

KOSOVAR FILM NARRATIVES IN A TRANSNATIONAL CONTEXT

Kosovar filmmakers aim to address their audiences as citizens of a globalised, multicultural society. As Rascaroli (2013: 28) has argued with reference to other European films, the connection between film and real, historical events reinforces the medium's participation in the public discourse. Kosovar films are transnational by history, content and necessity: by history, given that Kosovo is a territory in which different ethnicities coexist; by content, as most of contemporary Kosovar films deal with the topic of migration and diaspora; by necessity, because in order to have their movies produced and released Kosovar filmmakers have to rely on European and extra-European partnerships. Kosovar films are products of a globalised production and distribution system, and a means to raise issues around ethnic conflicts, gender identity and coexistence among different cultures, switching between 'epiphanic' and 'affinitive transnationalism' (Hjort 2010b: 15–16).

The vast majority of Kosovar film narratives explore the recent history of the country, dealing with war-related topics and the consequences of ethnic conflicts and focusing on the collective physical and psychological traumatisation, especially on war rapes and gender violence. Although there are no official statistics, it is believed that around 20,000 women were victims of sexual violence during the war in Kosovo (Kakissis 2016; Human Rights Watch 2000). Rape as a specific theme is present in short films such as *Kthimi/The Return* (Blerta Zeqiri, Kosovo, 2012), *Home* (Daniel Mulloy, UK/Kosovo/Albania, 2016) and *Fence* (Lendita Zeqiraj, Kosovo/Croatia/France, 2018), and in the following feature films: *Anatema* (Agim Sopi, Kosovo, 2006), *Agnus Dei* (Agim Sopi, Kosovo, 2012), *Tri dritare dhe një varje/Three Windows and a Hanging* (Isa Qosja, Kosovo/Germany, 2014), *Heroi/The Hero* (Luan Kryeziu, Kosovo, 2014), *Martesa/The Marriage* (Blerta Zeqiri, Kosovo/Albania, 2017) and *T'padashtun/Unwanted* (Edon Rizvanolli, Kosovo/Netherlands, 2017).

Agim Sopi's *Agnus Dei* is one of the most ambitious and disturbing films produced in postwar Kosovo showing a devastated and violated society, in which even a monastery used as an orphanage 'is only a front for child prostitution and white slavery organized by local gangsters and the Belgrade mafia' and 'demonising the ethnic Other' (Pavičić 2012). Reportedly based on a true story, it elaborates on the myth of Oedipus the King, and focuses on Petar, a Serbian soldier dehumanised by the war, who falls in love with a young Albanian woman without knowing she is his sister (see Figure 7.1). Produced by Kosovo's CMB Productions and Germany's NiKo Film,[5] *Three Windows and a Hanging* by Isa Qosja is probably the most prominent film on war rapes to get recognition from the international film community, with the movie being selected – for the first time in Kosovar film history – to represent Kosovo for Best Foreign Film at the Academy Awards 2014. With its focus on the life of

Figure 7.1   The aftermath of the Kosovar war: trauma, ethnic conflict and war rape in *Agnus Dei* (Agim Sopi, 2012).

a group of rape survivors in postwar Kosovo, *Three Windows and a Hanging* also marks an important change in war narratives: the marginalisation of war rape survivors is finally being considered a major political issue. Amnesty International (2017: 7) confirms that only three prosecutions for wartime rape have been completed in Kosovo, and each resulted in an acquittal after appeal. Isa Qosja publicly exposes a taboo concerning the lives of 20,000 women (Eleftheriou 2014), stigmatised and silenced by a culture of shame that is still predominant in socially prejudiced Kosovo.

In addition to war stories, Kosovar cinema is also characterised by a predominance of characters on the move: emotionally, like the conflicted gay husband of *The Marriage* (2017) or the women coping with the trauma of war rape in *Agnus Dei* (2012); philosophically, like the suicidal teen in the short film *Ballkoni/Balcony* (Lendita Zeqiraj, Kosovo, 2013); physically, like the Albanian interpreter turned into a prisoner trying to find her way out in Agim Sopi's *Anatema* (2006); or like Zana, an Albanian Kosovar refugee who lives in Amsterdam with her son Alban, in Edon Rizvanolli's *Unwanted* (2017).

In this sense, Kosovar cinema is to a large extent a diasporic cinema, not only because the films' narratives often focus on Kosovar migration, but also because – in many cases – the filmmakers are migrants themselves, such as the Los Angeles-based Antoneta Kastrati, Amsterdam-based Edon Rizvanolli and Cologne-based Visar Morina. As migrant filmmakers working across cultures, languages and histories, their work represents a cultural fusion (Sweet et al. 2008); aspects from homeland and host-land are combined to create a fused 'intercultural identity' (Croucher and Kramer 2017: 104). Kosovar filmmakers have turned to the outside world in order to find ways for producing their films and telling their stories. They have appealed to international investors, mobilised participation through the Internet and crowdfunding platforms, and turned Kosovar stories into transnational narratives that can address transnational audiences.

The Kosovo Cinematography Center and the Kosovar Film Industry

The main institution involved in developing Kosovar film industry is the Kosovo Cinematography Center, which was founded in 1969 as Kosovafilm in the former autonomous province of Kosovo, SFR Yugoslavia, as a state institution for film production, distribution and screening. In 1969, Kosovafilm signed the first co-production collaboration with institutions based in other Yugoslav republics, such as Filmske Novosti and Avala Film in Belgrade. Two years later, Kosovafilm established exclusive rights for its films to be distributed in the entire territory of the former Yugoslavia. Between 1969 and 1990, Kosovafilm produced about seventeen feature films and several short films and documentaries (Elsie 2011: 100; 2004: 60), of which seven were Serbian-Kosovar co-production collaborations within Yugoslavia. In 1990, the institution was taken over by the Serb authorities and 'dissolved for all intents and purposes' (Elsie 2004: 60).[6]

With the Law on Cinematography, in 2004 the Kosovar government established the Kosovo Cinematography Center (KCC) as the central authority for cinema under the auspices of the Ministry of Culture. Subsequently, Kosovafilm acquired a different role and currently functions as a film archive. KCC aims to adopt and implement film policies that reflect public interest, manages the film fund and announces a competition every year in the following categories: feature, short, documentary and animated film. Since Kosovo's declaration of independence in 2008, KCC has been extremely active in financing and supporting Kosovar film production. From 2008 to 2018 it has subsidized 154 films, 70 of which have been released (27 feature fiction, 13 feature documentaries, 27 shorts, and 5 animations – see the Tables at the back of the book). Two co-productions with Germany, Isa Qosja's *Three Windows and a Hanging* and Cologne-based Visar Morina's *Babai/Father* (Germany/Kosovo/North Macedonia/France, 2015)[7] were selected to represent Kosovo for best foreign film at the Academy Awards in 2014 and 2015, respectively. The KCC contributes to a maximum of 51 per cent of a film's budget (except for animated films and graduate filmmakers' projects, which may be funded up to 90 per cent). Since 2008, when the total amount of money available through the KCC was 300,000 euros, there has been a progressive film budget increase and the subsidised film number has grown. On 7 August 2018, in recognition of the promising results that Kosovar films have achieved, the Minister of Culture, Youth and Sports, Kujtim Gashi, declared an increase by 100 per cent of the KCC film budget, that is from 600,000 to 1,200,000 euros (Kosova Sot 2018).

The KCC plays a key role in promoting films internationally and gives the opportunity to Kosovar filmmakers to visit film industry events abroad, such as the European Film Market affiliated to the Berlin International Film Festival, the Cannes Film Festival and the Balkan Film Market in Albania, among others. In 2012, it joined the Germany-based European Film Promotion (EFP) network, and in 2017 the South Eastern Europe Cinema Network (SEE) that offers development funds to Balkan co-productions. The KCC also actively encourages co-productions, even though the country has not yet signed the European Convention on Cinematographic Co-Production and is not a member of Eurimages.[8] The year 2017 has been important for cooperation agreements. At the Berlinale, the KCC signed two memoranda of understanding: one with the European Audiovisual Entrepreneurs (EAVE) aiming to provide audiovisual education to the Kosovar citizens; and one with the regional film fund Balkan Cinema Cities. The Kosovar film industry is currently reinforcing its role in the Balkan area through bilateral oral agreements with nearby countries such as Bulgaria, Turkey and North Macedonia (KCC Annual Report 2018). The agreement signed in 2018 between the Kosovo Producers Association and the Macedonian Film Producers Association (MZFP), for example, has the purpose of developing relations and support in the field of film industry in both countries (Economou 2018a).

As of 2018, Kosovo has 202 registered production companies, two film associations (the Kosovo Producers Association and the Union of Film Artists of Kosovo), five major international film festivals (DokuFest, Anibar, PriFest, Hyjnesha në Fron – The Goddess on the Throne, FerFilm) and five cinemas (Armata, Cineplexx, ABC Cinema, DokuKino and Jusuf Gërvalla). Cineplexx, Armata, ABC Cinema and DokuKino are commercial cinemas. The first three operate in the capital city Prishtina, DokuKino cinema is located in Prizren, while Jusuf Gërvalla cinema is in Peja. The history of these cinemas somehow reflects the history of Kosovar society in the prewar and postwar years that marked the country. For example, Armata, located in an ex-Army House, reopened after thirty years in April 2018 as a regenerated public space to promote alternative arts.

Given the limited financial resources available to filmmakers in the country, filmmakers regularly seek European financial support. The Director of KCC, Arben Zharku, declared in 2015 that the total of foreign funds in Kosovar films, in co-productions with Kosovo and in minority co-productions, was 5,060,000 euros (GjilaniInfo 2015). Film projects are funded by private and public institutions, and NGOs, upon evaluation of the films' artistic, cultural, educational and social value such as Cinema Foundation – Ile De France Region, Municipality of Prishtina, Panavision New Filmmaker Grant, the United Nations Office in Kosovo, USAID and the Fondacioni i Kosovës për Shoqëri të Hapur/The Kosovo Open Society Foundation, and the Ministry of Foreign Affairs of Kosovo.

FILM FESTIVALS AND DISTRIBUTION

Apart from the state-funded KCC, three commercial distribution film companies operate in Kosovo, all based in Prishtina: Kooperativa, KDSHF Genci and Entermedia. Kooperativa was established in 2012 as a platform for the cooperation of independent culture organisations from the former Yugoslavia and in the South East European area (Slovenia, Croatia, Bosnia-Herzegovina, Serbia, Montenegro, North Macedonia). KDSHF Genci is a local film distribution company that owns ABC Cinema and supports workshops for young people and students interested in studying films. Entermedia is a communication and entertainment company established in 2004, now based in New York, Berlin and Prishtina: in 2012, Entermedia produced the successful nation-branding campaign 'The Young Europeans', meant to bring attention to the young Kosovar nation (Hapçiu and Sparks 2012).

With only five cinemas operating in the country and a limited exhibition infrastructure, Kosovar film festivals are significant, not only because they attract local audiences to watch international films that would otherwise not be shown, but also because they allow Kosovar filmmakers to showcase their films to international guests. These festivals depend financially on European and international communities. PriFest, for example, is supported by the Turkish Ministry of Culture and Tourism, the Croatian Embassy in Kosovo and the Kingdom of the Netherlands. DokuFest is co-sponsored by the Swiss Department of Foreign Affairs, the Government of the Grand Duchy of Luxembourg, USAID, the Austrian Embassy in Prishtina and the US Embassy in Kosovo, among others. Anibar relies on a variety of funds, especially from the Visegrad Group countries (Czech Republic, Hungary, Poland and Slovakia). All the above have established a rich network of exchanges. In 2018, DokuFest showcased more than a hundred films from forty different countries, while Anibar screened 220 films from more than thirty different countries. Film festivals are also important for developing awareness of political, educational and social issues that are still hotly debated in the country. They support democratisation and contribute to a pluralistic society. The idea that film festivals should also work as an intercultural bridge, promoting knowledge across borders, is clearly expressed by the themes or mission statements of the festivals, for example: Anibar 2016 'Culture for All', Bridge Film Fest 2016 'Welcome to the Other Side', DokuFest 2017 'Future (Future Is My Love, Future Is Not Dead)' and PriFest 2018 'Friendship. Forever.'

The commitment and support of film festivals helped re-establish two of the five cinemas currently operating in Kosovo. In the case of the DokuKino cinema in Prizren, it could not have been built without the financial support of the Municipality of Prizren, the European Union, the Norwegian Embassy and the US Embassy in Kosovo. Managed by DokuFest International Film Festival, the DokuKino opened in 2013 and marked the return of cinemas to the town. Similarly, Jusuf Gërvalla Cinema in Peja, which was established in 1955 and was the only cinema in the area at the time, had been left in ruins in the war. It was brought to new life thanks to the support of Anibar NGO. To prevent Jusuf Gërvalla's privatisation and preserve the cinema's cultural values and history (Mehtaj 2017), in 2017 the staff of Anibar NGO signed a fifteen-year contract with the Municipality of the city of Peja to revitalise the cinema and strengthen the sense of community around the arts.

Defining Kosovar Films in Postwar Kosovo

As Kosovar film industries, producers and filmmakers work and cooperate to expand Kosovar cinematic arts and make them visible on the global landscape, two of the most successful Kosovar co-productions on an international scale, short-films *Shok* (Jamie Donoughue, UK/Kosovo, 2016) and *Home* (2016), are directed by non-Kosovar filmmakers. *Shok* for example, which broke the record for being the first Kosovar film ever to reach the Oscar nomination (for Best Short Film) in 2016, was written and directed by British filmmaker Jamie Donoughue after a five-week stay in Kosovo. Based on true events, the film focuses on an episode of unprovoked aggression by Serb soldiers against two young boys. *Shok* counts a Kosovar cast and crew. Similarly, BAFTA-winning short film *Home* by Daniel Mulloy is a Kosovar and British co-production, co-funded by Kosovar DokuFest and by British Bartle Bogle Hegarty, Black Sheep Studios and Somesuch. Produced under the UN flag and released on World Refugee Day, *Home* was funded and supported by several international public institutions (United Nations Office in Kosovo and USAID, among others) and film production companies. Shot in the UK and in the Kosovar villages of Janjevo and Gračanica, *Home* is a twenty-minute short film about a British family forced to become refugees, reversing the roles of persecutor and persecuted and inviting an international audience to identify with the protagonists' plight (see Figure 7.2). Mulloy's interest in the history of Kosovo is in part personal, since Mulloy's partner is a former Kosovo's refugee. *Home* is important because it raises awareness about a major humanitarian issue such as the refugee crisis, but it is also problematic because it is too abstract and detached from Kosovo's history. In the film, Kosovo only works as a theatre of war: the country's real refugee crisis is marginal to the story of a white, middle-class

Figure 7.2   Kosovo as a "theatre of war" in *Home* (Daniel Mulloy, 2016).

British family's struggle to survive. As an English-spoken short film, made as a British majority co-production with a British cast, it reflects outsiders' perspectives on the Kosovar crisis. Its critical success seems to suggest that the topics of war and refugee crisis catch the attention of an international audience only when they are perceived as affecting affluent Western countries.

Despite their position on the margins of the European cultural and political landscape, Kosovar filmmakers – and in particular those who grew up during prewar and postwar Kosovo – consider cinema as a means of social and civil commitment. They use Kosovo as a narrative framework to explore urgent and relevant issues for contemporary Kosovar culture and society such as civil and human rights, inclusion, education, sex(ual) and ethno-racial discrimination. Some film narratives, as in the case of *Unwanted* and *The Marriage*, represent Kosovo as a country dominated by a strict heteronormative and patriarchal society. With its story of abuse and survival, *Unwanted* deserves particular attention. *Unwanted* tells the story of a Kosovar teenager, Alban, who lives in Amsterdam with his mother, as he had to leave Kosovo after being cast out for being raped by a Serbian soldier during the 1999 war. When Alban falls in love with Ana, the daughter of a Serbian Kosovar refugee, their parents are against the relationship, while Alban and Ana feel disconnected from national conflicts and consider themselves Dutch. Alban's self-identification with the host country is revealed by the fact that he speaks Dutch to his mother while she talks in Albanian (Petković 2017) (see Figure 7.3). *Unwanted* proves that wartime sexual violence and the subsequent discrimination against the victims

Figure 7.3   Diaspora and the experiences of the post-war Kosovar generations in *Unwanted* (Edon Rizvanolli, 2017).

is not only a Kosovar subject, but it is present 'in a wider geographical context, where societies have failed to work on the reintegration and de-stigmatization of victims' (Bilibani 2017), such as in Bosnia and Herzegovina.

While *Unwanted* focuses on the experiences of postwar Kosovar generations who grow up as members of the diaspora, and between cultures, the release of the Kosovar-Albanian film *The Marriage* marks a turning point in the representation of the LGBTQ community in Kosovo. Focused on a young newlywed man who is secretly in love with his best friend, *The Marriage* highlights the hypocrisy and contradictions within rigid patriarchal societies, while powerfully illustrating the multiple forms of structural violence to which the individual who fails to conform is subjected (Hasa 2018) (see Figure 7.4). The director of *The Marriage*, Blerta Zeqiri, is one of the many Kosovar female filmmakers whose films aim to sensitise the population about social inequalities. Zeqiri is also an activist at the virtual Women Activists Museum,[9] a platform for the defence of women's rights. Like Zeqiri, other female filmmakers are very committed to raising the voice of women in Kosovar film industry and culture.

One of the most active filmmakers is the Los Angeles-based Antoneta Kastrati. Originally from Peja, Kastrati studied at the American Film Institute but always looked back at Kosovo's history as an inspiration for her movies: 'I've spent the last 15 years making films about important social issues that need to be talked about; the environment, sex, homophobia, gender, things that the media in Kosovo hasn't made space for yet' (Travers 2017). She directed three short

Figure 7.4 Marginalised communities in *The Marriage* (Blerta Zeqiri, 2017), a Kosovar queer film.

films before her first full-length work *Zana* (Kosovo/Albania, 2019), a story of war, motherhood and black magic inspired by the director's experience as a war survivor.

With an MFA in Film and TV completed at NYU, Kosovar screenwriter Blerta Basholli had already shot her first short film *Lena dhe unë/Lena and Me* (Serbia/ USA, 2011) when she worked as a third assistant director to Daniel Mulloy on *Home*. Basholli's latest feature-length film project, *Zgjoi/Hive* (Kosovo/North Macedonia/Albania, 2019), about a woman who tries to run her own business in postwar Kosovo, was awarded 80,000 euros at PriFest 2017 and a minority co-production grant by Tirana International Film Festival in 2018.

The twenty-seven-year-old director and activist, Prishtina-based More Raça, dedicates her work as a filmmaker to the cause of women's rights, and considers herself an 'advocate for the challenges and problems facing my country as well as the region' (Raça 2018). Raça's films inform the audience about the women's silent fights in Kosovar patriarchal society, such as *Amel* (Kosovo, 2013) which tells the story of a young mother who gets a part in an audition for a foreign film production but faces difficulties from her family and cultural environment. Raça's second short *Home* (Kosovo, 2016), focused on property inheritance rights and the subversion of social norms – an issue ignored by Kosovar authorities until 2016 – and successfully opened a public discussion about inheritance equality (Jin 2018). Feminist issues are also addressed in her latest short, *Ajo/She* (Kosovo/France, 2018), in which a female teenager takes her mother away from her abusive husband, as a new generation of women takes courage to fight for their own freedom. The film addresses the often unreported issue of domestic violence as a public issue in direct contrast to the Kosovar 'cultural tradition to keep domestic violence hidden as a private family matter' (UNICEF 2013: 22).

The themes of memory and trauma, antagonistic ethnic identities and nationalism, a difficult past and turbulent changes – common themes in post-Yugoslav literary (Beronja and Vervaet 2016) and filmic texts (Murtic 2015) – also include the marginalisation of disadvantaged subjects and gender inequalities. Films become an engaging means of promoting anti-war values, cosmopolitanism, (gender) equality and human rights. Kosovar cinema reflects society and makes society reflect; it documents and illustrates interconnected questions, socio-cultural dynamics, complexities and transformations. Kosovar films aim at bringing social changes through public discussion and engagement and pierce the veil of silence in developing Kosovo.

Conclusions: A New Framework for Kosovar Cinema

The context in which Kosovar cinema was built and is currently being developed is extremely complex: as a country that proclaimed its independence in 2008, Kosovo seems to have immediately identified cinema as the best and most popular tool to sensitise the population on controversial issues such as ethnic divisions and identity, gender and LGBTQ. This has been possible through the KCC, local associations, agencies for international cooperation and NGOs specialising in social development and conflict management operating in Kosovo.

From *Gomarët e kufirit/Donkeys of the Border* (Jeton Ahmetaj, Kosovo, 2009), one of the first films produced in independent Kosovo and the first to get international attention through its participation at the PriFest Film Festival, to Kosovo's official selection for the 2019 Oscars the LGBTQ-themed *The Marriage*, Kosovar cinema has made significant improvements and developed into a well-established industry, thanks to important connections with major European film production and distribution companies. However, the public funding available through the KCC together with the few other private sources is not enough to cover the requests from filmmakers.

As agreements signed by the KCC with international film distribution companies support the circulation of Kosovar films not only in the Balkan area but across Europe and in the United States, film festivals work as frameworks for audiences, stakeholders and funding procedures. Even though Kosovar cinema is alive and evolving into a well-established cultural reality and productive platform, it still needs the support of nearby countries. With a population of 1,830,000 inhabitants in a country of 4,212 square miles, Kosovo can be considered a 'small state' (Hjort 2010a: 48). With more than ten film festivals across the country, over 200 production companies listed in the KCC website and between five and twenty films funded every year up to 2017, the Kosovar film scene is more productive than ever, with twenty-eight projects in production in 2018. Kosovar film projects are developed within a young, vibrant and creative environment, but require the support of a network of international film productions and institutions for the films to be completed, released and distributed. Kosovar cinema is therefore *de facto* transnational. The increasing quantity (and quality) of films co-produced in Kosovo, the collaborations between Kosovar private and public film companies and institutions, both European and extra-European production and distribution companies and the ability of Kosovar 'small-nation filmmakers' (Hjort 2011) to overcome financial constraints by reaching beyond national borders in search of cross-border solidarities and partnerships are all evidence of Kosovar cinema's transnational dimensions.

In this geopolitical scenario, where films focus mainly on representing conflicts and sensitising audiences toward human rights, a definition of Kosovar cinema has to take into consideration the peculiarity and urgency of such themes and stories for the Kosovar society. In the Kosovar context, cinema functions as a way to overcome the ethnocentric dynamics that legitimised hate, violence, sufferings and atrocities against ethnic others. It expresses the collective unspoken aim to reveal problems, and conceptualises a multicultural perspective on identity for a peaceful coexistence and the tackling of social fragmentation.

There are various initiatives aiming at developing a united and collaborative society between Serb Kosovars and Albanian Kosovars, such as those undertaken in the tourism and judicial sectors.[10] With regard to film production,the KCC has financed not only Albanian Kosovar directors, but also foreign directors such as, Italian filmmaker Laura Bispuri, French artist Mathieu Jouffre, American writer and producer Pamela Cohn, Macedonian film directors Igor Ivanov and Borjan Zafirovski, Slovenian director Marija Zidar and Croatian filmmaker Simon Bogojevic-Narath. While there were no Kosovar filmmakers of Serbian ethnicity in the film projects funded by the KCC, one hopes that the values of a multicultural society and country will prevail and there will be no further need to focus on the Albanian-Serbian division within Kosovo.

Cinema in Kosovo is currently undergoing a significant transformative phase: as evident in the latest films, local dynamics serve as a background for reflecting on global issues, and addressing universal problems. In this passage from local to global, the Kosovar narrative framework is forming its new identity, sharing its story with the world and being part of it.

NOTES

1. The clashes between Serbs and Albanian Kosovars in Kosovo culminated in 1999 during the regime of Milošević. In the spring of the same year, NATO conducted a 79-day bombing campaign against Serbia to protect Albanian Kosovars from Serbian hostilities (Waller et al. 2001).
2. The President of Kosovo, Hashim Thaçi, reaffirms this concept stating: 'Kosovo will remain multi-ethnic (society). But we have to solve animosities that exist for more than 200 years' (KoSSev, 2018).
3. At the time of writing, five European Union member states – Spain, Slovakia, Cyprus, Romania and Greece – as well as three Balkan countries – Bosnia and Herzegovina, North Macedonia and Serbia – do not recognise Kosovo's statehood. However, Kosovo has been in close contact with the EU, having signed in 2015 the Stabilisation and Association Agreement (SAA) with the purpose of implementing EU-related reforms, including political dialogue and cooperation opportunities. Moreover, the European Reform Agenda (ERA) was launched in November 2016 with the goal of maximising the economic and political benefits of the SAA (Republic of Kosovo 2016). In addition, the Berlin process, launched in 2014, is boosting cooperation in the Western Balkan area. Kosovo has signed cooperation agreements with Albania, North Macedonia and Montenegro and continues to maintain good economic and cooperation ties with Turkey. Kosovo concluded the border demarcation agreement with Montenegro in 2018, fulfilling one of the key criteria for its visa liberalisation (see USAID Final Report 2017; European Commission Kosovo 2018 Report).
4. As the constitution defines the Republic of Kosovo as 'a multi-ethnic society consisting of Albanian and other Communities' (Article 3), recognising both Albanian and Serbian as official languages (Article 5) and stressing that 'the flag, the seal and the anthem are the state symbols of the Republic of Kosovo all of which reflect its

multi-ethnic character' (Article 6), the implication is that the term 'Kosovar' no longer refers only to citizens of Albanian ethnicity.

5. NiKo Film also co-produced *Babai* (Visar Morina, 2015).

6. From 1945 to 1980 during Tito's presidency 'a series of policy and constitutional changes occurred aiming to stimulate peaceful development in the region, and the granting of certain autonomous powers to ethnic Albanians in Kosovo' (Shan 2014: 53). More specifically, in 1974 the Yugoslav constitution recognised the autonomous status of Kosovo, giving the province *de facto* self-government. Following Tito's death in 1981, a series of protests and riots took place in Kosovo, suppressed by the army. In 1989, the Yugoslav president Slobodan Milošević removed the status of Kosovo as an autonomous province of Serbia within Yugoslavia laid down by the 1974 constitution, thus stripping it of the modest degree of self-determination it enjoyed thus far.

7. With a budget of 1.7 million euros, *Babai* is the most expensive Kosovar film to date (Morton 2015).

8. However, Kosovo participated in October 2018 in the Balkan Film Market in Tirana (Albania), which is an event under the patronage of Eurimages.

9. More information can be found at <https://womenactivistsmuseum.com>.

10. As reported by SPARK (2015), on 16 June 2015, a 'multi-ethnic round table discussion' was held in Prishtina with Serbian and Albanian Kosovar representatives to promote Kosovo's tourism. On the judicial sector, see European Commission Kosovo Report (2018: 3).

References

Albertini, Matteo (2012) 'Kosovo: An Identity between Local and Global', *Ethnopolitics Papers*, 15 (2) <https://www.psa.ac.uk/sites/default/files/page-files/EPP015_0.pdf> (last accessed 7 December 2018).

Amnesty International Report (2107) *Wounds That Burn Our Souls. Compensation for Kosovo's Wartime Rape Survivors, But Still No Justice* <https://www.amnesty.org/download/Documents/EUR7075582017ENGLISH.PDF> (last accessed 31 March 2019).

Andersen, Aasmund (2002) *Transforming Ethnic Nationalism in Kosovo – The Potential of 'Kosovar' Identity*, Paper presented at the Regional Meeting for the SouthWest/Texas Popular Culture Association and American Culture Associations, New Mexico, pp. 1–6.

Beronja, Vlad and Vervaet, Stijn (2016) *Post-Yugoslav Constellations: Archive, Memory, and Trauma in Contemporary Bosnian, Croatian, and Serbian Literature and Culture*. Berlin/Boston: De Gruyter.

Bilibani, Eroll (2017) 'Fighting Stigmatization on Film. Kosovo's Latest Oscar Entry Tackles the Aftermath of Wartime Sexual Violence', *Kosovo 2.0*, 21 October <http://kosovotwopointzero.com/en/fighting-stigmatization-film/> (last accessed 7 December 2018).

Council of Europe (2018) *European Convention on Cinematographic Co-Production*, Chart of signatures and ratifications of Treaty 147, Status as of 7 December <https://www.coe.int/en/web/conventions/full-list/-/conventions/treaty/147/signatures> (last accessed 7 December 2018).

Croucher, Stephen M. and Kramer, Eric (2017) 'Cultural Fusion Theory: An Alternative to Acculturation', *Journal of International and Intercultural Communication*, 10 (2), pp. 97–114.

Economou, Vasilis (2018a) 'Kosovo and Macedonia sign a co-production agreement at Cannes', *Cineuropa*, 16 May <http://cineuropa.org/en/newsdetail/354554> (last accessed 7 December 2018).

Economou, Vasilis (2018b) 'LGBT Drama *The Marriage* Aiming for an Oscar Nomination', *Cineuropa*, 4 September <https://cineuropa.org/en/newsdetail/359745/> (last accessed 9 December 2018).

Eleftheriou, Anastasia (2014) 'Isa and Donat Qosja on *Three Windows and a Hanging*', *East European Film Bulletin*, November <https://eefb.org/interviews/isa-and-donat-qosja-on-three-windows-and-a-hanging/> (last accessed 23 March 2019).

Elsie, Robert (2004) *Historical Dictionary of Kosovo*. Lanham, MD: Scarecrow Press.

Elsie, Robert (2011) *Historical Dictionary of Kosovo*, 2nd edn. Lanham, MD: Scarecrow Press.

European Commission (2018) *Kosovo 2018 Report*, Commission Staff Working Document, Strasbourg, 17 April <https://ec.europa.eu/neighbourhood-enlargement/sites/near/files/20180417-kosovo-report.pdf> (last accessed 7 December 2018).

GjilaniInfo (2015) 'Kineastët dyshojnë në 5 milionë investime të huaja', 9 February <https://www.gjilani.info/?p=25550> (last accessed 18 February 2019).

Grater, Tom (2017) '*The Marriage* Director Talks Emerging Kosovan Film Industry', *Screendaily*, 1 December <https://www.screendaily.com/features/the-marriage-director-talks-emerging-kosovan-film-industry/5124619.article> (last accessed 7 December 2018).

Hapçiu, Annea and Sparks, Robert (2012) *The Internal Effect of the Kosovo: The Young Europeans Branding Campaign on the Kosovar People*. Friedrich Ebert Stiftung. Friedrich Ebert Foundation, October <http://library.fes.de/pdf-files/bueros/kosovo/09780.pdf> (last accessed 7 December 2018).

Hasa, Gresa (2018) 'Martesa(t) e pakurorëzuara', *Kosovo 2.0*. 3 April <http://kosovotwopointzero.com/martesat-e-pakurorezuara> (last accessed 7 December 2018)

Hjort, Mette (2011) 'Small Cinemas: How They Thrive and Why They Matter', *Mediascape: UCLA's Journal of Cinema and Media Studies*. 29 March <http://www.tft.ucla.edu/mediascape/Winter2011_SmallCinemas.html> (last accessed 7 December 2018).

Hjort, Mette (2010a) 'Affinitive and Milieu-building Transnationalism: the *Advance Party* Initiative', in Dina Iordanova, David Martin-Jones and Belén Vidal (eds), *Cinema at the Periphery*. Detroit, MI: Wayne State University Press, pp. 46–66.

Hjort, Mette (2010b) 'On the Plurality of Cinematic Transnationalism', in Nataša Ďurovičová and Kathleen E. Newman (eds), *World Cinemas, Transnational Perspectives*. New York: Routledge, pp. 12–33.

Holdsworth, Nick (2017) 'Oscars: Kosovo Selects "Unwanted" for Foreign-Language Category', *The Hollywood Reporter*, 13 September <https://www.hollywoodreporter.com/news/oscars-kosovo-selects-unwanted-foreign-language-category-1038462> (last accessed 7 December 2018).

Human Rights Watch (2000) 'Kosovo: Rape as a Weapon of "Ethnic Cleansing"', *RefWorld*, UNHCR, The UN Refugee Agency, 1 March. <https://www.refworld.org/docid/3ae6a87a0.html> (last accessed 8 December 2018).

Iordanova, Dina (2016) 'Foreword. The Film Festival and Film Culture's Transnational Essence', in Mareike de Valck, Brendan Kredell and Skadi Loist (eds), *Film Festivals: History, Theory, Method, Practice*. New York: Routledge, pp. xi–xvii.

Ivic, Sanja (2016) *European Identity and Citizenship: Between Modernity and Postmodernity*. London: Palgrave Macmillan.

Jin, Katusha (2018) 'Director More Raça: Telling Women's Stories, One Film at a Time (Part I)', *FF2 Media*, 29 July <http://ff2media.com/blog/2018/07/29/director-more-raca-telling-womens-stories-one-film-at-a-time-part-i/> (last accessed 8 December 2018).

Kakissis, Joanna (2018) 'In Kosovo, War Rape Survivors Can Now Receive Reparations. But Shame Endures for Many', *NPR*, 6 April <https://www.npr.org/sections/parallels/2018/04/06/598832041/in-kosovo-war-rape-survivors-can-now-receive-reparations-but-shame-endures-for-m> (last accessed 8 December 2018).

Kosova Sot (2018) 'Ministri Gashi: MKRS-ja rrit 100% buxhetin për Qendrën Kinematografike të Kosovës', *Kosova Sot Online*, 7 August <https://mobile.kosova-sot.info/lajme/297286/kosovasot/> (last accessed 8 December 2018).

Kosovo Cinematography Center (2018) *Film Catalogue 2017*, Prishtina <https://qkk-rks.com/uploads/files/2018/March/15/QKK_Catalog_20171521126632.pdf> (last accessed 8 December 2018).

Kosovo Cinematography Center (2019) *Annual Report 2018*. Prishtina <https://qkk-rks.com/uploads/files/2019/January/04/Raporti_Narrativ_i_QKK-se_per_vitin_20181546592493.pdf> (last accessed 29 March 2019).

Kosovo, Constitution of the Republic (2008), 15 June <http://www.kryeministri-ks.net/repository/docs/Constitution1Kosovo.pdf> (last accessed 8 December 2018).

Kosovo, Republic of (2016) *Memorandum of Understanding Entered into Between the Ministry of Culture, Youth and Sports of the Film and Television School of the Academy of Performing Arts in Prague (FAMU) and Kosovo Cinematography Centre (KCC)*, 25 November <https://qkk-rks.com/uploads/files/2019/January/04/Raporti_Narrativ_i_QKK-se_per_vitin_20181546592493.pdf > (last accessed 8 December 2018).

KoSSev (2018) 'Thaci: No Partition of Kosovo, No Land Swap', N1 English Edition. 27 August. <http://rs.n1info.com/a415009/English/NEWS/Kosovo-s-Thaci-says-there-won-t-be-eitherppartition-or-territory-swap-between-Belgrade-and-Pristina.html> (last accessed 8 December 2018).

Mehtaj, Valmir (2017) 'Not Another Supermarket. Arts NGO Anibar's Fight Against the Privatization of Kino Jusuf Gervalla', *Kosovo 2.0*, 30 March <http://kosovo-twopointzero.com/en/not-another-supermarket/> (last accessed 8 December 2018).

Ministria e Kulturës, Rinisë dhe Sportit, Republika e Kosovës (Ministry of Culture, Youth and Sports, Republik of Kosovo), 'Kosovafilmi' <https://www.mkrs-ks.org/?page=1,125> (last accessed 30 March 2019).

Morton, Elise (2015) 'Kosovo Enters Its Most Expensive Film for the Oscars', *Calvert Journal*, 10 September <https://www.calvertjournal.com/news/show/4672/kosovo-enters-its-most-expensive-film-for-the-oscars> (last accessed 31 March 2019).

Muco, Albana (2018) 'Albanian as a Pluricentric Language', in Rudolf Muhr and Benjamin Meisnitzer (eds), *Pluricentric Languages and Non-Dominant Varieties Worldwide: New Pluricentric Languages – Old Problems*. Frankfurt and Vienna: Peter Lang Verlag, pp. 171–83.

Murtic, Dino (2015) *Post-Yugoslav Cinema: Towards a Cosmopolitan Imagining*. London: Palgrave Macmillan.

Pavičić, Jurica (2012) 'Post-Yugoslav Film: Style and Ideology', *Moveast* <http://moveast.eu/103/post-yugoslav-film-style-and-ideology> (last accessed 7 December 2018).

Petković, Vladan (2017) 'Unwanted: A Release from Set Identities as a Path to Love', *Cineuropa*, 7 March <https://cineuropa.org/en/newsdetail/330803> (last accessed 8 December 2018).

Raça, More (2018) 'Telling Women's Stories to Drive Change', *#DirectedbyWomen*, 28 June <https://directedbywomen.com/more-raca-telling-womens-stories-to-drive-change/> (last accessed 31 March 2019).

Ramet, Sabrina P., Simkus, Albert and Listhaug, Ola (eds) (2015) *Civic and Uncivic Values in Kosovo. History, Politics, and Value Transformation*. Budapest: Central European Press.

Rascaroli, Laura (2013) 'On the Eve of the Journey: Tangier, Tbilisi, Calais', in Michael Gott and Thibaut Schilt (eds), *Open Roads, Closed Borders: The Contemporary French-Language Road Movie*. Bristol: Intellect, pp. 19–38.

Shan, Lanhe S. (2014) 'Analysis of Tito's Policies on Ethnic Conflict: The Case of Kosovo', *Journal of Living Together* ICERM, 1 (1), pp. 53–9.

Skutsch, Carl (2015) 'Yugoslavia', in Carl Skutsch (ed.), *Encyclopedia of the World's Minorities*, Vol. 1, A–F. New York and London: Routledge, pp. 1325–8.

'SPARK' (2015) 'Kosovo Develops a United Tourism Sector', *Spark Online*, 14 September <http://www.spark-online.org/kosovo-develops-a-united-tourism-sector/> (last accessed 9 December 2018).

Sweet, William, McLean, George F., Imamichi, Tomonobu, Ural, Safak and Faruk, Akyol O. (2008) *The Dialogue of Cultural Traditions: A Global Perspective*. Washington, DC: Council for Research in Values and Philosophy.

Travers, Eve-Anne (2017) 'Kosovo Filmmaker Explores Motherhood and Black Magic in Forthcoming Feature', *Prishtina Insight*, 12 December <https://prishtinainsight.com/kosovo-filmmaker-explores-motherhood-and-black-magic-in-forthcoming-feature-mag/> (last accessed 8 December 2018).

Tv21 (2015) 'Shala: Ministria e Kultures ka rreth 1.4 milion borxhe nga 2014-ta', *Tv21*, 1 August <https://tv21.tv/web/shala-ministria-e-kultures-ka-rreth-1-4-milion-borxhe-nga-2014-ta/> (last accessed 5 December 2018).

UNICEF (2013) 'Study on Dimensions of Domestic Violence Gender-based Violence in Kosovo Municipalities: Dragash/Dragaš, Gjakovë/Djakovica and Gjilan/Gnjilane 2013'. Prishtina: UNICEF Kosova. <https://www.unicef.org/kosovoprogramme/media/156/file/Final_Gender_based_violence_ENG.pdf> (last accessed 31 March 2019).

USAID (2017) *Kosovo Political Economy Analysis. Final Report 2017*, 26 December <https://usaidlearninglab.org/sites/default/files/resource/files/pa00n87p.pdf> (last accessed 31 March 2019).

Waller, Michael, Drezov, Kyril and Bülent, Gökay (eds) (2001) *Kosovo: The Politics of Delusion*. London and New York: Routledge.

Women Activists Museum <https://womenactivistsmuseum.com> (last accessed 07 September 2019).

Zajec, Špela (2014) 'Narcissism of Minor Differences? Problems of Mapping the Neighbour in Post-Yugoslav Serbian Cinema', in Ewa Mazierska, Lars Kristensen and Eva Näripea (eds), *Postcolonial Approaches to Eastern European Cinema: Portraying Neighbours on Screen*. New York: I. B. Tauris, pp. 201–26.

8. MONTENEGRO: A SMALL, OPEN AND FORWARD-LOOKING FILM INDUSTRY

Sanja Jovanović

With a population of 640,000 and an area of less than 14,000 square kilometres, Montenegro is the smallest country to emerge out of former Yugoslavia. Like its neighbours, it has faced many social, economic and political challenges related to the post-communist transition and to the establishment of a new independent country. Until Montenegro's independence in 2006, the country's cinematic history developed in the context of the Yugoslav Federation, and as a result, the process of identifying a national account has been rather difficult. Gojko Kastratović's (1999) history of Montenegrin cinema offers the first attempt to provide such an account, while the rest of the scholarship on Montenegrin cinema consists mainly of studies of individual Montenegrin authors active during the Yugoslav period.[1]

During the Yugoslav war and the breakup of the country, Montenegro joined Serbia in forming the Federal Republic of Yugoslavia in 1992, which later became a state union of Serbia and Montenegro from 2002 to 2006, when Montenegro proclaimed independence in June 2006 through a majority-backed referendum. For a decade, both countries endured a socio-economic crisis, intensified by the United Nations' embargo, which in the case of Montenegro led to an almost effective halt in film production, both local and foreign. During these years, the only films made were four short documentaries by Momir Matović and one never distributed feature film. Over the last decade, the conditions for the establishment of a Montenegrin cinema have gradually been improving, through a series of reforms and institutions that support film education, film preservation and, most crucially, local film production.

Since its independence, Montenegro has undergone a series of changes mostly as a result of its integration into a number of global and European contexts, which opened up new opportunities for the film sector. These included the Euro-Atlantic integration processes (such as joining NATO in 2017), membership in the Council of Europe, and the adoption of several European conventions, which served as blueprints for the drafting of the national cinema legislation.[2] Montenegro has also joined the European Film Promotion network, the EU's MEDIA programme, and the European Audiovisual Observatory. In the last decade or so, the country has experienced rapid social, cultural and economic development, a strengthening of national identity and also direct benefits from international cooperation and inward investment.

In the same period, Montenegrin cinema has also started to gain increased international visibility. It is regularly showcased at the Cannes Film Festival market as part of the Southeast Europe Pavilion, while a Montenegrin candidate for the nomination of American Film Academy is elected every year. A key development in the consolidation of what promises to be a thriving film industry in Montenegro is the founding of the Montenegrin Film Centre in 2017, which is the last of the former Yugoslav countries to establish a film centre. Furthermore, in January 2019 the country joined Eurimages, establishing Montenegro's presence in transnational film networks, and rewarding the film community's decade-long efforts to put Montenegro on the map of European collaborations.

In the process of this growth, a great number of small production companies have emerged, which helped to further promote an image of Montenegro across the world both as a location for foreign productions and as a small country that participates in successful regional co-productions. Nowadays, Montenegrin films premiere at prestigious film festivals such as Ivan Salatić's *Ti imaš noć*/*You Have the Night* (Montenegro/Serbia, 2018) at the Venice International Film Critics' Week, and Andro Martinović's *Između dana i noći*/*Never-ending Past* (Montenegro/Serbia, 2018) at the Montreal World Film Festival.[3]

This chapter aims to show how the last decade has been important in terms of building institutions and capacity for the development of a small but thriving film industry in Montenegro. The first part will explore how the industry has been successful in attracting foreign production shooting to generate profit and contribute to the professionalisation of film practitioners. The second part will focus on the establishment of institutions and laws which offer funding and development of national films, and provide an overview of film festivals and distribution networks. In addition to more funds being allocated for the production of national films, regional co-productions have become reignited after a period of stagnation, while Montenegro is increasingly geared towards even more European co-productions. The third part will provide an overview of contemporary Montenegrin feature and short films, and a discussion of the themes and stylistic tendencies of this new generation of Montenegrin filmmakers.

FOREIGN FILM PRODUCTIONS SHOT IN MONTENEGRO

Montenegro has attracted foreign film crews for its evocative and picturesque locations since cinema's early days. The first known film to be shot in Montenegro was the actuality *U crnim brdima, na Crnogorskom knjaževskome dvoru/ In the Black Hills, on Montenegrin Principal's Court* (1902) made by Hungarian Ferdinand Somogy and later shown in Vienna. Since then, many political and social occasions provided reasons for foreign filmmakers to shoot their films in the country, such as *Proglašenje Crne Gore za Kraljevinu i krunisanje kralja Nikole/The Proclamation of Montenegro as a Kingdom* in 1910.[4] In the late 1950s and 1960s, foreign film producers, mostly Italian, came to Montenegro not only for the breath-taking beauty of the nature as scenery for historical dramas, but also because the country offered the filmic know-how, through the production company, technical studio and distribution company (Lovćen Film, Mediteran Film and Zeta Film respectively) which were established in the federal republic in the context of socialist Yugoslavia. The blockbuster film production *The Long Ships* (Jack Cardiff, UK/Yugoslavia, 1964) distributed by one of the Hollywood majors, Columbia Pictures, and with an all-star cast Richard Widmark and Sidney Poitier was partly shot in Budva, a seaside town on the Adriatic coast of Montenegro. After the shooting, one of the main beaches was named 'Richard's head' and the giant bell which was made for filming purposes still remains by the fortress wall as a tourist attraction.

Montenegro was rediscovered again as an attractive film location in 2003, when the Italian director Ermano Olmi shot the adventure-drama film *Cantando dietro i paraventi/Singing Behind Screens* (Italy/UK/France) loosely inspired by the real-life events of a Chinese pirate Ching Shih on the Skadar lake (Koprivica 2017). More recently, it was the widely seen James Bond franchise *Casino Royale* (Martin Kempbel, UK/Czech Republic/USA/Germany/ Bahamas, 2006) that put Montenegro back on the global cinema map and drew tourists – who soon realised that there are no Eurostar trains in Montenegro, and that, besides the name of the hotel Splendid, nothing in the film was Montenegrin. Throughout the decade under examination, several foreign film productions were made in Montenegro, drawing many Hollywood celebrities to the country: Mark Ruffalo, Rachel Weisz and Adrien Brody for *The Brothers Bloom* (Rian Johnson, USA, 2008), Ralph Fiennes and Gerard Butler for *Coriolanus* (Ralph Fiennes, UK, 2011), Pierce Brosnan for *November Man* (Roger Donaldson, USA/UK, 2014) and Charlie Hunnam and Rami Malek for *Papillon* (Michael Noer, Czech Republic/Spain/USA, 2017). Montenegro's

Figure 8.1   Pierce Brosnan in *November Man* (Roger Donaldson, 2014), shot in Perast, Montenegro.

picturesque seacoast and old towns were used as the backdrop for events unfolding in all these films: the boat scene in *The Brothers Bloom* was shot in Petrovac, the old town of Kotor provided establishing shots for *Coriolanus*, the streets of Perast can be seen in action and driving scenes in *November Man*, while the small island and fortress Mamula stood for the French Guinea's Devil's Island in *Papillon*.

The importance of promoting Montenegro as a film destination was recognised by the state and Film Centre of Montenegro in 2017, which introduced incentives for foreign producers that intend to film in Montenegro, such as the cash rebate up to 20 per cent on the invested funds for a film or television project (not as high, but comparable to the cash rebates given by neighbouring countries, such as Slovenia and Serbia 25 per cent, Malta 27 per cent and Cyprus 35 per cent). Since December 2018, the refund increased to up to 25 per cent to cover eligible expenditures spent in Montenegro for the making of the film and is granted to producers if they meet certain conditions (Filmski Centar Crne Gore 2019). These foreign film productions brought well-needed foreign capital into the country and the industry, and provided opportunities for local film production crews and companies to improve their practice. One local company, Artikulacija, which uses the slogan 'Bringing the World to Montenegro', has been providing production services to foreign companies for film, TV commercials and music video shoots since 2001. Together with other factors further discussed below, such as the founding of the Montenegrin Cinémathèque and a university filmmaking department, the activity and investment of these international productions in the country has contributed to the professionalisation of the Montenegrin film industry.

INSTITUTIONALISATION AND THE ROAD TO EUROPE

The founding of the Faculty of Dramatic Arts in Cetinje in 1994, notably the departments for acting, direction, screenwriting and production, was the first step toward rejuvenation and development of contemporary Montenegrin cinema. This was followed by the establishment of the Montenegrin Cinémathèque in 2000, which aimed at the preservation and restoration of old Montenegrin films – often with the participation of international partners – and the promotion of contemporary works.[5] Support in film production began in 2002, when the Ministry of Culture of Montenegro released funds for feature films, shorts, documentaries and animations. This enabled a new generation of filmmakers to develop a new aesthetic direction, differentiating the image of Montenegro from its stereotypical cinematic representations, as established during the Yugoslav era – especially through what Sehad Čekić (2016) called the 'swords and fiddles' genre. These new films deal with contemporary urban stories and introduced a cinema of author-directors. In *Opet pakujemo majmune/Packing the Monkeys, Again* (Marija Perović, Serbia and Montenegro, 2004), the story of a young couple is told from the perspective of a man with amnesia; *Imam nešto važno da vam kažem/I Have Something Important to Tell You* (Željko Sošić, Serbia and Montenegro, 2005) adopts the Dogme 95 approach to follow the life of a young musician; *Pogled sa Ajfelovog tornja/A View from Eiffel Tower* (Nikola Vukčević, Serbia and Montenegro/Slovenia/Croatia, 2005) explores sexual exploitation and the tough choices faced by a young woman in the Balkans. The critical and commercial success of these films within the region (*Packing the Monkeys, Again* was awarded Best Film, Best Actress and Best Supporting role at the Film Festival in Novi Sad, while *A View from Eiffel Tower* had the largest admission rates in Serbia and Montenegro in 2005), along with the emergence of a new generation of directors, producers and screenwriters, led the way for the establishment of a solid film industry in Montenegro.

These foundations were further reinforced in 2015 with the adoption of the Law on Cinematography, which led to the establishment of the Filmski centar Crne Gore/Film Centre of Montenegro in 2017. This institution has diversified and expanded the sources of revenue for film production, as besides the government's annual budget allocated to film support, there is also a dedicated film fund that draws on levies from cinematographic works. These include income from marketing, commercial broadcasters with national coverage, cable, satellite and Internet distribution providers, cinema tickets and video-on-demand rental services. This income leads to the significantly larger fund for development and production of around 900,000 euros ('Nacionalni Program Razvoja

Kinematografije' 2018). The Centre also supports film promotion and complementary film activities, such as film festivals, as well as the work of professional associations such as the Association of Film Producers and Directors, and the Actors' Association of Montenegro. These endeavours have greatly helped to professionalise the film sector, rendering it increasingly visible and engaged in agreements for future cooperation.

The institutionalisation process also resulted in the reorganisation of old film festivals, and the foundation of new internationally oriented ones, which signalled the readiness and willingness of the Montenegrin film community to form transnational links and communicate through the art of film. There are currently seven international film festivals in Montenegro, with different programme orientations, among which the most important is the Montenegro Film Festival Herceg Novi, founded in 1987 as the Festival of Yugoslav Film. While in the 1990s the festival showcased Serbian and Montenegrin cinema, since independence it has become international and regional, focusing on cinema from South Eastern Europe. Since 2009, its significance for Montenegrin culture was recognised by the Ministry of Culture as it provides it with regular funding, while the other festivals receive support only through public calls. The Herceg Novi festival takes place at the peak of the tourist season, in August, attracting large and diverse audiences. It offers both competition programmes (feature, documentary and student film) and non-competition programmes (for example Kino Evropa or Midnight Screening). In 2018, the festival introduced a mini-pitch programme aimed at students to present their projects and compete for the production prize. Among other festivals, of great importance for the local film scene is UnderhillFest, established in 2010 in Podgorica, an independent festival dedicated to full-length documentary films from around the world, which also focuses on developing the documentary scene in Montenegro through the organisation of professional workshops. In this context, in 2018, it introduced CIRCLE, an international platform helping to finance documentary film projects made by women. Held every year in June in open-air improvised locations, UnderhillFest has built its own regular audience.

In addition to film festivals, Montenegro still has a fairly successful cinema theatre circuit, even though similarly to other former Yugoslav countries, piracy is a real issue and cinema audience numbers have dwindled since the breakup. In 2008, the oldest cinema theatre Kultura in the capital city of Podgorica closed down, and the first multiplex cinema, part of the Greek chain Ster Cinema, opened. The multiplex offered a quality viewing experience to Montenegrin audiences and a regular repertoire of Hollywood blockbusters released simultaneously to the rest of the world. According to the director of Ster Cinema in Montenegro Goran Škuletić (now director of Cineplexx Podgorica), the multiplex brought back the cinema-going habit to the Podgorica community. In 2011, Ster Cinema was acquired by the Austrian Cineplexx, which introduced 3D projections. Four years later, as a result of private-public partnership, Cadmus Cineplex opened in Budva, the most visited tourist town in Montenegro. By 2019, the country had two fully operating digital cinemas (Cineplexx in Podgorica and Cadmus Cineplex in Budva) with regular screenings on ten screens. The other two digital cinemas operating in Nikšić (in the projection hall of the Hotel Yugoslavia) and Tivat (in the Cultural Centre) since 2007, do not offer a regular repertoire, while some municipal cultural centres occasionally organise screenings.

Montenegrin Cinema Goes Out to the World

Under socialist Yugoslavia, each republic of the federation had an autonomous production and distribution film company, but films were made collaboratively with artistic, technical and financial resources shared among companies from different republics (Čekić 2016). Montenegro's film company, Lovćen Film, was founded in Cetinje in 1949, and its first production was *Lažni car/The Fake Tzar* (Velimir Stojanović, Yugoslavia, 1955), a historical biopic about a self-proclaimed tsar, Šćepan Mali (Šćepan the Little), at the end of eighteenth century. In terms of successful film professionals of Montenegrin origin working across pan-Yugoslav productions, we can note the renowned animator Dušan Vukotić for the Oscar-winning animated short *Surogat/Surrogate* (Yugoslavia, 1961) produced by the Zagreb Animation School, Veljko Bulajić the director of the partisan war epic *The Battle on the River Neretva*, and the Montenegrin-born Croatian director Krsto Papić for the political thriller *Lisice/Handcuffs* (Yugoslavia, 1970). Known for his provocative films that explored Montenegrin mentality and identity, Živko Nikolić (1941–2001) was one of the most prominent Montenegrin authors active in the 1970s and 1980s. In films such as *Beštije/Beasts* (Yugoslavia, 1977), *Čudo neviđeno/ Unseen Wonder* (Yugoslavia, 1984) or *U ime naroda/In the Name of the People* (Yugoslavia, 1987) he developed a unique style that juxtaposed people and natural beauty, myth and reality, poverty and wealth, humour and tragedy.

Since independence, Montenegro, due to its size and output, seems to fit Bordwell and Thompson's definition of 'smaller producing countries' (2005:79), referring to a country that produces a small number of films or a small country that produces films. In pursuit of quality productions and greater visibility for the films, Montenegro turned to cross-border collaboration with the countries from the former Yugoslavia (in most of the film productions), which came natural as all of the countries share similar languages, history, cultural values, production models and practices, institutions – and similar problems! The co-production arrangements were triggered by insufficient finances for completing films and the lack of film post-production facilities in Montenegro. This model of production, as well as the thematic focus of the films, resonates with the transnational character of Montenegrin cinema and in particular Mette Hjort's (2010) 'affinitive transnationalism'.

From 2008 to 2018, nine films made in Montenegrin majority co-production arrangements with countries in the region have been of great importance for Montenegrin cinema, not only in financial terms, but also as recognition that Montenegrin filmmakers had interesting stories to tell. The first film to receive any official support from one of the regional funds, in this case from the Croatian Audiovisual Centre, was *Gledaj me/Look at Me* (Montenegro, 2008), directed by Marija Perović (known for her first feature film *Packing the Monkeys, Again*), which featured two Croatian actors in the leading roles. Based on the novel *Dječak iz vode/A Boy from the Water* by the Montenegrin author Ksenija Popović, the film tells a story about generational conflicts in a small town. During the same period, eleven films directed by prominent authors from the region were supported by the Ministry of Culture of Montenegro as minority co-productions. Worth highlighting here is *Ti mene nosiš/You Carry Me* (2015) by the Croatian female director Ivona Juka, a co-production with Croatia, Slovenia, Serbia and Montenegro. This film did not receive any official funding from Montenegro; however, the Montenegrin Galileo production was involved in providing some production services. This suggestive social drama is about three daughters coming to terms with their criminal father and his illness. It was entirely made in Croatia and in Croatian, and does not have any distinctive Montenegrin cultural features. However, the participation of several Montenegrin creative collaborators allowed it to fill the required quota to qualify as Montenegrin, and it was selected as the Montenegrin nominee for Best Foreign Language Film at the 88th Academy Awards.

Judging from the international festival success and critical reception,[6] the most interesting Montenegrin film was *Posljednje poglavlje/The Ascent* (Montenegro/ Slovenia, 2011), the debut feature film of a young director and script co-writer Nemanja Bečanović. It was produced by the aforementioned company Artikulacija, in collaboration with the Slovenian production company Arkadena Studio, which provided technical equipment for the shoot and finally joined the project as a co-producer.

The main female role was played by the Slovenian actress Inti Šraj, and cinematography was signed by the Slovenian Jure Verovšek. The film received funding from the Ministry of Culture in 2008, and had a world premiere at the Sarajevo Film Festival, having been developed through the festival's Cine-Link co-production programme. This horror story revolves around a writer struggling to finish his first novel, who, in pursuit of inspiration, goes to a friend's remote country estate, where he meets an alienated, illiterate family of farmers that have no contact with civilisation. The strange family, headed by the hardened old man, has merged with the surrounding nature. Regardless of their unfriendly attitude, harsh nature and suspicious sexual relations, the writer decides to stay with the family, wandering the surrounding mountains and watching them in their everyday routine. The writer's intellectual control

Figure 8.2   Official poster for *The Ascent* (Nemanja Bečanović, 2011).

is just an illusion; his fate is in their hands from the moment he entered their lives. The obscure mountain landscape, shot in remote Montenegrin locations, in combination with the use of rich stylistic tools, builds an oppressive atmosphere that holds the viewer's attention through the whole film.

With the exception of 2009 when the Ministry of Culture did not finance any films due the global economic crisis, between 2002 and 2017 (the year the Film Centre of Montenegro was established), the Ministry of Culture supported ninety-two film projects, with an average annual budget of 253,333 euros, including feature fiction, documentary, short fiction and animated films, and co-productions (Filmski Centar Crne Gore and 'Nacionalni Program Razvoja Kinematografije' 2018). Although the average annual number of films supported may seem significant in terms of Montenegrin production potentials, they take a long time to develop and complete, usually because state budgets are insufficient and alternative models of financing are limited.

As only legal entities can apply for film production support through the ministry's open calls, a large number of small production companies have opened to take advantage of these opportunities. This was further intensified by the increasing interest of foreign productions to shoot in Montenegro. By 2018, thirty-three film production companies operated in the country (sixteen run by producers and seventeen by directors), producing various audio-visual projects

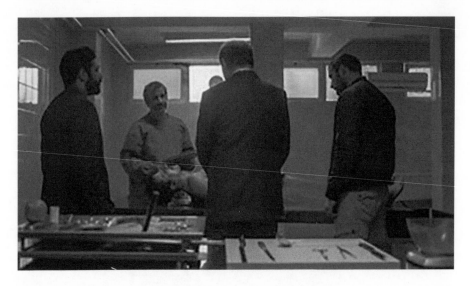

Figure 8.3   Still from *Lowdown* (Pavle Simonović, 2016).

and providing services for foreign productions wanting to film in picturesque Montenegrin locations. The leading Montenegrin production companies are Artikulacija, Galileo production, B-Film Montenegro, Cut-Up, Adriatic Western, Meander film, Montenegro Max Film and ABHO Film. From 2008 to 2018, they produced twenty-five feature fiction films – only five of them entirely national. The most successful national films were: an action film starring Michael Madsen, *As pik/Ace of Spades – Bad Destiny* (Draško Đurović, Montenegro, 2012), a stylistically fresh, dark thriller set in contemporary Podgorica entitled *Ispod mosta, među stijenama/Lowdown* (Pavle Simonović, Montenegro, 2016) and *The Books of Knjige – Slučajevi Pravde/The Books of Knjige – Cases of Justice* (Zoran Marković, Montenegro, 2017), a comedy made by the famous comedy group called 'The Books of Knjige', greatly anticipated by the audiences in the region.[7]

Evident from the majority of the films produced in last decade, contemporary Montenegrin films draw inspiration from the people and small communities with their secrets, while the authorial approach of each director suggests a diversity of style and genre. The most successful Montenegrin film in terms of visibility and circulation is the family drama *Dječaci iz ulice Marksa i Engelsa/The Kids from the Marx and Engels Street* (Montenegro/Slovenia, 2014), directed by Nikola Vukčević. The film brought back domestic audiences to cinema theatres and scored the highest admission rates at home, gaining third place in the domestic box office with over 12,500 tickets in one cinema (Cineplexx in Podgorica). It travelled the world and received numerous nominations and awards at international festivals (among others, the SEE Festival in Paris, Raindance, Cairo, Cottbus and the Boston Independent Film Festival). The film revolves around a story of two brothers exploring existential and economic problems typical of all post-Yugoslav societies and often leading to emigration in pursuit of a better life. The project received funding from the Ministry of Culture of Montenegro and from the Slovenian Film Fund in 2010, and was made in collaboration with Croatian and Serbian production companies as minority partners. Vukčević, an experienced commercial, music video, TV and film director, adopted a dynamic and lively visual style and, due to the regional success of his previous film, managed to attract a great number of actors from former Yugoslavia – all of which contributed to the film's popularity.

Igla ispod praga/The Black Pin (Montenegro/Serbia, 2016), directed and written by Ivan Marinović, is a comedy about a priest, Father Petar, who, due to a series of personal misfortunes, is afraid that the universe is indifferent and God no longer intervenes. As he tries to find peace, a large property sale is about to happen in his seaside parish in Montenegro and he becomes deeply involved in complicated intrigues between the inhabitants, which give meaning to his life again. Produced by the director's own company, Adriatic Western and in co-production with EED Production from Serbia, the film involved several Serbian actors and film crew members. The film's dialogue is full of local jokes drawn from the customs of the inhabitants of this small seaside village. The film plays with stereotypical representations of Montenegrins, which appeals to a regional audience familiar with these traits, but places them in the novel context of real-estate speculation. The film had significant success in the domestic and

Figure 8.4   Nikola Ristanovski as Father Petar in *The Black Pin* (Ivan Marinović, 2016).

regional markets (4,170 admissions in Montenegro; 7,035 in Serbia, North Macedonia and the Republic of Srpska), winning several awards at film festivals and becoming Montenegro's submission to the Academy Awards in 2017.

The most recent example of a successful Montenegrin transnational project is *You Have the Night*. A co-production between Montenegro and Serbia, it was also supported by Qatar's Doha Film Institute, introducing a new global partner in film production. This existential drama follows Sanja on her way back home from a cruiser where she had been working. She returns to the small Montenegrin seaside town Bijela, where a historical shipyard is being shut down leaving much of the population without a job. These dire circumstances are presented through a characteristic atmosphere where slow pace, gray winter colours and rare dialogues merge with the sound of the sea and wind. The film was selected for the Settimana della Critica programme at the Venice Film Festival 2018, and the success of this film, made by young Montenegrin filmmakers, marks a positive trend in Montenegrin cinema.

Finally, a new wave of short films with a captivating style made by young Montenegrin filmmakers who had graduated from Faculty of Drama Arts in Cetinje has gained recognition throughout Europe in the last decade. The short film, *Sve to/All of That* (Branislav Milatović, Montenegro, 2012), is based on the story by a young award-winning Montenegrin author Ognjen Spahić and focuses on a father and son relationship. In order to draw the boy's attention away from the funeral of a school friend, the father takes him on a fishing trip. Through a series of beautiful scenes and spectacular landscapes, the author creates a singular narrative, which reveals the difficulty of a father's natural intention – to protect his own son, as the boy shows maturity beyond his age. This touching drama had a successful presentation at more than thirty festivals, including Sarajevo, Zagreb, Tirana, Drama, Ljubljana, regionally, but also Hamburg, Nice, Portugal, Poland, Lithuania and Morocco further afield.

Umir krvi/Tranquillity of Blood (Senad Šahmanović, Montenegro/Serbia, 2015) is another short film based on the story of the young Montenegrin novelist, Stefan Bošković that had a very successful festival life. This picturesque drama deals with a theme deeply rooted in the Montenegrin tradition – that of blood feud. The story revolves around Drago and Persa who, having lost their son ten years ago, stage Drago's death and funeral in order to attract their son's murderer back to the village. However, an unexpected twist occurs at the end leaving viewers with the possibility of forgiveness. The film won major awards in Drama (Greece) and Banja Luka (Bosnia-Herzegovina) in 2015. Another young director, Dušan Kasalica, was awarded in Sarajevo for *Biserna obala/A Matter of Will* (Montenegro/Serbia, 2015), and a year later for *Soa* (Montenegro, 2017). Kasalica became widely known for his exceptional style and the uniqueness of the themes. Supported by the Montenegrin Ministry of Culture, *A Matter of Will* is a charming but sad story about the monotony of everyday life, inspired by the Montenegrin reality in which young people suffer from the lack of opportunities (Minić 2016). The story takes place in a weight loss camp for children, located in a ruined seaside resort, led by an authoritarian instructor using the ideology of 'Men's Health'. The success of these young directors and their short films has greatly contributed to promoting Montenegrin cinema in the region and beyond, paving the way for new possibilities and collaborations.

Conclusion

Through an overview of the institutional developments and transnational processes after independence, this chapter has provided a picture of the contemporary developments in Montenegrin cinema highlighting the extent to which it has both dynamically embraced new opportunities and asserted established links. The opening of the country to international productions has offered financial benefits, but has also contributed to the professionalisation of a new generation of producers and crew members. Furthermore, limited national funding and restricted visibility, partly due to the country's small size, has led to a further reinforcement of co-productions with the countries from the former Yugoslavia, illustrating 'affinitive transnationalism' as these countries share a lot of cultural, social, political and linguistic references.

The progressive institutionalisation of the national film industry over the last decade, the establishment of film departments, film festivals opening up internationally, the creation of the Montenegrin Cinémathèque and the Film Centre of Montenegro, have all provided crucial steps towards building a fruitful cinema industry and a thriving film community. Nowadays, aside from attracting foreign action films and Hollywood blockbusters for the beauty of its picturesque locations, the small country of Montenegro and its film industry has produced a number of aspiring and successful young authors who are slowly emerging on the international film festival circuit, gaining critical acclaim and winning awards.

Notes

1. Among the most prominent Montenegrin authors from the Yugoslav period: Živko Nikolić, Velimir Stojanović, Ratko Đurović, scriptwriter of the famous partisan epic *Bitka na Nerevti/The Battle of Neretva* (Yugoslavia/Italy/West Germany/USA, 1969), and Dušan Vukotić, the first animator from the former Yugoslavia to win an Oscar.
2. Namely the following: the European Convention on Cinematographic Co-Production, the European Cultural Convention and the European Convention on the Protection of Audio-visual Heritage.
3. Other titles include: the shorts *Peloid* (Bojan Stijović, Montenegro, 2018) and *Tam 4500* (Momir Matović, Montenegro, 2018); the features *Sam samcat/All Alone* (Bobo Jelčić, Bosnia-Herzegovina/Croatia/Montenegro/Netherlands, 2018) and *Granice,*

kiše/*Borders, Raindrops* (Nikola Mijović and Vlastimir Sudar, Bosnia-Herzegovina/ Montenegro/Serbia, 2018) – all at the Sarajevo Film Festival; the short *Glava puna radosti*/*A Head Full of Joy* (Branislav Milatović, Montenegro/Serbia, 2018) at the Festival de Cine de Alicante, and *Lijenština*/*Lazy Guy* (Aleksa Stefan Radunović, Montenegro, 2018) at the Motovun Film Festival.

4. In August 1910, the ceremony and declaration of Montenegro as a Kingdom and Prince Nikola I Petrović as king, in the presence of the European courts, such as the Princess Jelena of Savoy, King Vittorio Emanuele and the Great Prince of Russia, was attended by many cameramen who recorded the event, and drew great interest from the European public according to Kastratović (1999).

5. Since 2010, the Montenegrin Cinémathèque has been a member of FIAF (the Fédération Internationale des Archives du Film) and ACE (Association des Cinémathèques Européennes).

6. The Raindance Film Festival, London; the Izmir Film Festival, Turkey; the European Film Festival, Palić; the Sarajevo Film Festival; the Montenegro Film Festival, Herceg Novi.

7. TBOK is a popular comedy group that has been running a radio show since 1994; from 2000 they started creating various TV formats – sketches, commercials. This is their first feature film and it attracted 40,000 spectators in local cinemas. After the producer's decision to bypass regional television distribution channels and upload it onto the RTCG (Montenegrin National Television Channel) YouTube channel, it received 120,000 views.

REFERENCES

Bordwell, David and Thompson, Kristin (2005) *Film History: An Introduction*. New York: McGraw-Hill.

Čekić, Sehad (2016) 'Crnogorski film: u potrazi za nacionalnim stilom', in Radmila Vojvodić and Janko Ljumović (eds), *Crnogorske studije kulture i identiteta*. Cetinje: Fakultet dramskih umjetnosti, pp. 46–83.

Filmski Centar Crne Gore (2017) 'Law on Cinematography of Montenegro 2015', *fcgg. me*, <http://fccg.me/wp-content/uploads/2017/12/Zakon-o-kinematografiji.pdf> (last accessed 10 April 2019).

Filmski Centar Crne Gore/Film Centre of Montenegro (2019) *fccg.me* <http://fccg.me/> (last accessed on 22 August 2019).

Hjort, Mette (2010) 'On the Plurality of Cinematic Transnationalism', in Nataša Ďurovičová and Kathleen E. Newman (eds), *World Cinemas, Transnational Perspectives*. New York: Routledge, pp. 12–33.

Hjort, Mette and Petrie, Duncan (2007) *The Cinema of Small Countries*. Edinburgh: Edinburgh University Press.

Kanzler, Martin (2008) *The Circulation of European Co-Productions and Entirely National Films in Europe 2001–2007*. Strasbourg: European Audiovisual Observatory.

Kastratović, Gojko P. (1999) *Crnogorska kinematografija i filmovi o Crnoj Gori*. Podgorica: Društvo za očuvanje baštine.

Koprivica, Veseljko (2017) 'Hoće li kauboji opet jahati po Durmitoru', *Al Jazeera Balkans*, 5 February < http://balkans.aljazeera.net/vijesti/hoce-li-kauboji-opet-jahati-po-durmitoru > (last accessed 18 March 2019).

Minić, Milica (2016) 'Dušan Kasalica: *Biserna obala*. Crna Gora kao filmski studio bez struje', *Camera Lucida*, 21–3 <https://cameralucida.net/test/index.php?option=com_content&view=article&id=555%3Aduan-kasalica-biserna-obala&catid=23%3Acl-21-23&Itemid=17> (last accessed 18 March 2019).

'Nacionalni Program Razvoja Kinematografije 2018–2023' (2018) *Ministarstvo Kulture/ Ministry of Culture* <http://webcache.googleusercontent.com/search?q=cache:b4Ty PcPWBn4J:www.gov.me/ResourceManager/FileDownload.aspx%3FrId%3D320318 %26rType%3D2+&cd=1&hl=en&ct=clnk&gl=me&client=safari> (last accessed 10 April 2019).

9. NORTH MACEDONIA: A NATION AND CINEMA IN TRANSITION

Vessela S. Warner

Whereas the history of North Macedonia's cinema has its official beginning in 1947, when the Film Skopje (Filmovo Skopje) agency and the producing company Vardar Film were established, the foundational history of the country which put a national stamp on over seventy decades of film productions is not that specific. The prolonged birth of the Republic of North Macedonia (RNM) has been guided by modernist models of collective identities and challenged by the postmodern currents of transnationalism, regionalism and globalisation for over a century. During modern history alone, the country's territory was part of various empires, kingdoms and states,[1] and developed a national culture based on autonomous language, literature and art only within communist Yugoslavia (1945–91). Between 1991 and 2018, following the federation's breakup, the independent Former Yugoslav Republic of Macedonia (FYROM), began to aggressively promote a sovereign nation-state. Its aspirations to construct a monolithic cultural identity often conflicted with the histories it shared with neighbouring Greece, Bulgaria and Serbia, as well as with its inherent ethnic and religious heterogeneity. After almost three decades of conservative nation-building, the 2018 agreement with Greece on the official name – North Macedonia – marked a victory for the country's international recognition, regional integration and economic stabilisation, which also became a 'victory for NATO [and] the European Union' (Zeneli 2019).

In the quagmire of refracting cultural politics that have accompanied its post-communist and particular post-Yugoslav transition, the North Macedonian film industry, especially during 2008–18, has developed various artistic and marketing strategies to attract local as well as international audiences and tackle national, but also global issues. The trajectory of this development relates to the social and aesthetic hybridity of postcolonial communities, which reveals the 'symbolic interaction' of differences: public and private, past and future, imperial and national (Bhabha 1994: 9). Using interdisciplinary frames, such as film and cultural studies, data analysis, and the theoretical junctions of postcolonialism and post-communism that inform all transitional cultures of the former Eastern bloc, this chapter analyses the economic and artistic tenets of North Macedonian cinema between 2008 and 2018. It focuses on its progressively expanding producing and co-producing abilities, and the effect they have on the films' aesthetic qualities alongside governmental cultural politics. The topical examination of North Macedonian fictional features advances a thesis of multiple and merging national representations, which are provisionally defined by their recollective, symbolic and reflective modes of collective unification. Ultimately, this study argues that in RNM, as well as in other post-communist countries, national but also regional – Balkan and ex-Yugoslav – narratives have become frequent and often successful cinematographic commodities on the global capitalist market, as well as constant modifiers of what is often read as European or transnational values.

Postcolonial Legacies and Transitional Politics

The Macedonian region, the most north-western parts of which falls in the RNM's borders, became internationally known as a knotted Balkan borderland with a predominantly 'Christian-orthodox population speaking an Eastern South Slavic (call it Macedonian or Bulgarian) dialect', which was the last to break out of the Ottoman colonisation (Voss 2007: 164–5). As a result of the World Wars' outcomes and significant international pressure, the territory was included in the Serbia-dominated Kingdom of Yugoslavia during 1918–41 and in 1945 became one of the six republics in the Socialist Federal Republic of Yugoslavia. The Yugoslav communist system created another distinct postcolonial legacy for RNM, which affected its relations within the former Yugoslavia, the larger Balkan region, and Europe.

Socialist Yugoslavia thrived as a supra-national totalitarian state with a dual east–west orientation as well as a centralised economy boosted by limited capitalist practices and foreign loans. During the 1950s and the 1960s the Yugoslav multiculturalism, although ideologically enforced as a proletarian brotherhood and unity among all the ethnic groups, enabled the Macedonian national idea, which was shaped after the modernist 'perennial' model of 'fundamental ethnic ties' and the cultural model of shared common language, faith, folklore, literature and art (Smith 1998: 223). This national self-determination, nevertheless, evolved parallel to the cultural self-expression also granted to the Turkish and Albanian minorities living within the territories of the Socialist Republic of Macedonia.[2] After the republic's secession in 1991, the largest minority group of Macedonian Albanians – about one third of the total population[3] – has actively sought political and cultural representation.[4] It has critically pitted the two largest parties of the Slavic Macedonian majority: the right-wing, ethnic-nationalist Internal Macedonian Revolutionary Organisation-Democratic Party of Macedonian National Unity (VMRO-DPMNE) and the centre-left and more ethnically inclusive Social Democratic Union for Integration (SDSM). Despite their political rivalry, both of these parties have tried to wedge nineteenth-century ethnic-state forms of nationalism into the heterogeneous multicultural models of civic nationalism exemplified by developed western democracies and, to some extent, the supra-national entity of the European Union (Smith 1998:121; Sutherland 2012: 34–40).

The still continuing post-communism of North Macedonia demonstrates postcolonial practices common for the rest of the former East European bloc, of which the most important are how the new country 'struggles to memorize, rewrite and reinterpret its history . . . and how it negotiates its continued semi-peripheral status in the European Union' (Şandru 2016: 169). Additionally, the consequences of communism's 'internal colonisation' – that is, the ideologically based political-economic oppression of one class over another – are manifested in authoritative mechanisms of governing and lacking civil activism and an independent judicial system. In general, the quasi-democratic politics of North Macedonia have been defined as "clubbish', dirty and corrupt', showing visible signs of conservative and neo-totalitarian party methods enabled in part by a slowly reforming legislature (Macedonia-Politics).[5] However, the underlined presence of VMRO-DPMNE as a leader of four coalition governments from 1998 to 2002 and from 2006 to 2016 has decisively shaped the country's political life. The party's most pronounced nationalistic (that is ethnic Macedonian) exclusionism materialised in an artistic 'renaissance', which embraced the ideas of ethnic purity and classical and Christian Europeanness, and became affirmative of the country's cultural branding.[6] VMRO-DPMNE's conflicting treatment of the Albanian minority[7] has bolstered the confidence of the Macedonian nationalist electorate and its tolerance of stereotypical representations of Albanians in mass media and TV production (Alagjozovski 2012: 175–6). The longest ruling party also halted diplomatic relations with Bulgaria by allowing fraudulent historical claims and the appropriation of its cultural heritage, and fuelled the dispute with Greece over the country's name and Hellenism-inspired state insignia. Paradoxically, the vigorous antiquisation of North Macedonian culture through the imperial legacy of Alexander the Great became VMRO-DPMNE's stratagem for closing the ethnic and religious cleavage, and cooperating with Albanian political parties in compliance with the requirements for EU membership. RNM's agrarian and light industrial economy, backed up by a conservative banking system, did not significantly feel the quivers of the 2007–8 world-market crisis, but it remained unstable and contributed to the increase of the social class gap. To counterbalance that, a false facade of prosperity and unity, often achieved through unreasonable spending and illegal activities, created a thin veneer of comfort and self-esteem. As a result of these neo-totalitarian contradictions, and the ensuing 2016 political crisis, a SDSM-led government came in power in 2017 and immediately began to repair the damage to the country's diplomatic relations and international image.

The post-communist RNM has honed particular cultural fluidity and adaptability in order to conduct a political decolonisation while entertaining its colonial imagination. Yugoslav nostalgia has projected a certain longing for a lost ancient glory and the material security provided by imperial belonging. Simultaneously, the continuous de-communisation has produced self-orientalising refractions of western views of the Balkans previously epitomised by the Macedonian Question[8] and epistemised in the Balkanist discourse.[9] Skewing national essentialism that originates in official as well as populist discourses, artistic reflections of North Macedonia's colonial legacies have made visible a rather 'hybrid nationalism . . . which cannot be contained within the nation-state' and which is reasoned by a complex desire for historical evaluation, regional/supra-national affiliation, and transcendence of human experiences (Sutherland 2012:45).

The Economies of North Macedonian Cinema

The post-2008 history of North Macedonian cinema is an integral part of the overall evolution of national film industry that could be characterised as compensatory yet conservative and simultaneously market-driven and tradition-centred. The most determining factor for RNM's film production after 2008 was the country's prior cinematographic cooperation, including shared resources and marketing, with the rest of the Yugoslav republics. After the collapse of communist regimes, their international relations continued to be viable, followed by North Macedonia's renewed ties with the rest of the Balkan neighbours and with old Western partners such as Germany, Italy and France. Priority in these relations was nevertheless given to the regional – ex-Yugoslav and Southeast European – cooperation, which acted as a safeguard for many smaller economies in the region after the 2007–8 global financial crisis (Stojcheska 2018).

The interest of the North Macedonian government to build a vibrant film industry as a tool of national self-identification and pride, but also as a capital investment, prompted the adoption of the Film Industry Law, which introduced economic incentives and European business standards, as well as led to the founding of the Macedonian Film Fund in 2006. The Fund, renamed as the Film Agency in 2014 and the North Macedonia Film Agency (NMFA, Agentzija za film na Republika Severna Makedonija) after 2018, manages state capital and some foreign grants,[10] and is the country's only legal entity for sponsoring films of national interest and national film festivals. It maintains that '[a] minimum of 75% of the budget should be spent locally . . . [and on] films that can return some of the invested money' (Teodosievski 2018: 35). A return of the investment, however, has been a less feasible task since 'the film industry in the former Yugoslavia is vastly underfunded' and local productions have not made any return on their input in the last ten years (Brownell 2011; Zikov 2019).

Business opportunism and the political significance of national film production explain the Agency's increasing budget: from 800,000 euros in 2007 to 5.2 million euros in 2018, with the highest budget of 6 million euros recorded for 2017 (Kostova 2019; Lazarevska 2017; North Macedonia 2018).[11] The overall cinematographic production during 2008–18 is impressive for the country's size and resources: over 150 films, of which fifty-five fictional motion pictures classified as follows: eight fully national productions national productions, twenty co-productions with majority financing and thirty minority co-productions (Kostova 2019; Stojcheska 2018).[12] Additionally, during the same period, the Film Agency has funded over fifty feature documentaries, seventy shorts and fifteen animations (Kostova 2019; NMFA). Whereas the majority financed productions fulfilled the Film Agency's primary goal to provide 'a continuous support to the production of films of national interest', they have struggled on the local and international markets (NMFA). The steady and more prolific release of minority productions, on the other hand, have compensated for the lack of 'infrastructure, including equipment, crews and post-production' facilities' (Brownell 2011). Moreover, they have assured the viability of national film production by chartering new artistic territories and attracting international audiences.

Between 2016 and 2018, two minority financed films entered the Official Selection at Cannes: *Sieranevada* (Cristi Puiu, Romania/Bosnia-Herzegovina/Croatia/North Macedonia/France, 2016) and *Ahlat agaci/The Wild Pear Tree* (Nuri Bilge Ceylan, Turkey/France/Germany/Bulgaria/North Macedonia/Bosnia-Herzegovina/Sweden, 2018). Additionally, *Posoki/Directions* (Stephan Komandarev, Bulgaria/North Macedonia/Germany, 2017) was included in the Cannes Festival programme Un Certain Regard. From the majority pool, the internationally co-produced and distributed by Sisters and Brother Mitevski Production, *Zhenata koja si gi izbrisha solzite/The Woman Who Brushed Off Her Tears* (Teona Strugar Mitevska, North Macedonia/Germany/Slovenia/Belgium, 2012) premiered at the Berlin Film Festival (Panorama Special). Since then, it has also been presented at the 2013 Busan International Film Festival and 2014 edition of Visions Social, a side section to the Cannes Film Festival.

Figure 9.1   *Secret Ingredient* (Gjorce Stavreski, 2017).

In regard to international visibility, it is also important to note Gjorce Stavres-ki's feature debut *Izcelitel/Secret Ingredient* (North Macedonia/Greece, 2017), a majority funded co-production with Greece, which surprisingly won the Best Film Award given by the audience in the Balkan Survey selection of the 58th Thessaloniki International Film Festival (see Figure 9.1). The international cooperation in both majority and minority films productions has impacted the advancement of North Macedonian film professionals, while also building Europe's trust in the young country that still remains in the periphery of the democratic world.

Despite the increasing number of feature movies and generally steady box office between 2008 and 2018, the NMFA exhibited the flaws of any major state institutions in the country, such as nepotism, political complic-ity and financial mismanagement.[13] As a result, the national film production became less of a long-term business and cultural investment and more of a lucrative financial opportunity for appropriating state and foreign capi-tal (Teodosievski 2018: 35). This observation supports the notion of North Macedonia's hybrid – market-driven as well as centralised – economy, and explains the fast multiplication of producing companies: up to 100 private and, until 2013, only one, Vardar Film, state-owned, all of which apply for financing through the NMFA. In its turn, the state Film Agency has made significant efforts to revamp its marketing strategies by promoting local film-ing locations and taking into consideration the number of technical staff and shooting days in North Macedonia in the projects' evaluation for funding. Additionally, the NMFA offers 20 per cent cash rebate to foreign producers, and generally provides 'affordable taxes [and] low prices' for all filmmakers working in the country (Stojcheska 2018).

Regardless of the lucrative business incentives and local distribution efforts, the main source of box office revenue – slightly over 1 million euros each year for the period between 2014 and 2018 – continues to be foreign film imports. The numbers are realistic, considering that, as of 2018, there are only five movie theatres in the country (three commercial and two arthouse cinemas) in addition to eighteen cultural centres with film screening facilities: a stark contrast with the eighty-six theatres operating in 1972 (Teodosievski 2018: 35). Nevertheless, a positive sign for the local film market is the fact that in 2014 the number of cinema screenings and the size of audience returned to pre-2007 levels.

The opportunity to fund creative and cultural projects locally as well as to promote a national image to the world has led to the fast proliferation of film festivals – between twenty and twenty-five, most of them international (North Macedonia 2018). The Manaki Brothers Film Camera Festival, held annually in Bitola, celebrates forty years in 2019. Founded in 1979 by the Cinémathèque of Macedonia and the Association of Macedonian Filmmakers and the Stage as a national (that is Yugoslav) event, the festival became international in 1991, attracting serious world talent while also premiering and celebrating its own. Founded in 2003, the international Cinedays Festival of European Films, held annually in Skopje, features a CineBalkan section as well as Retrospectives and Student Film, among other programmes. It also offers educational workshops for audiences of various ages and interests. The annual Skopje Film Festival, celebrating its twentieth edition in 2019, offers selections from different genres, including shorts and documentaries, and focuses on European together with national productions. Part of the larger film-distribution circuit, the North Macedonian film festivals provide the best advertising for the industry and extend the knowledge of Balkan and European cinema history, artistic achievements and professional opportunities. Additionally, they strongly benefit the country's visibility and support its burgeoning tourist industry.

After a rather uncertain production development during 2008–13, mostly due to the industry's post-communist transformation of administrative and financial structures, North Macedonian cinematography underwent a deep reorganisation through the adoption of the Film Industry Law and the establishment of the NMFA. These changes provided a new infrastructure that set the basis for improving the industry's technical and artistic capabilities, as well as aligning it with the European film-production standards and global trades. Embracing the ideas of exchange and cooperation, the North Macedonian cinematography has made strong efforts to expand its co-producing and business opportunities internationally, driven by the country's attempt to promote aggressive capitalist reforms and recharge its economy.

CINEMATIC IMAGE OF A NATION IN TRANSITION

The cultural and artistic economies of twenty-first-century North Macedonia exhibit disparate postcolonial perceptions and self-representations, which are often steered by deep-nested populism and challenged by global multicultural-ism. In response to these tendencies, the national cinema after 2008 has shown a penchant for the quasi- and mytho-historical narratives fraught with traditional, exotic and even orientalising idioms. Many of the films produced between 2008 and 2018 have retreated to familiar at home and marketable abroad formulas of epic or comedic plots, often tapping into successful literary and theatre works to ensure high quality dramatic content. Similar cinematographic practices marked the emergence of the national discourse in the 1950s, when most of the pioneer screenwriters came from literary backgrounds – fiction and/or drama – to bring artistic expressiveness to the Macedonian language and empower the perfor-mances of Macedonian actors in joint productions of the Yugoslav republics (Holloway 1996: 9–15). During the period discussed in this chapter, the sce-narios of some of the most notable films were written by established North Macedonian playwrights such as Dejan Dukovski, whose *Balkanot ne e mrtov/ Balkan Is Not Dead* (Aleksandar Popovski, North Macedonia, 2013) adapts for the screen his award-winning play, Zanina Mirčevska, who scripted *Soba so pijano/The Piano Room* (Igor Ivanov, North Macedonia/Slovenia/Serbia, 2013), and Goran Stefanovski, who co-wrote the scenario of *Do balcak/To the Hilt* (Stole Popov, North Macedonia, 2014). These artists, among other screenwrit-ers or writers-directors, delivered strong dramatic structure and characters and introduced genre varieties. They often managed to transcend national boundar-ies and tell moving human stories set against a local background, thus integrat-ing a Macedonian historical narrative into the European master narrative and offering memorable, thought-provoking and self-examining images of a nation.

Regardless of its funding, certain characteristics can 'legally define the national identity of a film, [such as] language, location, the nationality of its makers, etc.' (Papadimitriou 2018: 218). National values and/or importance of a film, however, are much more nebulous categories, which consider a complexity of contextual, referential and stylistic aspects in a cinematographic work. Whereas dramas with a conflict between an individual and his/her specific historical background serve to recover past collective memories, relationship-centred stories set up against a distinct cultural and physical topography play a self-reflective role and often universalise the local milieu or exploit it for additional dramatic enhancement. The following analysis filters a decade of film productions in North Macedonia by using three provisional and often overlapping dimensions of the term 'national importance': national-recollective, national-symbolic and national-reflective. These categories emerge from and are emblematic of the different relations to col-lective identity presented by three feature films, which received funding directly from the government, rather than as a result of the NMFA's competition. In this case, state subsidy not only provided a 'helpful solution to the [Film Agency's] limited funds' but also recognised projects that the government deemed to be of national importance (Teodosievski 2018: 35). Evoking the recollective, symbolic and reflective sides of the national imaginary, respectively, the three films and the funding they received are: *Treto poluvreme/The Third Half* (Darko Mitrevski, North Macedonia/Czech Republic, 2012) – 1 million euros; *To the Hilt* – 2 million euros; and *Majki/Mothers* (Milcho Manchevski, North Macedonia/France/Bulgaria, 2010) – 500,000 euros.

Usually found among the documentaries created since 1991, the movies qualifying as national-recollective, revive histories of origin and past experiences of great importance for the national community. The choice of such historical cornerstones is not accidental as filmmakers attempt to restore specific collective memories and reset the nation's historical flow. Emblematic of this category, *The Third Half* offers subject matter and narrative mode that have a strong effect on local audiences. Based on a true story about a Macedonian football team coached by a German Jew, the film recounts the Nazi occupation of Skopje and the deportation of local Jews, which they carried out together with their ally, the Bulgarian fascist government. Composed as a romance set against the Second World War background and with the added tension of a football competition (see Figure 9.2), *The Third Half* emphasises the characters' ethnic identities by featuring dialog in six different languages. Its simplified melodramatic form, nevertheless, evokes expectable national-cathartic experiences through the love story and survival of the Jewish woman Rebecca and Macedonian athlete Kosta. This story symbolically endows Macedonians with the qualities of martyrdom and continuity, as it joins the larger Holocaust and European histories of survival and triumph. *The Third Half* became a national hit and was the official submission to the Best Foreign Language Film

Figure 9.2   *The Third Half* (Darko Mitrevski, 2012).

competition at the 85th Academy Awards (Nedelkovska 2012). Nevertheless, it did not receive the expected international attention and was critiqued for the insensitive, even provocative, depiction of the Bulgarian military – the only villains in this heroic epic.[14] Paradoxically, the ethnic castigation of the Bulgarian characters due to the film's simplified narrative form has also triggered a simplified political response in the opinion that North Macedonian attitudes professed in *The Third Half* strongly oppose 'our European values' ('Macedonian Film Infuriates Bulgaria' 2011).

Another film dealing with the same historical period was released in 2016: the adaptation of Dušan Jovanović's play *Osloboduvanje na Skopje/The Liberation of Skopje*, co-directed by internationally famed Croatian actor Rade Šerbedžija and his son, Danilo Šerbedžija (North Macedonia/Croatia /Finland). The little impressive fiction draws more unsettling juxtapositions of North Macedonia's Second World War enemies by employing cultural stereotypes and alluding to old East–West dichotomies. Film critic Sheri Linden writes: 'By comparison with the Bulgarian collaborators, who move through the town like mobsters, the Nazi is a genteel man of culture – which doesn't preclude rape from his social arsenal' (2011). At the end, the young German officer is assassinated by the communist guerilla-fighters, but is secretly mourned by Lica (Lucija Šerbedžija), his lover-by-necessity and a helpless mother constructed in the iconography of a 'Slavic Madonna'. Tackling the motif of power and violence – in war, politics and the family unit – the film appears to condemn foreign (mostly Bulgarian) occupation as well as communist dictatorship altogether. Consequently, it implies moral judgement foregrounded in perceptions of the tribal East versus the civilised West.

Only a few of the movies in the period examined deal with the crimes during totalitarianism, which not only suggests a movement away from this topic after 2000, but also resonates with the advancements of the Macedonian nation within the more relaxed Yugoslav communism. In *Zlatna petorka/The Golden Five* (Goran Trenchovski, North Macedonia, 2016), party loyalties are viewed as tools of human betrayal and personal pursuit of domination and possession. The movie, which deals with one of the most explored communist periods – the 1950s purges of Stalinist supporters in the former Yugoslavia – is based on true events that had initially inspired Bratislav Tashkovski's 2011 novel *Rascepen um, ili odneseno so chavkite/Split Mind, or Taken by the Craws*. The three works, briefly discussed here, put strong emphasis on historical memory and appear similar in their choices of realistic-romantic representation of the past. They pursue the recovery of collective events of national importance as well as their validation by and inclusion in major discourses of modern European history.

Noticeably outnumbering the above national-recollective narratives, the North Macedonian films with national-symbolic markers strive to mythologise the local through larger regional experiences. They tap into themes entrenched in the Balkan histories and reverberated after the Yugoslav wars, such as ethnic conflicts and knotted multicultural interrelations. Quite often, these films employ exotic images of national topography and/or present marginalised ethnic communities – their decor, livelihood, natural behaviours and simple desires against a crumbling world.

The most honourable representatives of the national-symbolic category are the national production *To the Hilt* and the co-production *Balkan Is Not Dead*. The films' plots are set in one and the same historical period – the disintegration of the Ottoman Empire and the escalation of Macedonia's national-liberation struggle in the beginning of the twentieth century. They envision the origin of the Macedonian nation in the anti-colonial struggle, which symbolically parallels the country's independence movement during the collapse of the Yugoslav 'empire' a century later. *To the Hilt*, with the subtitle *Tales from the Wild East*, weaves a love-and-death conflict among a local patriot and revolutionary, a Europeanised student and a brutal Turkish officer, in the centre of which is a young English woman. Written by the most prominent at home and abroad Macedonian playwright Goran Stefanovski, this 'historical fairytale' (Nastoski 2014) contains a hyphenated drama dressed as a parody of the Balkanist clichés, but also of the Hollywood westerns to which the creators wittily counterpoint their own genre of 'eastern'. It holds recollective and ethnographic faculties that please the domestic audiences, while also create a marketable brand through ironically sensationalised and overly Balkanised local history.[15]

Using similar aesthetics, *Balkan Is Not Dead*, a screen adaptation of the famous play by Stefanovski's student, Dejan Dukovski,[16] represents an intelligent, complex and deconstructive view of North Macedonia's nationalistic discourses. It denies the authenticities of the plot's multiple storylines by employing explicitly theatrical set design (see Figure 9.3), similar to the experimental *Anna Karenina* (Joe Wright, 2012). Coming from a theatre background, director Aleksandar Popovski chooses to emphasise the poetry rather than the parody of the original text in an attempt to create a hybrid form of post/modern myth of the Balkans as seen from the Macedonian lands. He contemporises the storytelling and transposes the region's historical 'question of freedom or death' to the one of 'love or hate'.[17]

Twentieth-century Balkan history, including the Yugoslav legacy, is also treated in more realistic film language, mixed with elements of drama, suspense or humour. Some of the films, which engage the themes of people's displacement, immigration and loss, especially in nests of divisiveness and violence like Albania and Kosovo, are: *Vojnata zavrshi/The War Is Over* (Mitko Panov, North Macedonia/Switzerland, 2010); *Tatko/My Father* (Shqipe N. Duka, North Macedonia, 2010), the first North Macedonian movie in the Albanian language; *Lazar/Lazarus* (Svetozar Ristovski, North Macedonia/Croatia/Bulgaria/France, 2015);

Figure 9.3   *Balkan is Not Dead* (Aleksandar Popovski, 2013).

and *Ruganje so Hristos/Mocking of Christ* (Jani Pojadzi, North Macedonia/ Slovenia, 2018). Additionally, broad-based variation on national-symbolic themes attempt to expose culturally entrenched oppressions still extant in smaller Balkan communities. Some of these films include parallel stories of characters from different nationalities experiencing gender or political oppression, such as in *The Woman Who Brushed Off Her Tears* and *Zemjata pomedzu granitzite/The Land between the Borders* (Arben Kastrati, North Macedonia, 2010). Other movies of that category offer critical perspectives of the local cultural practices in the aesthetics of comedy and the absurd, such as *Vrakanje/ The Return* (Kastriot Abdyli, North Macedonia/Kosovo, 2018) and *Godina na majmunot/The Year of the Monkeys* (Vladimir Blazhevski, North Macedonia/ Serbia/Kosovo/Slovenia, 2018). Displaying self-colonising attitudes in a variety of forms, the films dealing with national-symbolic subjects embrace cultural binaries. In that vein, they echo the Balkan 'primordial sins' of tribalism, sexism and nationalistically fuelled violence, adopting them as 'Macedonian own' and thus exonerating the national imaginary from the stigma of communism.

The category of national-reflective goes farthest from generalising or orientalising the national community. It seeks 'the heart of a nation' in ethical and civil values, such as class equality, social justice and generational differences. The ethnic-cultural markers of such narratives, for instance traditional practices, historical references, landscapes and local vernaculars, are still part of the films' aesthetics and they enhance their background, atmosphere and styles. To local audiences, this secondary plane of imagery gets inadvertently 'in focus' to inform a very particular cultural-symbolic discourse. It creates a specific performative connection between fiction and reality that keeps the viewer's perception simultaneously aware of both, thus generating meanings beyond the confinement of the plot. The duality of cinematographic fiction, when reflecting on local topics, finds an intricate representation in Milcho Manchevski's authored and directed *Mothers*. Manchevski is a well-known name in world cinema, making his early career breakthrough with the Macedonia-based 'mythistory' *Pred dozhdot/Before the Rain* (North Macedonia/France/UK, 1994).[18] His principle of 'telling myths in a new language' (Mancevski [*sic*] 1995) thrives in the plot structure of *Mothers*, which comprises two fictional segments loosely based on events that had happened to the director's friends and one documentary segment about the investigation of serial murders in the town of Kichevo. As Manchevski explains, 'all three stories were based on real events, but they were treated differently; I applied radically different approaches,' therefore debating 'the nature of truth' in artistic/mediated representations (Manchevski 2012: 17–18, 12). Despite its preoccupation with form, *Mothers* can also be read literally, as a revelation of 'political and social notions . . . the corruption of authorities, especially of the police; the generation conflict between those who have known Tito's era, who live in the past . . . and those who are occupied with the future . . .' (Bonnefoy 2011). Manchevski's experimental yet dramatically and visually arresting picture captures fleeting moments of contemporary life in North Macedonia, similar to Gjorce Stavreski's black comedy *Secret Ingredient*, which follows a son's desperate and amusing struggle to alleviate his father's cancer with a secret herb that turns out to be marijuana. Stavreski's feature film debut renders a candid and sympathetic view of the poverty and poor health system in post-communist North Macedonia. As Wendy Ide rightfully observes, 'The comedy is underplayed, with the kind of deadpan naturalism. . . . Locations – all weeping concrete, rust and decay – are evocatively used' (2017).

Most of the films dealing with the notion of the national-reflective recreate the styles of neo-realism and dark social satire, also known as the Black Wave of the 1960s Yugoslav cinema. They reflect on a fragmenting reality where violence is unavoidable and unpunished as in *Ova ne e amerikanski film/ This Is Not an American Movie* (Sasho Pavlovski, North Macedonia, 2011) and *Koga denot nemashe ime/When the Day Had No Name* (Teona Strugar Mitevska, North Macedonia/Slovenia/Belgium, 2017). Acts of revolt extend beyond an individual's coming-of-age to depict the anxiety of a politically divided society in *Pankot ne e mrtov/Punk Is Not Dead* (Vladimir Blazevski, North Macedonia/Serbia, 2011) and *Amok* (Vardan Tozija, North Macedonia/ Albania, 2016), whereas destroyed human lives and dreams are depicted in *The Piano Room* and *Medna nok/ Honey Night* (Ivo Trajkov, North Macedonia/Slovenia/Czech Republic, 2015). The 'national' in these films does not manifest itself through traditional and exotic images that presuppose a distant or detached look at North Macedonia's time-space, but by an immediate reflection of the socially diversifying community. In them, character varieties and exclusions assume a representative function, as narratives validate contemporary vernaculars and assert new moral agencies. Still, many of these films continue to rely on already constructed East–West polarities and tropes of Balkan extremities. Furthermore, they nostalgically revive memories of the Yugoslav cultural and cinematographic revolution in the 1960s.

North Macedonian cinematography between 2008 and 2018, as represented by motion pictures with national identity and values, shows a progressively increasing number of co-productions, the majority of which remain within the realms of the former Yugoslavia (Serbia, Slovenia, Croatia and Kosovo) and the Balkan region (Greece, Bulgaria and Albania). Funding from west European and non-European countries is scarce and is mostly associated with films by North Macedonian directors who studied and currently reside abroad, and who have received recognition at international film festivals, such as Milcho Manchevski (United States and France), Teona Strugar Mitevska (Germany and Belgium), Svetozar Ristevski (Switzerland) and Ivo Trajkov (Czech Republic). Nevertheless, local funding and regional cooperation have not prevented newcomers such as author-directors Gjorce Stavreski and Vardan Tozija to successfully take a step on the big international stages. Moreover, they have not limited or skewed the thematic opportunities for cinematic representation of a nation in historical transition.

After 2008, open-market opportunities, adaptive party politics and new legislature have created favourable conditions for North Macedonian film producers and their international collaborators. The main artistic objective for the following decade of filmmaking has been finding new stories and aesthetic approaches that best capture a nation located in the *liminal* space of political and cultural currents: capitalist, but still much neo-authoritarian; European, but also Balkan and post-Yugoslav. Although global awareness and shared European values have significantly influenced North Macedonian politics and culture, they have hardly become a norm, precipitating cinema's focus on national narratives with recovering, symbolic and reflective denominators. In particular, the North Macedonian fictional feature films produced between 2008 and 2018 have persistently performed a postcolonial re-evaluation as well as synchronisation with resurging Balkan and European histories. To that end, they critically discuss universal topics, such as cultural marginalisation, ethnic/religious divergences and gender hierarchies, but they artistically render them through the double lenses of anti-colonial and postcolonial standpoints in order to emphasise the stories' national-recollective and national-symbolic values. The targeted effect of such an approach is the temporal and spatial externalisation of the national imaginary, which is positioned in comparison to other national models prominent during modernism. In contrast, by focusing on inter-cultural differences and new social divisions, a number of films with national-reflective value discuss similar topics through internalised and inadvertently post-modern – either self-examining or art-questioning – perspectives. They critique and rebuild the local civil-national community, which emerges under the external threats of economic neo-colonialism, imposed liberalism and cultural assimilation in a globalised world. Ultimately, the *glocal* representations analysed in this chapter seem to serve overlapping goals: they attract both domestic and foreign audiences by means of mythologised local histories, thus satisfying co/producers' marketing goals and filmmakers' career pursuits. Moreover, they contribute to the cultural and aesthetic branding of the new Balkan and European country of North Macedonia, which firmly places it on the world map.

NOTES

1. Historically, the country's territory was part of the ancient Kingdom of Macedon and, later, the Empire of Alexander the Great (800s–300s BC). From the 200s BC to the 1900s, it was successively included in the Roman, Byzantine, Bulgarian, Serbian and Ottoman empires. It was repetitively torn among the states of Bulgaria, Serbia and Greece during the Balkan Wars (1913, 1914) and the two World Wars.
2. For example, one of the state-owned theatres in Skopje since 1950 was the Teatar na narodnosti /Theatre of Nationalities, which included Turkish and Albanian troupes performing in their native languages ('Albanski teatar – Skopje' 2004).
3. According to the 2002 census, the Albanian minority constitutes 25.17 per cent of the total population of 2,022,547 with other ethnic minority groups, such as Turks, Roma, Serbs, etc. making another 10.65 per cent of the population. The Macedonian majority is 64.18 per cent (Teodosievski 2018: 15).
4. The support by the US and EU 2001 Framework Agreement prevented a separatist war between the Macedonian Albanians and Slavs and led to changes in the constitution in recognition of the Albanian cultural and electoral minority. A current objective of the two ethnic Albanian parties has been the passing of the 'controversial Law on Language, which aims to advance the use of the Albanian language in official communication' (Bliznakovski 2018: 3).
5. For more information about the transitional status of North Macedonia, see the Freedom House country report ('Macedonia: Country Profile' 2018). For the exact corruption charges filed against VMRO-DPMNE officials, see 'Anti-Corruption Digest, Republic of North Macedonia' 2019.
6. Some of the most ostensible ethnic-nationalistic displays include the 66-metre-tall Millennium Cross raised over Skopje in 2009 and the capital enhancement project Skopje 2014, which architecturally and artistically redesigned the centre and parts of the capital city with neoclassical style buildings and commemorative statues.
7. VMRO-DPMNE formed several coalition governments with the most prominent Albanian-based Democratic Unity for Integration (DUI), while at the same time it continued to employ populism and promote uni-ethnic policies.
8. The term 'Macedonian Question' refers to the turn-of-the-twentieth-century dispute over the Ottomanised Macedonian territories, the liberation of which sparked inter-Balkan conflicts as well as nationalistic and even self-damaging internal revolutionary actions.
9. Drawing on the different attitudes and treatment of the Balkans since the Enlightenment, Maria Todorova concludes: 'In the realm of ideas, balkanism evolved partly as a reaction to the disappointment of the West Europeans' "classical" expectations in the Balkans, but it was a disappointment within a paradigm that had already been set as separate from the oriental' (Todorova 1997: 20).

10. The Film Agency's local funding comes mostly from casino proceeds, taxes on media companies and imported audiovisual equipment (2–3 per cent), and box office and distribution (Zikov 2019). Since becoming a member in 2009 until 2011, North Macedonia has received half a million euros for the distribution and screening of 97 films by Eurimages, the European Cinema Support Fund at the Council of Europe (Kjuka 2011). In 2015, the NMFA also became a member of the European Film Commission Network (EUFCN), which 'works closely with European public institutions, promoting the interests of film commissions, carrying out projects funded by the European Union, and conducting seminars and conferences' ('Macedonian Film Agency Joins European Film Commission Network' 2015). Other outside funding sources include the Social Entrepreneur Empowerment Network, which helps with film developing, as well as an Italian-Macedonian Co-production Development Fund established in 2016.

11. Another report for 2017 states an annual budget of approximately 6 million euro for 2017 (see NMFA 2017).

12. As Stojcheska explains, major productions require the project to be submitted for funding by a North Macedonian producer as the leading co-producer and that 4 per cent of the requested funds are in place as a private investment.

13. In 2017, after the SDSM took power over the government and the presidency, the Acting Director of the NMFA was quickly replaced with a suitable professional, who could ensure the institution's political support for the new ruling party.

14. For more information about all positions on this issue, see 'Director of Controversial Holocaust Film Rejects "Revisionist" Criticism' (2012) and Leviev-Sawyer (2012).

15. Somewhat similar to the post-Soviet *Sibirskiy tsiryulnik/ The Barber of Siberia* (Nikita Mikhalkov, Russia/France/Italy/Czech Republic, 1998), *To the Hilt* exercises self-evaluation through the foreign gaze, but without the strong cultural judgment and heavy sentimentalism.

16. The play's full title is *Balkan Is Not Dead ili Magija Edelvais [sic]/Balkan Is Not Dead, or the Magic of Edelweiss*. It won the 1993 Best National Drama award at the Vojdan Černodrinski's Theatre Festival.

17. The teaser-line 'It is not a question of freedom or death; it is a question of love or hate' appears on the film's official poster (*Balkan Is Not Dead*, IMDb).

18. *Before the Rain* won the Venice Film Festival's Golden Lion award, the Independent Spirit Award for Best International Film and David di Donatello, and was nominated for an Oscar in the Foreign Film category, among other awards.

References

Alagjozovski, Robert (2012) 'The Nationalistic Turn and the Visual Response in Macedonian Art and Cinema', in Daniel Šuber and Slobodan Karamanić (eds), *Retracing Images: Visual Culture after Yugoslavia*. Leiden: Brill.

'Albanski teatar – Skopje' (2004) *Teatri vo republica Makedonia* <http://www.mactheatre.edu.mk/avtor.asp?lang=mac&id=3> (last accessed 2 June 2019).

'Anti-Corruption Digest, Republic of North Macedonia' (2019) Council of Europe, May <https://www.coe.int/en/web/corruption/anti-corruption-digest/the-former-yugoslav-republic-of-macedonia> (last accessed 7 June 2019).

Balkan Is Not Dead (2013) IMDb <https://www.imdb.com/title/tt1942808/media-viewer/rm1021100032> (last accessed 28 July 2019).

Bhabha, Homi K. (1994) *The Location of Culture*. London and New York: Routledge.

Bliznakovski, Jovan (2018) 'Macedonia', *Freedom House* (pdf file) <https://freedom-house.org/report/nations-transit/2018/macedonia> (last accessed 25 July 2019).

Bonnefoy, Claire (2011) 'Two Truths and One Hubbab: Milcho Manchevski's *Mothers* (Majki, 2010)', *East European Film Bulletin* 3 (March 2018) <https://eefb.org/per-spectives/milcho-manchevskis-mothers-majki-2010/> (last accessed 20 August 2019).

Brownell, Ginanne (2011) 'Balkans Reclaim a Place in Cinema', *New York Times*, 28 December <https://www.nytimes.com/2011/12/29/arts/29iht-balkanfilm29.html?mtrref=www.google.com&gwh=4AAC79CE927DA86BAC71004F884B899D&gwt=pay> (last accessed 3 July 2019)

'Director of Controversial Holocaust Film Rejects "Revisionist" Criticism' (2012) *Radio Free Europe/Radio Liberty*, 12 December <https://www.rferl.org/a/mitrevski-third-half-controversial-macedonian-holocaust-film/24805049.html> (last accessed 3 July 2019).

Holloway, Ronald (1996) 'Macedonian Film. A History of Macedonia Cinema 1905–1996)', *Kino* (Cinémathèque of Macedonia, December 1996).

Ide, Wendy (2017) 'Secret Ingredient: Tallinn Review', *Screen Daily*, 29 November <https://www.screendaily.com/reviews/secret-ingredient-tallinn-review/5124518.article> (last accessed 7 July 2019).

Kjuka, Deana (2011) 'Eurimages Probes Abuse of Macedonia Movie Funds', *Balkan Insight*, 25 July <https://balkaninsight.com/2011/07/25/eurimages-to-probe-macedonian-movie-scandal/> (last accessed 26 July 2019).

Kostova, Marina. Email to the author, 17 April 2019.

Lazarevska, Marina (2017) 'Macedonia: Country Report 2016', *FilmNewEurope.com*, 17 February <https://www.filmneweurope.com/news/macedonia-news/item/114051-macedonia-country-report-2016> (last accessed 9 June 2019).

Leviev-Sawyer, Clive (2012) 'Bulgarian FM Mladenov Speaks on Macedonia's "Third Half" Film Controversy', *Sofia Globe*, 14 September <https://sofiaglobe.com/2012/09/14/bulgarian-fm-mladenov-speaks-on-macedonias-third-half-film-controversy/> (last accessed 9 July 2019).

Linden, Sheri (2011) ' "The Liberation of Skopje": Film Review', *Hollywood Reporter*, 6 December <https://www.hollywoodreporter.com/review/liberation-skopje-952790> (last accessed 7 June 2019).

'Macedonia: Country Profile' (2018) *Freedom House*, <https://freedomhouse.org/report/nations-transit/2018/macedonia> (last accessed 27 July 2019).

Macedonia – Politics (2018) *GlobalSecurity.org* <https://www.globalsecurity.org/military/world/europe/mk-politics.htm> (last accessed 7 June 2019).

'Macedonian Film Agency Joins European Film Commission Network' (2015) *The Calvert Journal*, 16 October <https://www.calvertjournal.com/articles/show/4855/macedonian-film-agency-joins-european-film-commissions-network> (last accessed 13 July 2019).

'Macedonian Film Infuriates Bulgaria' (2011) *Euractive*, 28 October <https://www.euractiv.com/section/enlargement/news/macedonian-film-infuriates-bulgaria/> (last accessed 20 August 2019).

Mancevski, Milco (1995) 'Interview', 48 (7) *UNESCO Courier* (July–August 1995) <https://www.questia.com/magazine/1G1-17382443/milco-mancevski> (last accessed 14 July 2019).

Manchevski, Milcho (2012) *Truth and Fiction: Notes on (Exceptional) Faith in Art.* Brooklyn, NY: Punctum Books.

Nastoski, Zharko (2014) ' "Do Balcak": banalno i zdodevno', *Okno.mk.*, 22 October <https://okno.mk/node/41754> (last accessed 27 July 2019).

Nedelkovska, Maja (2012) 'Tears and Standing Ovations for "The Third Half"', *Balkan Insight*, 17 September <https://balkaninsight.com/2012/09/17/the-third-half-receives-tears-and-standing-ovation/> (last accessed 7 June 2019).

NMFA (North Macedonia Film Agency) <http://filmfund.gov.mk/en/home-3/> (last accessed 27 July 2019).

NFMA (North Macedonia Film Agency) (2017) *European Film Promotion* <https://www.efp-online.com/en/members/219/Republic-of-North-Macedonia/North-Macedonia-Film-Agency> (last accessed 25 July 2019).

'North Macedonia' (2018) *FilmNewEurope.com* <https://www.filmneweurope.com/countries/malta> (last accessed 20 August 2019).

Papadimitriou, Lydia (2018) 'Greek Cinema as European Cinema: Co-productions, Eurimages and the Europeanisation of Greek Cinema', *Studies in European Cinema*, 15 (2–3) pp. 215–34.

Șandru, Cristina (2016) 'Postcolonial *Post-communism?*' in Anna Bernard, Ziad Elmarsafy and Stuart Murray (eds), *What Postcolonial Theory Doesn't Say*. London: Routledge, pp. 156–77.

Smith, Anthony D. (1998) *Nationalism and Modernism*. London and New York: Routledge.

Stojcheska, Anita (2018) Interview with Teresa Vena, *Cineuropa*, 20 September <https://cineuropa.org/en/interview/360617/> (last accessed 24 July 2019).

Sutherland, Claire (2012) *Nationalism in the Twenty-First Century: Challenges and Responses*. Hampshire and New York: Palgrave Macmillan.

Tashkovski, Bratislav (2011) *Rascepen Um, ili Odneseno so Chavkite*. Skopje: Makavej.

Teodosievski, Zlatko (2018) 'FYP of Macedonia' Compendium: Cultural Policies and Trends', *Compendium of Cultural Policies & Trends* <https://www.facebook.com/173617236024674/posts/zlatko-teodosievski-updated-the-cultural-policy-profile-of-fyr-macedonia-the-gov/1908923059160741/>

Todorova, Maria (1997) *Imagining the Balkans*. New York and Oxford: Oxford University Press Press.

Voss, Christian (2007) 'Great Macedonia as a "Mental Map" in the 20th and 21st Century', in Jolanta Sujecka and Wojciech Józef Burszta (eds), *Terytorializm i Tożsamość Balkany Słowiańskie i Niesłowiańskie [Territorialism and Identity: The Slavonic and non-Slavonic Balkans]*, *Sprawy Narodowościowe*, vol. 31, pp. 163–9.

Zeneli, Valbona (2019) 'North Macedonia: A Name Agreement in the Age of Nationalism?' *National Interest*, 14 February <https://nationalinterest.org> (last accessed 7 June 2019).

Zikov, Aleksandar (2019) Email to the author, 7 May.

10. ROMANIA: TRANSNATIONAL AND NATIONAL TENSIONS BEYOND THE NEW WAVE

Raluca Iacob

In 2005, a Romanian three-hour long film about a misanthropic old man suffering from abdominal pains and carted from one Bucharest hospital to another won the Un Certain Regard Prize at the Cannes Film Festival. The film, *Moartea domnului Lăzărescu/The Death of Mr Lazarescu* (Cristi Puiu, Romania, 2005), coalesced into what quickly became known as the Romanian New Wave or, more broadly, New Romanian Cinema.[1] Starting in 2001 with Puiu's debut feature film *Marfa și banii/Stuff and Dough* (Romania), the movement gained momentum in 2006 when two Romanian films were presented in Cannes: Corneliu Porumboiu's *A fost sau n-a fost/12:08 East of Bucharest* (Romania) – which went on to become one of the most seen Romanian films abroad[2] – and Cătălin Mitulescu's *Cum mi-am petrecut sfârșitul lumii/The Way I Spent the End of the World* (Romania/France), and culminated in 2007 with Cristian Mungiu's film *4 luni, 3 săptămâni și 2 zile/4 Months, 3 Weeks and 2 Days* (Romania/Belgium) winning the Palme D'Or. Over the next decade, the New Wave continued to produce notable films and assert its presence on the international film festival circuit, cinema theatres and across a variety of distribution channels (DVDs and streaming services). The impact of the New Romanian cinema has also been felt outside national borders, most notably on other cinemas in the Balkans, such as post-Yugoslav films (Pavičić 2011). For Pavičić, embracing this influence is a 'political gesture' for filmmakers, who aim to distance themselves from the excessive and carnivalesque Kusturica-style often associated with Balkan films in the West, and forge a different, subtle and yet recognisable, personal but also observational style (Țuțui and Iacob 2019).

For a cinema on which little had been written in English prior to the new millennium, this surge in interest and the consistent presence of Romanian films gave rise to reviews, journal articles and special issues, and the publication of several books, covering the subject from a number of different perspectives and approaches (Nasta 2013, Pop 2014, Strausz 2017, Batori 2018, Stojanova 2019). Drawing formalistic connections to minimalism and realism, the majority of film scholarship on New Romanian cinema establishes some common characteristics: a predilection towards 24-hour narrative structures; a focus on individuals dealing with some form of existential crises living in austere environments; the use of black humour as a form of dealing with problems; and the adoption of an aesthetic characteristic of slow cinema – mainly the use of observational, long takes.

Romanian cinema has evolved significantly since the 1990s, a period dominated by struggles triggered by the post-communist transition, which led to radical restructuring of the systems of production, distribution and exhibition. This crisis culminated in 2000, when no Romanian films premiered. The mid-2000s saw the emergence of the New Wave and the consequent rejuvenation of Romanian cinema. With their films made between 2005 and 2007, directors Cristi Puiu, Cristian Mungiu, Radu Muntean, Corneliu Porumboiu and Cătălin Mitulescu changed the fate of Romanian cinema, turning it from obscurity into one of an internationally recognisable and highly influential movement. Following the emergence of the New Wave, the years 2008–18 became one of the most productive and mature periods of Romanian cinema. The number of films produced grew, including films that departed from the New Wave aesthetic approach. Alternative or do-it-yourself forms of distribution and exhibition were also introduced, while Romanian cinema also saw an increased level of cross-border interactions and cooperation, including with other countries in the Balkans.

In this chapter, I explore the dynamics of Romanian cinema over this decade, in order to highlight the interplay between national and transnational structures. A part of Romanian cinema remained strictly national, with genre-specific films that were financed, produced and exhibited exclusively within national borders. Despite the heterogeneity of approaches and styles, New Romanian cinema remains the core of this national output, especially as its international visibility has facilitated engagement with transnational systems of production and distribution. Using some of Mette Hjort's identified types of transnationalism, I will trace recognisable patterns of transnational co-productions involving Romanian cinema. In the final part of this chapter, I will examine the diverse distribution opportunities and the multiple ways in which Romanian films can reach an audience, including film festivals, to offer a more holistic overview of contemporary Romanian cinema and the challenges it faces.

ROMANIAN CINEMA: FROM NATIONAL TO TRANSNATIONAL

The fall of the Berlin Wall in 1989 and the consequent geopolitical impact of the collapse of communism in Europe renewed questions of national identity and their representation in cinema (Galt 2006). The concept of a national cinema itself started to become challenged, with an increasing emphasis since the 1990s on the transnational, a concept 'at once useful and problematic, liberating and limiting' (Higbee and Lim 2010: 10). These contradictions are largely due to the elasticity and metamorphic nature of the transnational, or in Mette Hjort's words (2010), to the paradoxical situation that the 'plurality' of cinematic transnationalisms has played a 'strangely homogenising role' (2010: 13). To counter these limitations, Hjort proposes identifying 'strong or weak' forms of transnationality (2010: 13) and types of transnationalism. She then proposes nine distinct categories, while acknowledging that these are neither mutually exclusive nor final. In what follows, I will outline some of the transnational characteristics of post-2008 Romanian cinema referring to both industrial and textual dimensions.

Most New Wave Romanian films from the 2000s that have had extensive international visibility were defined by an aesthetic of 'kitchen sink realism' (Pop 2014) that displayed the economic and social precarity of the late Ceausescu era or the early post-communist years. In a contribution to discussions on New Romanian cinema, Doru Pop has observed a more recent tendency towards transnationalisation, by which he refers to the tendency of post-2010 Romanian films to remove local specificities and instead present 'characters and narratives that are decreasingly linked to a particular cultural milieu' and socio-economic situation (2019: 233). Pop notes that many of these films focus on upper-middle-class individuals, whose problems are more readily translatable across borders. He also argues that this led to a different stylistic representation of their milieu that removed the specificity of time and place that can be found in the early examples of the New Wave. Films such as *Marți după Crăciun/Tuesday After Christmas* (Radu Muntean, Romania, 2011), *Poziția copilului/Child's Pose* (Călin Peter Netzer, Romania, 2013), *Când se lasă seara peste București sau Metabolism/ When Evening Falls on Bucharest or Metabolism* (Corneliu Porumboiu, Romania/France, 2013), Pop argues, are characteristic of this tendency. Pop suggests that part of the reason for this change is the increasing integration of Romanian cinema into a transnational system of funding, production, distribution and exhibition. This is also evident in the transnational lives that a lot of Romanian filmmakers increasingly lead – even if the majority continue to be based mainly in Romania.

Diasporic or exilic filmmakers (Naficy 2001) predated the fall of communism. Lucian Pintilie had lived in France between 1975 and 1990, while Radu

Gabrea was an émigré in Germany between 1974 and 1997 – both returned to Romania in later years. Others chose to stay abroad: Romanian born Radu Mihăileanu emigrated to France in the 1980s to study at L'Institut des hautes études cinématographiques (IDHEC). His films deal with questions of migration and identity focusing on people from different ethnic and linguistic backgrounds: Jewish – *Train du vie/Train of Life* (France/Belgium/Netherlands/Israel/Romania, 1998) and *Va, vis et deviens/Live and Become* (France/Israel/Belgium/Italy, 2005); Romanian – *Trahir/Betrayal* (1993, France/Switzerland/Spain/Romania, 1993); North African/Arabic – *La source des femmes/The Source* (France/Belgium/Italy, 2011); or French – *Le concert/The Concert* (France/Italy/Romania/Belgium, 2009). His most recent film to date, *L'histoire de l'amour/The History of Love* (2016) is perhaps the epitome of a transnational film: a French, Canadian, Romanian, US and Belgium co-production, shot in Montreal, New York and Romania, with an international cast of world-renowned actors such as Derek Jacobi, Gemma Arterton and Elliott Gould, with dialogue in English and Yiddish, and an adaptation of the homonymous, bestseller book about star-crossed lovers by Nicole Krauss.

Another distinct type of transnational filmmaker is Nae Caranfil. After he graduated in 1984 from the 'I. L. Caragiale' Institute of Theatre and Film in Bucharest, he spent some years in Brussels, where he attended the European Screenwriter's Programme within the FEMI (Flemish European Media Institute). While there, sometime between 1988 and 1991, he wrote the scripts for *E pericoloso sporgersi/Sundays on Leave* (France/Romania, 1993) and *Restul e tăcere/The Rest is Silence* (Romania, 2007). While he directed *Sundays on Leave*, his first feature film, after his return to Romania, he has maintained close connections with francophone countries as almost all his films have subsequently been co-produced with French and/or Belgian partners. His cinematic style contrasts with the minimalist aesthetics of the New Wave, prompting film critic and scholar Dana Duma to label it as 'maximalist aesthetics' (2013). This refers partly to the blockbuster-like budget of some of his historical dramas, such as *The Rest Is Silence* and *Closer to the Moon* (Romania/USA/Italy/Poland/ France, 2013). *Closer to the Moon*, for example, had a budget of 4 million euros, an international cast (including Vera Farmiga, Mark Strong, Harry Lloyd, Anton Lesser), and was spoken entirely in English but its screenplay was based on true events that happened in 1959 in Bucharest. This was the story of a six-person gang that carried out the biggest bank robbery in communist Romania – a story with evident parallels with Hollywood films about outlaws. While Caranfil is based in Romania and his stories are drawn from its setting, his high-budget filmmaking represents a kind of transnationalism motivated by the need for international co-producers in order to complete the budget and, by extension, reach more publicity and various national markets.

In 2018, two Romanian films which won major awards at international film festivals were also co-productions – a *de facto* transnational mode of production: Adina Pintilie *Nu mă atinge-mă/Touch Me Not* (Romania/Germany/Czech Republic/Bulgaria/France, 2018) won the Golden Bear at the Berlin International Film Festival; and Radu Jude's *Îmi este indiferent dacă în istorie vom intra ca barbari/I Do Not Care If We Go Down in History as Barbarians* (Romania/Germany/Bulgaria/France/Czech Republic, 2018) won the Crystal Globe award at Karlovy Vary International Film Festival. Interestingly, these co-productions involved the same four partner countries: Germany, Czech Republic, France and Bulgaria. The recurrence of this transnational model of production contrasts with the fact that the award-winning films of the mid-2000s – *The Death of Mr. Lazarescu*, *12:08 East of Bucharest* or *4 Months, 3 Weeks and 2 Days*, to give just a few examples – were nationally produced films. The recent festival successes of Pintilie and Jude's films also point to the increasing stylistic variety of the Romanian films, as neither can be said to follow the minimalist aesthetic and concentrated, linear story-time of the New Wave. *Touch Me Not* is an experimental film that mixes documentary, fiction and visual art, and explores the idea of intimacy and personal relationships. *I Do Not Care If We Go Down in History as Barbarians* deals with the subject of historical guilt and interrogation of the past, focusing on an omitted episode in Romania's history, the murder of tens of thousands of Jews following the capture of Odessa by Romanian troops in 1941 – a topic of unaddressed historical guilt that could be extrapolated to many other national contexts. While revisiting recent history has been the topic of a number of New Wave films the theatricality adopted by Jude in this film in terms of the style of performance and the depiction of events is markedly distinctive from the realist, austere style of the Romanian New Wave. Despite not fitting into the minimalist aesthetic of the New Wave aesthetic, these two films are representative of the broader category of New Romanian cinema, which refers to art films enabled by the success of their New Wave predecessors.

Indeed, many New Romanian films are now made as co-productions, while films produced solely with national funds tend to be genre-orientated, and are often adaptations of American originals. These are usually comedies or romantic comedies, which gain some modest success at the box office but are usually critical flops. One example are the films directed by Jesus del Cerro (and produced in large part by one of the private TV stations, PRO TV), such as *Ho Ho Ho* (Romania, 2009), a loose adaptation of the premise of the very successful American Christmas comedy *Home Alone* (Chris Columbus, US, 1990) or the comedy *Cuscrii/The In-Laws* (Radu Potcoava, Romania, 2014), a loose adaptation of the American homonymous films *The In-Laws* (Arthur Hiller, US, 1979) and its Andrew Fleming directed 2003 remake.

Tough Roads to (Co-)production

Customarily, transnational collaborations are dependent on a project having already secured funding from national resources, which in the case of Romanian productions are most commonly supplied through the Centrul Naţional al Cinematografiei (CNC)/Romanian Film Center. With a budget drawn from several resources, the CNC organises two yearly public rounds of contests for film productions,[3] structured on a point-based system which takes into account several aspects of the film's production (the screenplay, the director, the producers, the box office numbers and festival selections of their previous films). This system has been frequently criticised by filmmakers due to the tendency of the institution and its administration to revert to old ways of cronyism and bureaucracy. Following his experience as one of the jury members in December 2008, Cristian Mungiu wrote an open letter, highlighting issues and inconsistencies in the functioning of the film fund and its administration, which led the Ministry of Culture to suspend funding competitions in 2009 and ask filmmakers and production companies to submit suggestions for improving regulations and systems of state financing. Yet, 'in 2010 the competition was back with virtually no changes in the regulations, except for a more rigorous and precise list of the international film festivals that can count for company or director "quality" points' (Uricaru, 2012: 435). Even in the case of a best possible outcome of a production receiving financial support from the CNC, the contribution cannot exceed 50 per cent of the budget, forcing producers to look for sources of financing elsewhere. Oftentimes, these sources are found in transnational TV companies (for example, HBO Europe offers support to some fiction and documentary productions), foreign production companies, supra-national entities (such as Creative Europe-MEDIA, through either single project or slate funding, or through Eurimages) or through festival funds – though this is the least frequent avenue, seeing that such initiatives usually offer either (script) development or post-production support.

In the wider framework of the Romanian film production landscape between 2013 and 2017, the number of co-productions over that five-year period across short and feature-length fiction, documentary and animation films only reach fifty-nine out of a total of 200 films produced (CNC 2018). Concerning feature length fiction films, co-productions represent a significant margin of the market, in 2016 even exceeding the number (13 co-productions) of those made solely with national funding (12 films financed with 100 per cent national funds). Among these, Western European partners are predominant, France, Germany and sometimes Sweden, and only more rarely Eastern European countries. This is because, aside from their main national cinema funds, Western European partners also have substantial regional and other specialist resources, some geared to supporting 'world cinema'. For example, *Sieranevada* (Cristi Puiu, 2016, Romania/France/Bosnia and Herzegovina/Croatia/Republic of Macedonia) received funding from a number of national funding sources, which included six different partners from France. The national film funds that supported the film were the Romanian National Centre for Cinema, the Bosnian Fondacija za Kinematografiju Sarajevo, the Macedonian Film Agency, the Croatian Audiovisual Centre and, from France, the Centre National du Cinéma et de l'Image Animée. Other French sources of funding were from the world cinema fund L'Aide aux Cinémas du Monde and France's Ministry of Foreign Affairs, the regional partner Région Île-de-France, the French Institute, and the television channel Arte France. Larger and wealthier European partners, in other words, have both more, and more dispersed, resources, providing therefore very attractive propositions as co-producing partners.

These co-productions usually involve either an established New Romanian cinema filmmaker or one of the more prominent production companies such as HiFilm, Mobra Film, Mandragora, Libra Film or Strada Film – or both. In trying to maintain creative control over their films, New Romanian cinema filmmakers have set up their own production companies, for, as Ioana Uricaru observes, all versions of the Romanian legislation concerning cinematic productions 'state funds would always be awarded to a Romanian production company, never to individual writers or directors', prompting film directors to take this role as a way to ensure 'financial independence as a prerequisite for creative freedom' (2012: 438).

Returning to Hjort's discussion of the transnational, it is important to engage with some of the specific categories she proposes. 'Opportunistic transnationalism' (2010: 19), which refers to a purely economic motivation for cross-border co-operation, represents one of the primary modes of co-production for Romanian films. Co-production conditions usually require some form of obligation in exchange for financial support, for example some members of the cast or certain services (e.g. post-production) need to originate from the co-producing partner. For example, in *Sieranevada* post-production was done by the French company Film Factory, the original music was provided by Croatian multimedia artist Bojan Gagić, Adnan Besirovic (a Bosnian producer) is credited as a food stylist, while Croatian actress Petra Kurtela appeared in a small role as the friend of the daughter of the family. Such co-production agreements commonly also include deals for the rights of distribution in the contributing company's area –in the case of *Sieranevada*, Arte Film, for example, retained the TV rights for France and Germany. The above system of exchanges offers opportunities and restrictions, whose creative impact on the final product is variable, but whose economic impact is primarily positive, as there are a number of different financially interested parties.

Hjort's 'epiphanic transnationalism' refers to the 'cinematic articulation' of shared regional cultural identities that can be found in the overlap between national cultures (2010: 16). This can be observed in some co-productions between neighbouring countries, such as the primarily Romanian-Bulgarian *Aferim!* (Radu Jude, Romania/Bulgaria/Czech Republic/France, 2015). Set in the first part of the nineteenth century, the film follows a gendarme, Constandin, and his son as they travel across Wallachia – Romania's southern-most region – searching for a gypsy slave who is accused of running away from his master after having an affair with the nobleman's wife. Shot in stark black and white, the film constructs a discourse about identity, prejudices, history and cultural memory, in a way that is both connected to and patently distinct from the New Romanian cinema (Figure 10.1). Funded by the Romanian Film Center (CNC), the Bulgarian National Film Center, the Czech Cinematography Fund and the Creative Europe Media programme, the film was partly shot in the Bulgarian Nu Boyana studios with a Romanian cast and majority of the crew. Often identified as a Balkan western, the film is a departure from the minimalist aesthetics of the New Wave because it uses more elements of genre and drama. While set in Romanian and spoken predominantly in nineteenth-century Romanian, the film and the story reflects some wider regional Balkan characteristics. This refers to the use of the so-called 'Red Western' genre, popular throughout the region during the communist period. The Red Westerns combined traits of the American Western with specific tropes from local culture, such as the romanticised hero figure of the *haidouk*, a kind of outlaw found throughout the Balkans, who opposed and rebelled against Ottoman rule.

It should be noted, however, that despite undeniable historical and cultural commonalities between the Balkan countries, Romanian filmmakers generally reject their classification as Balkan. As Pop notes, one of the most renowned

Figure 10.1   *Aferim!* (Radu Jude, 2015).

Romanian film directors, Lucian Pintilie, whose films displayed evident traits of Balkan black humour 'clearly rejected his affiliation to this Balkan tradition' (2014: 155). This is not uncommon, as customarily filmmakers reject all manner of labels, including, but not limited to, that of pertaining to a Romanian New Wave.[4] However, a predilection towards (dark) humour across many Romanian and more widely Balkan films has been acknowledged by film scholars, who have noticed a shared sensibility among Romanian films made before the year 2000 (Dan Pita, Lucian Pintilie and Nae Caranfil) and after 2000 (especially Cristian Mungiu and Cristian Nemescu's debut films). Identified as a means of social endurance, dark humour, whether expressed as satire or irony, is seen as a way to counterbalance the tragic existential crises of the characters, which can be pervasive in Balkan films (Stojanova and Duma 2012).

Hjort's 'affinitive transnationalism', the 'tendency to communicate with those similar to us' (2010: 17) is not usually found in Romanian cinema, as it maintains a focus on shared commonalities, manifested in 'core values, common practices' and 'partially overlapping or mutually intelligible languages' (ibid.), more applicable to Nordic cinemas, and among post-Yugoslav countries. Romanian is the only Latin-based language in the region (also spoken in the Republic of Moldova) and the distinctiveness of its language, together with the legacy of isolationist politics from the communist period which distanced Romania from Eastern bloc countries, resulted in few affinitive links with neighbouring countries being developed. One possible exception and an example of 'affinitive transnationalism' may be Marian Crisan's debut feature, *Morgen* (Romania/Hungary/France, 2010), which is set close to the Romanian-Hungarian border. This New Wave film tells the story of a Kurdish illegal immigrant who attempts to cross the border on the way to Germany with the help of a local man. It deals with the question of borders and transnational flows, but it also represents a fusion of languages, as some of the characters, having lived their whole lives in a multi-ethnic community, are bilingual and communicate in both Romanian and Hungarian. Another example could be some of the work of the Moldovan filmmaker, Igor Cobileanski, who studied film directing at the Theatre and Film Academy in Bucharest in the 1990s, and directed *La limita de jos a cerului/The Unsaved* (Moldova/Romania, 2013), a film co-written by Corneliu Porumboiu and filmed by Oleg Mutu, cinematographer of *The Death of Mr Lazarescu* and *4 Months, 3 Weeks and 2 Days*.

'Globalising transnationalism', which Mette Hjort describes as belonging to a commercial strand whereby high budgets are integrally connected to a broad reach in terms of audience (2010: 21–2), is not very common in Romanian cinema, yet it can be found in the case of some Nae Caranfil films as mentioned before, or in the film *A Farewell to Fools* (Bogdan Dumitrescu, Romania/Germany/Belgium, 2013), a remake of the 1972 film *Atunci i-am condamnat pe toţi la moarte/Then I Sentenced Them All to Death* (Sergiu Nicolaescu,

Romania). Starring Harvey Keitel and Gerard Depardieu as the leaders of a small community in interwar Nazi-occupied Romania, who in order to save themselves from execution try to place the blame of the murder on the village idiot. This 2013 remake with an estimated budget of over 3 million euros only reached 7,400 spectators and was a Box office flop in contrast to its successful predecessor which had garnered almost 2.2 million spectators. This particular example points to the risks and potential failures of globalising transnationalism, while Caranfil's films tend to be more successful examples.

In summary, though sometimes difficult to put together and complicated to manage, co-productions have been a fundamental mode of financing, production and distribution for Eastern European and Balkan films, and as Angus Finney observes, 'remain a vital strategy for continental territories as a means to harness additional finance and distribution potential beyond their national support system' (2010: 75). In the case of Romanian cinema, international distribution is indispensable, even if it happens on a small scale, or only through festival networks, as national audiences alone cannot sustain national cinema – especially when it concerns art-house films. In the next part, I will discuss the importance and significance of film festivals and international distribution for the visibility and sustainability of New Romanian cinema. I will then cast light on the state of national distribution, within the climate of post-1990s closure of many cinemas and the disappearance of audiences.

SEEKING AUDIENCES: FILM FESTIVALS AND NATIONAL DISTRIBUTION

As Romanian films gained critical recognition and accolades at European festivals in the mid-2000s, their distribution and exhibition nationally was seriously hindered by the disintegration of the exhibition system and the progressive loss of audiences. This generated anxiety and pressure towards finding creative solutions to reach the public. During the communist era there had been a strong infrastructure with cinemas across the country and a robust cinema-going audience even in smaller towns. However, after 1990 the majority of cinemas closed down and their spaces were repurposed, leaving a large portion of the population without access to cinemas and redirecting them towards entertainment on television or, more recently, via the Internet. Nowadays, cinema theatres can be mostly found in urban centres, showing mostly Hollywood blockbuster fare, while Box office numbers for national productions are, for the most part, inconsequential. Even though the percentage of European films screened in Romania has increased in the last decade compared to the previous period – with US productions around 50 per cent, European films 30 per cent, Romanian films 15 per cent and the rest 5 per cent (CNC 2018) – US films are by far the most lucrative, bringing in more than 90 per cent of the revenue.[5]

The increase in the number of European and world cinema titles shown in Romania is explained by the rise of film festivals, which bring the public in contact with arthouse cinema. Available data shows that the majority of European films that reach Romania come from well-developed national cinemas – France, the UK, Germany, Italy, Spain (CNC 2018). Data regarding screenings of films from low-production countries, including Balkan countries, is not systematically available, but film festival catalogues show evidence of such screenings. For example, the Transylvania International Film Festival presented a Focus on Bulgaria in the 2018 edition, while the same year the Greek film *Oiktos/Pity* (Babis Makridis, Greece/Poland, 2018) was selected in the official competition. The previous year, the Focus country was Slovenia and included, among others, a retrospective dedicated to Damjan Kozole. Croatia was one of the focus countries in 2016, Greece in 2013, and so on.[6]

The 'discovery' and success of New Romanian cinema is indelibly linked to film festivals – originally Cannes, but then a multitude of smaller festivals which have been showing the films in subsequent screenings. Dina Iordanova has written on the network flow of films through film festivals 'where a small film from an obscure source can be picked up by a succession of festivals and shown consecutively in various localities, thus getting truly global exposure' (2009: 24). This has been the main *modus operandi* for the films of the Romanian New Wave, especially for those titles that emerged in the mid-2000s. As exposure to festivals can build a film's 'critical capital' (Czach 2004: 81) Romanian producers and directors target premieres at one of the major European festivals (Cannes, Berlinale or Locarno) to increase the chances that a film will be picked up for distribution in different territories and receive critical recognition. Festivals have increasingly become sites for co-production networking and deals, and filmmakers therefore aim to maximise their exposure there both for different purposes.

Aside from Western European film festivals, three prominent festivals in the region – the Sarajevo International Film Festival in Bosnia and Herzegovina, the Thessaloniki International Film Festival in Greece and the Transylvania International Film Festival in Cluj-Napoca, Romania – take an active role in promoting Romanian cinema. In Thessaloniki, Romanian cinema has a prominent place in the non-competitive programme the Balkan Survey, with Cristian Mungiu (2012) and Mircea Daneliuc (2015) having also been offered special tributes. In Sarajevo, Romanian films can be found in both the competition and non-competition sections. In Cluj, the major film festival of the country, national productions of all lengths and styles, from feature, short, documentary and sometimes genre films too, are showcased in the 'Romanian Days' strand.[7]

While film festivals support the visibility of Romanian cinema abroad, it is important to also look at what films Romanians watch, and how these reach them. A good starting point is to focus on the distribution trajectory of *Child's*

Pose, the most successful Romanian film critically and commercially in Romania in the decade since 2008 (Figure 10.2). The film tells the story of a controlling matriarch of a bourgeois Bucharest family who tries through any means necessary to get her lethargic, adult son out of a hit-and-run conviction. Having won the Golden Bear for Best Film at the 2013 Berlinale, within the next few months its German sales agency, Beta Cinema, sold it for distribution to twenty-one European countries and overseas territories, such as Japan, Brazil and Israel. The film reached over 30,000 spectators in France, Germany, Italy and Spain, and altogether over 300,000 spectators, of which about 100,000 were within Romania,[8] as it was retained in cinemas for thirty-nine weeks (from early March until December), and shown in up to forty screens at a time (European Audiovisual Observatory).

While *Child's Pose* capitalised on the Golden Bear win for its success, a different type of Romanian films with a significant Box office presence are comedies. One example is *Selfie* (Cristina Iacob, Romania, 2014), a film about three teenagers who decide to take an adventure-filled trip to the seaside, forgoing the preparation for the upcoming exams. An inane comedy filled with silly dialogue and to some degree poor casting, the film had nonetheless around 87,000 spectators for its 22-week run on Romanian screens, and led to a sequel *Selfie 69* (Cristina Iacob, Romania, 2016), which had 150,000 spectators, and at the time of writing both films are available to be streamed on Netflix. Other successful comedies are *America, venim!/America, Here We Come* (Răzvan Săvescu, Romania, 2014) which attracted only 28,000 spectators in the cinema but has

Figure 10.2 *Child's Pose* (Calin Peter Netzer, 2013).

reached over 800,000 views on YouTube through the online platform Cinepub, or *Două lozuri/Two Lottery Tickets* (Paul Negoescu, 2016, Romania), a comedy made with a micro-budget of 30,000 euros, which attracted 27,000 spectators in its opening week and 135,000 for its complete theatrical run.

While the popularity of these and other genre-driven films demonstrates that Romanian cinema is more heterogenous than it might first appear, it also highlights the fact that conventional, theatrical distribution is only one of the ways for films to reach audiences. Though access to non-Hollywood films in cinema theatres is limited by the aggressive marketing and focus on mainstream films, national and European films sometimes get distributed through alternative forms, which not only include festivals, but also cineclubs or other small events organised by dedicated cinephiles, as well as online platforms.[9]

However, the international success of a New Romanian cinema production does not always facilitate the reach of local audiences. One such example is *Un etaj mai jos/One Floor Below* (Radu Muntean, Romania/France/Germany/ Sweden, 2015). The film had its world premiere in the Un Certain Regard strand of the 2015 Cannes International Film Festival, and a sales agent (Films Boutique) from the very start. After Cannes, the film was presented at festivals in Transylvania, Karlovy Vary, Melbourne, Sarajevo, Toronto, Vancouver, Haifa, Hamburg, Rio de Janeiro, London, Gent, Denver, Buenos Aires, Jeonju, and a Romanian film festival in New York, travelling in one year to five continents. Between 2015 and 2018 the film also opened in theatrical distribution in Romania, Switzerland, Czech Republic, Hungary, Netherlands, Slovenia, Slovakia and France. In Romania, the film premiered in cinemas in September 2015 where it remained for eleven weeks. Aside from the opening week when it was shown on twenty-five screens and had an audience of almost 2,800 people, in the remaining ten weeks it was shown only on one screen at a time, reaching altogether the rather disappointing 3,200 total admissions.[10] Except for the opening week the film was shown in a peripatetic operation, screened in each new city for one week.

Such roadshowing of acclaimed but not widely available films is not a new initiative. Some have been organised as extensions of film festivals, in which audience favourites are taken to other cities around the country and screened free of charge for the local audience. The Transylvanian International Film Festival, which takes place every June in Cluj-Napoca, has mushroomed into several mini-festivals in other cities (Bucharest, Oradea and Sibiu in Romania, and Chișinău in the Republic of Moldova), and organises open-air screenings for a summer-long film 'caravan' in 15 other cities around the country. Following its Palme d'Or at Cannes and the subsequent wide coverage in the national and international press, a caravan was organised for *4 Months, 3 Weeks and 2 Days* taking the film to multiple cities around the country without cinemas, and drawing around 18,000 spectators during its one-month run. The case is

Figure 10.3   *Pororoca* (Constantin Popescu, 2017).

particularly notable as the filmmakers documented the film's journey around the country and even released it as a DVD extra, underscoring the problems with film exhibition and the struggles to reach national audiences.

Pororoca (Constantin Popescu, Romania/France, 2017) is another film that underlines the tensions between a positive transnational reception (festival selections and positive reviews) and the limited national audience numbers. A film about a man whose life is ruined when his young daughter disappears during a short outing at the park, *Pororoca* premiered in the San Sebastian Film Festival in 2017, where Bogdan Dumitrache won the first of several Best Actor awards for his portrayal of the suffering, guilt-ridden Tudor (Figure 10.3). Recognised as one of the Romanian New Wave films that uses the characteristics specific to the movement, namely wide-angle cinematography and long takes that delve deep into the existential crisis of a human being, the film was deemed by one reviewer as 'muscular hard-art fare that [. . .] could propel Popescu into the upper ranks of his country's auteurs' (Lodge 2017). Aside from San Sebastian, the film travelled among other places to Rotterdam, São Paolo, Transylvania, IndieLisboa, Moscow, Jeonju, Tallinn Black Nights and Fajr, however, its 'hard-art fare' made it very difficult to sell to general audiences. In Romania, the film garnered around 5,000 spectators for its seven-week run, displaying an equally low number for the film's distribution in the country of co-production, France, where, according to the Lumiere database, attracted fewer than 8,000 spectators. The film, however, is available through HBO's subscription service HBO Go in Romania, Hungary, Czech Republic and Slovakia, as well as on three different VOD platforms in France, allowing it to reach audiences beyond the confines of theatrical or festival release – although so far we cannot quantify its reach.[11]

CONCLUSION

Of the twenty feature length fiction films produced yearly between 2008 and 2018 on average, about a quarter were New Wave films. While this is a fraction of the overall national production, it is a very significant one, as it has garnered the interest of both critics and scholars to watch what this previously obscure national cinema had to offer. Beyond bringing international visibility the New Wave has also contributed to the growth of transnational collaborations in terms of production and distribution.

With limited opportunities for film funding from the Romanian Film Center and increased opportunities for transnational co-productions, Romanian film-makers have resorted to more and more cross-border collaborations. Whether driven by financial need or a shared creative vision – or both – these collabora-tions represent an integral part of New Romanian cinema film production. Even though they are transnationally produced, the characters and stories of these films remain set within the national framework and circumstances. While a typi-cal co-production arrangement includes at least one Western European country in its slate (usually France or Germany), there is a more recent inclination to (also) collaborate with other regional cinemas, such as Bulgaria, Hungary, Czech Republic or Croatia.

While in the case of film productions Romanian filmmakers seek out interna-tional partners, the limited opportunities for exhibition and distribution create tensions between national and transnational structures. Since the very start of New Romanian cinema, festivals played an integral role in its recognition, pro-motion and distribution, without which it would have remained confined within national borders. Instead, a number of Romanian films have had international distribution, including in home media and streaming formats, and form part of a transnational production and distribution network. Meanwhile, national distribution, which is dominated by mainstream cinema and suffers from a pro-nounced lack of exhibition spaces, has pushed filmmakers to find alternative forms of reaching an audience, demonstrating the need for adaptability. Roma-nian cinema in the last decade or so exists in the interstices of world cinema, situated neither fully in the national sphere nor in the international realm.

This extension beyond the national sphere is perhaps most striking in the case of the latest works from key directors of the New Wave, such as Corneliu Porumboiu or Cristi Puiu. Porumboiu's *La Gomera/The Whistlers* (Romania/France/Germany, 2019) is a genre-driven gangster film in which a police officer, intending to carry out a heist, travels to La Gomera, one of the smaller islands in the Canary archipelago, in order to learn a new language of whistling that is used by the locals to communicate. Complete with the figure of a femme fatale[12] the film embraces genre moving beyond the purview of the Romanian New Wave and beyond Romania as a geographical space. Meanwhile, Cristi Puiu's *La conac/Malmkrog* aka *The Manor House* (Romania/Serbia/Switzerland), due to be released in 2020, an adaptation from a book by Russian philosopher Vladimir Solovyov, is a period drama set at the turn of the twentieth century and centred around discussions about death and the Antichrist, morality and progress. This is the first film directed by Puiu with dialogue in a language other than Romanian – French. Combined with Porumboiu's film that is also multilingual and that was partly shot outside Romania, these two films indicate the transnationalisation of Romania cinema, a process that will likely mark Romanian cinema even deeper in the future.

NOTES

1. The two terms are almost used interchangeably. There is, however, a subtle distinction, with the 'New Romanian cinema' being a more inclusive term and referring also to Romanian films that have travelled at international film festivals, even if they do not strictly follow the rigorous formal characteristics introduced by the first 'New Wave' films.
2. It was distributed in thirty countries, garnering 100,000 spectators in France and 13,000 spectators during the opening weekend in Argentina. It attracted about the same number of spectators in Romania, highlighting the limited local appeal of Romanian New Wave films (Blaga 2007).
3. Despite being set to be organised twice yearly, the financing sessions were held only once in 2011, 2012, 2013 and 2017, as well as having no financing sessions for film projects in 2009 and 2015.
4. See Stojanova (2019) on Cristi Puiu's stance on the subject and, more broadly, the discussion on New Romanian cinema. Also, Andrei Gorzo's entry on Romanian cinema after 2000 notes how several contemporary filmmakers reject all manner of labels (2016).
5. Statistics compiled by the non-profit organisation Romanian Film Development (https://romfilmdevelopment.org/en/industrie/statistics-facts/) show that between 2012 and 2016 productions originating from Romania, France and Germany garnered between 1 and 5 million euros combined; US productions would take in between 28 and 46 million euros.
6. For more references to Kazale, see the chapter on Slovenia in this collection.
7. Perhaps interestingly enough, this section – which was introduced officially in 2004 – and the festival itself is run by a team that is involved also in film production (Libra Film), distribution (Transilvania Film) and film promotion as they run an organisation that is involved in the promotion of Romanian cinema (Asociația pentru promovarea filmului românesc/ Romanian Film Promotion), that is a part of the European Film Promotion.
8. *Child's Pose* is available on the Romanian online platform Cinepub (without any paywall, yet with geo-blocking exclusively to the Romanian territory), where it has amassed close to 120,000 spectators, in addition to 118,500 admissions during the national theatrical run.

9. Cinepub – an online platform dedicated solely to the distribution of Romanian films (fiction, documentary, animation, shorts, experimental) – is one such example.

10. See: https://www.cinemagia.ro/boxoffice/romania/

11. According to the European Audiovisual Observatory report on the inclusion of European films in VOD catalogues, Romania ranks 48th in the world and 15th among the European Union countries with fifty-two identified titles and forty-two titles on subscription-based VOD services – such as Netflix, Amazon Prime, etc. (Grece 2018: 106). The 'official' numbers found in institutional reports give only an incomplete portrait of the situation of Romanian film distribution, as it does not include information from streaming services or from what Ramon Lobato calls 'shadow economies of cinema' (2012) – the illegal or semi-legal channels of film distribution – in effect disregarding the presence of films online.

12. This is the character Gilda, who is played by Catrinel Marlon, born Catrinel Menghia, a Romanian-Italian model and actress. Prior to *The Whistlers* she appeared primarily in Italian films and TV series.

References

Batori, Anna (2018) *Space in Romanian and Hungarian Cinema*. Cham: Palgrave Macmillan.

Blaga, Iulia (2007) '*A fost sau n-a fost?* primit elogios de presa americană', *Romania Liberă*, June <http://agenda.liternet.ro/articol/4839/Iulia-Blaga/A-fost-sau-n-a-fost-primit-elogios-de-presa-americana.html> (last accessed 14 May 2020).

CNC (2018) 'Yearbook Cinema. 2018', *Anuar Statistic 2018* <http://cnc.gov.ro/?page_id=52615#1517992957387-91f2468e-12c5> (last accessed 30 November 2019).

Czach, Liz (2004) 'Film Festivals, Programming, and the Building of a National Cinema', *Moving Image*, 4 (1), pp. 76–88.

Finney, Angus (2010) *The International Film Business: A Market Guide Beyond Hollywood*. New York: Routledge.

Galt, Rosalind (2006) *The New European Cinema: Redrawing the Map*. New York: Columbia University Press.

Gorzo, Andrei (2016) 'Realism and Ideology in post-2000 Romanian Cinema', in *Lucruri care nu pot fi spuse altfel*, 25 July <https://andreigorzoblog.wordpress.com/2016/07/25/realism-and-ideology-in-post-2000-romanian-cinema/> (last accessed 30 November 2019).

Grece, Christian (2018) *Films in VOD Catalogues. Origin, Circulation and Age – Edition 2018*. Strasbourg: European Audiovisual Observatory.

Higbee, Will and Lim, Song Hwee (2010) 'Concepts of Transnational Cinema: Towards a Critical Transnationalism in Film Studies', *Transnational Cinemas*, 1 (1), pp. 7–21.

Hjort, Mette (2010), 'On the plurality of cinematic transnationalism', in Nataša Ďurovičová and Kathleen Newman (eds), *World Cinemas, Transnational Perspective*. New York: Routledge, pp. 12–32.

Iordanova, Dina (2009) 'The Film Festival Circuit', in Dina Iordanova and Ragan Rhyne (eds), *Film Festival Yearbook 1: The Festival Circuit*. St Andrews: St Andrews Film Studies, pp. 23–39.

Lobato, Ramon (2012) *Shadow Economies of Cinema. Mapping Informal Film Distribution*. London: British Film Institute/Palgrave Macmillan.

Lodge, Guy (2017) 'Pororoca', *Variety*, 27 September <https://variety.com/2017/film/reviews/pororoca-review-1202573205/> (last accessed 30 November 2019).

Naficy, Hamid (2001) *An Accented Cinema: Exilic and Diasporic Filmmaking*. Princeton, NJ: Princeton University Press.

Nasta, Dominique (2013) *Contemporary Romanian Cinema: The History of an Unexpected Miracle*. London and New York: Wallflower Press.

Pavičić, Jurica (2011) *Postjugoslavenski film: stil i ideologija*. Zagreb: Hrvatski filmski savez.

Pop, Doru (2014) *Romanian New Wave Cinema. An Introduction*. Jefferson, NC: McFarland.

Pop, Doru (2019) 'The "Transnational Turn": New Urban Identities and the Transformation of Contemporary Romanian Cinema', in Christina Stojanova (ed.), *The New Romanian Cinema*. Edinburgh: Edinburgh University Press, pp. 225–39.

Stojanova, Christina (ed.) (2019) *The New Romanian Cinema*. Edinburgh: Edinburgh University Press.

Stojanova, Christina and Duma, Dana (2012) 'New Romanian Cinema Between the Tragic and the Ironic', *Film International*, 10 (1), pp. 7–21.

Strausz, László (2017) *Hesitant Histories on the Romanian Screen*. Basingstoke: Palgrave Macmillan.

Țuțui, Marian and Iacob, Raluca (2019) 'New Romanian Cinema: Geography and Identity', in Christina Stojanova (ed.), *New Romanian Cinema*. Edinburgh: Edinburgh University Press, pp. 211–24.

Uricaru, Ioana (2012) 'Follow the Money: Financing Contemporary Cinema in Romania', in Anikó Imre (ed.), *A Companion to Eastern European Cinemas*. Hoboken, NJ: Wiley-Blackwell, pp. 427–53.

11. SERBIA: RECO(R)DING THE CINEMATIC TURN

Nevena Daković, Aleksandra Milovanović and Iva Leković

Unlike elsewhere in Europe, such as Portugal, Ireland, Italy, Spain and Greece, the effect of the 2008 financial crisis was only indirectly and mildly present in Serbia, as the country still strongly felt the effects of the deep crisis that followed the breakup of the Socialist Federal Republic of Yugoslavia (SFRY) in 1992. Raging wars, corrupt governments, civic protests and huge hyperinflation devastated the country in the 1990s and by 2008 it was still in too weak a position to be significantly affected by the European crisis. Despite short periods of relative stability and progress (notably the early 2000s prior to the assassination of Prime Minister Zoran Đinđić on 12 March 2003), political tensions, confrontations and controversial topics, such as the status of Kosovo and EU integration, have continued to dominate the Serbian public sphere to this day. This has enabled Aleksandar Vučić (Prime Minister 2012–17; President 2017–), whose firm rule has often been compared to the Milošević era in international media, to highlight Serbia's East–West crossroads positioning in order to develop new opportunities for cooperation with EU partners, maintain links with traditional allies (such as Russia and Turkey) and nurture links further afield (China, Saudi Arabia, Azerbaijan).

Since the Yugoslav breakup, the country's socio-economic and political situation has been reflected in the genre broadening and diversification of Serbian film productions. This points to the fact that national cinema moves in two directions – one is outward-orientated, forward-looking and determined to reach and assimilate European and global patterns of popular cinema; the other is more inward-looking and often burdened with gloomy reflections on the country's troubled past and present. These processes are visible in the emergence of new genres and the redefinition of old ones, i.e. via re-genrefication – in other words the development of new genres, or the redefinition of existing ones. Notable among such developments is the exploration of the troubled past through a revival of historical epics and war dramas in feature films, and the engagement with nuanced (hi)stories of familial, local, national and regional topics set in both the past and present in documentaries. This chapter explores genre developments since 2008, and highlights the positive role that a series of institutional changes – notably the introduction of a sustainable and viable national film financing system and the strengthening of regional and European partnerships – have played in supporting the recent successes of Serbian cinema, both at home and abroad.

The founding of the Film Center Serbia (FCS) in 2004, under the auspices of the Ministry of Culture and Information, was crucial for the restructuring of the Serbian film industry, paving the way for a line of internationally recognised and awarded titles. During the first decade of its existence, the Film Center's most important achievement 'was the reorganization of the national cinema structure according to European models' (Daković 2006: 95) that included the creation of a lasting and durable system of national financial subsidies. In the decade since 2008, the FCS has financially supported more than 800 projects (fiction feature and short films, feature and short documentaries, animation and experimental films) many of them being awarded winning titles in Cannes, Berlin or Venice. Indicatively, in 2018 the FCS distributed nearly eight million euros that secured the production of 18 fiction feature films, 31 short features (including student films), 21 documentary films, 12 short documentaries and 23 minority co-productions (Janković 2019a). Serbia joined Eurimages in January 2005 and since then it has received over one million euros (Janković 2018) while ten years later, in December 2015, when it joined the MEDIA programme and until 2019, it has received almost 1.8 million euros – the highest amount in the region – for different projects.[1] At the same time, due to the work of Film Center Serbia, the production of domestic TV series – sometimes made simultaneously with the films – has also flourished,[2] while the number of incentives to attract foreign productions has surpassed all expectations. The FCS is also responsible for the digitalisation (of all aspects of cinema), education and the modernisation of cinema theatres. All the above mentioned activities have strengthened the financial and creative status of Serbian cinema and positioned it as a major regional player in the post-Yugoslav context.

INSTITUTIONS AND THE RISE OF EUROPEAN AND REGIONAL CO-PRODUCTION

Despite delays due to organisational problems, governmental intervention, infrastructure and international relations as well as financing and legal frameworks,

Film Centre Serbia launched a series of reforms. The creation of the Group for Cinematography in 2014 allowed the public to see the cumulative effect of the reforms. The Group consists of representatives of all professional associations of filmmakers in Serbia and functions under the Chamber of Commerce and Industry of Serbia. The work of the Group led to the increase and steadying of the funds available to film production, the harmonisation of the co-production with European and world standards and the inclusion of cinema in the strategic planning and work of the country's creative industries. The most important result of the joint work of the Group and the Film Centre is arguably the introduction of the new cash flow system that allows financial assets from the budget of Ministry of Culture to be relocated to the FCS and then re-distributed through open calls as it enables continuous and regular funding for film production.[3]

The active participation of Serbian companies, as either majority or minority partners in European co-productions, has assured access to bigger markets, richer and global funds, new technologies and skills, desired locations and the overall transfer of knowledge. These co-production initiatives reflect Serbia's specific position in the regional/Balkan/post-Yugoslav and European context, and represent an important step in the country's long and hectic process of EU integration. Additionally, they resonate with the varieties of transnationalism proposed by Mette Hjort (2010): 'epiphanic' – being the projects between post-Yugoslav states that revise the notion of 'Yugoslavhood'; 'affinitive' – referring to Balkan and post-Yugoslav co-productions organically built upon common language and cultural or political heritage; and 'globalizing' – that encompass co-productions with other EU countries.

All national actors in Serbia – i.e. the cultural scene (ministries, institutions, associations, festivals), creative industries (artists and experts), education system (schools, universities, research institutes, conferences, workshops, publishing) and cultural heritage centres (museums, archives, libraries, cinemas) – actively participate in the creation and implementation of a balanced and well-defined cultural policy. The assimilation of EU standards progressively influences sustainable models for the consolidation of the Serbian creative industries, which are based on diversifying funding sources and improving quality. In times of transition, Europeanisation and regionalisation (understood as cooperation and standardisation with both EU and non-EU neighbours, and including both post-Yugoslav and non post-Yugoslav countries) are both evident in Serbian cinema, whether in relation to each other or as separate processes. Regionalisation focuses on individual post-Yugoslav states, while also addressing the whole Balkan region (i.e. Romania, Bulgaria, Greece, Turkey). Regional networking as a long-term strategy for the development of film (co)productions, (new) audiences, festivals and cinema associations, transnational digital platforms for media distribution, interdisciplinary film studies, digital preservation of cultural heritage, is a *sine qua non* for Europeanisation. Although Serbia has

Figure 11.1 *The Load* (Ognjen Glavonić, 2018).

always been part of Europe and European cultural space, its accession to the
EU – EUpeanisation – is still slow, complicated and uncertain. The actual date
of becoming a fully-fledged member is continuously being postponed, while
pro-European opinion among the public is oscillating. Within this context, the
standardisation of education and culture emerges as the easiest way for making
some progress on the road to the EU, and particularly the growing number of
projects supported by Eurimages is a good indicator of success.

While Serbia has not yet been able to become an EU member state, its
active membership in pan-European cultural institutions and networks,
such as Eurimages and the MEDIA programme, has already yielded positive
results in terms of invigorating the local film industry. In the period 2008–18,
Eurimages financed thirty-five feature fiction and documentary films (seventeen major and eighteen minor co-productions) allowing Serbian cinema
to gain transnational visibility and recognition due to the growing number
of awards at prestigious film festivals.[4] However, films supported by Eurimages with Serbia as the major co-production partner seem to have a nar-
rowly defined thematic scope, addressing issues with obvious transnational
appeal. More specifically, they narrate the stories about the disintegration of
Yugoslavia (*Turneja/The Tour* Goran Marković, Serbia/Bosnia-Herzegovina/
Croatia/Slovenia, 2008; *Krugovi/Circles*, Srdan Golubović, Serbia/Germany/
France/Slovenia/Croatia, 2013) or explore the notion of otherness (*Enklava/
Enclave*, Goran Radovanović, Germany/Serbia, 2015; *Parada/Parade*, Srđan
Dragojević, Serbia/Slovenia/Croatia/France/North Macedonia/UK, 2011; *Kad*

Figure 11.2   Poster for *Requiem for Mrs. J* (Bojan Vuletić, 2017).

svane dan/When the Day Breaks, Goran Paskaljević, Serbia/France/Croatia, 2012). These films reinterpret the Balkan conflicts of the 1990s through the dialectics of nationalism, ethnic conflicts and war crimes (*Teret/The Load*, Ognjen Glavonić, Serbia/France/Croatia/Iran/Qatar, 2018), while often stressing the overall dehumanisation and moral decay (*Vlažnost/Humidity*, Nikola Ljuca, Serbia/Netherlands/Greece, 2016; *Rekvijem za gospođu J./Requiem for Mrs. J.*, Bojan Vuletić, Serbia/Bulgaria/North Macedonia/Russia/France/Germany, 2017; *Šavovi/The Stitches,* Miroslav Terzić, Serbia, 2019). Most of them are co-productions with partners from other post-Yugoslav countries and address common topics explored in the cinema of the region: memory and trauma, war crimes and dehumanisation, the ever increasing rate of crime, corruption and poverty.

Regional co-productions are well established among the countries of the former Yugoslavia. Shared experiences before and after the wars of the 1990s provide common thematic ground for cinematic narratives, while pre-existing collaborations across the federal republics in the socialist years have resulted in the establishment of common practices. Post-war/post-Yugoslav narratives often evoke life in former Yugoslavia and its traumatic breakup, scrutinising and criticising post-Yugoslav societies. As Dina Iordanova notes, 'it seems that all important films from the region ultimately deal with historic memory. More specifically, history is treated as something to endure, to live through, a process where one does not have agency but is subjected to the will power of external forces' (Iordanova 2007: 22). Each of these films also plays an important role in public debates and institutional processes – developing along the lines of truth, peace and reconciliation – in its distinctive way. For example, the Serbian minority productions *Aleksi* (Barbara Vekarić, Croatia/Serbia, 2018), and *Ti imaš noć/You Have the Night* (Ivan Salatić, Montenegro/Serbia, 2018) are evidence of such regional cross-cultural projects. The Bosnian film *Žaba/ The Frog* (Elmir Jukić, Bosnia-Herzegovina/North Macedonia/Serbia/Croatia, 2017) in which Serbia participates as a minority co-producer together with a number of former Yugoslav partners explores collective guilt and trauma in an apparently cosmopolitan and tolerant society. Dalibor Matanić's *Zvizdan/ The High Sun* (Croatia/Serbia/Slovenia, 2015), a minority co-production with Croatia, depicts the love story between a Croat man and a Serbian woman and the fragility and enduring strength of their forbidden love across three decades, from the time of prewar ethnic tensions to the aftermath of the wars of 1990s.

The provision of services for foreign productions in Serbia (as in other Balkan and European countries, such as Bulgaria, Hungary and the Czech Republic) is another dimension of the transnational and globalising tendencies that characterise the audiovisual industries in recent years. The Serbian Film Commission (Srpska filmska asocijacija, branded as Film in Serbia) was established in 2009 in order to facilitate cross-cultural filmmaking and promote Serbia as an attractive destination for investments (Simić 2015). In 2018, the Serbian government adopted a new Decree on Incentivising Investments in Production of Audio-visual Works that raised a percentage on the cash return from 15–20 per cent to 25 per cent for all direct film productions. According to the authors of the *Film Production Guide*, 'the quality services, low production costs and professional labour force [make] Serbia one of the most attractive filming locations in the region' (Karanović and Nikolić 2016: 16). The new system secured an effective platform for the branding and promotion of Serbia, facilitating networking between foreign and local filmmakers and professionals while simultaneously raising the employment rate in the film industry and related sectors. The top companies servicing the production of foreign films in Serbia are Work in Progress, Red Production and Art & Popcorn with projects such as *A Series of Unfortunate Events* (Barry Sonnenfeld, USA, 2017), *The White Crow* (Ralph Fiennes, UK/France/ Serbia, 2018) and *Anna* (Luc Besson, France/USA, 2019). By the end of 2017, foreign production services in Serbia made a profit of 58.5 million euros, out of which 35 million were reinvested in the national feature film production budget (Janković 2019a).

New and Old Genres

The emergence of new genres that broadened and diversified the rather limited genre spectre of the cinema of former Yugoslavia and the transformation of existing ones (re-genrefication) reflect a range of changes in Serbian cinema and culture since 2008. The 1990s were marked by a new generation of filmmakers – the 'generational turn' – and the appearance of a 'new wave' in national cinema – 'the New Belgrade School or Belgrade's guerrilla' with emblematic films such as *Mi nismo anđeli/We Are No Angels* (Srđan Dragojević, Yugoslavia, 1992) and *Kad porastem biću kengur/When I Grow Up I Want to Be a Kangaroo* (Raša Andrić, Serbia, 2004). The New Belgrade school films were highly self-conscious and richly intertextual (with quotations, allusions and references), while their dominant urban atmosphere is presented as escapist (the characters' world is protected from the gloomy reality), cosmopolitan (bridging the gap with the world) and postmodern (eclectic in style). The topics of these films point to and reflect the beginning of re-genrefication 'as a process deeply contextualised within socio-economic and cultural conditions; shaped through the traces of the changing cinematic cityscape of New Belgrade as the site of the shifts brought about by socialist/ postsocialist transition' (Daković 2008). Many new genres, often involving hybridisation, assimilation and appropriation of Hollywood models, were introduced in subsequent years. These included horror (*T.T. Sindrom/T.T. Syndrome*, Dejan Zečević, Federal Republic of Yugoslavia, 2002; *Šejtanov ratnik/Sheitan Warrior*, Stevan Filipović, Serbia, 2006; *Mamula /Nymph*, Milan Todorović, Serbia/Montenegro, 2014), neo-noir (*Mehanizam /The Mechanism*, Đorđe Milosavljević, Federal Republic of Yugoslavia, 2000; *Četvrti čovek/ The Fourth Man*, Dejan Zečević, Serbia, 2007), zany comedies (*Ringeraja/ Ringeraja,* Đorđe Milosavljević, Federal Republic of Yugoslavia, 2002; *Mala noćna muzika/Little Night Music*, Dejan Zečević, Federal Republic of Yugoslavia, 2002), (meta)melodramas (*Skoro sasvim obična priča/An Almost Ordinary Story*, Miloš Petričić, Serbia, 2003); melodrama/ethno-Westerns (*Čarlston za ognjenku/Tears for Sale*, Uroš Stojanović, Serbia, 2008), ghetto films (*Apsolutnih sto/Absolute Hundred*, Srdan Golubović, Federal Republic of Yugoslavia, 2001; *1 na 1/One on One,* Mladen Matičević, Federal Republic of Yugoslavia, 2002), fiction-faction films (*Beogradski fantom/The Belgrade Phantom*, Jovan Todorović, Serbia/Hungary/Bulgaria, 2009), Dogme-like stories (*Sutra ujutru/Tomorrow Morning*, Oleg Novković, Serbia, 2006), workers' opera (*Beli, beli Svet/White White World*, Oleg Novković, Serbia/ Germany/Sweden, 2010) or musical (*Praktični vodič kroz Beograd sa pevanjem i plakanjem /Practical Guide to Belgrade with Singing and Crying*, Bojan Vuletić, Serbia/Germany/France/Hungary/Croatia, 2011) and science fiction films (*Ederlezi Rising/A.I. Rising*, Lazar Bodroža, Serbia, 2018).

The growing number of co-productions and public calls for funding – aimed for thematic or otherwise defined categories – supports the creation of new genres, or the transformation of existing ones. There are different calls for films with a national theme, for commercial films, for documentaries and, since 2019, for children's and new directors' films. A number of films made within these categories brought audiences back to cinemas, allowing us to speak about the emergence of (national) blockbusters. Traditionally in Serbia, the biggest box office hits are romance, comedy or action films (*Mali Budo/ Little Buddho*, Serbia/Slovenia/Bosnia and Herzegovina/Switzerland, Danilo Bećković, 2014; *Jesen samuraja/The Samurai in Autumn*, Danilo Bećković, Serbia, 2016). Two films directed by Dragan Bjelogrlić, *Montevideo, Bog te video!/Montevideo, Taste of a Dream!* (Serbia, 2010) and *Montevideo, vidimo se!/See you in Montevideo!* (Serbia, 2014) managed to come close to the record held by Zdravko Šotra's *Zona Zamfirova* (Federal Republic of Yugoslavia, 2002), the most popular Serbian film of the millennium with 1,200,000 admissions in a country with a population of barely over 7 million. Bjelogrlić's films are based on the true event of the victory of the Serbian football team in the World Cup in Uruguay in 1930, which is presented in a romantic manner skilfully combining love, sport and politics. References to the glory of the Great War gave the film the tone of national melodrama and boosted the sense of national pride.

In the decade under examination, the most recent box office record for a Serbian film was set by Miloš Avramović's *Južni vetar/The South Wind* (Serbia, 2018) with 700,000 admissions.[5] The film tells the story of a young hero (played by Miloš Biković) from the Belgrade 'pavilions' (poor, ghetto-like high-rise blocks such as the *HLM* in the Parisian banlieu) who is involved in the selling of stolen cars, and is accidentally caught up in the war between two rival drug-dealing gangs. In an ending that meets the ambivalent moral standards of a society in transition, he volunteers to serve the prison sentence with a mischievous smile promising that he would return afterwards only to start new adventures. This is an action-packed thriller, a typical drug-trafficking crime film that follows standards established by Hollywood action films, which include explicit violence, street language, ghetto humour, expert camera work and tight plots. The film represents a trend evident in other Serbian blockbusters, of adopting Hollywood-derived narrative and stylistic formulas in stories set in Serbia and, sometimes, the wider Balkans.

Table 11.1 offers a map of the current generic regime in Serbian cinema, suggesting some of the complexities related to re-genrefication and genre diversification, as developed by combining familiar and established genre conventions with new local elements, or by adapting world narratives to the regional social context. It should be noted that the genre terminology used here reflects common use by audiences, critics and the creative industry.

Table 11.1 Feature fiction film production (2008–18) classified according to genre.

Genre	Production	Total	Examples
Comedy: Zany Urban Musical Worker's opera	National productions	17	*Čitulja za Eskobara/Obituary for Escobar* (2008) *Falsifikator/Falsifier* (2013) *Mali Budo/Little Buddho* (2014)
	Majority co-productions	15	*Turneja/The Tour* (2008) *Parada/The Parade* (2011) *Stado/Herd* (2016)
	Minority co-productions	10	*Nije kraj/Will Not End Here* (2008) *Cirkus Kolumbija/Cirkus Columbia* (2010) *Godina majmuna/Year of the Monkey* (2018)
Drama: Social drama Romance Ethno-melodrama	National	24	*Krugovi/Circles* (2013) *Na mlečnom putu/On the Milky Road* (2016)
	Majority	28	*Beli beli svet/White White World* (2010) *Vlažnost/Humidity* (2015) *Rekvijem za gospodju J./Requiem for Mrs. J.* (2017) *Teret/The Load* (2018)
	Minority	26	*Kenjac/Donkey* (2009) *Zvizdan/The High Sun* (2015) *Žaba/The Frog* (2017)
War Historical themes with national importance	National	5	*Sveti Georgije ubiva azdahu/St. George Shoots the Dragon* (2009) *Kad svane dan/When Day Breaks* (2012) *Kralj Petar I/King Peter I* (2018)
	Majority	7	*Neprijatelj/The Enemy* (2011) *Branio sam Mladu Bosnu/The Man Who Defended Gavrilo Princip* (2014) *Zaspanka za vojnike/Soldier's Lullaby* (2018)
	Minority	4	*Brat Dejan/Brother Deyan* (2015)
Adventure Fantasy Horror	National	11	*Čarlston za Ognjenku/Tears for Sale* (2008) *Život i smrt porno bande/The Life and Death of a Porno Gang* (2009)
	Majority	3	*Mamula/Nymph* (2014) *Ederlezi Rising/A.I. Rising* (2018)
	Minority	2	*Noć grešnika/Night of the Sinner* (2010)
Action Thriller Crime Ghetto film Dogme stories	National	19	*Beogradski Fantom/The Belgrade Phantom* (2009) *Južni vetar/South Wind* (2018)
	Majority	4	*Ustanička ulica/Redemption Street* (2012) *Izgrednici/Offenders* (2017)
	Minority	5	*Metastaze/Metastasis* (2009)
Children *La jeunesse désaffectée* *(disaffected youth)*	National	24	*Klip/Clip* (2012) *Pored mene/Next to Me* (2015)
	Majority	10	*Tilva Roš/Tilva Ros* (2010) *Kutija/The Box* (2011) *Neposlušni/The Disobedient* (2014) *Varvari/Barbarians* (2014)
	Minority	3	*Aleksi* (2018)

Data from Film Centre Serbia and the book *Kritički Vodič Kroz Srpski Film/A Critical Guide of Serbian Film, 2000–2017* (Bajić et al. 2018).

Of the genre categories listed in the table, the one that stands out as distinctive is the new subgenre of mainly debutant films of the new generation of directors that emerged in the 2010s, and which can be labelled as *la jeunesse désaffectée* ('disaffected youth'). The term was coined by the French philosopher Bernard Stiegler and used to describe the universal phenomena of unmotivated, impatient, disoriented, unsatisfied and deprived youth communities. In the local context, it also denotes young filmmakers 'born at the beginning of the 1990s (. . .) – those who matured in poverty, sanctions, and transitions without a certain and/or clearly envisioned future' (Daković and Seničić 2019: 147). The films are thematically consistent and offer a critical depiction of the situation that their young protagonists find themselves in, without, however, morally condemning them. Titles include *Tilva Roš/Tilva Ros* (Nikola Ležaić, Serbia, 2010), *Klip/Clip* (Maja Miloš, Serbia, 2012), *Varvari/Barbarians* (Ivan Ikić, Serbia/Montenegro/Slovenia/Bosnia-Herzegovina, 2014), *Neposlušni/The Disobedient* (Mina Đukić, Serbia, 2014), *Panama* (Pavle Vučković, Serbia, 2015). The new wave of young directors in Serbia brought a fresh perspective on socio-political changes, adolescent violence, intolerance and bigotry, dysfunctional family relationships, sexuality and drug addiction, disillusionment and life at the margin, while framing these within formal devices reflecting the virtual digital world shared by young people in all the Balkans – and beyond.[6]

Cultural Memory in Fiction and Documentary

Other prominent genres in Serbian cinema since 2008 are, on the one hand, historical epics and dramas dealing with key moments in national history (eleven and seventy-eight films produced respectively – see Table 11.1), and on the other, the growing number of documentary and docu-fiction films tackling socialist, post-socialist and post-national stories, and getting the critical acclaim at international film festivals (four and sixteen documentaries produced respectively – see the Tables at the back of the book). In this respect, the new categories of the Film Centre Serbia's funding calls, as indicated above, reinforced genre changes that had already manifested themselves, thus playing both a reactive and a proactive role in shaping up future films. The cultural and political atmosphere in the country during the two decades following the Yugoslav breakup led to a nationally biased historical revisionism reflected to a large extent on the emphasis on public anniversaries of historical events. The emergence of fiction films dealing with suffering and martyrdom and Serbia's glorious past should be seen in the context of such broader developments. Such historical revisionism is evident in all constitutive members of the former Yugoslavia as every republic sought to rewrite past and history – from medieval times through to the Great War and the Second World War – in order to construct a firm national identity and tradition of a sovereign country. Previously shared national narratives underwent an ideological revision especially with reference to Second World War (hi)story. Examples of such revisionism in the region include the Serbian TV series, *Ravna Gora* (Radoš Bajić, Serbia, 2013–14) and the film *Za kralja i otadžbinu/For King and Homeland* (Radoš Bajić, Serbia, 2015), as well as the Croatian films *Četverored/In Four Rows* (Jakov Sedlar, Croatia, 1999) and *Duga mračna noć/Long Dark Night* (Antun Vrdoljak, Croatia, 2004) that rewrite the history of the Second World War, depicting Chetniks and Ustashas as national liberators and freedom fighters that consensually take over the role played by the Partisans.

The wave of films about anniversaries and celebrations of the Great War began with *Sveti Georgije ubiva azdahu/St. George Shoots the Dragon* (Srđan Dragojević, Serbia/Bosnia-Herzegovina/Bulgaria, 2009) followed by *Branio sam mladu Bosnu/The Man Who Defended Gavrilo Princip* (Srđan Koljević, Serbia, 2014), *Zaspanka za vojnike/Soldier's Lullaby* (Predrag Antonijević, Serbia, 2018), only to end with the first film subsidised in the new open call for films with a national theme (of national importance) – *Kralj Petar I/King Peter I* (Petar Ristovski, Serbia/Greece, 2018). Constructed as a national spectacle, in many ways it echoes the nation-building historical melodrama D. W. Griffith's *Birth of a Nation* (USA, 1915), as it recounts a historical episode of the withdrawal of the Serbian Army through the Albanian mountains. Ordinary people, hungry and sick soldiers and King Peter I – the warm and beloved figure of Serbian history – march through snow and cold to the Albanian shore with the help of the Allies only to reach Corfu, Africa and other places of recovery – and death, since many thousands died of exhaustion on the Greek island of Vido near Corfu. Impressive camera work, the solid reconstruction of the epoch and the well-measured acting of Lazar Ristovski as King Peter, amply compensate the problems of a story originally made for a TV series and not for a feature-length film. Ideologically, the film reinforces Serbian national sentiments reproducing the myth of Serbian martyrdom, with respect both to the fourteenth-century Battle of Kosovo (1389) and the 1915 withdrawal (in the context of the First World War) when the fate of the country was again decided in the same place. In the decisive withdrawal – for saving the people, the king and the government – the Serbian army fought against dangerous attacks (including robberies and massacres) of the Albanian and Kosovo outlaws, paramilitaries and gangs. The events of the First World War even today strongly echo and shape the contemporary relations between Serbia, France and Albania as well as the question of Kosovo.

While the fiction films tend to promote a fairly simplistic and nation-boosting account of an ideologically charged national narrative, several Serbian documentaries in the recent decade have achieved international success and critical acclaim, proposing a more nuanced and multi-perspectival vision of the country's complex past and equally challenging present. Despite 'the market, the conditions in which

Figure 11.3   *The Other Side of Everything* (Mila Turajlić, 2017).

films are being produced, taboos and conformity' (Otašević 2018: 5), Serbian documentary filmmakers have been well-received within national, regional and European contexts and at film festivals.

The unprecedented success of Mila Turajlić's *Druga strana svega/The Other Side of Everything* (Serbia/France/Qatar/Germany/Hungary, 2017) – winning the award of the main competition at IDFA in Amsterdam and automatically becoming a candidate for the Oscars – confirmed the wide international outreach of Serbian documentary production. Turajlić's film follows the pattern set by several documentaries that explore the complex functioning of cultural memory that prevails over simplistic or propagandistic accounts of history. These include her own *Cinema Komunisto* (Mila Turajlić, Serbia, 2010), *Jugoslavija: kako je ideologija pokretala naše kolektivno telo/Yugoslavia: How Ideology Moved our Collective Body* (Marta Popivoda, Serbia/France/Germany, 2013), and *Valter: Mit. Legenda. Heroj/Valter: Myth, Legend, Hero* (Andrej Aćin, Serbia, 2012). These films 'symptomatically explore the history of SFRY, its birth, crises and decline under the rule of Josip Broz Tito', and 'due to hybridization and montage principles the film texts build up to docu-fiction of socialism in post socialism', and 'recount the post-Yugoslav (after the breakup of SFRY), post-socialist (after the collapse of socialism) and post-national tales' (Daković 2017: 68). Most recently, due to the 2016 refugee crises, which rendered Serbia one of the principal transit routes for many Middle East refugees, the migrant destinies became the topic of several documentaries – by the veteran filmmaker Želimir Žilnik (*Destinacija Serbistan/Logbook Serbistan*, Serbia, 2015; *Najlepša zemlja na svetu/The most Beautiful Country in the World*, Austria/Serbia, 2018) and the considerably younger Marko Grba Singh (*Abdul & Hamza*, Serbia and Montenegro, 2015). The strong presence of female authors in documentaries – following in the vein of Eurimages' gender equality strategy of 50/50 by 2020 – is evidence that Serbian documentary filmmakers have been acting as human rights activists within the national, regional and wider European context. Their films – including *Zvezda je rođena/A Star is Born* (Vanja Kovačević, Serbia, 2010), *Kosma* (Sonja Blagojević, Serbia and Montenegro, 2013), *Okupirani bioskop/ Occupied Cinema*, Senka Domanović, Serbia, 2018) and *Wongar* (Andrijana Stojković, Serbia, 2018) – have been in the spotlight of the international festivals. At the same time, one notices the revival of animated films, due to award-winning films such as the short *Rabbitland* (Nikola Majdak and Ana Nedeljković, Serbia and Montenegro, 2013) that was awarded the Crystal Bear at the Berlinale.

FILM FESTIVALS, DISTRIBUTION AND EXHIBITION

In order to increase and promote the transnational and global circulation of films, the Ministry of Culture provides annual financial support for national film festivals. Thus in 2018 and 2019 almost 60 festivals received more than half a million euros (FEST, the Auteur Film Festival, Kusturica's Kustendorf Film Festival, the European Film Festival Palić, among others). European funding by the MEDIA programme (2016–18) has supported industry-orientated events, such as film markets and audience development activities at one feature and two documentary film festivals. The Film Center Serbia regularly promotes Serbian films at international film festivals and in 2018, 15 films (seven documentaries and two animated films) benefitted from such subsidies. The positive changes in Serbian documentary film – increased production, interest in art documentaries demonstrated both by directors and producers, the quality of the films as proven by numerous awards at international film festivals, the growing popularity of documentary film festivals and the diversification of their programme to include workshops, debates and seminars – are primarily the result of the systematic joint work of the Film Center and the professional association DOKSerbia – Docu- mentary Filmmakers of Serbia (DOKSrbija – Udruženje Dokumentarista Srbije). The association was founded in 2015 with the aim of sustaining Serbian filmmak- ers and documentary films both locally and internationally. Consequently, the number of documentaries, institutionally and financially supported by the FCS, has almost tripled: from 15 supported projects in 2014, it had gone up to 43 in 2018 (Milošević 2018: 1). The affirmation of documentary film is also reinforced by well conceptualised and specialised film festivals that support decentralisation and the development of industry programmes. In Belgrade alone there are five of those: Belgrade Documentary and Short Film Festival (Martovski Festival, the oldest, founded in 1954), Dock #1 (the newest, first organised in January

2019), Magnificent 7 Festival, Free Zone Film Festival and Beldocs. Supported by the MEDIA programme, the latter is a multifunctional platform that includes screenings of national documentary films, industry activities, including a pitching forum, sales and distribution, and educational events such as master classes and educational workshops.

Another important step towards the strengthening of the local film industry is the ongoing digitalisation of the cinema infrastructure, in other words, the equipment of film theatres with facilities for digital, 3D and 4D projection. In 2017, the FCS and the MEDIA programme Serbia supported the digitalisation of 22 cinema theatres across the country. This process resulted in the doubling of the number of the cinema-goers suggesting that the audience had been eagerly waiting for the modernised European-like conditions of film-viewing. The results shown in Table 11.2 present the number of cinemas in Serbia in the last decade: the big drop in 2013 and, more importantly, the immediate success of 75 per cent of digitally equipped cinema halls in 2017.

Table 11.2 Cinemas in Serbia.

Year			Digital screens and cinemas	Number of spectators	Box office total (in euros)
2008	Number of screens	124	–	1,486,500	4,037,586
	Number of cinemas	101			
2009	Screens	123	–	1,713,600	4,624,978
	Cinemas	92			
2010	Screens	110	–	2,062.200	5,824,800
	Cinemas	80			
2011	Screens	117	13	2,625,000	7,105,800
	Cinemas	82	6		
2012	Screens	123	24	2,369,900	6,617,900
	Cinemas	81	11		
2013	Screens	102	27	2,368,300	6,926,400
	Cinemas	71	11		
2014	Screens	114	43 (38 3D)	3,157,300	9,573,000
	Cinemas	74	14		
2015	Screens	118	47 (42 3D)	3,161,700	9,441,200
	Cinemas	75	15		
2016	Screens	118	78 (63 3D)	3,530,700	10,939,600
	Cinemas	61	28		
2017	Screens	134	102 (83 3D)	4,148,700	13,645,000
	Cinemas	65	34		
2018	Screens	158	130 (115 3D)	4,476,000	14,613,200
	Cinemas	70	42		

Data: Film Center Serbia and the Statistical Office of the Republic of Serbia.

Digitalisation also had a positive impact on archives, as films and associated documents from the past can now be not only preserved but also more effectively disseminated. The digitalisation of film related documents and cultural heritage began with a highly successful project, the digital repository of *Filmske Sveske* (1968–86) in 2017. *Filmske Sveske* is the most important film review in the former Yugoslavia and Eastern Europe – conceptualised and named after legendary French review *Cahiers du Cinéma*. The digital repository – made as the joint venture of the Faculty of Dramatic Arts in Belgrade, the mathematical institute of SASA (Serbian Academy of Science and Arts) and Film Center Serbia – contains all published issues of *Filmske Sveske*, a specially developed advanced search system and additional space for the entry of new critical notes. The online platform, thus made important and relevant theoretical film heritage accessible to all generations of film scholars and all those interested in film theory.

The digitalisation of archival material related to cinema and the material related to digital literacy does not only comply with the Council of Europe's directives regarding the preservation of cultural heritage but is proclaimed by the Film Center Serbia as one of the main strategic goals for the next decade. The digitalisation project of the greatest treasures 'of national film history', coordinated by the Yugoslav Film Archive, includes film classics such as: *Ko to tamo peva/Who's Singin' Over There?* (Slobodan Šijan, Yugoslavia, 1980), *Nacionalna klasa/National Class Category Up to 785 ccm* (Goran Marković, Yugoslavia, 1979), *Skupljači perja/I Even Met Happy Gypsies* (Aleksandar Petrović, Yugoslavia, 1967) and *Kad budem mrtav i beo/When I Am Dead and Pale* (Živojin Pavlović, Yugoslavia, 1967). The digitalised copies of the classics were shown at national and international film festivals (Cannes Classic programme in 2017 and the Forum at the Berlin Film Festival in 2018).

Conclusion

The Film Centre Serbia has played a key role in planning and supporting the development of Serbian cinema, and the last decade (2008–18) saw the positive results of the organisational and infrastructural investments it initiated. Since its foundation in 2004, the FCS placed emphasis on achieving self-sustainability, developing strategic policies and implementing a new legal and administrative framework according to EU standards. After the post-communist, postwar and post-democratic revolution turmoil, Serbian efforts for Europeanisation and EUpeanisation led to membership in Eurimages and the MEDIA programme, which have helped the dynamic progress of various kinds of co-productions and partnerships (post-Yugoslav, Balkan and European).

The widening and diversification of the genre spectrum, as discussed above, testifies that national cinema moves in two directions. On the one hand, it is moving away from direct political premises as it becomes determined to reach and assimilate European and world patterns of commercial and popular cinema. On the other hand, it offers innovative insights into the past and turbulent social present that determine its gloomy future.

While the impact of the post-2008 economic crisis on national cinema has been almost negligble, Serbia continues to be permanently affected by low-profile crises since the 1990s. The cinematic turn in Serbian cinema – recognised both by film scholars and policy-makers – is the cumulative result of the period from 1990 and the ongoing crises till today. The 'cinematic turn' is reflected in the consolidation of institutions and the legislative framework; the thematic and genre shifts that include genrefication and genre diversification; the digitalisation of cinemas and audiovisual heritage; the regional co-production development and the transnational integration within European cinema. Serbian cinema heads along the rhizomatic roads between post-Yugoslav states, the Balkans and Europe – and an unstable EU in crisis – while strengthening its presence and position in the region.

NOTES

1. MEDIA-supported projects from Serbia (2016–18) include: *Zlogonje/The Witch Hunters* (Rasko Miljković, Serbia/North Macedonia, 2018), *Otac/Father* (Srdan Golubović, Serbia/France/Germany/Slovenia/Croatia, 2019), *Strahinja* (Stefan Arsenijević, Serbia/France/Luxembourg/Bulgaria, 2019) and *The Labudović Files* (Mila Turajlić, in production).

2. The most popular TV series are: *Ubice mog oca/My Father's Killers* (Predrag Antonijević, Serbia, 2016), *Senke nad Balkanom/Shadows over Balkan*, also known as *Black Sun* (Dragan Bjelogrlić, Serbia/Russia/Bosnia-Herzegovina/North Macedonia, 2017) and *Jutro će promeniti sve/Morning Changes Everything* (Goran Stanković and Vladimir Tagić, Serbia, 2018).

3. The budget of the Ministry of Culture revolves around 0.7 per cent of the total GDP while the film industry contributes with 0.06 per cent to the national GDP, as estimated in 2014.

4. *Circles* received around twenty-six awards among which were the Special Jury Prize (Sundance), the Prize of Ecumenical Jury (Berlin) and the Audience Award (Sarajevo); *Requiem for Mrs. J.* won twenty-two awards (Grand prix Fest, Grand prix Otranto film festival); *Load* won the Cineuropa award (Trieste) and the Heart of Sarajevo for the leading actor, and widely circulated at film festivals around the world.

5. In 2016, the most popular domestic film in Serbian cinemas was *Stado/Herd* (Nikola Kojo, Serbia) with 163,395 admissions, while in 2017 *Zona Zamfirova 2* (Jug Radivojević, Serbia) had 190,442 admissions and *Na Mlečnom putu/On the Milky Way* (Emir Kusturica, Serbia/UK/USA) had 64,466 admissions. Total admissions increased from 3,754,368 in 2017 to 4,193,755 in 2018, mostly due to the blockbusters *South Wind* and *King Petar I* (168,447 admissions) (comp. Janković 2019b).

6. The topic of youth delinquency and borderline behaviour is also strongly present in the work of the experienced Dejan Zečević in a minimalistically stylised neo-noir/thriller *Izgrednici/Offenders*, Serbia, 2017). The plot revolves around three sociology

students who conduct an experiment – 'they set up surveillance cameras in a neighbourhood of apartment blocks in New Belgrade, infamous for dilapidation, graffiti and various criminal groups, from petty thieves and drug dealers to football hooligans' (Petković 2018) – led by their Machiavellian professor.

REFERENCES

Bajić, Đorđe, Janković, Zoran and Velisavljević, Ivan (2018) *Kritički vodič kroz srpski film 2000–2017*. Beograd: Filmski Centar Srbije.

Daković, Nevena (2006) 'Europe Lost and Found: Serbian Cinema and EU Integration', *New Cinemas: Journal of Contemporary Film*, 4 (2), pp. 93–103.

Daković, Nevena (2008) *Balkan kao (filmski) žanr: slika, tekst, nacija*. Fakultet dramskih umetnosti: Institut za pozorište, film, radio i televiziju.

Daković, Nevena (2017) 'The Other Side of Socialism: History and Cinematic Memory of Socialism', *Contemporary Southeastern Europe*, 4 (2), pp. 61–78.

Daković, Nevena and Seničić, Maša (2019) 'La jeunesse désaffectée in contemporary Serbian cinema', in Betty Kaklamanidou and Ana Corbalán (eds), *Contemporary European Cinema: Crisis Narratives and Narratives in Crisis*. New York: Routledge, pp. 147–60.

DokSerbia /DokSrbija <http://doksrbija.rs> (last accessed 8 January 2019).

Film in Serbia (2019) 'Serbia increases cash rebate to 25%', 13 February <http://www.filminserbia.com/news/serbia-increases-cash-rebate-to-25/> (last accessed 10 March 2019).

Filmske sveske (1968–86) <www.filmskesveske.mi.sanu.ac.rs> (last accessed 12 May 2019).

Hjort, Mette (2010) 'On the Plurality of Cinematic Transnationalism', in Nataša Ďurovičová and Kathleen E. Newman (eds), *World Cinemas, Transnational Perspectives*. London: Routledge, pp. 12–32.

Iordanova, Dina (2007) 'Whose Is This Memory? Hushed Narratives and Discerning Remembrance in Balkan Cinema', *Cineaste*, 32 (3), pp. 22–7.

Janković, Zoran (2018) 'Nakon uspešne 2018. godine, veći budžet za srpski film za godinu pred nama', FCS, 25 December <http://www.fcs.rs/nakon-uspesne-2018-veci-budzet-za-srpski-film-za-godinu-pred-nama/> (last accessed 28 December 2018).

Janković, Zoran (2019a) 'Serbia, Market Analysis 2018', *Film New Europe* <https://www.filmneweurope.com/countries/serbia> (last accessed 22 April 2019).

Janković, Zoran (2019b) 'Gordan Matić je novi direktor Filmskog centra Srbije', FCS, 21 July <http://www.fcs.rs/32272/> (last accessed 22 July 2018).

Karanović, Dragan and Nikolić, Dejan (2016) *Film Production Guide*. Beograd: Film in Serbia.

Milošević, Nenad (2018) *Catalog Serbian Docs 2018/2019*. Beograd: FCS and DokSerbia.

Otašević, Ana (2018) 'Extending the Borders of Possible', in Nenad Milošević (ed.), *Catalog Serbian Docs 2018 /2019*. Beograd: FCS and DokSerbia, pp. 4–5.

Petković, Vladan (2018) 'Review: Offenders', *Cineuropa*, 6 March <https://cineuropa.org/en/newsdetail/349222/> (last accessed 15 February 2019).

Simić, Vladimir (2015) 'Analiza organizacione i upravljačke strukture na primeru Srpske filmske asocijacije', *Ekonomija teorija i praksa*, 8 (4), pp. 28–46.

Statistical Office of the Republic of Serbia/Republički zavod za statistiku <http://www.stat.gov.rs/sr-Latn/oblasti/kultura/institucije-kulture> (last accessed 28 August 2018).

12. SLOVENIA: A SMALL NATIONAL CINEMA IN THE PHASE OF TRANSNATIONAL SYNERGY

Polona Petek

For nearly two decades film scholars have produced books, articles, journals and conferences suggesting the paradigm of national cinema is out of fashion, if not indeed completely outdated, and 'transnationalism' is the new catchword of informed film scholarship. More recently, critical voices have emerged questioning the utility of the term that seems to be used either as a self-evident or a catch-all term; as Mette Hjort has put it, 'the term "transnational" has assumed a referential scope so broad as to encompass phenomena that are surely more interesting for their differences than their similarities' (2009: 13). Therefore, to retain its critical purchase, the term's plurality must be taken into account, while it is also imperative to bear in mind 'the persistence of nation in various transnational constellations' (Hjort and Petrie 2007: 2). Particularly small national cinemas, as defined by Mette Hjort and Duncan Petrie (2007), exhibit this persistence while exemplifying the emergence of regional networks and alliances as transnational alternatives to both any rigid idea of national cinema and the culturally homogenising model of contemporary global Hollywood.

Slovenia fits Hjort and Petrie's definition of small national cinema perfectly. Since the declaration of independence in 1991, which brought Slovenian national cinema proper into being, it has met its criteria of size (population, area, gross national product) and, to some extent, the criterion of having a history of being subject to domination (in three different political formations). The latter meant that the 1990s and the first few years of the new millennium were the period of laying the groundwork, and establishing a new infrastructure for film in Slovenia. In 1994, the Slovenski filmski sklad/Slovenian Film Fund was established, which was succeeded in 2011 by the still functioning Slovenski filmski center/Slovenian Film Centre (SFC). The year 2001, when Slovenia joined Eurimages, is another landmark. Other major milestones are 2004 and 2007, the years Slovenia joined the European Union and the Eurozone respectively, which significantly improved transnational and international connectivity of Slovenian filmmakers.[1] However, throughout this formative period Slovenian cinema remained fairly 'closed', with national productions by far outnumbering majority and minority co-productions and with very few films reaching international audiences. It is only in the last decade that Slovenian cinema has begun to display the most enabling aspect of Hjort and Petrie's definition of small national cinema: its active, strategic participation in transnational networks and alliances. This is evident in the films themselves, their casts and crews, their funding sources and their authors' thematic and stylistic preoccupations; even more importantly, however, the ramifications of this recent transnationalisation are visible in Slovenia's film culture at large, its investment in improving film literacy, developing film scholarship, exploring its own history and maintaining a lively festival culture.

It makes sense then, to start this journey through the recent history of Slovenian cinema in 2008. Obviously, as the year that marks the onset of the most recent global economic crisis, its consequences were felt globally and Slovenian film production was no exception.[2] More importantly, however, 2008 is a legitimate point of departure because it marks the beginning of a truly transnational phase in Slovenian cinema. To map this profound transformation of filmmaking and of Slovenian film culture as a whole, this chapter is divided into two sections. The first section discusses the work of established auteurs and provocative emergent figures, detecting some shared features and speculating about the reasons for the emergence of a fairly distinctive aesthetics among such different filmmakers. It also identifies women as a specific group on the rise not only within the new generation of filmmakers, but also among decision-makers and educators. The second section presents a broader picture of contemporary Slovenian film culture. It outlines the vibrant culture of film festivals; it sketches the recent efforts invested in the cultivation of film literacy and further development of institutionalised film scholarship; and it observes the ramifications of Slovenia having developed a flair for celebrating its cinematic pioneers and searching for forgotten figures. The chapter concludes with the observation that Slovenian cinema has developed into a cosmopolitan present-day incarnation of small national cinema: its filmmakers are concerned less with consolidating or critiquing national identity and more with exploiting newly accessible transnational networks and funding structures to be able to perfect their authorial signatures and establish their standing at home and abroad; Slovenian film culture complements and supports these ambitions for it is thoroughly invested in mobilising national and transnational resources to cultivate film appreciation and erudition.

ESTABLISHED AUTEURS AND EMERGENT FIGURES

Contemporary Slovenian film production is a mixture of commercially reasonably successful genre attempts (such as Miha Hočevar's youth film *Gremo mi po svoje/Going Our Way* (Slovenia, 2010); Tomaž Gorkič's horror film *Idila/Killbillies* (Slovenia, 2015); Luka Marčetič's comedy *Pr' Hostar* (Slovenia, 2016) and arthouse projects displaying thematic interests similar to other ex-Yugoslav countries, such as dysfunctional public services (*Družinica/The Basics of Killing*, Jan Cvitkovič, Slovenia/Serbia, 2017), corruption, sordid affairs in elite social circles (*Nočno življenje/Nightlife*, Damjan Kozole, Slovenia/Republic of Macedonia/Bosnia and Herzegovina, 2016), poverty, migrants and social exclusion (*Čefurji raus!/Southern Scum Go Home!*, Goran Vojnović, Slovenia/Bosnia and Herzegovina, 2013; *Adria Blues*, Miroslav Mandić, Slovenia/Croatia, 2013) and coming to terms with recent history (*Circus fantasticus/The Silent Sonata*, Janez Burger, Slovenia/Ireland/Finland/Sweden, 2010; *Rudar/The Miner*, Hanna Slak, Slovenia/Croatia, 2017). Some reasons for the success of genre films will be sketched out in the second section. In this section, we turn to a selection of authorial projects illustrating not only the transnational consolidation of established auteurs and up-and-coming figures but also the emergence of a distinctive, audacious aesthetics of contemporary Slovenian cinema.

Twenty years ago, commentators welcomed Janez Burger's first feature *V leru/Idle Running* (Slovenia, 1999) as a sign of change, the 'rebirth' or at least a significant reinvention of Slovenian cinema (Vrdlovec 2008), which at the time seemed too focused on commercial success and pleasing the audiences (Vrdlovec 2013: 697). Burger, a graduate of the Prague film school FAMU, created something very different: a low-budget, austere-looking black-and-white vignette of student life in Ljubljana, populated with characters unable to grow up and based on a script Burger had co-written with Jan Cvitkovič, the lead actor in his film. *Idle Running*, which won more than twenty national and international awards and was screened at more than sixty film festivals abroad, was not only a critical and commercial success (with more than sixty thousand viewers in Slovenia); it also launched the careers of two of the most prominent figures in present-day Slovenian cinema.

Burger went on to direct five more fiction feature films (and several documentaries and shorts). His latest feature, *Ivan* (Slovenia/Croatia, 2017), is a compelling example of an ambitious cinematic attempt at holding a mirror to contemporary Slovenian society. It stages a personal drama against the backdrop of a society pervaded by violence and corruption: a young woman, Mara (Maruša Majer in an award-winning performance), finds herself in a desperate situation after giving birth to her son, Ivan. The child's father disappears and Mara learns her lover is not only a married man, but also a criminal. She is brutally beaten by his wife's cronies and eventually forced to choose between her son and her lover. But the film is much more than a socially critical drama. It is also the latest example of the maturity and aesthetic mastery Burger reached in this decade. Not unlike *Idle Running*, which revels in its protagonist's world-weariness and indolence, *Ivan* with its bruised-looking photography (by cinematographer Marko Brdar) and minimalist, yet semantically heavily charged *mise-en-scène* and acting style does not simply stage the desperate situation of its protagonist; rather, it positively incarnates it (see Figure 12.1).

Aesthetically, *Ivan* is an outstanding film. In terms of its production background, however, it is a typical product of contemporary Slovenian cinema: it falls into the majority of film projects in Slovenia today, which are transnational or international co-productions. This visible shift of Slovenian producers' focus to co-productions has occurred in the last few years, whereas foreign producers' share in the investments in Slovenian majority projects has also increased, and is now close to a relatively high number of 30 per cent (Lešničar 2019). This is a result of Slovenia being a member of Eurimages, which encourages authors to seek (in Hjort's terms 'opportunistic') transnational connections not only for creative reasons but also to make their projects eligible for international funding schemes. It is also the effect of the latest novelty introduced by the SFC in 2016: the interest in Slovenia as a shooting location and a potential production partner, has increased due to the 25 per cent cash rebate scheme with a simple application procedure and no minimum spend (Vinter 2019a). Yet it is not just

Figure 12.1   Bruised-looking photography incarnates perfectly the desperate situation of Mara (Maruša Majer) in *Ivan* (Janez Burger, 2017). Photographer: Marko Brdar. Courtesy of Staragara.

that co-productions in general are on the rise – a much more specific pattern of (Hjort's 'affinitive') transnationalism, also exemplified by *Ivan*, is observable among majority and minority co-productions: as a rule, networking and collaboration involve producers and crews from the former Yugoslav region. *Ivan* was produced by the Slovenian production company Staragara, co-produced by RTV Slovenija and the Croatian Propeler Film, and co-funded by HAVC (Croatian Audiovisual Centre), Eurimages and SFC. Such 'affinitive' transnationalism seems a natural result of collaboration channels established in Slovenia's Yugoslavian past and cultivated further in the present, particularly through festival circuits.

The other prominent figure in present-day Slovenian cinema whose career started with *Idle Running* is Jan Cvitkovič. Cvitkovič, an archaeology graduate, followed his successful acting appearance in Burger's first feature with a stunningly accomplished directorial debut, *Kruh in mleko/Bread and Milk* (Slovenia, 2001), two years later. The black-and-white portrayal of a family drama triggered by the father's alcoholism and set in a small Slovenian town won the Lion of the Future, the Luigi De Laurentiis award for the best debut film at the Venice International Film Festival and put Cvitkovič firmly on the list of up-and-coming Slovenian filmmakers. Like Burger, he reached his prime in this decade, having directed four more features (and several shorts). In contrast to Burger, Cvitkovič has been less successful in exploiting international funding schemes, while his films have been successful in attracting international attention and accolades. His latest film, *The Basics of Killing*, premiered in the same year as Burger's *Ivan* and it shows similar social and aesthetic concerns. The story about the dismal fate of an average middle-class family, triggered by a student complaint levelled unjustly against the father, a grammar school teacher (Primož Vrhovec), and then sealed by the dysfunction of public services in present-day Slovenia, is painted in dark, gloomy colours (by cinematographer Marko Brdar) and supported perfectly by the haunting soundtrack (Damir Avdić), creating a suffocating, visceral spectatorial experience.

The third prominent auteur in contemporary Slovenian cinema is Damjan Kozole, whose career had already started in socialist Yugoslavia (with two features made in the late 1980s) and reached its most prolific stage in this decade. Kozole has directed ten fiction feature films to date, four of which were made in the past ten years. His fifth film, *Rezervni deli/Spare Parts* (Slovenia, 2003), was nominated for the Golden Bear award at the Berlin International Film Festival and ranked among the ten most important films of the 'New Europe' by *Sight & Sound* in 2008 (SFC 2008). The film about human trafficking set the tone for Kozole's future projects: bleak colours, harsh exteriors and barren interiors, laconic dialogues, and characters so overcome with fear, despair or hatred they appear numb, almost drained of life. Nowhere is this signature more palpable than in Kozole's 2016 film *Nightlife*, yet another 'ex-Yu' co-production, which was awarded the Crystal Globe for Best Director at the Karlovy Vary International Film Festival. *Nightlife*'s story, inspired by a highly publicised affair about the death of a Slovenian doctor and the alleged sexual abuse of his dogs, could have been rendered as a gripping genre exercise; instead, Kozole decided to focus on creating the sinister atmosphere of the hours following the protagonist's death, in which his wife (Pia Zemljič), framed relentlessly in claustrophobic close-ups (DoP Miladin Čolaković), is gradually consumed by fear and hopelessness (see Figure 12.2). Kozole and his co-writers (Urša Menart and Ognjen Sviličić) show little interest in conventional action- or dialogue-driven storytelling: *Nightlife* does not narrate its story; rather, it plunges its viewer into a whirl of almost non-verbal, but poignant affect.

In this sense, Kozole – but also Burger with *The Silent Sonata*, Cvitkovič with *Arheo/Archeo* (Slovenia, 2010), Miha Knific with *Vztrajanje/Perseverance* (Slovenia/Croatia/Italy/Serbia, 2016), Ema Kugler with *Odmevi časa/Echoes of Time* (Slovenia, 2013) and *Človek s senco/Man With the Shadow* (Slovenia/Czech Republic, 2019), and others – come astonishingly close to the non-narrative cinematic poetics developed systematically by the newest rising star of Slovenian cinema, Sonja Prosenc. Like Burger, Cvitkovič, Kozole and Kugler, Prosenc did not study filmmaking in Slovenia; she completed her undergraduate studies in journalism and cultural studies at the University of Ljubljana, and found her way into filmmaking via an international path. She took part in Berlinale and Sarajevo Talent Campuses, and was selected for the Script & Pitch postgraduate programme at the TorinoFilmLab. She has also completed a Midpoint course in script development and film dramaturgy at FAMU. Prosenc has directed six titles to date, two of which are feature-length fiction films. Already with her first project, the short film *Nič novega, nič pretiranega/Free Spirited Friends* (Slovenia,

Figure 12.2 Claustrophobic framing captures the sinister atmosphere of *Nightlife* (Damjan Kozole, 2016). Photographer: Željko Stevanič, IFP. Courtesy of Vertigo.

2005), she established herself as an unconventional filmmaker whose primary interest is neither the story nor the action, but rather the psychological states of her characters and the emotional charge of the story. This impression was confirmed with her first feature, *Drevo/The Tree* (Slovenia, 2014), and cemented with her second feature, the Eurimages and MEDIA-supported international co-production *Zgodovina ljubezni/History of Love* (Slovenia/Italy/Norway, 2018), Prosenc's most accomplished and critically most successful project to date. *History of Love* is a film about a teenage girl (Doroteja Nadrah) whose mother has suddenly died and who is now struggling to come to terms with her loss and the discovery that her mother had a secret life. Prosenc uses this story as a springboard from which she pushes the viewer into the strange, almost dream-like world of the protagonist's inner life, in which numerous extreme close-ups of grief-stricken human faces are interwoven with shots of water of all shapes, beautifully photographed by Mitja Ličen (see Figure 12.3). Intense emotions run wild and words are silenced by often completely inarticulate sounds which are interspersed with the film's mesmerising soundtrack, designed by Riccardo Spagnol, Julij Zornik and Gisle Tveito.

In short, although contemporary Slovenian film production at first sight resembles many other European cinemas as a mixture of arthouse projects with similar thematic interests and genre titles with fairly satisfactory commercial success, it becomes clear upon closer inspection that, over the past decade, projects and authors of very different backgrounds have developed what might even be called a distinctive, audacious aesthetics of contemporary Slovenian cinema. It is a cinema of affect and austerity, suffused with an ever-growing lack of interest in conventional action- or dialogue-driven storytelling.

Figure 12.3 The dreamlike world of *History of Love* (Sonja Prosenc, 2018) interweaves close-ups of grief-stricken human faces and shots of water of all shapes. Courtesy of Monoo.

This is particularly interesting if we consider these projects' backgrounds. Slovenia is a proverbially small country, so it is not surprising that people working in cinema meet sooner or later. And indeed, there is plenty of evidence of creative exchange among the creators of these films: Burger and Cvitkovič have a history of collaboration on several projects since *Idle Running*, they have both worked with cinematographer Marko Brdar, Cvitkovič has also worked with Prosenc's cinematographer Mitja Ličen, and so forth. Another important figure overlooking several of the above-mentioned projects from behind the scenes is the established Slovenian producer Daniel Hočevar, director of E-motion Film and Vertigo. Yet it is important to stress these authors belong to different generations (some of them were born in the mid-1950s, some in the 1980s) and have very different educational and professional training backgrounds (none of them studied filmmaking in Slovenia). In short, there is no 'new wave' or 'school' of Slovenian cinema, yet a number of films produced over the last decade display a very similar, distinctive and thought-provoking aesthetic. What is it then that has brought all these different authors and projects into such taciturn yet poignant harmony? The answer must, of course, remain speculative. Yet I cannot ignore the fact that these projects possess a particular variation on what Laura Marks (2000) has termed 'haptic visuality'. Increasingly indifferent to conventional action- or dialogue-driven storytelling, they seem focused on engulfing the viewer in intense, extreme emotion and making this non-verbal experience comprehensible beyond linguistic or national borders. While Marks identifies this as a virtue made of necessity in intercultural cinema's 'configurations of sense perception different from those of modern Euro-American societies' (Marks 2000: xiii), I see it as an inspired response of Slovenian filmmakers to the newly accessible transnational circuits. As we have seen above, the currently available structures of funding and the history of the now independent country have prepared the ground for a mixture of opportunistic and affinitive transnationalisms. But Slovenian filmmakers have responded even more ambitiously: they are carving a space for themselves in this transnational arena with an aesthetic whose appeal is decidedly cosmopolitan (see Hjort 2009: 20–1).

Prosenc is representative of this aesthetic, and although her directorial curriculum vitae is short, she is such a consistent, focused and highly recognisable new author that her work more than deserves to be discussed on its own merits (Petek 2019). Yet she is also representative of a broader phenomenon in contemporary Slovenian cinema: the visible upsurge in numbers of women filmmakers and decision-makers. In fact, it might not be unreasonable to expect that the next decade might be the women's decade in Slovenian cinema. While the first feature film directed by a woman in Slovenia was only released in 2002 (*Varuh meje/Guardian of the Frontier*, Maja Weiss, Slovenia/Germany/France), in June 2019 the seventeenth feature film directed by a female director premiered in Ljubljana.[3] All but four of these 17 films were released in the last decade. It should be noted though that the situation is still alarming: the number of female directors and completed projects has increased, but women's projects still represent only about 10 per cent of all SFC-supported projects (Gričar 2018: 3) and their achievements are often swept under the carpet. In the 2018 edition of FSF, director Urša Menart was the first ever woman to receive the Best Feature Film award for her directorial debut *My Last Year as a Loser*.[4] She was also the first ever woman to receive the Best Screenplay award at FSF.[5] Sonja Prosenc's *History of Love* won several special festival awards, including the Crystal Globe at the Karlovy Vary Film Festival and a Vesna for Best Original Work at the Slovenian Film Festival, and has recently been submitted for the Academy Award for Best International Feature Film. Hanna Slak's *Miner* won awards at festivals in Los Angeles, Trieste and Tuzla, and Ema Kugler's *Echoes of Time* won 11 awards at different festivals in North America and Asia.

In addition to these creative achievements and accolades, it is also worth mentioning that a number of top positions in the industry are currently held by women: Nataša Bučar is director of the Slovenian Film Centre; Jelka Stergel (former director of SFC) is director of the Slovenian Film Festival; Urša Menart is president of the Directors Guild of Slovenia (DSR), while there are two female professors teaching in the Film and Television department at the Academy of Theatre, Radio, Film and Television (AGRFT). Most importantly, women are finally becoming a more prominent part of decision-making bodies and expert commissions, in which they had thus far been most meagrely represented (Gričar 2018: 2). It is particularly important that this is so at the time when a significant budget increase has been announced. In 2018, SFC received 4,859,000 euros for film funding and other activities. Based on the unanimous vote by the Slovenian parliamentary Culture Committee in November 2018, the annual budget for film production will gradually increase to reach 11 million euros by 2022 (Vinter 2019a). In short, Slovenian cinema does not seem to be a sinking ship deserted by men and left to women.

This welcome change is not a fortuitous coincidence. It is a result of individual enterprise and institutional change, and hopefully a sign of cultural change as well. Institutional change is manifested especially in SFC striving to follow *Gender Equality in the Audiovisual Sector – A New Council of Europe Recommendation* (Council of Europe 2018b) and to implement the *Eurimages Strategy for Gender Equality in the Film Industry* (Council of Europe 2018a) to come as close as possible to their stated aim of '50/50 by 2020'. Unlike the Swedish Film Institute, for instance, which now distributes public funding equally between male and female directors, the SFC has not introduced gender quotas for funding; it has, however, initiated monitoring, public debate and research (like Gričar's 2018 study) and it has been careful to include women in all its decision-making bodies. Another enabling novelty is SFC's funding for first features: the first such call was announced in 2012 and 27 per cent of supported projects have been directed by female debutants since then (Gričar 2018: 4).

Even more importantly, the new generation of women filmmakers in Slovenia has found further encouragement and empowerment in national, transnational and international connections and networks beyond those coordinated by the SFC. The European Women's Audiovisual Network (EWA) is one such network, whereas more locally the closed Facebook group Filmarke** (Women Filmmakers**) functions as a 'self-managed anarchist group providing exchange of information, dialogue, inspiration, promotion, support and mutual encouragement to Slovenia-based women filmmakers of all professions, generations and backgrounds'.

The importance of such networks and exchange could not be overemphasised. Access to knowledge and information is crucial, especially for marginalised groups. Women, for instance, have all too often been cast as 'newcomers' to film; yet, there was a female student, Marija Milkovič, who graduated in 1973 with the very first generation of film directors in Slovenia (Inkret et al. 1996:197). Knowledge provides one not only with the proverbial power but also with a sense of history, including histories denied by dominant discourses. This is why changes outlined in the next section of this chapter should prove extremely important not only in terms of improving general film literacy in Slovenia, but also in terms of empowering and providing encouragement for emergent and future generations of filmmakers and filmviewers, especially those from marginalised groups.

Institutions: From Film Production to Film Erudition and Appreciation

In this section, I provide a broader picture of contemporary Slovenian film culture to demonstrate how this culture complements the filmmakers' ambitions discussed above. To show its investment in mobilising national and transnational resources to support film production and cultivate film erudition and appreciation, I sketch the vibrant culture of film festivals and outline the recent efforts invested in the cultivation of film literacy and further development of film scholarship.

According to the SFC (n.d.) and the Slovenian Ministry of Culture (MK n.d.), there are thirteen film festivals organised annually in Slovenia. According to Rok Govednik (2019), the director of the Film na oko festival and the head of the 'Mad About Film' project, the number is more than double: his list contains 29 festivals (including those not subsidised by the state, but excluding those that have only had one edition thus far). This sounds more than decent for a country with the population of 2.08 million, 50 operating cinemas with 108 screens, and admissions usually around 2.5 million (Vinter 2019b).[6]

Not surprisingly, the longest running festival is the Festival of Slovenian Cinema (FSF),[7] the national showcase and the central film event of the year. The second oldest festival is the LGBT Film Festival,[8] established in 1984 in Ljubljana, which makes it the oldest festival of gay and lesbian cinema in Europe. In contrast to the FSF – which has never been banned, has always enjoyed reasonable state support and would no doubt have existed also without any international partners – the LGBT Film Festival had a more turbulent history.[9] The third oldest film festival in Slovenia is the Ljubljana International Film Festival (LIFFe), established as Film Art Fest in 1990.[10] Since its inception, the global arthouse-oriented festival has provided a welcome yearly antidote to the otherwise mainstream cinema-dominated programme of Slovenian movie theatres.[11]

This trio of festivals is the legacy of the Yugoslavian chapter in the history of Slovenian cinema. It forms the basis of Slovenian film festival culture, which kept growing through the first two decades of independence and has virtually exploded in the past few years. According to Wikipedia (2019), 26 new festivals were established in the last decade (although some of them only had one edition and several years have passed since then). Such proliferation of festivals (that exceeds the official account cited above) underscores a desire to broaden the horizons of all stakeholders – audiences, artists and decision-makers – and shift their attention from the traditionally privileged fiction features to other kinds of film production. To illustrate this claim and demonstrate the first achievements of this desire, I will closely examine four clusters of more recent (state-recognised and independent) festivals: short film festivals, documentary film festivals, animated film festivals and festivals of genre films.

There are two short film festivals in Slovenia: the FeKK Ljubljana Short Film Festival has been running since 2015, and SHOTS, the short film festival taking place in Slovenj Gradec, a year less. Both festivals are emphatically international in terms of programmes and juries, and almost exclusively Slovenian in terms of funding. *SHOTS* screens approximately twenty Slovenian and international films in competition, whereas FeKK has separate Slovenian and 'Yugoslavian' competition sections in addition to several other programmes displaying the festival's deeper ambitions (presentation of a 'Visiting Festival', selection of best international short films of the year, retrospective of a prominent author from abroad, short film programme for children). In brief, the two short film festivals celebrate short film production and have found a niche to exploit in the current film festival offer in Slovenia. Even more importantly, FeKK has played an important role in cultivating short film appreciation and gain recognition for short film production, as two years after its first edition, in 2017, the SFC introduced a separate call for short film projects (whereas previously short film projects competed with features).

The energy behind documentary film festivals in Slovenia is also drawn from the desire to increase financial support and visibility for the genre. Yet, despite the fact that some documentary film festivals, such as the Documentary Film Festival, which celebrated its twentieth anniversary in 2018,[12] are a lot older than its short film counterparts, they have not managed to affect the SFC's structure of funding: documentary film projects still compete with fiction in all categories. Yet, despite this financial disadvantage, documentary films produced in Slovenia have always been the backbone and the flagship of its film culture: film production in Slovenia in the early twentieth century started with documentaries, while Slovenian (and Yugoslavian) cinema first gained international recognition in 1947 also with a documentary, France Štiglic's short *Mladina gradi/Youth Builds* (Yugoslavia, 1946) which was awarded a Bronze Lion in Venice. Furthermore, two recent and often provocative additions to the genre gained far more success and publicity than any fiction film. These are the international co-productions *Houston, imamo problem!/Houston, We Have a Problem!* (Žiga Virc, Slovenia/Croatia/Germany/Czech Republic/Qatar, 2016), a mockumentary about Tito selling NASA Yugoslavia's space programme to be able to finance Yugoslavia's socialist experiment; and *Družina/The Family* (Rok Biček, Slovenia/Austria, 2017), a *cinéma vérité* style documentary about a family of people with special needs.

The third segment of Slovenian film production that has benefited from Slovenian film festival culture is animation. While solitary pioneers such as Saša Dobrila and Miki Muster laid the foundation for film animation in Slovenia (and Yugoslavia) as early as the 1950s, animation only started to be taught at university in the last decade at the University of Nova Gorica. The most successful present-day animators such as Špela Čadež and Kolja Saksida were educated abroad. Yet, despite the lack of educational opportunities until recently, the Animateka International Animated Film Festival taking place in Ljubljana every December, has familiarised Slovenian audiences with the genre. Although formally established in 2004, its roots go back to 1998 when the Slovenian Cinémathèque introduced a special monthly programme focusing on animated film. Over the past two decades, Animateka has developed into an ambitious venture with nine sections including a rich programme of retrospectives and additional screenings, workshops and events. Not unlike FeKK for short films, Animateka systematically cultivates an appreciation for animated film, which has often been a completely ignored segment of production: for instance, animated film was never mentioned as a separate, autonomous category in the SFC's publications prior to 2016. Furthermore, Animateka is very active in mobilising regional transnational connections and collaborations, as evident in the 'Cartoon East' project (initiated in 2010) which facilitates collaboration and exchange between six regional festivals.[13]

Within the realm of fiction features, it is worth noting the recent prominence of two genre film festivals with a taste for blood and gore and an appreciation for cult film viewing practices: Kurja polt; and Grossmann Fantastic Film and Wine Festival. Engaging with a marginalised, if not derided, kind of cinema, they bridge an important gap in Slovenian film culture. In 2007, the Slovenian film publicist Samo Rugelj argued that the traditional division between entertainment and arthouse cinema still persisted in Slovenia. In fact, he argued that it should be considered a systemic feature, which had resulted in a highly polarised situation with lay audiences who flocked to multiplexes to consume primarily Hollywood products at the one end, and with connoisseurs, professionals and experts who believed that (domestic) film production was and should remain synonymous with auteur-driven arthouse cinema at the other end of the spectrum (see also Petek 2017). Over the past decade, Kurja polt and Grossmann have significantly contributed to closing this gap, Grossmann especially with its clever promotion strategies[14] and Kurja polt with an increasing emphasis on academic research focusing on cult and genre films.[15]

This outward reach of academic research is an important novelty in Slovenian film culture. Exploring film used to be the prerogative of Slovenian academic circles, notably philosophers, sociologists and literary scholars, performed in the form of publishing rather than as a university course or module (for a representative publication see Vrdlovec 1988). Over the past decade or so, Slovenian film scholarship has matured into an academic discipline, albeit one still searching for its institutional domicile (currently split between two faculties and one art academy at the University of Ljubljana). At primary and secondary school levels, until recently film used to be the domain of extracurricular activities and teachers' personal initiatives, even though pioneering figures such as Mirjana Borčič and Tone Rački were organising film education workshops, lectures and round tables as early as the 1960s (see Borčič 2007 and 2014). More recently, their ground-breaking work has been eagerly carried on by locally and internationally funded projects such as 'Kino katedra' (series of lectures for children, students and teachers organised by the Slovenian Cinémathèque), 'Filmska osnovna šola' (educational programme for teachers organised by the Slovenian Art Cinema Association in partnership with Kinodvor and the Slovenian Cinémathèque, co-funded by the Slovenian Ministry of Culture and the European Social Fund), 'Kino Balon' (Kinodvor's educational programme for children and youth), 'Kinotrip' (Kinodvor's film club and festival for youth) and 'Mad About Film' (a versatile project featuring seminars, online publications, the Eye on Film festival and a summer camp, organised by the non-profit organisation the Vizo Institute). Over the past decade, all these and other initiatives have provided a rich programme of lectures, workshops, screenings, festivals, summer camps and two international conferences on film education.

We have now reached a new milestone with regard to film education in Slovenia, a phase of synergy which all stakeholders seem to have entered simultaneously. This can be demonstrated by four further developments. First, in 2016, the Slovenian government adopted a strategy regarding the development of a national programme of film education (SFC 2016). Since then 'Film Education' has been introduced as an elective primary school subject with 'History and Theory of Theatre and Cinema' as a compulsory subject in the art programmes of grammar schools or as an elective subject in classical, general and specialist programmes of grammar schools. Second, in 2018, the DSR published a 'National Programme for Film 2018–2023' (DSR 2018) in which Slovenian film directors recognised the need for film education to become institutionalised and demanded a systemic change securing film education at all levels. Third, the first university courses on film education (that is, courses designed for future teachers of film education) are being developed at the University of Ljubljana and the University of Primorska. Once accredited, these courses and their alumni should bring the implementation of film education programmes in primary and secondary schools to a whole new level, infusing it not only with enthusiasm but also with academic rigour. And fourth, the determination to make film education a regular part of curricula at all levels of schooling is also visible among those who shape film history most actively. At the time of writing, the SFC was preparing a *Regional Seminar of Film Education in Central Eastern and South Eastern Europe* on the 'Next Steps in Film Education' to be held in Ljubljana in April 2020, organised as part of the project 'Film Education: From Framework to Impact'. The project – a consortium of the British Film Institute (BFI), the Danish Film Institute (DFI), Vision Kino (Germany) and the Cinémathèque française, supported by the European Film Agency Directors (EFADs) and their Film Education Working Group – is funded by Creative Europe and the SFC is thus becoming its regional partner. In short, while this phase of synergy of all local stakeholders might have been long in the making, it has now reached unprecedented proportions also due to transnational incentives.

The orchestrated efforts to improve film literacy and cultivate film erudition and appreciation, including the appreciation of local film history, are an extremely welcome phenomenon in Slovenian film culture. In an article on the issue of gender in Slovenian cinema (Petek 2017: 136–7), I observed that Slovenian film culture was 'a culture that often ignores its key figures and only grants them entry into its history and canon after a long period of neglect'. This 'culture of forgetfulness' virtually stumbled upon its 'father' Karol Grossmann almost half a century after he had shot the first films in Slovenia, and it only discovered the pioneers of its film distribution (Pavla Jesih), production (Anton Codelli), sound design (Emilija Soklič and Rudi Omota) and others in the last twenty years. Combined with the inquisitive nature of the new generation of filmmakers, the celebratory atmosphere of proliferating festivals, the favourable conditions for the development of film scholarship and some additional funding opportunities, these discoveries have initiated a profound transformation of Slovenian film culture.

For just over a decade, the Slovenian Cinémathèque has been publishing *Tributes*, a series of short monographs dedicated to key figures in the history of Slovenian cinema. In 2010, the hall of the Slovenian Cinémathèque was dedicated to Silvan Furlan, the first director and one of the founders of film scholarship in Slovenia. In 2011, the Museum of Slovenian Film Actors was established in Divača, the birthplace of the first Slovenian movie star, Ita Rina. In 2012, a theme path was opened leading through the shooting locations of the first Slovenian sound feature film *Na svoji zemlji/On Our Own Land* (France Štiglic, Yugoslavia, 1948). In 2016, the Slovenian Cinémathèque celebrated the twentieth anniversary of its establishment with a year-long series of events.[16] In 2019, the centenary of the birth of France Štiglic, the director of the first Slovenian sound feature film and of the first internationally awarded Yugoslavian film, will be celebrated with another long series of events supported and coordinated by the SFC and the Slovenian Cinémathèque, including a new film festival, the 'Week of Slovenian Cinema'. We could continue listing anniversaries, awards and recently rediscovered figures, but suffice it to say that this list of commemorative events illuminates an important and positive change in Slovenian film culture – its transformation from a culture of forgetfulness into a culture of festive remembrance, providing a more inclusive sense of history and encouragement for emergent and future generations of filmmakers and filmviewers, especially those from marginalised groups.

To avoid sounding complacent, this section should end with some more critical observations. First, it seems that the climax of the transformation into a culture of festive remembrance occurred in the middle of the decade under consideration: in 2013, three hefty monographs on the history of Slovenian cinema were published (Stankovič 2013; Štefančič 2013; Vrdlovec 2013), followed shortly by another two (Majcen 2015; Štefančič 2016). In other words, the climax of historical research activity roughly coincided with the peak of the crisis in film production. Individual scholars' research and the publication of their findings were not just what film culture in Slovenia needed at the time, but also what Slovenian film institutions could *afford* in times of severe austerity measures. That this remark is not too cynical is demonstrated further by the second fact we need to draw attention to. Surely, an economically healthy culture of remembrance would adopt a systematic approach to preserving its heritage; yet, as regards the digitalisation of its cinema, Slovenia is still without any viable strategy (see AIPA 2018). Third, this 'archaeological' groundwork as we might call a great deal of historiographic efforts in Slovenian cinema is still unfinished: as already mentioned, women's contribution to Slovenian cinema has not been properly addressed by film scholarship yet. Even more glaring is the lack of a critical assessment of the position of LGBT filmmakers and films in Slovenia. The first Slovenian film featuring openly queer characters and queer themes is the already mentioned *Guardian of the Frontier* (2002). Since then, only a handful of films have joined the list, most notably *Posledice/ Consequences* (Darko Štante, Slovenia/Austria, 2018), the first Slovenian film with one explicit scene of gay sex. Obviously, a strong LGBT community exists in a culture with the oldest LGBT film festival in Europe; yet, there is hardly any evidence of this in its creative output.

Conclusion

To round off this journey through contemporary Slovenian cinema, let me draw attention once again to the above-mentioned women filmmakers' networking and DSR's publication of a 'national programme for film 2018–2023'. Aimed in different directions – the former rather outwardly and the latter emphatically inwardly – they encapsulate the profound change in contemporary Slovenian cinema. Filmmakers in Slovenia no longer await (national) support, but rather seek and demand (transnational) participation and control. This demonstrates that Slovenian national infrastructure has solidified, while the awareness of the importance of transnational connections and international collaboration has also deepened. Combined with the above discussed ingenuity of Slovenian filmmakers, the vibrancy of the local film festival culture, the increasingly orchestrated efforts of all stakeholders put into the development of film education, and the festive remembrance of the celebrated as well as the previously forgotten figures from the history of cinema in Slovenia, this transnational orientation suggests that Slovenian film culture has developed into a cosmopolitan present-day incarnation of national cinema. In other words, a culture concerned less with consolidating or critiquing national identity and more with exploiting transnational networks and funding structures to support original production and cultivate film erudition and appreciation.

Notes

1. I differentiate between 'transnational' and 'international' in agreement with Tim Bergfelder (2005) drawing on Ulf Hannerz's (1996) definition of the terms.
2. Already in 2009 the annual film production numbers had decreased significantly, but the effects of the crisis became evident in 2011, the year with the lowest number of completed feature-length projects in Slovenia (see Tables at the back of the book). In Slovenian culture and society in general, the crisis culminated in 2012, the year marked by the introduction of severe austerity measures, which were then followed by uprisings in several Slovenian cities and towns and the fall of Janez Janša's government that had imposed the public funding cuts. The impact of austerity measures on Slovenian cinema was immense for the majority of filmmakers in Slovenia who are self-employed and thus dependent upon state funding.

3. Given the past marginalisation of women and their projects, it is certainly appropriate to list them all. In addition to the aforementioned *Guardian of the Frontier*, *The Miner, The Tree, History of Love, Echoes of Time* and *Man with the Shadow*, the following are the titles directed by women (in chronological order): *Slepa pega/ Blind Spot* (Hanna Slak, Slovenia, 2002), *Phantom* (Ema Kugler, Slovenia, 2003), *Le Grand Macabre* (Ema Kugler, Slovenia, 2005), *Instalacija ljubezni/Installation of Love* (Maja Weiss, Slovenia/Germany, 2007), *L kot ljubezen/L . . . for Love* (Janja Glogovac, Slovenia, 2007), *Teah/Tea* (Hanna Slak, Slovenia/Bosnia and Herzegovina/ Croatia/Poland, 2008), *Realnost/Reality* (Dafne Jemeršić, Slovenia, 2008), *Za konec časa/For the End of Time* (Ema Kugler, Slovenia, 2009), *Neke druge zgodbe/ Some Other Stories* (Ana Marija Rossi, Ivona Juka, Ines Tanović, Marija Džidževa and Hanna Slak, Serbia/Slovenia/Croatia/Bosnia and Herzegovina/Republic of Macedonia/Ireland, 2010), *Panika/Panic* (Barbara Zemljič, Slovenia, 2013), and *Ne bom več luzerka/My Last Year as a Loser* (Urša Menart, Slovenia, 2018).

4. This was the third time a woman was awarded one of the two most prestigious awards; the first woman to receive the Best Director award was Maja Weiss in 2002 for her directorial debut *Guardian of the Frontier*, followed by Hanna Slak in 2017 for her third feature *The Miner*.

5. In fact, Melina Pota Koljević received the award for Best Screenplay the year before, but she shared the award with Janez Burger, Aleš Čar and Srdjan Koljević, the co-authors of the screenplay for *Ivan*.

6. The golden age of filmgoing in Slovenia was in the late 1950s (in 1960, 17 million tickets were sold), whereas in the independent Slovenia admissions peaked in 1995 (more than three million) and reached their all-time low in 2014 (less than two million), according to Lešnik and Koren (2015).

7. The FSF was established in Celje in the 1970s as the 'Week of National Film' (which showcased the entire Yugoslavian film production). After the declaration of independence, it was first renamed the 'Slovenian Film Marathon' and then the 'Festival of Slovenian Cinema' (1998) and moved to Portorož, a cosmopolitan town on the Slovenian riviera. FSF is funded by a number of national and regional institutions, and the EU's Creative Europe.

8. Established as the 'Magnus Festival', it was initiated by the gay section Magnus at the non-profit student cultural organisation ŠKUC-Forum. It drew visitors from the broader European LBGT community and relied heavily on the resourcefulness and personal transnational connections of individuals such as Brane Mozetič in Suzana Tratnik to secure guests from abroad and films to be screened.

9. Not surprisingly, it did not please the Yugoslavian homophobic authorities, which – via the Social and Health Care Council of the Socialist Alliance of Working People and the Ljubljana Sanitary Inspection Service – managed to cancel the festival's fourth edition in 1987, capitalising on the global Aids panic: 'The gathering of this risk group from the entire Europe would pose a serious threat due to the aids epidemic' (Velikonja n.d.).

10. LIFFe is hosted by the Slovenian cultural and congress centre Cankarjev dom, and supported by a number of local and international partners.

11. The majority of Slovenian screens are now owned by two major multiplex chains: Kolosej Kinematografi and Cineplex. Their programme consists of mainstream

new releases. Members of the Slovenian Art Cinema Asociation, which currently has twenty-seven active members, cater for audiences with more arthouse-oriented tastes.

12. At least three more documentary festivals should be mentioned here: the international documentary film festival DOKUDOC (held in Maribor since 2010), the international ethnographic film festival Days of Ethnographic Film (DEF, Ljubljana, since 2007), and the international Mountain Film Festival (several locations since 2007).

13. The participating festivals are: Animafest (Zagreb, Croatia), Animateka (Slovenia), anim'est (Bucarest, Romania), Balkanima (Belgrade, Serbia), Banja Luka International Animation Film Festival (Bosnia and Herzegovina) and FestAnča (Žilina, Slovakia).

14. Grossmann was launched in 2005, allegedly to honour the 100th anniversary of Slovenian cinema in Ljutomer, where the first Slovenian films were made by Karol Grossmann (who never made horror films). Initiated with the help of the European Structural Fund and supported by the SFC and several commercial partners, the festival managed to position itself as a marketable unconventional event with distinguished guests and a rich programme of accompanying activities (from wine tastings and art exhibitions to round tables and carnivalesque manifestations).

15. One of the key factors in this development of Kurja polt is the festival's partnership with Northumbria University (Newcastle, UK), leading to the introduction of an academic conference which has now become a regular part of the festival, and the establishment of collaboration with the University of Ljubljana which will now also participate in the preparation of the conference and an accompanying student workshop.

16. In fact, there has been a cinémathèque in Ljubljana since 1963. The institution was first established as a branch of the Yugoslavian Cinémathèque founded in Belgrade in 1949 (see Šimenc 1996).

BIBLIOGRAPHY

AIPA (Collecting Society of Authors, Performers and Film Producers of Audiovisual Works of Slovenia) (2018) 'Slovenija brez strategije pri restavraciji filmov' <http://www.aipa.si/sl/Novice/2018/Junij/Slovenija-brez-strategije-pri-restavraciji-filmov> (last accessed on 5 August 2019).

Bergfelder, Tim (2005) 'National, Transnational or Supranational Cinema? Rethinking European Film Studies', *Media, Culture & Society*, 27 (3), pp. 315–31.

Borčič, Mirjana (2007) *Filmska vzgoja na Slovenskem: Spominjanja in pričevanja 1955–1980*. Ljubljana: Slovenska kinoteka in UMco.

Borčič, Mirjana (2014) *Odstiranje pogleda: spomini, izkušnje, spoznanja*. Ljubljana: Javni zavod Kinodvor in Slovenska kinoteka.

Council of Europe (2018a) *Eurimages Strategy for Gender Equality in the Film Industry 2018* <https://rm.coe.int/strategy-gender-equality-in-the-film-industry-english/16809805b5> (last accessed on 22 September 2018).

Council of Europe (2018b) *Gender Equality in the Audiovisual Sector – A New Council of Europe Recommendation* <https://rm.coe.int/recommendation-on-gender-equality-in-the-audiovisual-sector/16809805dd> (last accessed on 22 September 2018).

DSR (Directors Guild of Slovenia) (2018) 'Nacionalni program za film 2018–2023' <http://www.dsr.si/files/2018/09/Filmarija-3.pdf> (last accessed on 1 August 2019).

Govednik, Rok (2019) 'Seznam: Filmski festivali v Sloveniji' <https://madaboutfilm.si/seznam-filmski-festivali-v-sloveniji/> (last accessed on 30 July 2019).

Gričar, Nika (2018) *Facts & Figures: Gender Equality*. Ljubljana: Slovenski filmski center <https://issuu.com/sfilmc/docs/sfc_2018_facts___figures_gender_equ_27512fe95c5704> (last accessed on 22 September 2018).

Hannerz, Ulf (1996) *Transnational Connections: Culture, People, Places*. London: Routledge.

Hjort, Mette (2009) 'On the Plurality of Cinematic Transnationalism', in Nataša Ďurovičová and Kathleen E. Newman (eds), *World Cinemas, Transnational Perspectives*. New York and London: Routledge, pp. 12–33.

Hjort, Mette and Petrie, Duncan (2007) 'Introduction', in Mette Hjort and Duncan Petrie (eds), *The Cinema of Small Nations*. Edinburgh: Edinburgh University Press, pp. 1–19.

Inkret, Andrej et al. (1996) *50 let: Zbornik ob petdesetletnici Akademije za igralsko umetnost/Akademije za gledališče, radio, film in televizijo*. Ljubljana: AGRFT.

Lešničar, Tina (2019) 'Nujno zlo ali okrepitev nacionalne kinematografije? Koprodukcije', *Delo*, 12 October, p. 15.

Lešnik, Andreja and Koren, Janja (2015) 'V slovenskih kinematografih vse manj obiskovalcev' <https://www.rtvslo.si/kultura/novice/v-slovenskih-kinematografih-vse-manj-obiskovalcev/376851> (last accessed on 30 July 2019).

Majcen, Matic (2015) *Slovenski poosamosvojitveni film: institucija in nacionalna identiteta*. Maribor: Aristej.

Marks, Laura (2000) *The Skin of the Film: Intercultural Cinema, Embodiment, and the Senses*. Durham, NC and London: Duke University Press.

MK (Ministry of Culture) (n.d.) 'Festivali' <http://www.mk.gov.si/si/kulturni_info/festivali/> (last accessed on 30 July 2019).

Petek, Polona (2017) 'The (M)Others of Slovenian Cinema? Gender, Border-crossing and the Conundrum of National Cinema', *Studies in European Cinema*, 14 (2), pp. 134–52.

Petek, Polona (2019) 'Women in the Way? Re-reading *The Monstrous-Feminine* in Contemporary Slovenian Cinema', in Nicholas Chare, Jeanette Hoorn and Audrey Yue (eds), *Re-reading the Monstrous-Feminine: Art, Film, Feminism and Psychoanalysis*. London: Routledge, pp. 230–40.

Rugelj, Samo (2007) *Stranpota slovenskega filma: Zapiski o kinematografiji 2000–2007*. Ljubljana: UMco.

SFC (Slovenian Film Centre) (2008) '*Spare Parts* among the Elite' <https://www.film-center.si/en/news/6840/spare-parts-among-the-elite>/(last accessed on 5 September 2019).

SFC (Slovenian Film Centre) (2016) 'Strategija razvoja nacionalnega programa filmske vzgoje', adopted by the Government of the Republic of Slovenia on 1 December 2016 <https://www.film-center.si/media/cms/attachments/2016/12/12/Filmska_vzgoja_-_strategija.pdf> (last accessed on 5 September 2019).

SFC (Slovenian Film Centre) (n.d.) 'Festivali v Sloveniji' <https://www.film-center.si/sl/film-v-sloveniji/festivali-v-sloveniji/> (last accessed on 30 July 2019).

Šimenc, Stanko (1996) *Panorama slovenskega filma*. Ljubljana: DZS.

Stankovič, Peter (2013) *Zgodovina slovenskega celovečernega filma. 1. Slovenski klasični film 1931–1988* Slovenia. Ljubljana: FDV.

Štefančič, Marcel, Jr (2013) *Maškarada: strašne fantazije slovenskega filma 1948–1990.* Ljubljana: UMco.

Štefančič, Marcel, Jr (2016) *Slovenski film 2.0: kritična enciklopedija slovenskega celovečernega filma 1991–2016.* Ljubljana: UMco.

Velikonja, Nataša (n.d.) '20 festivalskih let' <http://www.ljudmila.org/siqrd/fglf/20/20let. php> (last accessed on 30 July 2019).

Vinter, Damijan (2019a) 'FNE Market Analysis 2018: Slovenia' <http://www. filmneweurope.com/news/slovenia-news/item/117517-fne-market-analysis-2018-slovenia> (last accessed on 30 July 2019).

Vinter, Damijan (2019b) 'Slovenia' <http://www.filmneweurope.com/countries/slovenia-profile> (last accessed on 30 July 2019).

Vrdlovec, Zdenko (1988) *40 udarcev: slovenska filmska publicistika o slovenskem in jugoslovanskem filmu v obdobju 1949–1988.* Ljubljana: Slovenski gledališki in filmski muzej.

Vrdlovec, Zdenko (2008) '*Zadnji film* Marcela Štefančiča jr.', *Dnevnik*, 27 May <https://www.dnevnik.si/322263> (last accessed on 5 September 2019).

Vrdlovec, Zdenko (2013) *Zgodovina filma na Slovenskem.* Ljubljana: UMco.

Wikipedia (2019) 'Seznam filmskih festivalov v Sloveniji' <https://sl.wikipedia.org/wiki/Seznam_filmskih_festivalov_v_Sloveniji> (last accessed on 30 July 2019).

13. TURKEY: TRANSNATIONAL DIMENSIONS OF A LARGE NATIONAL FILM INDUSTRY

Melis Behlil

Turkey's cinematic landscape in the last decade is one filled with accomplishments. Total audience numbers nearly doubled since 2008, as the market share of local productions consistently surpasses 50 per cent in this country of 80 million, the largest national market in a single Balkan country. Arthouse films are featured at festivals around the world – such as Nuri Bilge Ceylan's *Kış Uykusu/Winter Sleep* (Turkey/France/Germany) snatching the coveted Golden Palm at Cannes in 2014. Meanwhile, the television industry is churning out hit after hit like *Binbir gece/1001 Nights* (Turkey, 2006–9), *Ezel* (Turkey, 2009–11) and *Muhteşem yüzyıl/Magnificent Century* (Turkey, 2011–14, followed by various spin-offs), series that are sold all across the world, from the Middle East to Latin America, and are particularly popular in Balkan countries. These achievements notwithstanding, difficulties still persist in Turkish cinema. Success at the box office is reserved for only a handful of films every year, exhibition venues are monopolised, and the polarised political environment has begun to be strongly felt by the film industry, especially after 2014. This situation is also reflected in the polarisation of films: the box office is dominated by vulgar comedies, while arthouse cinema recently produced a slew of dystopian narratives indirectly responding to the political climate.

This chapter will draw a multifaceted portrait of recent developments in Turkish cinema and its relationship to the local television industry, while situating them in the context of the Balkans. The size of the country and its industry is a key factor that differentiates it from its Westernmost neighbours. Among all the filmmaking nations in the Balkans, Turkey is by far the largest in terms of population, yearly domestic releases and box office figures. Between 2008 and 2017 average production was close to 100 films per year – a figure that not even the most productive of the other Balkan countries could reach – while the total box office figures in this period approached five billion Turkish lira (close to two billion euros corresponding to nearly half a billion admissions).[1] Due to the size of the domestic market, the national cinema in Turkey is for the most part self-reliant and commercially viable. However, the films that make up the bulk of the box office do not travel to international film festivals and are not popular abroad, save for a selected few in countries with significant Turkish diasporic populations such as Germany or the Netherlands. Conversely, the films that represent Turkey around the world at festivals and within the international critical discourse are not popular with domestic audiences. This creates a very divided system of a cosmopolitan, transnational and Western-orientated arthouse cinema, which forms the international corpus of Turkish cinema, on the one hand, and a popular but critically disregarded cinema consumed in large numbers at home, on the other. Indicatively, Nuri Bilge Ceylan's *Winter Sleep*, the 2014 Palme d'Or winner at Cannes and his commercially most successful film, sold 300,000 tickets in Turkey, an exceptionally high number for an arthouse film, where 100,000 are already considered a feat; conversely Togan Gökbakar's *Recep Ivedik 4* (Turkey, 2014), the fourth instalment of a comedy franchise starring the director's older brother Şahan Gökbakar, reached over 7 million tickets domestically and 700,000 across Europe, but is typically excluded from discussions about Turkish national cinema.

The 2008 financial crisis was felt only briefly in Turkey. While the country's economy shrank and unemployment increased, recovery was quick and reflected in the film industry's strong performance (Kutlu and Demirci 2011: 130, Oğuz 2009, Kaytaz and Gül 2014). Cinema attendance was not significantly affected by the crisis; the slight decline of 6 per cent in 2009 – after the record high of almost 37 million tickets sold in 2008 – was mostly due to the particular films released that year. In fact, due to ticket price increases, the box office income remained roughly the same both years. The effects of the crisis were felt in other sections of the media industry, as the reduction of advertising expenditure led to many layoffs in media conglomerates and, reputedly, in television personnel, too (Kara 2009: 75–6). The production of television drama series, however, began to flourish, largely because of an increase in exports to many Balkan and Eastern European countries due to the decline of their own local production as a result of the 2008 financial crisis (Yeşil 2015: 52–3). The relationship between the television and film industries in Turkey is symbiotic especially since the early 1990s, as one feeds on and relies on the other, hence television production and distribution will also be addressed here.

The chapter provides a critical overview of popular and arthouse Turkish cinema, exploring major themes, auteurs and box office trends. It situates these in the contexts of production, distribution and exhibition, placing an emphasis on their transnational dimensions. While the domestic commercial success of national productions often conceals the role of transnational reach and collaborations, the chapter argues for the significance of such exchanges in helping Turkey rise as a major regional and global film industry. A recent debate in Turkish film studies regarding terminology reflects concerns about transnationalism and the ways in which the term can meaningfully be applied in the Turkish context. It has been argued that the term 'Turkish cinema' (*Türk Sineması* in Turkish) excludes non-ethnically minority cinemas within Turkey (especially Kurdish), and does not take into account transnational filmmakers with Turkish origins such as Fatih Akin in Germany and Ferzan Özpetek in Italy. The term 'Cinema of Turkey' (*Türkiye Sineması*) has been offered as an alternative, more inclusive, term. However, since this discursive divide does not translate into English, I will employ the two terms interchangeably.

Symbiosis of Film and Television Industries

The size of the domestic market in Turkey enables the sustainability of its film industry, especially as the box office for Turkish films often exceeds that of foreign films. This phenomenon is not new. Between the 1950s and the late 1970s, the Turkish film industry – termed 'Yeşilçam' (Green pine) after the name of the street where most production companies of the time were located – was very prolific, churning out an average of 150–175 productions a year, which were enormously popular with audiences (Behlil 2010a: 2). Following a sharp decline from the mid-1970s due to several reasons such as the spread of television, economic crisis, and social unrest, and a 'sleeper' period through the 1980s and most of the 1990s, the industry slowly recovered in the 2000s. Arthouse cinema benefited from funds provided by the Ministry of Culture and Tourism from 2005, while popular cinema rode on the wave created by the impetus of the blooming television sector (Behlil 2010b).

As a result, Turkey's domestic productions have led in ticket sales almost uninterruptedly since 2005, with an average market share of 50–60 per cent (see Figure 13.1). This enormous share of national productions is only comparable to global behemoths like India and South Korea, and far exceeds any country in Europe. The fact that this has happened without a formal state or institutional strategy makes it both fascinating and essentially unpredictable. The steady rise of ticket sales (see Figure 13.2) can be tied to a sharp increase in the number of movie screens (from 987 in 2005 to 2,692 in 2017, TÜİK 2018), fuelled by the boom in construction, particularly of shopping malls, many of which host a multiplex cinema.

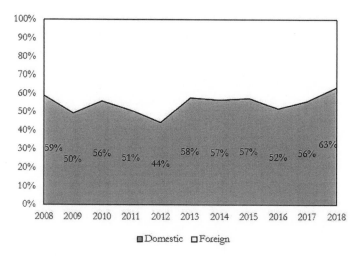

Figure 13.1   Market share of ticket sales for domestic releases.

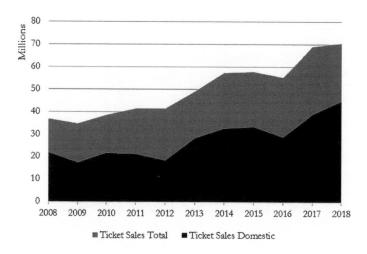

Figure 13.2   Total and domestic ticket sales.

Paralleling this growth in film production and cinema attendance is the afore-mentioned popularity of local television series, which mushroomed after the creation of the first private channels in the country in the early 1990s. As they needed to fill their airtime with affordable content, these channels purchased old Yeşilçam films in bulk from defunct production companies and broadcast them daily. A new generation of viewers, too young to have watched these films in the movie theatres, familiarised themselves with comedies and melodramas of the past. This reinforced the demand for locally produced content, leading to the production of a number of television series, which developed, together with advertising, into a sizeable industry (Çetin-Erus 2007). There is a clear link between the old film melodramas and the new television series, not just in terms of modality or narratives, but also in terms of industry practices. At the same time, the existence of a broader audiovisual industry allows for independent cinema to survive, as many members of the cast and crew of these films earn their living through series, commercials and mainstream films, and thus can afford to take part in independent productions for little to no salary. Nearly all film actors and actresses in Turkey work in television, save for a few exceptions like Cem Yılmaz and Yılmaz Erdoğan, who produce and direct the films they star in.

The popularity of Turkish TV dramas spread far and wide in the twenty-first century, with shows being broadcast all across Latin America, most of Europe and Asia, and some countries in Africa (Karlıdağ and Bulut 2014). However, this popularity has not translated to exportability of the theatrically released films. One possible reason behind this contrast is the fact that television and cinema are aimed at different target groups. The popular Turkish dramas are essentially soap operas influenced by the melodramas of Yeşilçam; they are directed at a gendered domestic audience that is mostly female. On network television, each episode lasts about 120 minutes excluding the commercials. To fill air time, their narration is stretched and filled with 'long takes, extremely long sequences, shaky camera techniques and long musical sequences' (Kesirli Unur 2015: 145), which is ideal for a domestic viewing experience where people chat and watch their mobile phones at the same time, but the cinema-going experience demands more dedicated viewing.

Audiovisual production has been further reinforced by the distribution opportunities offered by two online viewing platforms, BluTV and puhutv, which launched in 2016 and provide content different to that of network television in terms of style and subject matter. Both platforms produce their own content, webseries directed by arthouse filmmakers such as Seren Yüce (*Masum/Innocent*, Turkey, 2017) and Onur Saylak (*Şahsiyet/Personality*, Turkey, 2018). These shows feature scripts written by playwrights and novelists, with more daring content, complex narratives and shorter run times. Netflix launched in Turkey in 2016, connecting Turkish audiences with a wide variety of content from across the world. As announced in 2017, Netflix's first Turkish original, *Hakan: Muhafız/ The Protector* (Turkey, 2018) includes two full seasons shot by a crew that regularly works in film rather than television, with Can Evrenol (whose horror films have been shown at the Toronto International Film Festival) among the directors. This Netflix-produced series positions Turkey within a transnational distribution network opening the path for further transnational collaborations.[2] This is in many ways a new model for popular series, and certainly not one evident among theatrically released popular films, which despite their huge domestic popularity remain mostly unknown outside the country.

TRENDS AND THEMES IN POPULAR CINEMA

To illustrate the domestic popularity of Turkish films, it is useful to note that since records began in 1989, the first twenty-three spots belong to local productions, with only four foreign films (all Hollywood) in the top fifty.[3] The highest-grossing film of every year since 2005 has been a domestic release. Among these fourteen films, eleven are comedies, while a quick look at the top ten Turkish films of each year between 2008 and 2017 also shows a clear preference for comedies (see Figure 13.3). Comedies make up 60 per cent of tickets sold, while the horror intake is insignificant. This reign of comedy, partly due to traditional audience attachments to Yeşilçam formulas, owes a lot to the meteoric rise of one particular production company, BKM (Beşiktaş Cultural Center), which created exactly half of the sixty films in question (and several more that did not enter the top ten).

BKM was founded in 1994 as a private theatre company focusing on comedies in the Beşiktaş district of Istanbul. In its first decade, BKM concentrated on stage performances, providing a home for some of the most popular stand-up comedians in Turkey like Cem Yılmaz and Ata Demirer, who would both later successfully transition to cinema. Some of the stage shows were sold to television

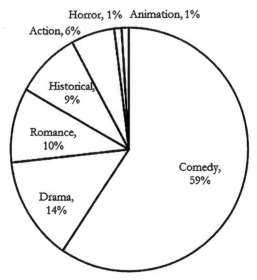

Figure 13.3   Distribution of genres in top ten domestic releases 2008–18.

233

channels, making BKM a household name in the late 1990s. In 2001 BKM started producing and distributing feature films. The first to be released was *Vizontele* (Turkey, 2001) directed by and starring Yılmaz Erdoğan, one of the company's co-founders. Telling the story of how television entered people's lives in a rural village in the 1970s, the film set the tone of BKM: wholesome comedies with a touch of nostalgia harking back to the golden days of Yeşilçam. Over the years, the company also made several romantic period dramas such as *Kelebeğin rüyasi/ The Butterfly's Dream* (Yılmaz Erdoğan, Turkey, 2013), Turkey's nominee for the Academy Award for Best Film in a Foreign Language in 2013.

BKM functions almost entirely at a national level, with two exceptions. In 2012, the company co-produced Iranian director Bahman Ghobadi's *Gergedan mevsimi/Rhino Season* (Iran/Turkey) with Ghobadi's Iran-based Mij Film. The film tells the story of Iranians in exile in Istanbul (mirroring the director's situation, as Ghobadi himself was in exile), with Yılmaz Erdoğan in one of the leading roles. In 2017, BKM released *İstanbul kırmızısı/Red Istanbul*, an Italian-Turkish co-production by Ferzan Özpetek, based on the director's own novel. Themes of exile and displacement also surface in this film, as the main character, an author named Orhan, returns to his hometown of Istanbul after having lived in London for over twenty years. These two instances of marked cinematic transnationalism are first and foremost opportunistic, to use Hjort's categorisation (Hjort 2009: 19): the two internationally known auteurs, Ghobadi and Özpetek provided BKM with prestige beyond popular comedies, as well as access to international funds and audiences. BKM continues its success on television and in the cinema, dominating the screens with films of relatively high production values and starring many of the country's popular comedians.

The most successful franchise in Turkish cinema is also the brainchild of a comedian, Şahan Gökbakar. Gökbakar started appearing on television in variety shows in 2004, and premiered his own show, *Dikkat Şahan çıkabilir/Warning, Şahan* (Turkey, 2005–6), the next year. The characters he created for the skits were enormously popular, and Gökbakar became one of the first Turkish comedians to go viral on then-new YouTube. Taking advantage of his online fame, Gökbakar adapted one of his characters into a feature length film in 2008's *Recep Ivedik*. The film, directed by his younger brother Togan, broke the all-time box office record with 4.3 million tickets sold. Over ten years, five Ivedik films were released, with the sixth instalment scheduled for 2019. Each one of those films topped the ticket sales in the year of its release, with the exception of *Recep Ivedik 3* (2010) which came in a very close second.[4] Ivedik is a vulgar, simple man from the lower classes, and the humour is largely scatological and sexual, with sexist and homophobic tendencies. The films have been criticised for setting a bad example for children, and it has been suggested that the Ivedik phenomenon 'can be seen as a reflection of the rapid transformation of Turkey during the AKP era' for its populist and anti-elite stance (Suner 2011: 147).

Figure 13.4   The title character of *Recep Ivedik 5* (Togan Gökbakar, 2017) in all his glory.

In addition to the productions of BKM and the Gökbakar brothers, many other comedies are released each year, particularly in the subgenres of mafia comedies and romantic comedies. Horror also proved to be popular with audiences, even if it never reached the ticket sales of comedies. While some horror films adopt generic syntax from Hollywood, especially in the vein of teenage slashers, a significant number utilise Islamic motifs, particularly the Djinn demons, mysterious beings mentioned in the Quran (Özkaracalar 2012). Even though there had not been a strong tradition of horror cinema in Turkey, the success of *Büyü/ Spell* (Orhan Oğuz, Turkey 2004), *D@bbe* (Hasan Karacadağ, Turkey, 2006) and *Musallat/Pestering* (Alper Mestçi, Turkey, 2007), was remarkable and led to a number of franchises, such as Hasan Karacadağ's *D@bbe* films and Alper Mestçi's *Siccin* (Turkey, 2014) and it sequels, all about possession by Djinns. Mestçi and Karacadağ have directed 14 of the top grossing 15 Turkish horror films, thus clearly dominating the field (Box Office Türkiye 2018).

INDEPENDENT, ARTHOUSE AND FESTIVAL FILMS

The indisputable superstar of arthouse filmmaking in Turkey is Nuri Bilge Ceylan, who has received awards at Cannes with every one of his films until his 2018 entry, *Ahlat ağacı/The Wild Pear Tree* (Turkey/North Macedonia/France/ Germany/Bosnia-Herzegovina/Bulgaria/Sweden). Many have tried to imitate his minimalist style with long takes and silent landscapes but without success. Semih Kaplanoğlu's Golden Bear win with *Bal/Honey* (Turkey/Germany/

Figure 13.5   Golden Palm winner *Winter Sleep* (Nuri Bilge Ceylan, 2014).

France, 2010) represents another major accomplishment for filmmakers who made their debuts in the late 1990s – often referred as the 'nineties generation'.

Others from this generation whose films have circulated regularly at prestigious international festivals include Zeki Demirkubuz, Yeşim Ustaoğlu, Reha Erdem and Turkish-Cypriot Derviş Zaim. All of these directors write their own scripts, and with the exception of Ceylan in his later work, act as their own producers. They are also exceptional among the independent directors in that they do not work for television or advertising to make a living.[5] Nonetheless, some of the crew and virtually all the cast these directors employ still work in television series. All of these directors tend to be referred to as 'arty' (often condescendingly by the mainstream press) and their cinema considered slow and challenging for general audiences. However, behind a broadly realist style, their themes are quite different from one another.

Zeki Demirkubuz often deals with alienated characters in urban settings, like the failed author Muharrem in his *Yeraltı/Inside* (Turkey, 2012), a very loose adaptation of Dostoevsky's *Notes from the Underground*. Yesim Ustaoğlu, the leading female director certainly of her generation, and of the country, tends to concentrate on female characters. In her *Araf/Somewhere in Between* (Turkey/France/Germany, 2012), Zehra, a naive young woman working at a truck stop, finds herself pregnant after falling for a handsome and brooding truck driver who promptly disappears from her life. Her more recent *Tereddüt/Claire Obscur* (Turkey/France/Germany/Poland, 2016) has two female leads, one oppressed by sexist traditions and one seemingly liberated, yet they discover that they have much more in common than would initially appear. Reha Erdem's characters inhabit fantastic worlds that seem to be located just on the precipice of the world as we know it. Films like *Hayat var/My Only Sunshine* (Turkey/Greece/Bulgaria, 2008), *Kosmos* (Turkey/

Bulgaria, 2009) and *Koca dünya/Big Big World* (Turkey, 2016) are not genre cinema, yet they reject the realist style that is common to most other art cinema directors in Turkey. Derviş Zaim makes a point of (limited) stylistic experimentation employing traditional Turkish/Islamic arts. In *Cenneti beklerken/Waiting for Heaven* (Hungary/Turkey, 2006), he told the story of miniature artists in the seventeenth century, in a style that imitated the Ottoman miniatures in portions of the film. *Nokta/Dot* (Turkey, 2008) emulated Arabic calligraphy using a single take, and *Gölgeler ve suretler/Shadows and Faces* (Turkey, 2010) took shadow plays as its starting point, an art that is often considered to be the precursor of cinema itself.

Furthermore, a new generation of filmmakers with unique styles and international recognition emerged in the mid-2000s. Seren Yüce, Emin Alper, Ali Aydın and Kaan Müjdeci all received awards in Venice, which appears to be the most welcoming of the three major festivals for Turkish filmmakers.[6] In his feature debut *Çogunluk/Majority* (Turkey, 2010), Seren Yüce focused on a regular young man from the middle class drawing a scathing yet extremely convincing portrait of the 'average man'. His acute sense of observation took a stab at the newly rich upper classes in his second feature, *Rüzgarda salınan nilüfer/Swaying Waterlily* (Germany/Turkey, 2016), but the film was neither critically nor commercially successful. Emin Alper's debut *Tepenin ardı/Beyond the Hill* (Turkey/Greece, 2012) told the story of a farming family in a rural area who are convinced that people from 'beyond the hill' have invaded their territory, arguably reflecting the current regime's 'external enemies' mentality in which threats are seen to come from the outside and everyone but ourselves are to blame for society's ills.

Another exponent of this new generation, Seyfi Teoman, received his formal training at the famed Lodz Film School in Poland. His first two films were contemplative yet joyful: *Tatil kitabı/Summer Book* (Turkey/Netherlands, 2008) is about a family in the provinces whose father falls in a coma, as told from the perspective of the family's ten-year-old son, while *Bizim büyük çaresizliğimiz/Our Grand Despair* (Turkey/Germany/Netherlands, 2011) is about two intellectual bachelors in their thirties in Ankara who share a home and who both fall in love with the young woman who moves in with them. Both films premiered in Berlin and received awards at various festivals, but Teoman passed away in a motorcycle accident in 2011, cutting a promising life and career all too short. Tolga Karaçelik's *Kelebekler/Butterflies* (Turkey, 2018) won the Grand Jury Prize at Sundance's dramatic competition in the world section, the first Turkish film ever to do so. This tale of three siblings who take a road trip to attend their estranged father's funeral in a small town is emotional, yet carries enough humour to attract audiences, a rare feat for independent films (still only around 134,000 tickets). Others like Pelin Esmer, Tayfun Pirselimoğlu, Hüseyin Karabey and Mahmut Fazıl Coşkun show their films at festivals around the world, with limited success at home. Nearly all of these filmmakers receive state funding for some of their productions, and many of their films are co-productions.[7] As such, the films are transnational in terms of production and consumption, but their content remains local in terms of stories, if not necessarily influences.[8]

As mentioned above, the spectre of Ceylan's cinema is felt in numerous examples of contemplative films set in rural areas. Ceylan's work itself manifests the mediation between the local and the transnational. These are transnational productions with stories firmly set in the local, featuring admitted nods to European literature, film and music (Diken et al. 2018). One trend in independent films often pointed out by critics is the emergence of symbolic narratives and dystopias that are set in the very near future, perhaps even the present. Tolga Karaçelik's *Sarmaşık/Ivy* (Turkey/Germany, 2015) is set on a cargo ship, where the crew is stuck for months because of the owner's bankruptcy. Emin Alper's *Abluka/Frenzy* (France/Qatar/Turkey 2015) depicts a derelict and tumultuous city where people live in constant terror and the leading character becomes an informant for the police, turning on his brother for political reasons that are not made entirely clear. Ceylan Özgün Özçelik establishes a similar setting in her debut, *Kaygı/Inflame* (Turkey, 2017), where the lead character questions her own suppressed traumatic memories, reflecting the country's own reluctance in facing traumatic events of its history. In Emre Yeksan's *Körfez/The Gulf* (Turkey/Germany/Greece, 2017), a young man returns home to Izmir, where an unexplainable stench has engulfed the city. These films can all be seen as examples of a tendency which reflects on the sense of feeling boxed in by an increasingly oppressive regime, particularly after its violent clampdown on anti-government protests in 2013.

In addition to popular and independent fiction features discussed above, there is a steady production of documentaries. These films circulate mostly in film festivals – when they are not banned for political reasons – or in independent exhibition circuits, as examined below. While documentaries belonged strictly to the realm of television until the 1990s, new technologies and a liberalisation of political climate resulted in a slew of documentaries giving voice to groups that had been previously silenced (Candan 2014). Among these groups are the Kurds, whose degree of oppression by the Turkish state is evident in the fact that they have not even had the possibility to express themselves in their own language since it was banned for decades. Filmmakers such as Kazım Öz, Çayan Demirel and Mizgin Müjde Arslan created works that question the Kurdish identity, as well as the official histories of the Kurdish region. Not surprisingly, their films have been censored at film festivals in Turkey and not allowed wider release (Başyiğit, 2016). These films have found limited release abroad at specialised events such as documentary or Kurdish film festivals. Others have been producing films on the fine line between documentary and fiction, especially on Kurdish topics. *İki dil bir bavul/On the Way to School* (Orhan Eskiköy and Özgür Doğan, Turkey/Netherlands, 2008), *Babamın sesi/ Voice of My Father* (Orhan Eskiköy, Turkey, 2012) and *Annemin şarkısı/Song of My Mother* (Erol Mintaş, Turkey/France/Germany, 2014) are just a few examples. All of these films feature non-professional actors and often personal stories. Another Kurdish director working in this vein is Ali Kemal Çınar. Paradoxically, Çınar makes micro-budget genre films set in his hometown of Diyarbakır, starring himself. These include *Veşarti/Hidden* (Turkey, 2015), where the protagonist faces the prospect of a magical gender reversal, and *Genco* (Turkey, 2017) about a superhero with very limited superpowers.

Short film production is also abundant; over 70 Turkish universities have Communication Faculties, where Cinema-TV departments or at least film-making courses are located. All major festivals have shorts competitions and there are numerous festivals and competitions devoted to short films. These include at least two that have pitching sessions and provide financial support to projects. One festival, Canlandıranlar, is solely for animated shorts, and animation has become a popular field throughout the decade. Several series produced for the national broadcaster TRT's children's channel have been adapted into feature films, but the most interesting and ambitious of the feature animations is strictly for adults. *Kötü Kedi Şerafettin/Bad Cat* (Ayşe Ünal and Mehmet Kurtuluş, Turkey, 2016), based on a popular comics character, features a swearing, stealing, womanising feline. The film, starring numerous celebrated voice actors, took nearly a decade to produce and was received well critically, but failed to make a significant box office earning. While it recuperated most of its budget through international sales, *Bad Cat* scared animators off producing any works that are not accessible to children.

Figure 13.6   Şerafettin the *Bad Cat* (Ayşe Ünal and Mehmet Kurtuluş, Turkey, 2016) raiding the fridge.

Financing, Co-productions and the Case of Mustang

Popular cinema in Turkey has been self-sustainable for the larger companies, and there has been some interest on the part of investment firms like hedge funds to invest in films. Independent films, as in most European countries, have been more reliant on national and international funds. The growth in Turkish independent cinema was preceded by the introduction of a cinema law which focused on classification and production support. Adopted in 2004, this law introduced a production support scheme that has been an imperative for independent films. A selection board comprised of industry members and state representatives convenes twice a year to determine the projects to be supported in development, production and post-production. While there is also support for short films and feature documentaries, the greater part of the funding the Ministry provides is allocated for feature films. Between 2005 and 2018, 543 feature films received roughly 74 million euros in support, with 327 for production, 171 first-time directors and forty-five post-production support (60 per cent, 31 per cent and 9 per cent, respectively) (Okur 2016: 2).[9] As the years progressed, the number of applications rose meteorically, rendering the committees ineffective, while the decisions became more and more politically charged. Yamaç Okur, a producer and a former selection committee member, points out that personal relations have become the leading factor in a film's evaluation, surpassing merit or eligibility (Akbulut 2015: 32).

Eurimages funds have also been valuable for Turkish independent films over the last three decades.[10] Turkey became the 18th member of Eurimages in 1990, and over a hundred films have benefitted from this source. Between 2008 and 2017, 31 projects in which Turkey is majority co-producer received a total of 5,928,000 euros. For minority co-productions, the amount was 1,870,000 euros for eight films. As a majority co-producer, Turkish companies overwhelmingly work with German firms (twenty-four of the projects), followed by French (eleven) and Dutch (6). This seems to have shifted from the previous decades, as Levent Yılmazok stated in 2010 that France, Greece and Hungary were the 'most preferred colleagues' between 1990 and 2010 (Yılmazok 2010: 91). Producers involved in co-productions indicate that Germany and France are favoured since they are much stronger filmmaking countries with a variety of funding schemes. Greece has been suffering from the financial crisis for a decade now, and countries like Hungary and Poland have experienced political instability in terms of cultural funding. Other Balkan countries, particularly ex-Yugoslav states, have much smaller funds available, and being a minority shareholder in co-productions with these countries is not supported by the Turkish state. Overall, the number of films where Turkey is the minority co-producer is much lower than its participation as the majority stakeholder, which has been pointed out as a weakness that is not sustainable in the long run by the Executive Director of Eurimages, Roberto Olla (SEYAP 2013).

Until 2008, the only films from Turkey that had any appeal to European audiences were European co-productions with Turkey as the minority partner. These included co-productions by transnational filmmakers such as Ferzan Özpetek and Fatih Akın, both of whom live and work in Europe. Ferzan Özpetek's *Hamam/Hamam: The Turkish Bath* (Italy/Turkey/Spain, 1997), *La finestra di fronte/Facing Windows* (Italy/Turkey/Portugal/UK, 2003) and *Saturno contro/ Saturn in Opposition* (2007), and Akın's *Auf der anderen Seite/The Edge of Heaven* (Germany/Turkey/Italy, 2007) lead the list in terms of admissions in the EU since 1996.[11] However, both directors gradually turned to making films set solely in their adopted homelands and stopped co-producing their films in Turkey (with the exception of Özpetek's *Red Istanbul* which has not performed very well outside of Turkey). Turkish majority Eurimages co-productions, festival award winners like all of Ceylan's films, Kaplanoğlu's *Honey* or Yeşim Ustaoğlu's *Pandora's Box* (Turkey/France/Germany/Belgium, 2008) also receive commercial releases in Europe, but most (or at least those who are not Ceylan) fail to reach large audiences. While these films are co-financed with European funding and employ crews from European countries, none of them have any transnational themes; in fact, many are set in rural parts of the country, focusing on characters trying to get away either from small hometowns or from the city back to their hometowns to rediscover themselves.

An interesting example of the state- and Eurimages-funded production model that reveals the ways in which co-productions problematise conceptions of national cinema is Deniz Gamze Ergüven's international hit *Mustang* (Turkey/ France/Germany/Qatar, 2015). The film received 100,000 euros in support from the Turkish Ministry of Culture in 2014, the highest amount given to first-time feature directors. Having also secured funds from the French Centre National de la Cinématographie (CNC) and the German federal Filmförderungsanstalt (FFA) and regional Film- und Medienstiftung NRW, it received Eurimages funding as a French/Turkish/German co-production the same year. *Mustang*'s story, about five orphan sisters oppressed by their guardians, takes place in Turkey with a Turkish cast and completely in the Turkish language. Nonetheless, the director Deniz Gamze Ergüven is a Turkish-born French citizen, and she had a French script co-writer. Sound and post-production were also done by French crews, providing a typical example of a European co-production that does not necessarily deal with transnational themes but takes advantage of transnational funding and technical expertise.

Following a premiere at the Directors' Fortnight section in Cannes, where it won the Label Europa Cinemas Award, the film travelled the world, receiving audience awards at festivals in Chicago, Glasgow, Seville, Stockholm, Sydney, Thessaloniki and Valladolid. It was nominated for a Golden Globe and a BAFTA, and due to its status as a co-production, it applied both in France and in Turkey to be the national selection for each country's Best Foreign Language Film

Figure 13.7 *Mustang* (Deniz Gamze Ergüven, 2015), not a Turkish favourite.

nominee at the Academy Awards. The Academy of Motion Picture Arts and Sciences (AMPAS) has fairly loose regulations regarding co-productions, stating that 'the submitting country must certify that creative control of the motion picture was largely in the hands of citizens or residents of that country' (AMPAS 2014). With a creative team that was Turkish-French, either submitting country would have been able to claim the film as their own. Which country's claim would have prevailed will never be known, however, as unlike France, Turkey did not choose *Mustang* as their nominee.[12] In France, *Mustang* sold over half a million tickets, but it was critically and commercially unsuccessful in Turkey, with 25,000 tickets sold and mostly negative reviews.

The reception of *Mustang* in Turkey was complicated, pointing also to the complexities of transnational productions. On the one hand, the plight of young girls for freedom drew sympathies from the traditionally secular viewers, who feel that the country's modern founding principles are under attack from the conservative government. On the other hand, the characters and situations felt inauthentic to many audiences and critics, and Ergüven was considered to have too much of an orientalist outsider's view on her subjects. Some of the frequent criticisms had to do with the fetishisation of the girls' bodies, as well as the incredulity of the main premise: how did a family this conservative allow these girls to create scandals to begin with? The appearance of the town as a nameless, timeless space, turning the film into a fairytale-like allegory for oppressed women everywhere was ruptured by inconsistent references to very concrete details. In her aptly titled review 'Five French Girls Walk into an Anatolian Village', Selin Gökçesu sums up everything Turkish audiences found problematic about the film and more, particularly drawing attention to the outsider status of Ergüven (Gökçesu 2016).

DISTRIBUTION AND EXHIBITION OF TURKISH FILMS
DOMESTICALLY AND BEYOND

When the recovery of the Turkish film industry became visible in the mid-2000s, one of the concerns was the sustainability of this success. The principal indicator for the weakness of the industry was how few films actually were able to turn a profit. Out of roughly 300 domestic films released between 2006 and 2011, forty sold more than a million tickets each, but more than half sold less than 100,000 (Behlil 2012a: 44). Box office success, in other words, was not equally shared, with by far the largest income going to the top ten Turkish films of each year. It is heartening to see that since 2015 a mid-range for films has emerged that are not blockbusters, but that can help their production companies sustain themselves (see Figure 13.8).

The major obstacle that films face in terms of box office is the monopolisation of exhibition. In 2011, two of the largest cinema chains in the country, Mars Sinema and AFM, merged to form a leviathan of a company which entered distribution and production as well, forming a classical Hollywood-style vertical integration model. Mars's dominance in urban centres means that the company determines the fate of many independent productions, which are not able to reach larger audiences if they are not shown within the Mars network. Mars 'has a box office market share of 50%, a cinema advertising market share of over 90% and is the leading distributor of movies in the country', according to Mars shareholder Actera's website. In 2016, Mars was sold

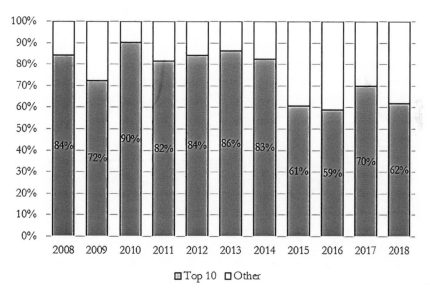

Figure 13.8   Share of Top 10 films in all local ticket sales.

to the South Korean conglomerate CJ Group, the fifth-largest theatre chain in the world (Noh n.d.). South Korea may be distant from Turkey geographically, but the two countries share certain characteristics, with this involvement highlighting another transnational dimension of exchange.

The Mars monopoly has been detrimental for independent productions, which already struggled for access to screens. In November 2013, an alternative distribution model called Başka Sinema (Another Cinema) was established to counter the hegemony of Mars and other commercial theatres. Backed by the Kariyo and Ababay Foundation, a small private institution established to develop activities in culture, arts and education, Başka Sinema was launched by the arthouse distribution company M3. Through its agreements with individual theatres, some of which it has helped with their digital upgrades, Başka Sinema releases both local and foreign independent films, securing them a month-long run and offering audiences three different films a day in each theatre (Carney 2014). From its creation until the end of 2019, Başka Sinema's theatres showed over 350 films in the network that now spans 49 screens in 21 cities. While this is not a powerful enough model to create a paradigm shift, it managed to provide cinephiles in Turkey with access to films they otherwise would not have been able to watch. These include primarily local independent productions – in fact, a great number of domestic independent films, among them documentaries, are only exhibited at Başka Sinema theatres. Başka Sinema does not show any US studio films, but exhibits old and new arthouse films from Europe, Asia and Latin America – a particularly significant function in the absence of a Cinémathèque in Istanbul (or anywhere else in Turkey). Among the film festivals that help promote Turkish arthouse cinema, the oldest was founded in the Southern coastal city of Antalya in 1964. This was followed by festivals in Adana in 1969, Istanbul in 1982 and Ankara in 1988. Istanbul and Antalya film festivals also feature co-production markets, facilitating transnational filmmaking.

Beyond distribution and exhibition opportunities within Turkey, the large diasporic communities of Germany, the Netherlands, Austria and, to a smaller extent, Switzerland and Great Britain provide significant markets for Turkish films. Germany-based distribution companies Cinemaxximum and Kinostar paved the way for this trend (Halle 2012: 130), followed by AF-Media, which started expanding into new territories across Europe, Asia the Middle East and South America, benefiting from the popularity of Turkish dramas in these regions (Meza 2018).

Table 13.1 shows the top ten highest grossing Turkish films in terms of EU admissions, showing a mix of nationally funded productions and transnational co-productions. Among the top ten, three are co-productions, fully transnational in terms of their production and finance. The other films on this list, produced only by Turkish companies, may not be transnational in terms

Table 13.1 Top ten films (co-)produced in Turkey in terms of EU admissions (excluding Turkish ticket sales).

Film	Producing country	Production year	Director	Admissions EUR EU
Mustang	FR/DE/TR	2015	Deniz Gamze Ergüven	1,177,310
The Water Diviner	AU/USA/TR	2014	Russell Crowe	1,151,300
Recep Ivedik 5	TR	2017	Togan Gökbakar	785,180
Recep Ivedik 4	TR	2014	Togan Gökbakar	703,636
Winter Sleep	TR/FR/DE	2014	Nuri Bilge Ceylan	593,972
Recep Ivedik 2	TR	2009	Togan Gökbakar	571,788
Recep Ivedik 3	TR	2010	Togan Gökbakar	463,391
Conquest 1453 (Fetih 1453)	TR	2012	Faruk Aksoy	437,830
Recep Ivedik	TR	2008	Togan Gökbakar	390,678
Nuptials and Merriments (Düğün dernek)	TR	2013	Selçuk Aydemir	389,045

of production, nor do they contain any transnational themes, but the fact that they are distributed in Europe and perform well is on account of the diasporic, transnational audiences. Hence, Table 13.1 is an excellent demonstration of the two facets of transnationality in regard to 'Turkish' cinema, three films in terms of production and the rest in terms of consumption. *Mustang*, at number one, as discussed above, is a noteworthy case. *The Water Diviner* (Russell Crowe, Australia/USA/Turkey, 2014) which had minimal Turkish involvement, benefited from Russell Crowe's star power, portraying an Australian man looking for his sons after the Battle of Gallipoli. It performed decently across Europe, with an exceptionally great popularity in Spain. Ceylan's Golden Palm winner *Winter Sleep* entered the top ten thanks to its popularity in France. *Conquest 1453* (Faruk Aksoy, Turkey, 2012) was a high-budget nationalist period drama that told the story of the invasion of Constantinople from the Turkish perspective. All other films are comedies; the phenomenon of *Recep Ivedik* has evidently found an audience in diasporic Turkish audiences in Europe as well, with all five films of the franchise placed in the top ten. These popular films all produced nationally and strictly without state funds. Turkish independent films making a name for Turkey at international festivals are of a different breed and have more in common with European art cinema in terms of production, distribution, style and content.

Conclusion

The year 2008 was not a particularly significant touchstone for cinema in Turkey; the country did not undergo the same experience of the financial crisis like some other countries in the region. In fact, as Yeşil suggested, the decline of production in other countries in the Balkan region may have benefitted Turkey in terms of its increasing exports of series (2015: 52–3). Arthouse films' opportunistic transnational positioning, whereby transnationality has been pursued in order to benefit from funds rather than explore transnational themes, has indeed presented opportunities for growth. Directors have explored a variety of themes, at times challenging narrative and narrational conventions set by previous generations. In popular cinema, the sheer number of productions have allowed different genres to emerge, with comedy and horror proving to be the most persistent.

Overall, the decade proved to be a very productive one for Turkish audio-visual industries. Turkish cinema developed into a viable commercial cinema and an occasional contender for festival laurels. This upward trend has promise to continue: audience numbers continue growing, international sales for films have prospective audiences in regions where Turkish TV dramas are popular, there are unexplored co-production possibilities and there is a significant young population, with many film schools at universities. Mirroring the region's conditions in 2008, the country has entered a financial crisis in 2018, with the Turkish lira losing about 40 per cent of its value in eight months. This loss can in fact benefit the industry by strengthening its transnational ties, and exporting its products more easily across the region and the world, but it would require some strategic momentum on the part of sales agents and distributors. The other challenge for the industry is presented by the stifling political environment and shifting diplomatic alliances. There is an ongoing brain drain, particularly among the intelligentsia, and media censorship sets serious restraints on the creative process. Again, one possible way through this impasse may be through transnational connections, relying on co-productions. While the film industry in Turkey has kept largely to itself over the last decade, it appears that now is the time for it to spread further and assume its position as a player in the world and a giant in the region.

Notes

1. All data for yearly numbers is provided by <http://www.antraktsinema.com>, courtesy of Deniz Yavuz. Data for individual films throughout the chapter is taken from <www.boxofficeturkiye.com>.
2. *Protector* is co-produced by O3 Medya, the Turkish branch of O3 Production Services, owned by the Dubai-based MBC Group.
3. These are: 24. *Furious 7* (James Wan, USA/China/Japan/Canada/United Arab Emirates, 2015); 25. *Titanic* (James Cameron, USA, 1997, rereleased in 2012); 31.

The Fate of the Furious (F. Gary Gray, China/USA/Japan, 2017), 36. *Avatar* (James Cameron, USA, 2009).

4. After the action-adventure film (*New York'ta beş minare/Five Minarets in New York* (Turkey/USA, 2010), directed by and starring a popular singer/actor, Mahsun Kırmızıgül.

5. Reha Erdem needs to be excluded from this, as his production company Atlantik Film is among the most prestigious advertising producers in the country.

6. Yüce's *Majority* and *Küf/Mold* (Ali Aydın, Turkey/Germany) won the Luigi de Laurentiis Award given to the best debut film in 2010 and 2012, respectively; *Sivas* (Kaan Müjdeci, Germany/Turkey, 2014) and Alper's *Frenzy* won the Special Jury Prize along with other smaller awards.

7. In recent years, political polarisation has limited the access of certain filmmakers to these funds. Directors who have been denied support, presumably because of their criticism of the government, include Alper and Karaçelik.

8. For a discussion of Tarkovsky's influence on Turkish directors, see Behlil (2012b).

9. This data combines Okur's report and the Ministry support reports as featured on Se-Yap's (Film Producers' Association of Turkey) website. The Ministry no longer provides these reports on its own webpage.

10. Nonetheless, many of the independents do not receive any of these funds. For a more detailed discussion of one of these, *El yazisi/One Way or Another* (Ali Vatansever, Turkey, 2012), see Behlil (2012a).

11. All data regarding admissions figures in the EU come from Lumiere, the European Audiovisual Observatory's Database on admissions of films released in Europe: <http://lumiere.obs.coe.int>.

12. Müjdeci's *Sivas* was selected instead, but failed to make the shortlist.

REFERENCES

Akbulut, Kültigin (2015) *Kültür Bakanlığı Sinema Destekleri* <http://kulturservisi .com/p/birinci-bolum-turkiyede-sinema-desteginin-dogusu> (last accessed 8 July 2018).

AMPAS (2014) *Academy Awards of Merit for Achievements During 2015* <https:// www.oscars.org/sites/oscars/files/88aa_rules.pdf> (last accessed 23 September 2018).

Anon. Destekleme Kurulu Kararlari Archives, *SE-YAP Sinema Eseri Yapımcıları Meslek Birliği* <http://www.se-yap.org.tr/category/destekleme-kurulu-kararlari/> (last accessed 26 October 2018).

Başyiğit, Veli (2016) 'Turkey's Film Festivals Face a Narrowing Space for Expression', *Index on Censorship*, 30 June <https://www.indexoncensorship.org/2016/06/film-festivals-artistic-freedom-expression-turkey/> (last accessed 22 April 2019).

Behlil, Melis (2010a) 'Better Late than Never? The Role of Policy in the Turkish Cinematic Revival', *Film International*, 8 (6), pp. 21–9.

Behlil, Melis (2010b) 'Close Encounters? Contemporary Turkish Television and Cinema', *Wide Screen*, 2(2), pp. 1–14.

Behlil, Melis (2012a) 'Majors , Mavericks and Contenders : Financing Practices in Contemporary Turkish Cinema', *Spectator*, 32, pp. 41–9.

Behlil, Melis (2012b) 'East Is East?: New Turkish Cinema and Eastern Europe', in A. Imre (ed.), *A Companion to Eastern European Cinemas*. Chichester: Wiley-Blackwell, pp. 504–17.

Box Office Türkiye (2018) 'Tüm Zamanların En Çok İzlenen 15 Yerli Korku Filmi' <https://boxofficeturkiye.com/haber/tum-zamanlarin-en-cok-izlenen-15-yerli-korku-filmi--1584> (last accessed 23 September 2018).

Candan, Can (2014) 'Documentary Cinema in Turkey: A Brief Survey of the Past and the Present', in H. Başgüney and Ö. Özdüzen (ed.), *The City in Turkish Cinema*. Istanbul: Libra Kitap, pp. 113–34.

Carney, Josh (2014) 'A New Distribution Model Gives Turkey's Film Fans Their Fill of Foreign Fare', *Variety*, January <https://variety.com/2014/film/global/a-new-distribution-model-gives-turkeys-film-fans-their-fill-of-foreign-fare-1201066391/> (last accessed 10 July 2018).

Çetin-Erus, Zeynep (2007) 'Son On Yılın Popüler Türk Sinemasında Televizyon Sektörünün Etkileri', *Marmara İletişim Dergisi*, 12, pp. 123–33.

Diken, Bulent, Gilloch, Graeme Peter and Hammond, Craig (2018) *The Cinema of Nuri Bilge Ceylan : The Global Vision of a Turkish Filmmaker*. London: I. B. Tauris.

Ezra, Elizabeth and Rowden, Terry (2006) *Transnational Cinema: The Film Reader*. London and New York: Routledge.

Gökçesu, Selin (2016) 'The Rumpus Review of Mustang: Five French Girls Walk into an Anatolian Village' <https://therumpus.net/2016/05/the-rumpus-review-of-mustang-five-french-girls-walk-into-an-anatolian-village/> (last accessed 22 April 2019).

Halle, Randall (2012) 'The German Turkish Spectator and Turkish Language Film Programming: Karli-Kino, Maxximum Distribution, and the Interzone Cinema', in S. Hake and B. Mennel (eds), *Turkish German Cinema in the New Millennium: Sites, Sounds, and Screens*. New York: Berghahn Books, pp. 123–35.

Hjort, Mette (2009) 'On the Plurality of Cinematic Transnationalism', in Nataša Ďurovičová and Kathleen E. Newman (eds), *World Cinemas, Transnational Perspectives*. New York: Routledge, pp. 12–33.

Kara, Tolga (2009) 'Küresel Ekonomik Kriz ve Medya Sektörüne Yansımaları', *Marmara İletişim Dergisi*, 15, pp. 65–79.

Karlıdağ, Serpil and Bulut, Selda (2014) 'The Transnational Spread of Turkish Television Soap Operas', *İstanbul Üniversitesi İletişim Fakültesi Dergisi*, II (47), pp. 75–96.

Kaytaz, Mehmet and Gul, Misra C. (2014) 'Consumer Response to Economic Crisis and Lessons for Marketers: The Turkish Experience', *Journal of Business Research*, 67 (1), pp. 2701–6.

Kesirli Unur, Ayşegül (2015) 'Discussing Transnational Format Adaptation in Turkey: A Study on Kuzey Güney', *International Journal of TV Serial Narratives*, 1 (2), pp.139–50.

Kutlu, Hüseyin Ali and Demirci, N. Savaş (2011) 'Küresel Finansal Krizi (2007–?) Ortaya Çıkaran Nedenler, Krizin Etkileri, Krizden Kısmi Çıkış Ve Mevcut Durum', *Muhasebe ve Finansman Dergisi*, 52, pp.121–36.

Meza, Ed (2018) 'Germany's AF-Media Pushes Out Turkish Films to International Markets', *Variety*, 8 May <https://variety.com/2018/film/news/af-media-turkish-films-international-markets-1202801042/> (last accessed 14 July 2020).

Noh, Jean (2017) 'South Korea's CJ CGV Pushes Past 400 Theatres', *Screen Daily*, 19 June https://www.screendaily.com/news/south-koreas-cj-cgv-pushes-past-400-theatres/5119199.article#:~:text=Leading%20South%20Korean%20exhibitor%20CJ,theatres%20under%20its%20Cinemaximum%20brand.> (last accessed 14 July 2020).

Oğuz, Şebnem (2009) 'The Response of the Turkish State to the 2008 Crisis: A Further Step towards Neoliberal Authoritarian Statism', in *Third IIPPE International Research Workshop*, pp. 1–21 <http://www.iippe.org/wiki/images/a/ac/Oguz_IIPPE_Ankara.pdf>.

Okur, Yamaç (2016) '*Kültür Bakanlığı Sinema Filmleri Destekleri 2005–2015*', Istanbul <https://drive.google.com/file/d/0B37XHub-ux8WaGg0bFVKNHFzWlk/view> (last accessed 14 July 2020).

Özkaracalar, K (2012) 'Horror Films in Turkish Cinema: To Use or Not to Use Local Cultural Motifs, That Is Not the Question', in P. Allmer, E. Brick and D. Huxley (eds), *European Nightmares: Horror Cinema in Europe Since 1945*. London & New York: Wallflower Press, pp. 249–60.

SEYAP (Sinema Eseri Yapımcıları Meslek Birliği) (2013) *Eurimages Meeting*. Istanbul <http://www.se-yap.org.tr/wp-content/uploads/2013/08/eurimages_toplanti_5_temmuz_2013.pdf> (last accessed 14 July 2020).

Suner, Asuman (2011) 'Between Magnificence and Monstrosity: Turkishness in Recent Popular Cinema', *New Perspectives on Turkey*, 45, pp. 123–54.

TÜİK (Türkiye İstatistik Kurumu) (2018) '*Sinema ve Tiyatro İstatistikleri, 201*, <http://www.tuik.gov.tr/PreHaberBultenleri.do?id=27604> (last accessed 14 July 2020).

Vivarelli, Nick (2018) 'Cannes: Turkish Sales Company Match Point Scores Sales to Asia', *Variety*, 17 May <https://variety.com/2018/film/global/cannes-match-point-sales-asia-1202813500/> (last accessed 14 July 2020).

Yeşil, Bilge (2015) 'Transnationalization of Turkish Dramas: Exploring the Convergence of Local and Global Market Imperatives', *Global Media and Communication*, 11 (1), pp. 43–60.

Yılmazok, Levent (2010) 'Turkish Films Co-produced within Europe: The Story after Twenty Years' Experience in Eurimages', *Sinecine*, 1 (2), pp. 87–108.

TABLES

NOTE

The tables of completed/released films below have been assembled to the best of the individual contributors' knowledge and checked, as far as possible, by the editors. Given that data collection is not coordinated across Balkan countries, and both criteria and methods for collection within institutions vary, we are aware of possible discrepancies across countries. In a number of cases, there were no institutionally collated data and the contributors identified the information by combining several different sources. At times, it proved too challenging to accurately collate from various sources, so the information is not provided. Despite such acknowledged limitations, the tables below offer an as accurate view as currently possible on the quantitative output of Balkan cinema between 2008 and 2018.

ALBANIA

Table 1 Overview of national film production

	2008	2009	2010	2011	2012	2013	2014	2015	2016	2017	2018
Feature films: Fiction	4	6	1	5	2	3	4	4	1	6	5
Feature films: Documentary	3	3	0	5	6	1	2	2	2	11	0
Short films: Fiction and documentary	8	10	16	5	1	3	3	6	8	9	1
Animation: Feature and shorts	6	4	4	1	0	1	1	3	2	3	0

ALBANIA

Table 2 Feature film (fiction) production and box office data

		2008	2009	2010	2011	2012	2013	2014	2015	2016	2017	2018
National productions		2	1	0	2	1	1	3	1	1	2	1
Co-productions	Majority	2	5	1	3	1	2	1	3	0	4	4
	Minority	0	1	0	0	1	0	0	1	0	2	1
Box office total (in euros)		n/a	n/a	n/a	n/a	n/a	n/a	n/a	n/a	n/a	n/a	n/a
Box office national (in euros)		n/a	n/a	n/a	n/a	n/a	n/a	n/a	n/a	n/a	n/a	n/a
Admissions total		n/a	n/a	n/a	n/a	n/a	n/a	n/a	n/a	n/a	n/a	n/a
Admissions national		n/a	n/a	n/a	n/a	n/a	n/a	n/a	n/a	n/a	n/a	n/a

Note: The vast majority of the above productions received funding or support from the Albanian National Center of Cinematography. Our research has shown that most films that did not receive such funding or support were made for television, had no theatrical release and did not participate in festivals, and are therefore not included here. The statistics on box office grosses and admissions in Albania are not made public by distributors and cinemas, consequently this data is not available.

Sources: Albanian National Center of Cinematography, Majlinda Tafa and Magali Perrichet (Marubi Academy of Film and Multimedia).

ALBANIA

Key institutions

Akademia i Filmit dhe Multimedia Marubi/
The Marubi Academy of Film and Multimedia
<https://afmm.edu.al/>

Arkivi Qendror Shetèror i Filmit/Albanian Central State's Film Archive
<http://www.aqshf.gov.al/>

Qendra Kombëtare e Kinematografisë/
Albanian National Center of Cinematography
<http://nationalfilmcenter.gov.al/>

Major festivals

Tirana International Film Festival
<https://tiranafilmfest.com/>

International Human Rights Film Festival Tirana
<http://ihrffa.net/>

DEA Open Air International Film Fest
Facebook: deafilmfestival

AniFest Rozafa
<www.anifestrozafa.al>

Balkan Food and Film Festival
<www.filmfreeway.com/festival/B3F>

Bosnia-Herzegovina

Table 1 Overview of national film production

	2008	2009	2010	2011	2012	2013	2014	2015	2016	2017	2018
Feature films: Fiction	2	1	7	1	2	5	6	2	2	6	4
Feature films: Documentary	2	1	6	5	5	1	3	11	10	13	4
Short films: Fiction and documentary	18	27	22	20	17	16	26	29	23	21	28
Animation: Feature and shorts	6	2	2	4	2	0	2	0	2	4	0

BOSNIA-HERZEGOVINA

Table 2 Feature film (fiction) production and box office data

		2008	2009	2010	2011	2012	2013	2014	2015	2016	2017	2018
National productions		1	1	2	0	0	2	4	1	0	3	1
Co-productions	Majority	1	0	5	1	2	3	2	1	2	3	3
	Minority	4	3	1	3	2	4	5	0	6	1	5
Box office total (in euros)		n/a	n/a	n/a	n/a	n/a	n/a	n/a	n/a	n/a	n/a	n/a
Box office national (in euros)		n/a	n/a	n/a	n/a	n/a	n/a	n/a	n/a	n/a	n/a	n/a
Admissions total		n/a	n/a	n/a	n/a	n/a	n/a	n/a	n/a	n/a	n/a	n/a
Admissions national		n/a	n/a	n/a	n/a	n/a	n/a	n/a	n/a	n/a	n/a	n/a

Source: The Association of Film Workers in Bosnia-Herzegovina.

Bosnia-Herzegovina

Key institutions

Udruženje filmskih radnika Bosne i Hercegovine/
The Association of Film Workers in Bosnia-Herzegovina
<http://bhfilm.ba/>

Kinoteka Bosne i Hercegovine Sarajevo/
The National Film Archive of Bosnia-Herzegovina
<https://www.kinotekabih.ba/>

Fondacija za kinematografiju Sarajevo/Cinema Fund Sarajevo
<http://fondacijakinematografija.ba/>

Filmski Centar Sarajevo/Film Center Sarajevo
<https://fcs.ba/>

Sarajevska filmska akademija/Sarajevo Film Academy
<https://www.sfa.ba/>

Akademija umjetnosti Banja Luka/Academy of Arts Banja Luka
<http://au.unibl.org/index.php/lat>/

Major festivals

Sarajevo Film Festival
<https://www.sff.ba/>

Bosnian-Herzegovinian Film Festival
<https://www.bhffnyc.org/>

Pravo ljudski Film Festival
<www.pravoljudski.org>

Banja Luka International Animated Film Festival
<http://www.banjalukanima.org/>

Mediteran Film Festival
<http://www.mff.ba/>

BULGARIA

Table 1 Overview of national film production

	2008	2009	2010	2011	2012	2013	2014	2015	2016	2017	2018
Feature films: Fiction	6	5	n/a	8	6	4	3	11	11	13	16
Feature films: Documentary	n/a	10	4	6	11	11	10	8	11	4	10
Short films: Fiction and documentary	6	16	8	6	4	5	7	12	11	19	11
Animation: Feature and shorts	6	7	4	7	8	9	6	8	17	11	5

BULGARIA

Table 2 Feature film (fiction) production and box office data

		2008	2009	2010	2011	2012	2013	2014	2015	2016	2017	2018
National productions		5	4	n/a	6	5	0	2	9	6	10	5
Co-productions	Majority	1	1	n/a	2	1	4	1	2	5	3	1
	Minority	4	4	n/a	1	2	0	0	5	6	5	5
Box office total (in euros)		9,809,100	12,889,700	16,511,000	18,749,000	17,366,500	20,362,800	21,024,200	23,457,500	24,758,900	25,922,700	23,537,900
Box office national films (in euros)		119,000	128,000	1,453,900	2,231,100	827,000	119,200	638,200	302,500	610,100	2,057,300	1,567,300
Admissions total		2,823,300	3,175,700	3,962,600	4,722,700	4,108,500	4,792,800	4,905,000	5,335,100	5,532,500	5,573,800	4,900,400
Admissions national		82,400	42,000	445,300	668,700	245,300	41,100	170,800	94,800	177,600	512,900	388,000

Note: Data includes only films produced with state subsidies provided by the Bulgarian National Film Center (a film can receive up to 75–80 per cent of its budget). Data for films funded through private sources is not collected by any institution and are therefore unavailable.

The figures provided are in EUR (1 EUR = 1.95583 BGN, 1 BGN = 0.511292 EUR).

Source: Bulgarian National Film Center.

Bulgaria

Key institutions

Bulgarska nacionalna filmoteka/Bulgarian National Film Archive
<www.bnf.bg>

Nacionalna akademia za teatralno i filmovo izkustvo Krastyo Sarafov/
National Academy for Theatre and Film Arts (NATFA) – Screen Arts Faculty
<www.natfiz.bg>

Nacionalen filmov centar/Bulgarian National Film Center
<www.nfc.bg>

Ministerstvo na kulturata na Bulgariya/Ministry of Culture of Bulgaria
<www.mc.government.bg>

Institut za izsledvane na izkustvata – Bulgarska akademia na naukite/
Institute of Art Studies, Bulgarian Academy of Sciences – Screen Arts Department
<www.artstudies.bg>

Suyuz na bulgarskite filmovi deitsi/Union of Bulgarian Filmmakers
<www.filmmakers.bg>

Major festivals

Golden Rhyton Bulgarian Documentary and Animated Film Festival
<www.zlatenriton.bg>

Golden Rose Bulgarian Feature Film Festival
<www.zlatnaroza.bg>

International Book and Movies Festival Cinelibri
<www.cinelibri.com>

International Film Festival Kinomania
<www.kinomania.bg>

International Sofia Film Fest
<www.siff.bg>

CROATIA

Table 1 Overview of national film production

	2008	2009	2010	2011	2012	2013	2014	2015	2016	2017	2018
Feature films: Fiction	7	8	7	11	6	16	13	8	10	9	15
Feature films: Documentary	3	6	5	7	8	6	10	10	14	8	10
Short films: Fiction and documentary	14	39	35	47	62	39	83	72	89	74	85
Animation: Feature and short	8	16	16	18	27	8	25	29	19	26	28

CROATIA

Table 2 Feature film (fiction) production and box office data

		2008	2009	2010	2011	2012	2013	2014	2015	2016	2017	2018
National productions		3	5	6	10	4	15	8	4	6	7	11
Co-productions	Majority	4	3	1	1	2	1	5	4	4	2	4
	Minority	1	2	2	7	5	4	8	6	6	9	7
Box office total (in euros)		11,740,000	14,350,000	14,350,000	16,610,000	17,250,000	19,150,000	17,430,000	15,080,000	16,800,000	18,330,000	20,140,000
Box office national (in euros)		162,500	230,300	221,200	461,400	1,356,300	1,740,000	358,500	262,800	685,300	381,000	210,800
Admissions total		3,000,000	3,250,000	3,290,000	3,340,000	4,060,000	3,990,000	3,790,000	3,930,000	4,300,000	4,500,000	4,600,000
Admissions national		37,400	52,500	51,200	114,000	328,200	436,100	94,200	76,000	181,900	119,700	54,000

Sources: Croatian Audiovisual Centre, European Audiovisual Observatory.

CROATIA

Key institutions

Hrvatski audiovizualni centar/Croatian Audiovisual Centre
<https://www.havc.hr/eng/>

Hrvatski filmski savez/Croatian Film Association
<http://www.hfs.hr/>

Hrvatski filmski arhiv (Hrvatska kinoteka)/
Croatian State Archive (Croatian Cinémathèque)
<http://zagreb.arhiv.hr/hr/hda/fs-ovi/kinoteka.htm>

Akademija dramske umjetnosti Sveučilišta u Zagrebu/
University of Zagreb Academy of Dramatic Arts
<https://www.adu.unizg.hr/>

Major festivals

Pula Film Festival
<http://www.pulafilmfestival.hr/hr/>

Motovun Film Festival
<http://www.motovunfilmfestival.com/>

ZagrebDox – International Documentary Film Festival
<http://zagrebdox.net/>

Animafest Zagreb – World Festival of Animated Film
<http://www.animafest.hr/en>

Mediterranean Film Festival Split
<https://fmfs.hr/en/news/>

CYPRUS

Table 1 Overview of national film production

	2008	2009	2010	2011	2012	2013	2014	2015	2016	2017	2018
Feature films: Fiction	1	n/a	2	2	n/a	2	3	4	n/a	3	6
Feature films: Documentaries	1	n/a	4	4	2	1	1	1	2	2	4
Short films	3	9	6	11	18	11	9	10	11	11	19
Animation: Feature and short	n/a	n/a	n/a	1	5	21	15	14	18	11	9

CYPRUS

Table 2 Feature film (fiction) production and box office data

		2008	2009	2010	2011	2012	2013	2014	2015	2016	2017	2018
National productions		1	n/a	1	n/a	n/a	n/a	3	3	n/a	2	3
Co-productions	Majority	n/a	n/a	1	2	n/a	2	n/a	1	n/a	1	3
	Minority	n/a	2	n/a	2	1	n/a	n/a	1	n/a	n/a	1
Box office total (in euros)		n/a	6,660,500	6,698,700	7,108,200	6,700,400	5,423,500	5,100,700	5,175,500	50,974,500	5,988,000	6,065,100
Box office national (in euros)		n/a	7,210	n/a	300	n/a	63,700	467,100	1,800	8,400	59,800	6,000
Admissions total		n/a	869,100	847,600	869,400	840,300	699,000	695,200	715,700	698,700	743,600	753,500
Admissions national		n/a	1,000	n/a	50	n/a	8,300	61,100	250	1,100	7,100	700

Sources: Cultural Services – Ministry of Education and Culture of the Republic of Cyprus, Cyprus Film Days IFF, International Short Film Festival of Cyprus, Countryside Animafest Cyprus – Views of the World, Lemesos International Documentary Festival.

Note: We have not been able to obtain data for the Turkish Cypriot film production, so the data here refers to films in the Greek Cypriot-controlled Republic of Cyprus.

CYPRUS

Key institutions

Klados Kinimatografou – Politistikes Ypiresies Ypourgeiou Paideias Politismou, Athlitismou kai Neolaias tis Kipriakis Dimokratias/ Cinema Department, Cultural Services – Ministry of Education and Culture of the Republic of Cyprus (renamed Ministry of Education, Culture, Sport and Youth of the Republic of Cyprus in 2019).
<http://filmingincyprus.gov.cy/?lang=en>

Enosi Skinotheton Kyprou / Directors Guild of Cyprus
<https://cyprusdirectors.com/>

University of Nicosia – BA in Digital Communications and Mass Media

Frederick University – BA in Audiovisual Communication

Major festivals

Cyprus Film Days International Festival
<www.cyprusfilmdays.com>

International Short Film Festival of Cyprus
<www.isffc.com.cy>

Images and Views of Alternative Cinema
<https://www.facebook.com/ImagesViewsOfAlternativeCinemaFilmFestival/>

Countryside Animafest Cyprus – Views of the World
<www.animafest.com.cy>

Lemesos International Documentary Festival
<http://filmfestival.com.cy/>

GREECE

Table 1 Overview of national film production

	2008	2009	2010	2011	2012	2013	2014	2015	2016	2017	2018
Feature films: Fiction	n/a	n/a	26	27	19	18	23	16	23	13	11
Feature films: Documentary	n/a	29	21	33	29	42	33	35	42	51	50
Short films: Fiction and documentary	n/a	n/a	n/a	n/a	n/a	n/a	n/a	n/a	n/a	n/a	n/a
Animation: Feature and shorts	65	68	66	79	73	50	68	59	50	40	24

GREECE

Table 2 Feature film (fiction) production and box office data

		2008	2009	2010	2011	2012	2013	2014	2015	2016	2017	2018
National productions		n/a	n/a	25	27	14	15	18	13	20	10	8
Co-productions	Majority	n/a	n/a	1	0	5	3	5	3	3	3	3
	Minority	n/a	n/a	0	2	0	3	2	3	2	4	3
Box office total (in euros)		n/a	100,240,000	99,440,000	92,990,000	70,180,000	59,310,000	58,000,000	63,386,600	64,400,000	65,000,000	60,000,000
Box office national (in euros)		n/a	n/a	n/a	n/a	n/a	n/a	n/a	n/a	n/a	n/a	n/a
Admissions total		n/a	n/a	11,720,000	10,850,000	10,100,000	9,210,000	8,973,000	9,806,000	10,025,000	10,100,000	9,355,000
Admissions national		n/a	n/a	1,400,000	1,160,000	1,145,000	758,000	310,000	826,000	902,400	1,005,000	655,000

Sources: Greek Film Centre, Thessaloniki Documentary Festival, <www.greekanimation.com>

Note: Data for feature films (fiction) refers to films in national distribution (with thanks to Christos Katselos of the Greek Film Centre). Data for feature films (documentary) refers to films shown at the Thessaloniki Documentary Festival. Data for animations refers to films produced in Greece (with thanks to Panayiotis Kyriakoulakos of ASIFA Hellas).

GREECE

Key institutions

Elliniko Kentro Kinimatografou/Greek Film Centre
<www.gfc.gr>

EKOME – Ethniko Kentro Optikoakoustikon Meson kai Epikoinonias/
National Centre of Audiovisual Media and Communication
<www.ekome.media>

ERT– Elliniki Radiofonia Tileorasi/Hellenic Radio Television
<www.ert.gr>

Hellenic Film Commission
<https://www.filmcommission.gr/>

Elliniki Enosi Kinoumenon Sxedion/ASIFA Hellas
<www.asifahellas.eu>

Major festivals

Thessaloniki International Film Festival
<https://www.filmfestival.gr/en/>

Thessaloniki Documentary Festival
<https://www.filmfestival.gr/en/documentary-festival>

Athens International Film Festival
<http://en.aiff.gr/>

Drama International Short Film Festival
<https://www.dramafilmfestival.gr/42_EN/>

Animasyros International Animation Festival
<https://www.animasyros.gr/>

Kosovo

Table 1 Overview of national film production

	2008	2009	2010	2011	2012	2013	2014	2015	2016	2017	2018
Feature films: Fiction	0	2	1	0	1	2	3	4	3	5	6
Feature films: Documentary	1	2	2	0	0	1	1	1	4	0	2
Short films: Fiction and documentary	0	3	1	1	3	1	4	4	3	1	4
Animation: Feature and shorts	0	0	0	1	0	0	2	1	0	1	0

Kosovo

Table 2 Feature film (fiction) production and box office data

		2008	2009	2010	2011	2012	2013	2014	2015	2016	2017	2018
National productions		0	2	1	0	1	0	1	0	0	0	3
Co-productions	Majority	0	0	0	0	0	0	0	0	1	3	1
	Minority	0	0	0	0	0	2	2	4	2	2	2
Box office total (in euros)		n/a	n/a	n/a	n/a	n/a	n/a	n/a	n/a	n/a	n/a	400,000
Box office national (in euros)		n/a	n/a	n/a	n/a	n/a	n/a	n/a	n/a	n/a	n/a	n/a
Admissions total		n/a	n/a	n/a	n/a	n/a	n/a	n/a	n/a	n/a	n/a	n/a
Admissions national		n/a	n/a	n/a	n/a	n/a	n/a	n/a	n/a	n/a	n/a	n/a

Note 1: The figures in both tables include only films that received public funds by Kosova Cinematography Center and do not reflect the total film production. The numbers of released films 2008–2018 were calculated based on the film projects annually subsidized by KCC. Information available at <https://qkk-rks.com/en-us/our-films/>.

Source: Kosova Cinematography Center, Statistical Yearbook of the Republic of Kosovo 2018.

Note 2: Given the relative scarcity of the films produced in Kosovo, and the fact that the minority co-productions listed are culturally Kosovar films, the total number of films listed under Feature Films (Fiction) in Table 1, includes national films and both majority and minority co-productions.

Kosovo

Key institutions

Qendra Kinematografike e Kosovës/Kosova Cinematography Center
<https://qkk-rks.com/en-us/>

Ministria e Kulturës, Rinisë dhe Sportit/Ministry of Culture, Youth and Sport
<https://www.mkrs-ks.org/>

Unioni i Artistëve të Filmit të Kosovës/Union of Film Artists of Kosovo
<http://uafk-ks.org/?page=2,1>

Fakulteti i Arteve i Universitetit të Prishtinës/
Faculty of Arts of University of Prishtina
<https://arte.uni-pr.edu/>

Major festivals

DocuFest – International Documentary and Short Film Festival:
<http://dokufest.com/>

PriFest – Prishtina Film Festival
<http://prifest.org/>

Anibar Animation Festival
<http://anibar.org/>

FerFilm – International Film Festival
<http://ferfilm.eu/>

Kosovo Film Festival – The Goddess on the Throne
<http://festfilmkosova.com/>

MONTENEGRO

Table 1 Overview of national film production

	2008	2009	2010	2011	2012	2013	2014	2015	2016	2017	2018
Feature films: Fiction	1	0	1	3	2	0	1	1	2	2	3
Feature films: Documentary	0	1	0	1	0	2	1	1	0	1	0
Short films: Fiction and documentary	0	3	1	2	2	2	0	6	1	1	3
Animation: Shorts and feature	0	0	0	0	0	0	1	0	1	0	0

MONTENEGRO

Table 2 Feature film (fiction) production and box office data

		2008	2009	2010	2011	2012	2013	2014	2015	2016	2017	2018
National productions		0	0	1	0	2	0	0	0	1	1	1
Co-productions	Majority	1	0	0	3	0	0	1	1	1	1	2
	Minority	0	0	0	2	1	0	3	2	0	1	2
Box office total (in euros)		n/a	n/a	n/a	217,500	766,300	760,800	997,250	1,010,950	1,042,800	1,056,750	1,082,200
Box office national (in euros)		n/a	n/a	n/a	38,600	8,500	400	64,550	163,000	8,550	100,900	3,350
Admissions total		n/a	n/a	n/a	63,300	221,600	219,900	258,900	267,000	277,200	281,500	285,400
Admissions national		n/a	n/a	n/a	11,300	2,500	100	17,000	36,400	2,600	27,200	1,000

Sources: Film Centre of Montenegro, Montenegrin Cinémathèque and Ministry of Culture, Cineplexx Podgorica and Cadmus Cineplex Budva.

Montenegro

Key institutions

Filmski centar Crne Gore/Film Centre of Montenegro
<www.fccg.me>

Crnogorska kinoteka/Montenegrin Cinemateque
<www.kinoteka.me>

Ministarstvo kulture Crne Gore/Ministry of Culture of Montenegro
<www.mku.gov.me>

Udruženje filmskih producenata i reditelja/
Association of Film Producers and Directors
<www.afpd.me>

Udruženje glumaca Crne Gore/Actors Association of Montenegro
<www.glumci.me>

Fakultet dramskih umjetnosti/Faculty of Drama Arts
<www.ucg.ac.me/fdu>

Major festivals

Film Festival Herceg Novi – Montenegro Film Festival
<www.filmfestival.me>

Podgorica Film Festival
<https://podgoricafilmfestival.me/>

UnderhillFest
<www.underhillfest.me>

Seanema Film Festival
<www.seanema.me>

NORTH MACEDONIA

Table 1 Overview of national film production

	2008	2009	2010	2011	2012	2013	2014	2015	2016	2017	2018
Feature films: Fiction	0	0	3	2	3	2	2	4	4	3	4
Feature films: Documentary	1	7	4	7	1	4	4	9	4	4	11
Short films: Fiction and	0	4	3	9	11	14	12	16	25	26	12
Animation: Feature and shorts	0	1	1	0	3	1	0	3	0	0	3

NORTH MACEDONIA

Table 2 Feature film (fiction) production and box office data

		2008	2009	2010	2011	2012	2013	2014	2015	2016	2017	2018
National productions		0	0	1	1	0	0	1	0	1	1	2
Co-productions	Majority	0	0	2	1	3	2	1	4	3	2	2
	Minority	0	3	3	4	0	0	5	3	4	4	4
Box office total (in euros)		n/a	n/a	n/a	n/a	n/a	n/a	1,041,800	1,222,700	1,198,800	1,180,600	1,166,400
Box office national (in euros)		n/a	n/a	n/a	n/a	n/a	n/a	76,200	17,700	30,000	29,800	14,900
Admissions total		n/a	n/a	n/a	n/a	n/a	n/a	357,900	432,800	366,900	427,700	401,300
Admissions national		n/a	n/a	n/a	n/a	n/a	n/a	34,800	7,100	15,700	17,500	8,200

Sources: Anita Stojcheska (Macedonian Film Agency), Macedonian Film Agency, IMDb, and NMFA database (for the 2018 data).

NORTH MACEDONIA

Key institutions

Agencijata za film/The North Macedonia Film Agency
<http://www.filmfund.gov.mk/>

Kinoteka na Makedonija/Cinémathèque of Macedonia
<http://www.maccinema.com/>

Ministerstvo za kultura – Vlada na Republika Severna Makedonija/
Ministry of Culture for the Republic of North Macedonia
<http://www.kultura.gov.mk/>

Društvoto na filmskite rabotnici na Republika Makedonija/
The Macedonian Film Professionals Association
<https://www.dfrm.org.mk/en/>

Major festivals

Manaki brothers International Cinematographers' Film Festival
<www.manaki.com.mk>

Skopje Film Festival
<www.skopjefilmfestival.com.mk>

Cinedays Festival of European Film
<www.cinedays.mk>

Asterfest International Film Festival
<www.asterfest.mk>

Makedox Creative Documentaries Film Festival
<www.makedox.mk>

Romania

Table 1 Overview of national film production

	2008	2009	2010	2011	2012	2013	2014	2015	2016	2017	2018
Feature films: Fiction	9	14	17	10	17	23	22	16	18	16	27
Feature films: Documentary	11	7	10	4	7	5	10	7	6	11	7
Short films: Fiction and documentary	11	23	10	11	9	5	6	10	14	12	7
Animation: Feature and shorts	0	2	1	1	2	2	4	9	4	2	8

ROMANIA

Table 2 Feature film (fiction) production and box office data

		2008	2009	2010	2011	2012	2013	2014	2015	2016	2017	2018
National productions		7	11	9	8	9	16	19	10	12	10	18
Co-productions	Majority	2	3	8	2	8	7	3	6	6	6	9
	Minority	0	4	2	1	2	2	5	1	7	1	1
Box office total		14,500,000	20,541,200	26,378,900	29,882,800	32,470,100	35,696,400	41,396,900	45,965,700	53,486,500	57,544,100	56,427,800
Box office national (in euros)		n/a	n/a	n/a	254,000	815,900	625,000	590,000	592,000	1,400,000	895,000	1,470,000
Admissions total		3,797,600	5,279,900	6,508,700	7,235,400	8,348,500	9,048,300	10,171,600	11,166,900	13,033,700	13,877,500	13,348,200
Admissions national		131,919	114,376	153,492	99,860	297,487	256,594	221,625	216,316	459,053	303,758	421,296

Sources: Romanian Film Center.

Romania

Key institutions

Centrul Național al Cinematografiei/Romanian Film Center
<http://cnc.gov.ro>

Ministerul Culturii și Identității Naționale/
Ministry of Culture and National Identity
<http://www.cultura.ro>

Arhiva Națională de Filme – Cinemateca Romana/
National Film Archive – Romanian Cinémathèque
<http://www.anf-cinemateca.ro>

Institutul Cultural Român/Romanian Cultural Institute
<https://www.icr.ro>

Universitatea Națională de Artă Teatrală și Cinematografică 'I.L. Caragiale'/
The National University of Theatre and Film 'I.L.Caragiale'
<http://www.unatc.ro>

Major festivals

Bucharest International Experimental Film Festival
<http://www.bieff.ro/ro/2018>

Transylvanian International Film Festival
<www.tiff.ro>

ANONIMUL International Independent Film Festival
<http://www.festival-anonimul.ro/en/home-page-en/>

Animest – Bucharest International Animation Film Festival
<https://www.animest.ro>

Astra Film Festival (Sibiu International Film Festival)
<https://www.astrafilm.ro>

Table 1 Overview of national film production

	2008	2009	2010	2011	2012	2013	2014	2015	2016	2017	2018
Feature films: Fiction	11	19	14	16	14	10	21	19	22	15	13
Feature films: Documentary	4	9	15	13	11	13	14	12	13	16	14
Short films: Fiction and documentary	34	30	36	46	58	48	64	67	32	36	19
Animation: Shorts and feature	8	33	14	9	11	7	5	12	4	3	5

SERBIA

Table 2 Feature film (fiction) production and box office data

		2008	2009	2010	2011	2012	2013	2014	2015	2016	2017	2018
National productions		7	15	6	8	10	7	8	13	14	8	6
Co-productions	Majority	4	4	8	8	4	3	13	6	8	7	7
	Minority	3	4	7	3	5	0	4	7	3	5	10
Box office total (in euros)		4,037,600	4,625,100	5,825,000	7,105,800	6,618,000	6,926,400	9,573,000	9,441,200	10,939,600	13,645,000	14,613,200
Box office national (in euros)		846,600	606,200	498,300	2,340,900	1,179,000	558,400	2,831,500	1,848,300	1,562,600	1,597,000	2,442,000
Admissions total		1,486,500	1,713,700	2,062,200	2,625,000	2,369,900	2,368,300	3,157,300	3,161,700	3,530,600	4,148,650	4,476,000
Admissions national		328,300	247,600	183,400	848,200	463,300	219,100	945,700	699,200	574,800	579,700	864,200

Sources: Film Centre Serbia, The Statistical Office of the Republic of Serbia, Eurimages – Co-production funding history, MEDIA Desk Serbia, and Đorđe Bajić, Zoran Janković, Ivan Velisavljević (2018) *Kritički vodič kroz srpski film, 2000–2017*, Beograd: Filmski centar Srbije.

SERBIA

Key institutions

Filmski centar Srbije/Film Center of Serbia
<http://www.fcs.rs/en/>

Republika Srbija – Ministarstvo kulture i informisanja/
Republic of Serbia – Ministry of Culture and Information
<http://www.kultura.gov.rs/en/>

Film in Serbia
<http://www.filminserbia.com/>

Jugoslovenska kinoteka/Yugoslav Film Archive – Yugoslav Cinémathèque
<http://www.kinoteka.org.rs/>

Filmske Novosti/Film news
<www.filmskenovosti.rs>

Fakultet dramskih umetnosti/Faculty of Dramatic Arts in Belgrade
<http://www.fdu.edu.rs/>

Univerzitet umetnosti u Beogradu/University of Arts in Belgrade
<http://www.arts.bg.ac.rs/en>

Major festivals

FEST – International Film Festival Belgrade
<http://www.fest.rs>

Auteur Film Festival
<http://www.faf.rs>

Magnificent 7 European Feature Documentary Film Festival
<http://www.magnificent7festival.org/en/index.php>

The Martovski Festival – Belgrade Documentary and Short Film Festival
<http://martovski.rs/en/>

Free Zone Film Festival
<http://www.freezonebelgrade.org>

Beldocs International Documentary Film Festival
<http://beldocs.rs/en/>

SLOVENIA

Table 1 Overview of national film production

	2008	2009	2010	2011	2012	2013	2014	2015	2016	2017	2018
Feature films: Fiction	8	4	8	2	5	8	5	8	10	9	7
Feature films: Documentary	2	1	2	1	7	2	3	2	2	5	10
Short films: Fiction and documentary	4	3	4	4	9	11	5	9	10	11	16
Animation: Feature and shorts	1	2	1	3	3	2	2	3	6	6	6

SLOVENIA

Table 2 Feature film (fiction) production and box office data

		2008	2009	2010	2011	2012	2013	2014	2015	2016	2017	2018
National productions		5	2	5	1	4	5	4	7	5	3	4
Co-productions	Majority	3	2	3	1	1	3	1	1	5	6	3
	Minority	2	1	3	3	3	4	3	8	1	3	3
Box office total (in euros)		9,599,300	10,877,600	12,811,400	12,982,200	11,955,900	11,090,800	9,228,700	10,172,200	11,704,200	11,637,000	n/a
Box office national (in euros)		71,700	106,400	780,500	463,900	403,300	1,094,600	262,500	147,400	1,197,100	526,100	n/a
Admissions total		2,418,000	2,558,200	2,888,400	2,867,200	2,637,800	2,277,600	1,849,900	1,989,700	2,295,500	2,306,800	2,549,100
Admissions national		23,500	27,800	194,000	114,300	104,200	247,800	70,500	39,700	241,900	146,700	n/a

Note: The admission data is from Cinemania Group's website (Slovenia's largest distributor).

Source: Slovenian Film Centre, Festival slovenskega filma.

Sᴌᴏᴠᴇɴɪᴀ

Key institutions

Slovenski filmski center/Slovenian Film Centre
<www.sfc.si>

Slovenski filmski arhiv/Slovenian Film Archive
<www.arhiv.gov.si>

Slovenska kinoteka/Slovenian Cinémathèque
<www.kinoteka.si>

Akademija za gledališče, radio, film in televizijo, Univerza v Ljubljani/
Academy of Theatre, Radio, Film and Television, University
of Ljubljana
<www.agrft.uni-lj.si>

Akademija umetnosti, Univerza v Novi Gorici/
School of Arts, University of Nova Gorica
<www.ung.si/en/study/school-of-arts/>

Major festivals

Animateka – International Animated Film Festival
<www.animateka.si>

Documentary Film Festival
<www.fdf.si>

Festival slovenskega filma
<www.fsf.si>

LGBT Film Festival
<www.lgbtfilmfest.si>

Ljubljana International Film Festival
<www.liffe.si>

TURKEY

Table 1 Overview of national film production

	2008	2009	2010	2011	2012	2013	2014	2015	2016	2017	2018
Feature films: Fiction	48	67	58	71	58	83	106	133	134	140	171
Feature films: Documentary	3	1	4	1	2	3	1	3	0	4	5
Short films: Fiction and documentary	n/a	n/a	n/a	n/a	n/a	n/a	n/a	n/a	n/a	n/a	n/a
Animation: Feature and shorts	0	2	0	1	0	1	2	2	3	4	4

TURKEY

Table 2 Feature film (fiction) production and box office data

		2008	2009	2010	2011	2012	2013	2014	2015	2016	2017	2018
National productions		43	62	54	65	54	75	96	126	127	140	167
Co-productions	Majority	5	5	4	6	4	8	10	7	7	0	4
	Minority	0	0	0	1	1	1	1	1	0	2	1
Box office total (in euros)		138,974,300	134,141,300	177,957,700	165,674,100	173,241,200	189,173,500	210,711,000	210,662,600	195,898,100	201,191,900	142,958,700
Box office national (in euros)		78,163,100	62,396,000	93,214,300	77,846,800	69,567,800	105,144,200	111,912,400	195,028,100	96,260,700	108,716,900	85,469,900
Admissions total		36,935,800	34,787,700	38,580,700	41,244,000	41,357,900	49,051,500	57,382,700	57,859,100	55,182,600	68,957,300	66,731,500
Admissions national		21,736,100	17,222,200	21,594,700	21,009,100	18,210,100	29,065,800	32,493,600	51,429,000	28,608,100	38,880,300	41,649,900

Note: Animation data in Table 1 includes feature films only, since short length animation numbers were unavailable.

Sources: Antrakt, Box Office Türkiye, Lumiere database.

Turkey

Key institutions

Kültür ve Turizm Bakanlığı, Sinema Genel Müdürlüğü/
Ministry of Culture and Tourism, General Directorate of Cinema
<http://sinema.ktb.gov.tr>

Belgesel Sinemacılar Birliği/
Association of Documentary Filmmakers in Turkey
<http://bsb.org.tr/>

Mithat Alam Film Merkezi/Mithat Alam Film Center
<https://www.facebook.com/groups/mithatalamfilmmerkezi/>

Türkiye Sinema Araştırmaları/Turkish Cinema Studies
<http://www.tsa.org.tr/>

Major festivals

Adana Golden Boll Film Festival
<https://www.altinkoza.org.tr/>

Ankara International Film Festival
<http://www.filmfestankara.org.tr>

Antalya Golden Orange Film Festival
<http://www.antalyaff.com>

Istanbul Film Festival
<http://film.iksv.org/>

Flying Broom International Women's Film Festival
<http://ucansupurge.org.tr/festival/>

GENERAL BIBLIOGRAPHY*

Akser, Murat (2018) 'Locating Turkish Cinema Between Populist Tendencies and Art Cinema', in Aaron Han Joon Magnan-Park, Gina Marchetti and See Kam Tan (eds), *The Palgrave Handbook of Asian Cinema*. London: Palgrave Macmillan, pp. 151–70.

Akser, Murat and Bayrakdar, Deniz (2014) *New Cinema, New Media: Reinventing Turkish Cinema*. Newcastle upon Tyne: Cambridge Scholars Publishing.

Atakav, Eylem (2013) *Women and Turkish Cinema: Gender Politics, Cultural Identity and Representation*. London: Routledge.

Batori, Anna (2018) *Space in Romanian and Hungarian Cinema*. Cham: Palgrave Macmillan.

Behlil, Melis (2012) 'East Is East? New Turkish Cinema and Eastern Europe', in Aniko Imre (ed.), *A Companion to Eastern European Cinemas*. Wiley-Blackwell, pp. 504–17.

Bjelić, Dušan (ed.) (2019) *Balkan Transnationalism at the Time of International Catastrophe*. London: Routledge.

Constandinides, Costas and Papadakis, Yiannis (eds) (2015) *Cypriot Cinemas: Memory, Conflict and Identity in the Margins of Europe*. London: Bloomsbury.

Daković, Nevena and Seničić, Maša (2019) '*La jeunesse désaffectée* in contemporary Serbian cinema', in Betty Kaklamanidou and Ana Corbalán (eds), *Contemporary European Cinema Crisis Narratives and Narratives in Crisis*. New York: Routledge, pp. 147–60.

---

[1] This bibliography complements those provided in the individual chapters and only includes sources in the English language.

Ďurovičová, Nataša and Newman, Kathleen E. (eds) (2010) *World Cinemas, Transnational Perspectives*. New York: Routledge.

Elsaesser, Thomas (2005) *European Cinema: Face to Face with Hollywood*. Amsterdam: Amsterdam University Press.

Ezra, Elizabeth and Rowden, Terry (2006) *Transnational Cinema: The Film Reader*. London and New York: Routledge.

Filimon, Monica (2017) *Cristi Puiu*. Urbana, IL: University of Illinois Press.

Galijaš, Armina and Paić, Hrvoje (eds) (2018) 'Special Issue on Film and Society in South-East Europe', *Contemporary Southeastern Europe: An Interdisciplinary Journal on Southeastern Europe*, 4 (2).

Gilić, Nikica (2017) 'Post-Yugoslav Film and the Construction of New National Cinemas', *Contemporary Southeastern Europe: An Interdisciplinary Journal on Southeastern Europe*, 4 (2), pp. 102–20.

Giukin, Lenuta, Flakowska, Janina and Desser, David (eds) (2015) *Small Cinemas in Global Markets: Genres, Identities, Narratives*, afterword by Dina Iordanova. Lanham, MD: Lexington Books.

Glenny, Misha (2012) *The Balkans 1804–2012: Nationalism, War and the Great Powers*, updated edition. London: Granta Books.

Gott, Michael and Herzog, Todd (eds) *East, West and Centre: Reframing Post–1989 European Cinema*. Edinburgh: Edinburgh University Press.

Grgić, Ana (2018) 'Recurrent Themes, Entangled Histories, and Cultural Affinities: Balkan Cinema at the 58th Thessaloniki International Film Festival', *Film Quarterly*, 71 (3), pp. 81–6.

Grgić, Ana, Kristensen, Lars and Peshkopia, Ridvan (eds) (2016) 'Special Issue 16: Albanian Cinema', *Kinokultura* <http://www.kinokultura.com/specials/16/albania.shtml>

Hammett-Jamart, Julia, Mitric, Petar and Novrup Redvall, Eva (eds) (2018) *European Film and Television Co-production: Policy and Practice*. London: Palgrave.

Hjort, Mette (2010) 'Affinitive and Milieu-building Transnationalism: The Advance Party Initiative', in Dina Iordanova, David Martin-Jones and Belén Vidal (eds), *Cinema at the Periphery*. Detroit, MI: Wayne State University Press, pp. 46–66.

Hjort, Mette (2010) 'On the Plurality of Cinematic Transnationalism', in Nataša Ďurovičová and Kathleen E. Newman (eds), *World Cinemas, Transnational Perspectives*. New York: Routledge, pp. 12–32.

Hjort, Mette and Petrie, Duncan (eds) (2007) *The Cinema of Small Nations*. Edinburgh: Edinburgh University Press.

Horton, Andrew J. (ed.) (2000) *The Celluloid Tinderbox: Yugoslav Screen Reflection of the Turbulent Decade*. Telford: Central Europe Review.

Hristova, Maria (ed.) (2015) 'Special Issue 15: Macedonian Cinema', *Kinokultura* <http://www.kinokultura.com/specials/15/macedonian.shtml>.

Imre, Aniko (ed.) (2012) *A Companion to Eastern European Cinemas*. Malden, MA: Wiley-Blackwell.

Iordanova, Dina (1996) 'Women in New Balkan Cinema: Surviving on the Margins', *Film Criticism*, 21 (2), pp. 24–39.

Iordanova, Dina (2001) *Cinema of Flames: Balkan Film, Culture and the Media*. London: BFI Publishing.

Iordanova, Dina (ed.) (2006) 'Special Issue 5: Bulgarian Cinema', *Kinokultura* <http://www.kinokultura.com/specials/5/bulgarian.shtml>.

Iordanova, Dina (ed.) (2006) *Cinema of the Balkans*. London: Wallflower Press.

Iordanova, Dina (2007) 'Contemporary Balkan Cinema: A Special Supplement', *Cineaste*, 32 (3), Summer.

Iordanova, Dina (2008) 'Intercultural Cinema and Balkan Hushed Histories', *New Review of Film and Television Studies*, 6 (1), pp. 5–18.

Iordanova, Dina (2008) *New Bulgarian Cinema*. College Gate Press.

Jameson, Frederic (2004) 'Thoughts on Balkan Cinema', in Atom Egoyan and Ian Balfour (eds), *Subtitles: On the Foreignness of the Film*. Cambridge, MA: MIT Press, pp. 232–56.

Jelača, Dijana (2016) *Dislocated Screen Memory: Narrating Trauma in Post-Yugoslav Cinema*. New York: Palgrave Macmillan.

Johnson, Vida (ed.) (2009) 'Special Issue 8: Serbian Cinema', *Kinokultura* <http://www.kinokultura.com/specials/8/serbian.shtml>.

Kaklamanidou, Betty and Corbalán, Ana M. (eds) (2019) *Contemporary European Cinema: Crisis Narratives and Narratives in Crisis*. London: Routledge.

Karalis, Vrasidas (2012) *A History of Greek Cinema*. London: Continuum.

Karanfil, Gökçen and Şavk, Serkan (eds) (2014) *Imaginaries Out of Place: Cinema, Transnationalism and Turkey*. Newcastle upon Tyne: Cambridge Scholars Publishing.

Krstić, Igor (2016) *Slums on Screen: World Cinema and the Planet of Slums*, Edinburgh: Edinburgh University Press.

Levi, Pavle (2007) *Disintegration in frames: aesthetics and ideology in the Yugoslav and post-Yugoslav Cinema*. Stanford, CA: Stanford University Press.

Mazaj, Meta (2008) *Once Upon a Time There Was a Country: National and Cynicism in the Post 1990s Balkan Cinema*. Saarbrucken, Ger: VDM Verlag.

Mazaj, Meta (2011) 'Freewheeling on the Margins: The Discourse of Transition in the New Slovenian Cinema', *Studies in Eastern European Cinema*, 2 (1), pp. 7–20.

Mazierska, Ewa (2013) 'Želimir Žilnik and Eastern European Independent Cinema', *Images. The International Journal of European Film, Performing Arts and Audiovisual Communication*, 13 (22), pp. 133–49.

Mazierska, Ewa, Kristensen, Lars and Näripea, Eva (eds) (2014) *Postcolonial Approaches to Eastern European Cinema: Portraying Neighbours on Screen*. New York: Tauris.

Milas, Nataša, Simmons, Cynthia and Jockims, Trevor L. (eds) (2012) 'Special Issue 14: Bosnian Cinema', *Kinokultura* <http://www.kinokultura.com/specials/14/bosnian.shtml>.

Murtic, Dino (2015) *Post-Yugoslav Cinema: Towards a Cosmopolitan Imagining*. Basingstoke: Palgrave Macmillan.

Nasta, Dominique (2013) *Contemporary Romanian Cinema: The History of an Unexpected Miracle*. London, New York: Wallflower Press.

Nedyalkova, Maya (2018) 'Spisanie Kino/Kino Magazine and Its Role in Reflecting and Developing Bulgarian Film Culture', *Studies in Eastern European Cinema*, 9 (1), pp. 112–14.

Papadimitriou, Lydia (2013) 'Greek Cinema and the Balkans: Connections, Divergences and Escapes', in Marian Tutui (ed.), *Escape from the Balkans*. Cetate: Divan Film Festival, pp. 62–87.

Papadimitriou, Lydia (2017) 'Cinema at the Edges of the European Union: New Dynamics in the South and the East', in Rob Stone, Paul Cooke, Stephanie Dennison and Alex Marlow-Mann (eds), *The Routledge Companion to World Cinema*. London: Routledge, pp.181–91.

Papadimitriou, Lydia (2018) 'European Co-productions and Greek Cinema since the Crisis: "Extroversion" as survival', in Julia Hammet-Jamart, Petar Mitric, and Eva Novrup Redvall (eds), *European Film and Television Co-production: Policy and Practice*. London: Palgrave, pp. 207–22.

Papadimitriou, Lydia (2018) 'Greek Cinema as European Cinema: Co-productions, Eurimages and the Europeanisation of Greek Cinema', *Studies in European Cinema*, 15 (2–3), pp. 215–34.

Papadimitriou, Lydia and Tzioumakis, Yiannis (eds) (2012) *Greek Cinema. Texts, Histories, Identities*. Bristol: Intellect.

Pavičić, Jurica (2010) ' "Cinema of normalization": Changes of Stylistic Model in Post-Yugoslav Cinema after the 1990s', *Studies in Eastern European Cinema*, 1 (1), pp. 43–56.

Petek, Polona (2017) 'The (M)Others of Slovenian Cinema? Gender, Border-crossing and the Conundrum of National Cinema', *Studies in European Cinema*, 14 (2), pp. 134–52.

Petek, Polona (2019) 'Women in the Way? Re-reading *The Monstrous-Feminine* in Contemporary Slovenian Cinema', in Nicholas Chare, Jeanette Hoorn and Audrey Yue (eds), *Re-reading the Monstrous-Feminine: Art, Film, Feminism and Psychoanalysis*. London: Routledge, pp. 230–40.

Pieniążek-Markovic, Krystyna and Szpulak, Andrzej (eds) (2018) 'New Western Balkans Cinema', *Images. The International Journal of European Film, Performing Arts and Audiovisual Communication*, 23: 32.

Radovic, Milja (2014) *Transnational Cinema and Ideology: Representing Religion, Identity and Cultural Myths*. New York and London: Routledge.

Ravetto-Biagioli, Kriss (2017) *Mythopoetic Cinema: On the Ruins of European Identity*. New York: Columbia University Press.

Raw, Laurence (2017) *Six Turkish Filmmakers*. Madison, WI: University of Wisconsin Press.

Samardžija, Zoran (2007) 'Bal-can-can', *Cineaste*, 3 (32).

Stojanova, Christina (ed.) (2019) *The New Romanian Cinema*. Edinburgh: Edinburgh University Press.

Stojanova, Christina and Duma, Dana (eds) (2007) 'Special Issue 6: Romanian Cinema', *Kinokultura* < http://www.kinokultura.com/specials/6/romanian.shtml>.

Strauss, Laszlo (2017) *Hesitant Histories on the Romanian Screen: Modernity and Social Construction in Cinema and Television*. Palgrave Macmillan.

Suner, Asuman (2010) *New Turkish Cinema: Belonging, Identity and Memory*. London: I. B. Tauris.

Todorova, Maria ([1997] 2009) *Imagining the Balkans*, updated edition. Oxford: Oxford University Press.

Trifonova, Temenuga (2011) 'Between the National and the Transnational: Bulgarian Post-communist Cinema', *Studies in Eastern European Cinema*, 2 (2), pp. 211–25.

Țuțui, Marian (2011) *Orient Express: The Romanian and Balkan Cinema*. Bucharest: Noi Media Print.

Țuțui, Marian (ed.) (2013) *Escape from the Balkans*. Cetate: Divan Film Festival.

Țuțui, Marian (ed.) (2014) *Balkan Comedy – Selected Papers from the 2013 Divan Film Festival Symposium*. Cetate: Divan Film Festival.

Țuțui, Marian (ed.) (2015) *Balkan Heroes and Anti-Heroes – Selected Papers from the 2014 Divan Film Festival Symposium*. Cetate: Divan Film Festival.

Țuțui, Marian (ed.) (2016) *Roads and Crossroads in the Balkans – Selected Papers from the 2015 Divan Film Festival Symposium*. Cetate: Divan Film Festival.

Vidan, Aida (2018) 'Framing the Body, Vocalizing the Pain: Perspectives by the South Slavic Female Directors', *Studies in European Cinema. Recent Quality Film and the Future of the Republic of Europe*, 15 (2–3), pp. 125–45.

Vidan, Aida and Crnković, Gordana P. (eds) (2011) 'Special Issue 11: Croatian Cinema', *Kinokultura* <http://www.kinokultura.com/specials/11/croatian.shtml>.

Vidan, Aida and Crnković, Gordana P. (eds.) (2012) *In Contrast: Croatian Film Today*. Zagreb, Oxford and New York: Croatian Film Association & Berghahn Books.

Vojković, Saša (ed.) (2008) Special Issue: 'Re-imagining the Balkans: Essays on Southeastern European Cinema', *New Review of Film and Television Studies*, 6 (1), pp. 1–95.

INDEX